James Gylby Lonsdale, Samuel Lee

The Works of Horace rendered into English Prose

With Introductions, Running Analysis, Notes and an Index

James Gylby Lonsdale, Samuel Lee

The Works of Horace rendered into English Prose
With Introductions, Running Analysis, Notes and an Index

ISBN/EAN: 9783337372040

Printed in Europe, USA, Canada, Australia, Japan

Cover: Foto ©Thomas Meinert / pixelio.de

More available books at **www.hansebooks.com**

The Globe Edition.

THE WORKS OF HORACE

RENDERED INTO

ENGLISH PROSE

WITH INTRODUCTIONS RUNNING ANALYSIS NOTES AND AN INDEX.

BY

JAMES LONSDALE M.A.

LATE FELLOW AND TUTOR OF BALLIOL COLLEGE OXFORD AND CLASSICAL PROFESSOR IN KING'S COLLEGE LONDON

AND

SAMUEL LEE M.A.

LATIN LECTURER AT UNIVERSITY COLLEGE LONDON AND LATE SCHOLAR OF CHRIST'S COLLEGE CAMBRIDGE.

London:

MACMILLAN AND CO.

1874.

PREFACE.

THIS version of Horace is a literal rendering of the original, the translators having kept in view the same objects as they had before them in their edition of Virgil in this series.

The style of the Satires and Epistles, "the prosaic Muse," as Horace himself calls it, appears to be not unsuited for actual prose; but with regard to the Odes, the case is certainly different. Yet, though few prose translations of the Odes have been written in this country, in France there have been many. Perhaps the most notable are the versions by M. Jules Janin and M. Léon Halévy. These are flowing and elegant, but have rather a tendency to paraphrase. It seems that one advantage is gained by adopting the form of rhythmical prose in translating the Odes: greater freedom is thus afforded for the attempt to make some approach towards the expression in another language of the exquisite felicity and delicate lightness of phrase, so difficult to handle without spoiling, which characterise the Odes of Horace above all other poems.

The space given to the Notes has necessarily been somewhat limited: but it is hoped that difficulties of construction have not been passed over, and that the illustrations and references explain sufficiently the very numerous and various allusions which are found in the writings of Horace.

CONTENTS.

GENERAL INTRODUCTION.

THOSE to whom the writings of Horace have given delight (and a great company they are, readers of various ages, countries, tastes, dispositions,) owe a debt of gratitude first of all to Horace's good father, then to the poets Virgil and Varius, and then to his friend and patron Mæcenas; for without all of them the life of Horace had been quite different, and literature had been without one of its most charming authors. No doubt even the childhood of Horace had influence upon his future life. He was born near the source of one of the southern tributaries of the impetuous Aufidus, now called Ofanto, the river of Apulia, often mentioned by him, and so dear to his early recollections, that he exalts it to be a representative stream, as had been used the harmonious names of Mæander and Eurotas, and the other rivers of the poetry of Greece. Venusia, now Venosa, his birth-place, is situate in a beautiful country on the side of the Apennines towards the Adriatic. In this romantic region he wandered as a child near the pointed peaks of the mountain Vultur, or under Acherontia, built like a nest on a steep hill, or amid the woods and glens of Bantia, or by the lowly village of Forentum. The Apennines with their sombre forests of pine, and summits rising over each other, described so well in the *Mysteries of Udolpho*, had charms for Goethe, though a foreigner; and a poetic child born amongst them would find them a meet nurse. In the poetry of the ancients there are none of those elaborate and idealized descriptions of scenery found so often in modern writers; yet Horace, like Virgil, often gives a picture of places by epithets carefully chosen. When his fame as a poet was established, he would look back with a natural gratitude to the scenery of his childhood, and fancy that the gods protected the spirited boy from bears and serpents in his roamings among the hills, and that doves, the birds of Venus, like the robin redbreasts of later stories, threw on the sleeping child leaves of sacred myrtle and holy bay. Venusia had been an important Roman colony for upwards of 300 years, ever since the days of the Samnite wars. Hither fled some of the Roman troops after the defeat at Cannæ. Nature never intended Horace for a soldier: but he, who was born in a military town, became for a short time a tribune or colonel in the Roman army, and often expresses an admiration for Roman courage in war.

Horace nowhere makes mention of his mother, and we do not know whether she was a freed-woman, or free-born; he only says in one place that he was the child of lowly parents. It is likely enough that she died when he was young; else Horace, whose character is marked by affectionate gratitude, would probably have mentioned her. There is hardly anything more beautiful in the writings of antiquity than the way in which he speaks of that good father, whom he says he would not change for any parent who had held high office in the state. His father spared no expense and pains in his education. By him was the boy guarded from every taint of evil. None of the other Roman poets (except Terence, who was a slave, but born at Carthage, and of what rank there we do not know,) sprang from so humble an origin. His father had been a slave. The man who enfranchised the father little thought what would be the consequence of that enfranchisement. No wonder, as Horace himself tells us, and as Suetonius in his Life of Horace observes, that his father's low estate and calling were made a reproach to the prosperous friend of Augustus and Mæcenas. How bravely Horace answered this taunt, every reader of the poet knows. Indeed, he owed all to his father. If he had not given his son such a liberal education, Horace would probably have passed his days in the obscure town of Venusia, engaged there in some petty trade, and been an entertaining companion at the suppers of the centurions and their families. A more striking example cannot be given of what may depend on some humble instrument, who at a certain time behaves with spirit and generosity. Horace must have profited much by the lessons which he had in Livius Andronicus, and the other early poets of Rome, though he did not, when a man, highly esteem those authors who had cost him many a flogging, even as he has caused many a flogging to schoolboys since. His teacher Orbilius was like many a teacher, sour-tempered, free-spoken, given to whipping, one who earned more fame than money, and had reason to complain of the interference of parents. But if Horace, when delivered from the rod of Orbilius the grammarian, had received no more education, he had never been the Lyric poet of Rome. To a school was to be added a University, and kindly Athens, the only city in the world that could do it, was to finish what Rome had begun, and Greek literature was to crown Latin, that he, like his friend Mæcenas, might be learned in both tongues. How Horace's father obtained the means to send his son to Athens we may well wonder, when we consider the expense of an education at that fashionable University. Horace, at the time he left Italy for Greece, must have taken leave of the good father, whom he was never to see again.

At Athens Horace became familiar with Greek literature, he was a seeker after truth in the groves of Academus, he tried his hand at Greek verses, Greek Iambics perhaps, or Greek Elegiacs, or Greek Lyrics, till, as he playfully imagines, one night when he was sleeping, behold, the divine founder of Rome, who recognised in him a true son of Italy, no mere imitator or translator of Greek poetry, appeared in a dream that issued after midnight from the gate of horn, and forbade his attempting such a superfluous work. Thus, as the scenery of the Apennines, the liberality of his father, his early residence at Rome, the teaching of severe Orbilius, all tended to make Horace what he was destined to be, so did Athens contribute its share towards this end, both directly and indirectly; directly by teaching him Greek literature and philosophy, indirectly by the circumstances into which he was thrown owing to the public events which were then taking place. There is hardly any one in whose case it is more plainly to be seen how all kinds of different things concur in training a man to be what he is meant to be. Walckenaer and Rigault both remark, that while Horace was a student at Athens the news came of the assassination of Julius Cæsar, that at that time Cicero sent his treatise on the Offices to his son, who then was also a student at Athens, in which treatise Cicero expresses his admiration of the act of the conspirators; that the students were many of them the sons of senators, that the statues of Brutus and Cassius were crowned with flowers together with those of Harmodius and Aristogiton. Horace would be carried away by this enthusiasm. Youth is the age for republican impulses. When Brutus, Cato's son-in-law, came there, he would appear to the young Horace the true representative of republican principles. Even supposing that Horace was at that time an Epicurean, of which however we cannot be certain, his zeal for republicanism would prevent his taking offence at the Stoic opinions of Brutus. How Horace, so young and of such lowly origin, became a military tribune in the army of Brutus is as difficult to understand as many points in history must always be. That in the service of Brutus, in the midst of his military life, he had those natural spirits and love of fun which were characteristic of his joyous nature, is plain from the seventh Satire of the first book, which is interesting, as being in all probability the earliest remaining production of the poet. The military career of Horace and his republican enthusiasm were soon terminated by the decisive defeat of Philippi, after which, as Tacitus says, the republic, as republic, fought no battles. To Horace the day was not fatal, as to many others: like the lyric poet of Lesbos, the future lyric poet of Italy threw away his shield, which was not well, as he himself confesses. But this short portion of the life of Horace, forming such a contrast to his earlier and latter days, contributed its part towards making him the writer he became. Three times has he mentioned Cato, the father-in-law of Brutus, speaking in one place of his unconquered spirit, in another of his virtue, in a third of his glorious death. The exploits of republican Rome are dear to the poet. The worthies of the ancient commonwealth, Regulus, Æmilius Paullus, Camillus and Fabricius, are not unsung by him. He has a feeling for the ancient simplicity, and a belief in the morality, of the days of old. No one sets forth more strongly than he does the madness and impiety of civil war. Had he not seen the evil with his own eyes, himself a part of it? A courtier he became afterwards, but still a patriotic poet.

After the battle of Philippi he returned to Italy, with farm lost, humbled in hopes, like a bird whose wings are clipped. These were his dark days. He says that bold poverty drove him to write verses. To poverty we owe *Rasselas* and the *Vicar of Wakefield.* The same necessity gave the impulse to the genius of Smollett as a novelist. But of what verses does Horace speak? Indeed it is probable that he is half jesting. This is the opinion of August Arnold in his Life of Horace. Certainly the Epistle in which Horace speaks of these verses drawn forth by poverty is an Epistle full of jests and pleasant irony. It will not do to interpret Horace literally always. The same August Arnold thinks that it was then he enrolled himself in the company or guild of clerks: and Suetonius says that he obtained the place of secretary to a quæstor. With what means, whether the remains of his fortune, or borrowed money, or by some interest, is unknown. Arnold says that it is to his credit that he did not then take up the life of a parasite. A man of his natural wit might have got a livelihood more or less agreeable in this way, and been not unlike the parasites Vibidius and Balatro, whom he himself so graphically describes in the last of the Satires. From the days of his poverty and obscurity he no doubt learnt something, as all wise men do. The remembrance of them would make him more grateful to the friend, who raised him from difficulties to competence and ease. Some of the sterner and more manly passages of his poetry, and those which recommend a spirit undisturbed by all the changes of fortune, owe something to his having known the hardships of adversity. However, the iron never entered deeply into his joyous soul. If it had, it might have crushed the poetic spirit and light heart within him. The evil days were few. Whether he knew Virgil in earlier days, or had met him at Athens, or whether Virgil, his elder by five years, had seen some of his youthful poems, he found in him and Varius friends in the hour of need. This was the turning-point of his life. Horace tells us shortly how he appeared before the great man on that eventful day so full of fate to Horace, to Mæcenas himself, to literature. He was diffident and shy, and his speech was broken and stammering. He told the simple truth of himself, his father, his means. Few were the words of the patron in reply. Mæcenas did not give his friendship lightly: but, nine months after, Horace became his friend. What Walter Scott imagines in *Kenilworth* when describing the meeting of Shakespeare and Leicester, may be applied here: the son of a freedman was honoured with an interview with the Emperor's great minister, so that age would have told the tale; in ours we should say, the immortal had done homage to the mortal. However, Horace owed not only the happiness of his life, but his fame as a poet and writer, to this interview with Mæcenas. Some poets, like Dante and Milton, may have been made greater by adversity, when the indignant Muse has drawn spirit and fire from misfortune, but such was not the case of Horace. Indignation could never make verses of the kind he wrote. The one or two Epodes which he probably wrote in the days of his adversity are not to be compared with the happy outpourings of his soul in the days of his prosperity. Juvenal was right, when he says that Horace was comfortable on the day that he burst out in the praises of the God Bacchus. A joyous, not a bitter spirit, was needed for the writer of the Satires and Epistles of Horace. His Sabine farm and his quiet valley inspired those of the Odes which breathe contentment and joy. The times of his adversity lasted about three years; the bright sun of prosperity shone upon him for full thirty years, and few and light were the clouds that passed over it, till the hour of his last illness, when death came swiftly upon him. Few men ever had a more pleasant life than the poet; he had a good father, a liberal education, genius, a Muse ready to his call, popularity, independence, contentment, honour, troops of friends. Against this are to be set troubles and difficulties soon over, a certain amount of rivalry and jealousy, and health that was not robust. Though he had not all the conditions of a happy life, which Martial enumerates, yet he had a goodly share of them.

Horace tells us that he wrote for his friends, not for the public. But we are all his friends now. The works of Varius are lost, and there was no opportunity for Virgil in his poems to mention his brother poet. Horace's name does not appear in the verses of Propertius or Tibullus, though to Tibullus Horace has written an Ode and an Epistle. Ovid is the only one of the contemporary poets who mentions him, saying that tuneful Horace charmed his ears by his finished odes sung to the Italian lyre. It is odd that Martial, enumerating the birth-places of famous Latin poets, has omitted Horace, for the Flaccus there spoken of is Valerius Flaccus, a very inferior Flaccus. However, in other places Martial joins Horace's name with Virgil; and it is plain from Persius, who lived only about sixty years after Horace, and from Juvenal and Quintilian, that Horace had soon become a standard author. In the middle ages his fame fell far short of that of Virgil, probably it did not equal even that of Lucan; but since the revival of classical literature Horace has been without comparison the most popular of Latin authors; indeed there is no Greek so popular, hardly any modern one. Dr Douglas, an eminent physician in the days of George II., collected even then no fewer than 400 editions of Horace. Mr Yonge, in his edition of Horace, says that the list of these editions given 50 years ago by Mitscherlich extends over a hundred pages. Great has been the learning and ingenuity devoted to the elucidation of the text and meaning of Horace. Bentley's famous edition is in its way the most remarkable of all editions of Horace. None of the productions of Bentley display greater merits and greater faults than his edition of Horace, never were his ability and his arrogance more clearly seen; but scholars have said that almost as much is to be learnt from the mistakes of Bentley as from the careful judgment of other editors. The edition appeared on the 8th of December, the birthday of Horace, 1777 years after that event. Mr Yonge says that he has lived at Eton in a Horatian atmosphere, and Eton men seem to regard Horace as an Etonian, an opinion in which other schools can hardly be expected to agree. Many who have little liking for the classics, and have an unpleasant recollection of their early drudgery in them, make an exception in favour of Horace, the one author in Greek and Latin whom they still read. And many scholars, who have not a few favourites among the ancient writers, give their dearest affection to Horace. With some men, as with the Abbé de Chaupy, and with the witty Galiani, this love has risen to a passion of enthusiasm. The latter went so far as to write a treatise on the principles of the Laws of Nature and Nations, deduced from the poems of Horace. The Abbé de Chaupy, says Rigault, used to thank those who spoke well of Horace. Old women that he disliked were to him so many Canidias; a young lady that pleased him was a Lalage. Malherbe said that he made Horace his breviary. If Horace's wit endears him to Frenchmen, his strong common sense no less recommends him to Englishmen. And German editions of the poet are almost innumerable. Horace is especially the poet of the man of the world, of the gentleman: but on so many points do his writings touch, that they have an interest for those whose life is more laborious and eventful. Condorcet had a Horace with him in the dungeon at Paris where he died; De Witt, the Pensionary of Holland, a man of capacity and integrity, is said, when the mob were about to murder him and his brother, to have repeated the verses of the Ode of Horace, which in Stoic style describe the righteous and resolute man as unshaken from his purpose by the fury of citizens who bid him do what is wrong. Lessing counted Horace as one of those spirits to whose name he, like the Abbé de Chaupy, was unwilling that any taint of dishonour should attach. Hooker, as Yonge tells us from Walton's Life, in the preface to his edition of Horace, was found in the fields tending his few sheep with a Horace in his hand. Many can remember with what enthusiasm Dr Butler at Shrewsbury and Dr Keate at Eton used to teach Horace. Yonge in his notes gives us many passages in modern writers suggested by Horace. It is true that Niebuhr, lecturing in the year 1827, speaks as if the admiration of Horace was a feeling that then wavered; and Niebuhr himself does scanty justice to his poetry, and still less to his character. A writer who is so singular in his views as to account Catullus the greatest poet of Rome, would not estimate Horace fairly; the wild and impulsive Catullus, with the loud wailings of his passion, moves him more than the mild and quiet Horace. But, in comparison with Horace, Catullus is little read and enjoyed. Allusions to Horace are expected to be at once recognized. In the short compass of the first Epistle of the first book there are many passages that have become almost proverbial. Adaptations of his lines, some dignified, some jocular, have been made continually. Thus, as Lord Lytton says in his Introduction to the Odes, Mr Pitt never moved the House of Commons more than when to England contending with Napoleon he applied the passage of Horace which compares Rome in her struggle with Hannibal to the oak, "which lopped by axes rude receives new life, yea from the very steel." When Dr Goodall, Provost of Eton, was asked what he thought of omnibuses, which had then just been introduced into London, he replied "Horace has settled this by saying 'Omnibus hoc vitium est.'" And again, being asked to take some trifle at dinner, he said "No thank you, 'hæ nugæ seria ducunt in mala.'"

What then are the causes of this marvellous popularity? The question has often been discussed, only too fully. Indeed there was no reason to say very much on the point, for the qualities of a writer who pleases so many must lie on the surface. It is said that his distinguishing characteristic is good common sense; and indeed, whether he is serious or jesting, he never forgets common sense. But this alone makes no poet popular. Boileau is considered the very impersonification of common sense. Yet Boileau is not popular as Horace is. So to common sense must be added his wit, a wit fine, good-natured, pleasant, not overstrained, sensible. Never was anything more untrue than what Niebuhr says of him: "He looks upon everything as a folly, and tries to sneer at everything, treating what is most venerable with irreverence; this becomes at last a bad habit in him." On the contrary, Horace gives honour where honour is due, he does not sneer at patriotism, temperance, modesty, courage, simplicity, kindness, contentment; he reverences virtue, the laws of his country, the temples of the gods, the memory of the great men of Rome; so far from sneering becoming a bad habit with him, in his later writings he shows more and more a serious and chastened temper. In him, as in Sydney Smith, is the union of wit and wisdom. He teaches the truth while he laughs. His irony does not weary his hearers as that of Socrates is said to have done, of whom it has been amusingly, though of course unjustly said "that he was put to death because he was such a bore." Horace plainly knew his own faults, and practised real self-examination, and does not blame himself, as we often do, for faults which we have not, while we ignore those which we have. To his wisdom and wit we must add, as another cause of his popularity, the form of his poetry. The ancients, inferior to the moderns in ideas, are superior in form. In this is a justification of their being used as a means of education. This is true of Horace in an eminent degree. In his Epodes and even in his Satires there is less neatness and terseness of expression than in the Odes and Epistles, in which writings all is put together as in mosaic. The very objection urged with truth against Horace, that he is common-place, lets us see one of the causes of his popularity. He says common things a little better than others say them, and, though often only a little above mediocrity, is still just above it. As we rightly honour a man, who "though he has done no remarkable single act, yet is remarkable for the steady and unbroken performance of many daily duties," so we are fond of the poet, who, though he has not been caught up into paradise, nor been in hell, though he does not fill us with the terrors of the imagination, or delight us with the magic forms of wonder, yet speaks happily and pleasantly of the ordinary sorrows and homely joys of life, whom we feel to be a genial companion, a trifler in small things, but no trifler in what is really good and grave. Wit, wisdom, terseness, grace, are the main causes of his popularity. Most of us like him best in his lighter vein, as Blair remarked long ago. He was free from Lucretius' awkwardness of form, Catullus' extravagance, Propertius' affectation, Virgil's solemnity, Ovid's conceits, Tibullus' excess of sadness, Lucan's pedantry, Persius' obscurity, Juvenal's bad taste. He has no fellow in literature. There was something in him that no Greek author, no modern has; Providence made but one Horace; we love him, and the reason why we cannot fully tell.

The man Horace is more interesting than his writings, or, to speak more correctly, the main interest of his writings is in himself. We might call his works "Horace's Autobiography." To use his own expression about Lucilius, his whole life stands out before us as in a picture. Of none of the ancients do we know so much, not of Socrates, or Cicero, or St Paul. Almost what Boswell is to Johnson, Horace is to himself. We can see him, as he really was, both in body and soul. Everything about him is familiar to us. His faults are known to us, his very foibles and awkwardnesses.

Yet in his account of himself there is nothing morbid. Like Walter Scott, he had a thoroughly healthy mind. In one epistle he speaks of himself as if he were not so-minded. But this was plainly only a passing malady of soul. He seems almost as a personal friend to each of us. What would we not give to spend one evening with him, to take a walk over his Sabine farm with him, to sit by his fountain, to hear him tell a tale, or discuss a point? We feel bound to defend him, as we would defend an absent friend.

Now the gravest charge brought against him is that of having been a servile flatterer in the court of a cruel and cold-hearted tyrant, of having been a coward who ran away in battle, a traitor to liberty, one who for a farm sold his independence, one who, knowing the sorrows and seeing the wounds of his country, "did not choose to let his heart bleed," but drowned his cares in cups of wine. If this charge against him be just, we are bound to answer it. Yet we must be on our guard against exaggeration on the other side. Our poet was no prophet or martyr, he was no Cato or Socrates, he was not made of the stuff of which those are made who die for an idea, whether it be a real idea or a phantasy. As we think of his life of 57 years, during full 30 of which he was an author, it is striking to consider the events that happened in that time. When he was born, Pompey was warring in the east. The name of the republic was still great. When he was three years old, the conspiracy of Catiline was put down. When he wandered as a child in the deep valleys of the Apennines, Julius Cæsar was subduing Gaul. When he died, the generation was fast passing away that remembered the days of republican liberty, and the Roman world was under the well-established power of Augustus. Goethe, quoted by Niebuhr, said that there never was a more senseless act than the assassination of Julius Cæsar. Rebellions against Augustus were quite as senseless. Horace was young when he served in the last army of the republic, but his strong common sense must have opened his eyes to the character of those who served with him, and he must have known quite well that at any rate after the battle of Philippi the republic was an idle dream. A person of his character adapted himself to circumstances. We perhaps judge severely of the principal persons of those times, because we know what sad years of despotism followed, and can see clearly how rapidly the new system was undermining all manly virtues. But one alive then, unable to see all that was to follow, but who had witnessed the evils and miseries of civil dissension, might fairly have regarded Augustus as the saviour of the state. Tacitus gives an epitome of the two opposite views of the character of Augustus. The unfavourable view represents him as ambitious, hypocritical, cruel, false even to his friends, the destroyer of religion by accepting equal honours with the gods, and as deliberately choosing Tiberius for his successor, that his own fame might gain by the contrast. It is likely that the historian inclines to this view, for he states it last and most fully. But Tacitus was a different man from Horace, and lived after, not during the reign of Augustus. And the opposite view, stated moderately by Tacitus, represents Augustus' earlier conduct as almost necessary; there was no resource for Rome but in the government of one who established peace, enlarged the boundaries of the empire, administered justice, restrained licence, and adorned the capital with magnificent structures of marble. Horace, in his praises of Augustus, speaks of him, as Virgil does, not as the subverter of the republic, but as the legitimate successor of the long line of the great men of Rome. That Horace's eulogies of Augustus are greatly exaggerated cannot be denied. But it was hard for a man like Horace to be proof against the repeated kindnesses of the Emperor, kindnesses substantial and most pleasantly conferred. Augustus' personal character and manners were simple, like those of Horace himself. Perhaps we are apt to be misled by the word Emperor. Augustus had no splendid court. His repasts were plain and homely. He was fond of fishing, and of playing with little children. He was a man that loved his joke. He was very liberal in his gifts. Suetonius expressly says that he was greatly beloved by many. On the whole he was a steady friend to those that he liked. He could forgive those who insulted him. Livy the historian praised Pompey, and Augustus' only revenge was to call him the Pompeian historian. According to Suetonius, the Emperor made advances to the son of the freedman, which he on his part was not eager to accept. When he declined them, the Emperor was not offended. The epistles of Augustus were extant in the time of Suetonius, but nothing of them is left now, except a few extracts preserved by Suetonius. The tone of them is kind and playful. As Augustus grew older, he certainly did not become a worse man, and the Emperor was very different from the triumvir. No Roman ever had received so many outward honours as Augustus. Thrice he closed the portals of Janus. The standards of Rome, taken by the Parthians from Crassus and Antony, were restored to him. In five wars he was successful. The ancients naturally regarded the fortunate as Heaven's favourites. The disasters that saddened his declining years did not fall upon him till after Horace's death. Tiberius would not have been named by him as his successor, had not death taken away Marcellus, Agrippa, Drusus. If we compare with the praises of Augustus, Boileau's flattery of Louis XIV., whose life in some respects is not unlike that of Augustus, the Latin poet will not seem so servile as the French. Horace's relations with the Emperor did not destroy his independence of spirit. While he was not out of place at the tables of the great, simplicity charmed him more, and prosperity did not spoil, but improved his character.

The philosophy of Horace is a subject not altogether wanting in interest. The popular opinion is that he was an Epicurean, a disbeliever in Providence, to whom expediency was the measure of right, a pig, as he calls himself, of the sty of Epicurus. Niebuhr speaks of the irony of his Epicurean philosophy. On the other hand, Lord Lytton says "Horace is the poet of Eclecticism." And August Arnold, in his Life of Horace, tries to prove from certain passages of his works that Plato was the poet's favourite philosopher. A fourth opinion is that Horace's philosophy is little more than strong common sense, contentment, and a large experience of the world and society. Many are the passages in his writings that bear on philosophy. This is not to be wondered at. For philosophy was to the educated in ancient times what theology is now. The Romans indeed originated no system of philosophy. They showed even less invention in philosophy than in poetry. What philosophy they had was moral rather than metaphysical. For questions of abstract truth they had little taste; but they professed to look to philosophy to guide them in practical life, to mould their character, to teach them moderation in prosperity, patience in adversity. Thus they cared more for the religion than the theology of philosophy. Cato was a Stoic, whose stern and harsh virtue refused to bend to the exigencies of the times. Atticus, the opposite of Cato, was an Epicurean, who professed to place his happiness in retirement, and passed his days in a calm and inactive repose. Cicero professed to choose the middle path, calling himself an Academic, but inclining somewhat more to Stoicism in his latter days; he had no very great genius for philosophy, but had the power of expressing Greek ideas in polished and flowing language. Horace is neither like Cato, nor Atticus, nor Cicero. Certainly Horace was no Stoic. He had too much sense, too much amiability, and too keen a sense of the ludicrous to be a Stoic. For the Stoics were the pedants of ancient philosophy, who affirmed all sins to be equal, accounted the robbing of a market garden as bad as sacrilege, maintained that all error was madness, that a wise man is king in all circumstances however absurd, knows all sciences, is jack-of-all-trades, is never angry, or pitiful, or wrong in judgment, never changes his mind, never repents. In Cicero's oration for Murena, they are held up to ridicule, and again, with much finer wit, in the Satires of Horace. And yet Horace, who had a feeling for all the sides of human life, never thought of his dislike of Stoicism or his obligations to Augustus, when he sang of the noble death of Cato, and the soul indomitable amidst the subjection of the world. When he describes the upright man firm of purpose, complete in himself, able to despise honours, and resist passions, more than a match for fortune, independent of the gods and their gifts, looking death steadily in the face, he uses the very language of Stoicism, surely not then in irony, but in sober earnestness and faith. Horace was not then exactly an Epicurean. He was bound in allegiance to no philosophic master. But his love of repose, his contentment, his irony, his easy good-nature, his simple habits, his dislike of vulgar pretence, of superstition, of arrogance, his bodily temperament, the prosperity of his life, inclined him to the gentlemanlike school of Epicurus. However, as he grew older, it is plain he longed for something better, and desired to free himself from his faults, and was not content with his own advancement in virtue, and wished to improve in old age; and whither then should he go for this, except to divine philosophy? In his later writings the expressions of this wish increase. Was he then the poet of Eclecticism? He was the poet of human nature in unaffected simplicity. He himself tells us how at one time he stood forth as true Virtue's guard and rigid sentinel, at another time glided insensibly into the adoption of the accommodating principles of Aristippus: but he does not speak as if he were satisfied with this inconsistency; rather, that he desires to make such progress as he may, though it may be little compared with perfection. Horace read and thought for himself, and doubtless judged differently at different times; but he was no eclectic philosopher in the sense of deliberately picking out and choosing parts from various schools. However, his philosophy was something more than mere common sense and experience. August Arnold, in his Life of the poet, appears to speak of his philosophy as the groundwork of his moral and poetical character. Rather, it was not so much the foundation of his character, as something added to it; not the groundwork, but the crown of his life, interesting him more and more in his latter days, his guide and support in old age, his comfort in those feelings of melancholy from which the tender and fine-strung nature of the poet was certainly not always free. The passages adduced to show that Plato was his favourite philosopher do not prove as much as this. We know that Horace in his youth studied in the groves of Academus, and that when older he read Plato, and advised others to do so, but the Roman poet both intellectually and morally was very different from the idealist Plato, or his master Socrates, and even his irony was of a distinct kind.

It has been often said that Horace's loves did not touch his heart deeply, or perhaps that they are almost imaginary, taken from Greek odes for the purposes of his poetry. But however this may be, at any rate his friendships were real and lasting. Aristotle in his *Ethics* devotes two out of ten books to the subject of friendship, its causes, various kinds, preservatives, how indispensable it is to happiness, its relation to the political life, and other points. Cicero has a treatise of a very different kind on the same subject, more historical and diffuse, entering far less into abstract questions, and abounding with platitudes expressed in rounded sentences. But neither Aristotle nor Cicero has written so forcibly on friendship as Horace has done. Horace is the poet of friendship. He tells us in one place that to rave is a pleasure, when a friend is regained; in another place, that so long as he keeps his senses there is nothing on earth he can compare to a pleasant friend, and that the light of that day is most welcome, which brings friends to him. The names of his loves scarcely appear in his Satires and Epistles; but the names of his friends are to be seen through all his writings. One of the first of the Odes expresses his wish for the safe voyage of his friend Virgil, while almost at the end of the *Art of Poetry* he pays a tribute to the sincerity of Quintilius. Horace's Muse is never so happily inspired as by the joys and sorrows of his friends. In other passages he wishes that friendship was as blind as love, and as partial as the affection of a parent; and longs for that mutual forbearance which would best form and maintain friendships.

Nowhere does he speak in such severe terms as when he condemns the wretch, who for the sake of raising a laugh can backbite an absent friend. A friend is to be chosen not for his rank, but for his character. Chance does not make true friends. Mæcenas' house is a happy one, because all live there as friends, free from envy and intrigue. Horace cares that his friends should like his writings, and would grieve if they found no pleasure in reading them. When he has obtained all that his own moderate wants need, he makes requests for his friends.

And never surely was a man blessed with more friends. In the last satire of the first book of Satires he enumerates some of them, Virgil and Varius, two names that always appear together, Mæcenas, Plotius, Pollio, Bibulus, Servius, and others; and yet those there enumerated are few out of the whole number. The dearest of his comrades was Pompeius Grosphus, with whom he shared the extreme dangers of the disastrous day at Philippi. His joy at welcoming him safe home is as keen as his sorrow at the death of honest Quintilius, the common friend of Virgil and himself, by whose criticisms it is likely enough that either poet profited. Virgil, Varius, and Horace formed a literary triumvirate, as Walckenaer calls it, and Addison in the *Spectator* has observed that these three poets lived together in a happy union, unsullied by envy. Of Varius we know but very little, for his writings have met with a different lot from that of his two friends, either through chance, or because they were less worth preserving; and yet Virgil speaks of him as a poetic swan, and Horace as the vigorous writer of epic poetry, and as one who can describe martial exploits; and Quintilian says he would dare to match his *Thyestes* with any Greek tragedy. But Niebuhr well remarks that it is an unhappy subject, and that he would rather have his poem *On Death* than his tragedy. Virgil and Horace differed in genius, yet had this in common, that they both took the greatest care to give their verses the last finish. Many of Horace's friends are scarcely known, save from his mention of them. One of the more famous was Pollio, a general of Julius Cæsar, who at one time reconciled Antony and Augustus, and to whom Virgil owed the recovery of his farm. When fresh troubles broke out between the two leading men of Rome, Pollio maintained an honest independence, and, after his successful expedition to Dalmatia, retired from the senate and forum, and wrote a history of the civil war between Pompey and Cæsar, in which he did not fear to praise Brutus and Cassius. Neither the history, nor any of his tragedies, compared by the grateful Virgil to those of Sophocles, have come down to us. But he appears to have been a man of a brave and noble spirit. Another of Horace's friends was Messala Corvinus. He had been third in command at Philippi, but was received into the friendship of Augustus; and yet he preserved a bold and independent bearing, never afraid to say that he had had the honour of being the lieutenant of Cassius. Horace and others mention him as a distinguished orator. He was the patron of Tibullus. Horace speaks of him as imbued with philosophic learning, and yet as one who did not scorn to be a pleasant companion. His writings, composed, according to Seneca, in pure Latinity, are all lost.

But the friendship of Horace which we know far the most of is that with Mæcenas, for Mæcenas is to be regarded much more as the friend than the patron of the poet. Horace dedicated eight odes and four epodes to him. Two satires are addressed to him, and in the Satires frequent mention is made of him. Three epistles are also addressed to him. Mæcenas shares with Melpomene the glory of his lyric poetry. Simple and even homely is the ode in which the poet invites his luxurious friend to a humble repast. Mæcenas clung to life with a fondness to be condemned by a Roman, but with which his affectionate friend could sympathize, and promised him his company in the last dreadful journey, a promise curiously fulfilled. If we had an ode on the death of his dearest friend, we might have known still more of their happy affection. It was the glory of the poet to think that he, the child of lowly parents, had been called "beloved" by Mæcenas. His friend who was content to remain a knight is the example to him of moderation. In one of the finest of his odes he tries to tempt his great friend to a pleasant change from his cares at busy Rome. He does not scruple, in the last satire of the first book of Satires, to mention Mæcenas as his friend on equal terms with others. Sometimes the poet was too abrupt in his visits, and yet always, as it would seem, welcome. There was nothing more he need trouble his powerful friend to give him, "blessed enough in his one Sabine farm." He can afford to disregard the jealousy which this distinguished intimacy had naturally caused him. In happy lines, imitated by Swift, he describes the harmless and easy conversation in his drives with the great man. Addressed to Mæcenas is the first of all the Epistles, in which he rises higher than his usual strain in the praises of philosophy, and virtue, and a good conscience, and yet for all that cannot help a joke at the expense of his usual butt, the Stoics. It is plain, and indeed not to be wondered at, that the minister, whose health was weak, and who had many cares and troubles, desired the company of such a delightful friend, and complained of his long absence. Horace, with a charming playfulness and a mixture of independence and respect, reminds his friend of his own weak health, his love for the country, his bashful modesty, his gratitude, his fondness for ease, his time of life, his willingness to resign all his patron's gifts rather than offend him, or mar the freedom of their intercourse. If we needed a proof of the truth of what Suetonius says about the independence of Horace in his dealings with Augustus, we have here an undesigned coincidence in his bearing towards Mæcenas. To the end their friendship lasted, and the dying statesman recommended the poet to the emperor, not knowing that his friend was so soon to follow him. Other friendships, as of Epaminondas and Pelopidas, Scipio and Lælius, Cicero and Atticus, have received a more distinct and marked attention, but never was one more lasting, more honourable, more unaffected; and if we love the memory of Horace as a lyric poet, a satirist, a master of the art of writing epistles, he has hardly fewer claims upon our admiration and affection, as giving us the pattern of a sincere and grateful friend.

LIFE OF HORACE BY SUETONIUS.

[The genuineness of this brief Life of Horace has, like that of so many of the writings of antiquity, been called in question; but Porphyrio, considered the most valuable of the ancient commentators on Horace, distinctly asserts that Suetonius wrote it, and the Delphin editor truly says that the style of Suetonius plainly appears in it. Niebuhr says: "The Life of Horace by Suetonius is very interesting." Walckenaer, in his Life of Horace, speaks of this Life as with good reason attributed to Suetonius.]

HORATIUS FLACCUS, born at Venusia, was the son, as he himself tells us, of a freedman, who was a collector of payments made at auctions (or, as there is a belief, of a salter, since a certain person wrangling with him taunted him thus: "How often have I seen your father wiping his elbow!") M. Brutus, the general in the war which ended at Philippi, stirred the spirit of Horace, who served as a military tribune: on the defeat of Brutus' side he was pardoned, and obtained a secretaryship to a quæstor. Having been introduced first to Mæcenas, then to Augustus, he became an intimate friend of both. Mæcenas' affection for him clearly appears from the following epigram: "If I love you not, Horace, more than my own bowels, may you behold your comrade leaner than any little mule:" and still more in his last moments, when he thus briefly recommended him to Augustus, "Remember Flaccus, as you would myself."

The post of private secretary was offered to him by Augustus, as is indicated by the following letter to Mæcenas: "Hitherto I have felt equal to writing to my friends; but now, being much occupied and infirm in health, I want to rob you of our common friend Horace.

He will leave then your table, where he dines as a parasite, and come to my palace to help me in writing letters." This offer was declined by Horace, but Augustus was not offended, and continued to press on him his friendship. Letters are still extant, from which I give, as a sample, a few extracts. "Assume the same amount of right at my house, as though you lived with me; for be sure you would act rightly and not without reason, since I would have as much of your company as your health will permit." And again: "What a lively recollection I have of you, you may learn from our friend Septimius; for it so happened that when he was present I mentioned your name. If you are so haughty as to scorn my friendship, I am not on that account disdainful in return." Often too, among other jokes, he called him "a pleasant mannikin," and enriched him by several acts of munificence. He admired his writings so much, and was so confident of their immortality, as to direct the composition of the Secular Hymn, and of the Ode on the victory of his step-sons, Tiberius and Drusus, over the Vindelici; and compelled the poet on this account to add, after a considerable interval, to the three books of Odes a fourth. Having read his Satires, he complained in the following terms of his having made no mention of himself in them: "Know that I am angry with you, because in most of your writings you do not choose to hold converse with me. Can you be afraid that your seeming to be intimate with me will discredit your name with future ages?" And he drew from him the Epistle, which opens with this preface: "Whereas alone you sustain the weight of so many duties, protecting the Italian Republic by arms, gracing it by morals, amending it by laws, I were a sinner against the public weal, were I by a long discourse to waste your time, Cæsar."

In form Horace was short and corpulent, as he is described by himself in his Satires, and by Augustus in the following letter: "Dionysius has brought me your little book, which I take in good part, though I find fault with the smallness of its contents. Indeed you seem to me to be afraid of your little books exceeding yourself in size. However if you lack inches, you lack not a dear little body. So you have my leave to write in a pint pot, since the compass of your volume is so very bulky, like your stomach." Horace lived generally in rural retirement at his Sabine or Tiburtine farm: and his house is still shown near the little grove of Tiburnus. I have also had put into my hands elegiacs ascribed to him, and an epistle in prose, in which he is made to recommend himself to Mæcenas; but I regard neither as genuine; for the elegiacs are common-place, and the epistle besides is obscure, a fault from which he was remarkably free. He was born on the 8th of December in the consulship of L. Cotta and L. Torquatus. He died on the 27th of November in the consulship of C. Marcius Censorinus and C. Asinius Gallus, when he had completed his 57th year, having in the presence of witnesses named Augustus his heir; for, owing to the violence of his illness, he had no strength to sign his will. He was buried at the end of the Esquiline Hill, close to the tomb of Mæcenas.

INTRODUCTION TO THE ODES.

THE poetry which Horace has left us is contained in the Odes, and, in a much slighter degree, in the Epodes. It is true that in them, as well as throughout the Satires and Epistles, he frequently appears as a moralist and a man of humour; but here only does he write as a poet, in the more usual sense of the word. Didactic verse is indeed in some points even better suited to his genius than the writing of lyric poetry; and so Dante, in the 4th canto of the *Inferno*, describes the poet as "Satirist Horace;" but the Odes have always been the most popular of his works, they were certainly his favourites and his pride, it was his glory to be pointed out as "the minstrel of the Roman lyre[1]," and he feels that in the Odes he has reared for himself "a monument more enduring than brass[2]."

Horace is ready to acknowledge his obligations to the lyric poetry of Greece, from which he derived his metres, and also not a few of his ideas. He speaks of his lute as one which had been "first tuned by the Lesbian citizen[3];" that is, by Alcæus, whom he seems to have taken as his model more than any other single poet; and he declares that Fate has granted to him "the delicate spirit of the Grecian Muse[4]." But in those passages of Horace where he has imitated verses of Greek poetry of which we possess the originals, there is nothing like plagiarism, or a servile reproduction of his author. Not only is the style everywhere completely his own, but a different turn is given to the idea, and such a change is made in its expression, that it becomes, as it were, fairly his property. This defence, which may justly be set up in behalf of Virgil, is even more strongly in favour of Horace. The fact that the fault of plagiarism, which has very often been imputed to Virgil, has but seldom been seriously charged against Horace, is due partly to the unquestioned originality of the Satires and Epistles; but in some degree it is to be explained by the chance which has lost to us most of the works which Horace appears to have chiefly adopted as his models; for he does not frequently imitate the extant Odes of Pindar.

Nor does Horace owe to any poet of his own country such obligations as Virgil owes to Lucretius. Catullus had indeed already

[1] IV. 3, 23. [2] III. 30, 1. [3] I. 32, 5. [4] II. 16, 38.

imitated Greek lyrics, and written odes in one or two of the metres used by Horace, in Sapphics and in Choriambics. But a perusal of the 11th and 51st Odes of Catullus, which are written in Sapphics, will show at once how little Horace is indebted to his predecessor. The latter of these pieces of Catullus has much merit as a translation of one of the extant poems of Sappho; but it wants the compactness and harmony and finish, which give to the Odes of Horace a character which belongs to them alone. With regard to the Alcaic metre, the boast made by Horace, that he was the first to introduce it into Latin literature, is, so far as we can tell, well-founded. "Alcæus, celebrated by no Roman tongue before, I first as Latin lyrist have made known[1]." Horace may truly be said to be, on the whole, an eminently original poet.

The Odes are written in numerous metres, which Horace selects with much skill to suit the many and various subjects of his poems. The two forms of the lyric stanza which he chiefly employs are the grave and stately Alcaic and the sprightly and rapid Sapphic. And yet sometimes, and especially in the Secular Hymn, he has succeeded in giving to the Sapphic verse an unwonted majesty and solemnity; and he has been no less happy in adapting the Alcaic stanza to some of his lighter songs.

If we divide the Odes into classes, we may enumerate those which sing of Love, Friendship, Religion, Morality, Patriotism; poems of eulogy addressed to Augustus and his relations; and verses written on miscellaneous subjects and incidents; and this latter class includes some of the most charming of the Odes.

It is a high compliment to the fascination of Horace's character, that those of his Odes which treat of love have attracted so much attention, and so much written disquisition. Out of about a hundred Odes of Horace which we possess, hardly a dozen can fairly be called love poems; and in every one of these the love is very clearly and unmistakably little more than an ornamental and fictitious emotion; there is no depth of feeling, no absorbing passion. It has often been attempted to make one genuine exception in the case of Cinara, who gained the poet's affection early in his life, and died young. Mr Theodore Martin says "She, if anyone, had touched his heart, and haunted his fancy." Horace mentions her name on four occasions; in the first Ode of the 4th Book he says, "I am not the man that I was beneath kind Cinara's sway;" in the 13th Ode of the same Book, "Fate to Cinara granted fleeting years;" in the 7th Epistle of the first Book he speaks of the time when he used "to lament over the wine-cup the flight of saucy Cinara;" and in the 14th Epistle of the same Book he refers to himself, when young, as one who, "without a present, could please the grasping Cinara." It would be going far to assert that allusions such as these express anything like tender regret or true affection. The poet seems to grieve, not for the loss of Cinara, but for the youth and health and

[1] Epist. I. 19, 32.

gaiety he once enjoyed. We do not see in Horace anything like the passionate fondness of Catullus; still less do we find in him Petrarch's deep and sad remembrance:

"Nè gran prosperità il mio stato avverso
Può consolar di quel bel spirto sciolto[1]."

"And high prosperity could ne'er console
My hapless lot for that fair spirit fled."

But those of Horace's Odes which may be called poems of friendship present an almost startling contrast to the unreality and absence of true feeling which we notice in his songs on love. Horace as a friend is always genuine and affectionate. The ode which prays for the safe return of Virgil from Greece[2], and that which so sorrowfully grieves for the death of Quinctilius, the friend of Virgil and himself[3], his song of joy on the return of his old comrade Pompeius Varus[4], the pleasing Ode addressed to Septimius[5], and the pathetic verses in which the poet promises Mæcenas that he will not outlive him[6], all these undoubtedly express a sincere and earnest friendship. If Horace, as the poet of love, is but weak and changeable, his Odes (and his other writings no less) show him to us as one of the best and truest of friends.

Horace, like his friend Virgil, mixes together the ideas of religion and fatalism. He has even coupled the names of Fate and the gods, as Powers of equal sovereignty. "Nothing more great or good than him have Fate and Heaven's grace bestowed on earth[7]." He once speaks of himself as "Heaven's niggard and unfrequent worshipper[8];" and tells how he was recalled from "Wisdom's foolishness" to a belief in the gods, by a peal of thunder in a clear sky. It is hard to decide how far this ode was intended to be understood seriously; at the same time, there is, perhaps, more religious feeling in the Odes than has been generally allowed. Horace constantly ascribes to the due worship of the gods the splendid growth of the Roman dominion; and he attributes the recent calamities of the civil wars, and other disasters, to the national neglect of religious observances. Addressing the Roman people, he says "'Tis because you own yourself lower than the gods, that you rule the world. From them is every beginning, to them ascribe every ending. Many a misfortune have the gods, when slighted, imposed upon afflicted Hesperia[9]." These ideas are repeated so persistently, and with so much emphasis, that it is almost impossible to doubt the sincerity of the poet. The Ode addressed to Phidyle[10] is clearly devotional in its spirit. Horace has been very successful in imparting to the Secular Hymn the tone of patriotic piety. He is fond of dwelling on the duty of resignation to the will of Heaven, as in the ode to Leuconoë[11]. In one passage, the words of Horace bear a striking resemblance to the

[1] Sonetto CCC. [2] I. 3. [3] I. 24. [4] II. 7. [5] II. 6. [6] II. 17. [7] IV. 2, 47. [8] I. 34, 1. [9] III. 6, 5. [10] III. 23. [11] I. 11.

precept in the Gospels, ("If any man will come after me, let him deny himself,") and the blessing which follows. "The more that each man has denied himself, the more he will receive from Heaven[1]." But it must be observed that the blessings which the poet contemplates are those only of contentment and peace of mind.

The morality which Horace teaches in the Odes is generally lofty and earnest in its spirit. He proclaims himself here, as he does elsewhere, the philosopher of moderation and contentment. In the Introduction to the Epistles, this leading feature of Horace's moral philosophy will be found to be more fully noticed. The moral teaching of Horace is well and concisely stated in the following lines, which conclude the 9th Ode of the 4th Book. "More rightly does he assume the title of 'blest,' who has learned how to use wisely the gifts of Heaven, and to endure stern penury, and who fears disgrace worse than death; he for his dear friends or fatherland is not afraid to die." Nor can it be said that the ideal character here described is wanting in excellence or dignity.

Horace, when he acts as a censor, has only too copious a subject on which to employ invective and regret. For in truth, owing partly to the long-continued civil wars, and the consequent prevalence of insecurity and lawlessness, partly to the introduction of foreign luxury, and the increase of political corruption, the morality of Rome had already advanced on the road to utter and irretrievable decay. "Alas," he exclaims, "we blush for our scars, and guilt, and brothers slain[2]!" Perhaps the most striking Odes on the universal degeneracy are the 6th and 24th of the 3rd Book: few readers of Horace will refuse to recognise in these odes, and also in others, the genuine lover of his country and of virtue.

In connection with the patriotic odes, those odes may be properly noticed, which are poems of compliment to Augustus and his relations. As to the flattery which these odes contain, the defence which may be put forth in behalf of the poet (and which seems to be good as an excuse, if not as a justification,) has already been stated in the General Introduction, and need not be repeated here. These two classes of Odes are alike at least in one point; namely, in their style and form. They are both written in Horace's grander and more elevated manner. Though Horace charms us far less here than he does in his lighter pieces, he is, notwithstanding, successful in a high degree. The march of the verse is firm and vigorous; the compliments and praises are expressed with much skill and dignity; and the feelings of patriotism are uttered with happiness and enthusiasm. The 2nd, 3rd and 5th Odes of the 3rd Book are good examples of Horace as a patriot, and many lines which they contain have become almost proverbs; the 4th, 6th and two last Odes of the 4th Book are specimens of panegyric; but still the eulogy is tempered with patriotism.

But the private Odes (as they may be called when compared with

[1] III. 16, 21. [2] I. 35, 33.

those which treat of public events and public men,) have always been the most popular and attractive. Love, Friendship, Religion, and Morality, are the subjects under which may be grouped the greater number of these Odes. Still, many of them are written on various other occasions; the legends of mythology, the changing seasons, the praise of wine, a quarrelsome party, an invitation, a fortunate escape from a wolf or the fall of a tree, such are some of the miscellaneous subjects of these poems. Sometimes they are sprightly and joyous, at other times they are more or less deeply marked by a tone of melancholy sadness. It is noticeable that the gayer of the Odes occur in the earlier Books; no doubt advancing years and failing health, added to the loss of many of his friends, subdued in no small degree the sprightliness of the poet's disposition. But indeed Horace has written very few Odes in a spirit of unmixed gaiety; when we have mentioned the lively and humorous remonstrance with Lydia[1], the ode of playful encouragement to Xanthias[2], the address to Barine[3], and the enthusiastic eulogy of the virtues of wine[4], it would not be easy to make any important additions to the list. More commonly, pensive and lively sentiments meet together in the same ode; as in that inscribed to his friend Quintius Hirpinus, where thoughts on the swift approach of age, the short-lived nature of youth and enjoyment, and the universal mutability of things, are introduced. "Spring flowers keep not always the same charm; nor beams the ruddy Moon with face unchanged; why harass with eternal designs a mind too weak to compass them[5]?" These somewhat gloomy reflections are used as a reason why we ought to enjoy wisely the pleasures of life, and not to fret. And Horace is fond of dwelling upon the interchange of these ideas; for he does the same in several others, and not the least pleasing of the Odes. As specimens of the excellence of the more or less serious of the private Odes, a few may be mentioned out of very many. The prophecy of Nereus[6] is perhaps the finest of those which are written on mythological subjects; the address to his page[7], to the fountain of Bandusia[8], and the dialogue between himself and Lydia[9], are composed in Horace's lightest and most elegant manner. In the Ode on the longing of all men for rest[10], the poet enforces his usual doctrines with much happiness and beauty of expression; while the two concluding Odes of the 3rd Book may be selected as good specimens, each in its different style, of Horace's more grave and elevated verse; the latter of these two Odes is probably the noblest of all poetical anticipations of immortality.

And never has an immortality of poetical fame been looked forward to with greater certainty and more surely-grounded confidence. It must of course be allowed that Horace is inferior to Pindar in power and sublimity, and to Burns in passion and spirit. Béranger in many points resembles, but does not equal Horace:

[1] I. 8. [2] II. 4. [3] II. 8. [4] III. 21. [5] II. 11, 9.
[6] I. 15. [7] I. 38. [8] III. 13. [9] III. 9. [10] II. 16.

perhaps, however, in tenderness and pathos he sometimes is at least not inferior to him. In writing of himself, for instance, Béranger is more pathetic than Horace. It may be that the language, which is natural and touching in the French poet, would have seemed too weak and plaintive to a Roman. As Horace tells us that poverty drove him to make verses, so Béranger says that, in his obscurity and destitution, Heaven inspired him to sing:

"Une plainte touchante
De ma bouche sortit;
Le bon Dieu me dit: 'Chante,
Chante, pauvre petit!'"

Though Horace so far resembles Béranger, that his lyric poetry almost defies translation, yet, in another point, he differs from him completely. If the Odes of Horace are hard to translate or imitate, his Satires and Epistles have been very successfully adapted by many eminent writers of modern Europe. An author, so open to imitation in one portion of his works, and yet almost inimitable in another, is surely entitled to the praise of especial originality. For thus he does not only prove his lasting influence on later poets, but also his command of two distinct and separate styles of composition: and, in each of these, Horace is still without a rival.

In the perfection of his taste, in delicacy of touch, in his power of so arranging words and phrases as to convey exactly the shade of thought which he intends, Horace has never been equalled; perhaps he has never been approached. But it is not only as an artist that Horace is remembered and beloved. His goodness as a moralist and a patriot, his true affection and faithfulness as a friend, the gentle and attractive pensiveness of his reflections, so pleasingly blended with happier and more cheerful thoughts, his delightful and polished humour, and the kindliness with which he uses his deep knowledge of the human heart to prove that vice, apart from its criminality, is a folly and a mistake,—all unite to render Horace that which he has ever so justly been, the most popular of poets.

ODES. BOOK I.

I.

The dedication to Mæcenas. Every man is governed by his ruling passion; the Olympian charioteer, the politician, the trader, the husbandman, the merchant, the man of pleasure, the soldier, the hunter. To win the title of a lyric poet is all that I desire.

MÆCENAS, sprung from royal ancestors, you that are both my shield and glory dear, some men there are who make it their delight to gather with the car Olympian dust; and the goal just cleared by the glowing wheels, and the ennobling palm, uplift them to the gods the lords of earth; one is blest, if the throng of fickle citizens rush to exalt him with the threefold honours; another, if he has stored in his own granary all that is swept from Libyan threshing-floors. Him whose joy it is to delve with the hoe his father's fields you can never tempt away, though you warrant him the wealth of an Attalus, to cleave with Cyprian bark the Myrtoan main, a timorous mariner. The merchant, while he dreads the African blast that wrestles with Icarian waves, praises the repose and fields of his native town; presently he repairs his shattered ships; for poverty to bear he cannot learn. One there is, who scorns not draughts of mellow Massic, nor to take a portion from the heart of the day, with limbs stretched now beneath a verdant arbutus, now at a hallowed streamlet's soothing source. Many the camp delights, and the clang of the trumpet mingled with the clarion, and wars that mothers abhor. Beneath the cold sky remains the hunter, and forgets his blooming bride, whether his faithful hounds have sighted a doe, or the Marsian boar has burst the fine-wrought nets.

Me the ivy-leaf, the meed of learned brows, makes the partner of the gods above; me the cool grove and the tripping companies of Nymphs blended with Satyrs sever from the people: if Euterpe keeps not back her flute, and Polyhymnia is not coy to tune the Lesbian lyre. But if among lyric bards you grant me a place, with crest exalted I shall strike the stars.

II.

The subject of this ode is the overflowing of the Tiber, which recalls to the poet the flood of Deucalion. He imagines that the disaster is caused by the wrath of Ilia, the wife of the Tiber, at the civil wars and the assassination of Julius Cæsar. Augustus, as Mercury in human shape, is invoked to save the empire.

Enough of snow and dreadful hail the Father has now sent upon the earth, and, smiting with red right-hand the sacred heights, has affrighted the city, has affrighted the nations, lest the troublous age of Pyrrha should return, who bewailed unwonted prodigies, when Proteus drove all his herd to visit the mountain-tops, and the tribe of fishes clung to the crown of the elm, which once had been the doves' familiar haunt, and timorous hinds swam on the o'erspreading flood. We have seen the yellow Tiber, his waves whirled back with fury from the Tuscan shore, advance to overthrow the monuments of the king, and Vesta's shrine; while the River boasts himself the avenger of Ilia that too grievously complains, and, wandering from his course, flows beyond his left bank through fondness for his spouse, though Jove approves it not.

Our youth, diminished by their parents' fault, will hear that citizens have made sharp the steel, wherewith the formidable Parthians would better perish, and shall hear of civil combats. Which of the gods shall the people invoke for the fortunes of the sinking empire? With what prayer shall the holy virgins solicit Vesta, who will not hear their hymns? To whom will Jove assign the duty of expiating guilt? Come at last, we entreat thee, thy brilliant shoulders robed in cloud, Diviner Apollo! Or thou, if thou choosest, laughing Erycina, around whom Mirth flits, and Love; or thou, our Founder, if thou dost regard thy race and children whom thou hast scorned, thou that art glutted with too long a show, thou whom the battle-cry delights, and polished helms, and the glance of the Marsian footman, fierce against his bloodstained foe; or thou, kind Maia's winged child, if on earth with change of shape thou dost take the form of a youth, deigning to be styled the avenger of Cæsar; late mayest thou return to heaven, and long be pleased to dwell among the people of Quirinus, and may not too early a gale waft thee away, offended at the crimes we commit! Here mayest thou rather love mighty triumphs, here mayest thou love to be called Sire and Sovereign, and suffer not the Medes to career unchastised, whilst thou art our chief, O Cæsar!

III.

The ode begins with a prayer for the safe voyage of Virgil to Athens, which suggests the daring of the earliest mariner. The boldness of man in overcoming difficulties set by Nature; which is poetically represented as presumptuous opposition to the will of Heaven.

So may the goddess who rules o'er Cyprus, so may Helen's brethren, those shining stars, and the father of the winds direct you, fast binding all the rest except Iapyx, O ship, you that carry Virgil as a pledge committed to your charge, give him up, I pray you, to the Attic shores unharmed, and keep safe the half of my soul.

Heart of oak and triple brass lay around the breast of him who first to the savage sea entrusted his frail bark, and feared not the African blast battling with the North-winds, nor the grisly Hyades, nor the fury of Notus, than whom there is no mightier lord of the Adriatic, whether it be his will to wake or smooth the deep. What form of Death's approach can he have feared, who viewed with tearless eyes the monsters swim, who viewed the surging sea, and your accursed rocks, Acroceraunia? In vain has God in his providence parted land from land by the estranging Ocean, if nevertheless impious barks bound across the waters that should not be touched. In its boldness to o'ermaster all things, the race of man dashes through forbidden sacrilege; in his boldness the child of Iapetus by guilty fraud brought fire among the nations. After fire had been filched from its home in heaven, wasting disease and a strange battalion of fevers swooped down on earth; and the doom of death, far removed before, made its coming swift. On wings not given to man Dædalus explored the void of air; through Acheron's barrier burst the toiling Hercules.

To mortals there is nought of difficulty; in folly we assail even heaven itself; and through our guilt we do not suffer Jove to lay his wrathful thunderbolts aside.

IV.

The return of Spring. The changing season warns us of the shortness of life.

Keen Winter is melting away beneath the welcome change to Spring and the Western breeze, and rollers draw the dry keels to the sea; and the herd no more delights in its stall or the ploughman in his fire, and with hoar-frosts the meadows are not white. Now Venus, Lady of Cythera, leads her quires, while the Moon looks down from above, and linked with the Nymphs the beauteous Graces shake the ground with measured tread, and fiery Vulcan kindles the Cyclops' ponderous forges. Now 'tis the time to twine the glossy head with myrtle green or the blossom which the unprisoned lands produce; now too 'tis the time to sacrifice to Faunus in the shady groves, either with a lamb if he require it, or, if he choose, with a kid.

Pale Death with impartial foot strikes at the hovels of the poor and the towers of princes. O my Sestius, blest though you be, life's short span forbids us to begin the fragment of a distant hope. Soon will darkness overwhelm you, and the fantastic Shades, and Pluto's narrow mansion; whither when once you have travelled, you will not by the dice's cast be elected monarch of the wine, nor admire the blooming Lycidas, with love for whom the maidens will presently glow.

V.

To Pyrrha, who is faithless as the winds or seas, and whose fancy no lover can fix.

What dainty boy amid a world of roses, and steeped in flowing perfumes crystal-clear, clasps you, O Pyrrha, in the pleasant cave? For whom do you bind up your yellow hair in a simplicity of gracefulness? Alas, how oft will he bewail your troth and Heaven's caprice, and stare, a novice, at the deep all wild beneath the gloomy blasts! Who in pure faith enjoys you now as gold; who dreams of you still unestranged, still kind, and knows not of the treachery of the gale. Hapless are they to whom unproved you shine! For myself, the holy wall by its votive tablet tells that I have hung up my dripping garments to the god that is lord of the main.

VI.

To Agrippa. His exploits will be better described in the epic poetry of Varius. The lightness of my lyric song suits not the grandeur of heroic subjects.

By Varius, a bird of Homer's strain, you shall be recorded a valorous warrior and the queller of the foe, what feat soe'er on deck or on his steed the soldier led by you has dauntlessly achieved.

We, Agrippa, essay not to sing these deeds, nor the direful wrath of Peleus' son, who knew not how to yield, nor shrewd Ulysses' voyages o'er the sea, nor Pelops' murderous house;—we, too slight for themes sublime; while reverence, and our Muse, the mistress of the unwarlike lyre, forbids us to mar by the fault of our genius illustrious Cæsar's praises, and your own.

Who shall record in worthy tones Mars clad in corslet of adamant, and Merion black with Trojan dust, and Tydides, by Minerva's aid a match for the gods above? 'Tis of feasts we sing, we sing of the battles of maidens, who fiercely ply with close-pared nails their lovers, whether we be free, or fired at all with love; and change not from our wonted playfulness.

VII.

Let others extol the famous cities of the world; the scenery of Tibur has the greatest charm for me. Wine drives away the sorrows of life; even Teucer, when banished from Salamis, consoled his companions with wine.

Let others praise famed Rhodes, or Mytilene, or Ephesus, and the walls of Corinth with its double sea, or Thebes made glorious by Bacchus, or Delphi by Apollo, or Thessalian Tempe. Some there are, whose only task it is to extol in long-drawn lay the city of virgin Pallas, and to set upon their brow a frontlet of olive, culled far and wide. Many a one, to render honour to Juno, will sing of Argos meet for steeds, and opulent Mycenæ. Myself neither enduring Lacedæmon nor the plain of fruitful Larissa has smitten with delight so keen as the home of echoing Albunea, and Anio's torrent, with the grove of Tiburnus, and the orchards watered by the bounding brooks.

As the fair South-wind ofttimes sweeps away the clouds from the gloomy sky, and does not ever beget the showers, so do you, my Plancus, wisely remember to put an end to sorrow and the troubles of life with mellow wine; whether the camp possesses you, all agleam with standards, or the tangled shade of your own Tibur shall possess you.

Teucer, while he fled from Salamis and his father, still is said in story to have bound with a poplar garland his temples dewy with the easeful god, and thus addressed his downcast friends: "Wheresoever a fortune kinder than a sire shall waft us, thither will we go, my partners and comrades. Let nothing be despaired of while Teucer is guide, and Teucer conductor: for unfailing Apollo has promised that on a new soil shall be a Salamis, whose name shall confuse it with the first. Come, my valiant men, ye who oft with me have suffered sorer woes than these, now with wine chase away your cares; to-morrow we will sail anew the boundless main."

VIII.

To Lydia, who has transformed Sybaris from a hardy athlete into a doting lover.

O Lydia, say, by all the gods I beg you, why haste to ruin Sybaris by your love? Why is it that he hates the sunny Plain, once able to endure the dust and heat? Why like a soldier does he prance no more among his peers, nor curb with sharp-toothed bits the mouths of Gallic steeds? Why fears he to touch the yellow Tiber? Why shuns he the wrestlers' oil more warily than vipers' blood; and no longer shows arms discoloured by his weapons, he who gained glory oft with the quoit, oft with the javelin sped beyond the mark? Why lies he hid, as they tell that the son of Ocean Thetis lay, just ere the woeful doom of Troy befel, lest his manly attire might drag him forth to the slaughter of the Lycian battalions?

IX.

To Thaliarchus. Description of winter scenery. Overcome the inclemency of the season with the warmth of hospitality. Leave the future to Heaven, and enjoy your youth while it lasts.

You see how stands Soracte, white with its depth of snow, and the groaning woods can no longer support their load, and the rivers are fast set with nipping frost.

Lavishly pile up logs upon the hearth, and melt the cold away; and with warmer cheer, my Thaliarch, draw from the two-handled Sabine jar the vintage four years old. To the gods commit all else; for when once they have laid to rest the blasts, that fiercely battle on the boiling deep, no more is the cypress tempest-tossed, and the ancient mountain-ash.

What is to be on the morrow, shrink from searching out; and each single day that Fortune shall grant, reckon it as gain; and scorn not you, in your youth, delightful loves or dances, so long as gray-haired sourness comes not near your bloom. Now too, let the Plain and squares, and tender whisperings at nightfall, again and again be sought at the preconcerted hour; now too, the pretty laugh from the depth of the nook, that betrays the hiding girl, and the forfeit snatched from her arm, or the finger that feigns to be unyielding.

X.

Hymn to Mercury.

Mercury, Atlas' grandchild eloquent, that didst skilfully fashion the savage manners of the earliest men by language, and the practice of the graceful gymnasium;—of thee will I sing, the herald of mighty Jove and of the gods, and the father of the curvèd lyre, cunning to hide away by playful theft whatever thing it please thee.

At thee, while of yore with threatening voice he tried to cow thy boyhood, unless thou wouldst restore the oxen that by craft had been taken away, bereft of his quiver Apollo smiled.

Likewise too with thee for his guide, the wealthy Priam, departing from Ilium, eluded the haughty sons of Atreus, and the Thessalian watch-fires, and the camp that was the foe of Troy. Thou in their blissful abodes dost lay the spirits of the pious, and with golden wand control the airy throng, darling of gods above and gods beneath.

XI.

To Leuconoë. It is vain to enquire into the future. Let us enjoy the present; for this is all we can command.

Forbear you to enquire, (for we may not know,) what ending Heaven has ordained for me, and what for you, Leuconoë; and essay not the Chaldæan tables. How much better 'twill be, to endure whatever shall befall! Whether Jove has granted many winters more, or this the last of all, which now against the barrier of pumice-stone crushes the might of the Etruscan sea, be wise, strain clear the wine; and since our span is short, cut off a length of hope. While we are speaking, envious Time will have fled: snatch To-day, and utterly mistrust To-morrow.

XII.

Address to Clio. The praise of Jupiter and others of the gods, and of the heroes of Roman history. The panegyric of Augustus, who on earth is second to Jove.

What man or hero choose you to record on the harp or the shrill flute, O Clio? What god? Whose name shall sportive Echo repeat, either on Helicon's shadowy spaces, or on the crown of Pindus, or on cool Hæmus? Whence the forests heedlessly followed melodious Orpheus, while by his mother's art he stayed the streams' fleet glidings and the nimble winds, and was strong in the charm of his tuneful strings to lead the attentive oaks.

What shall I speak before the accustomed praises of the Sire, who sways the estate of men and gods, who sways sea and earth and the firmament with its changing hours? From whom is begotten nothing greater than himself, nor thrives there aught his semblance or second; yet has Pallas assumed the honours next to him. Nor will I leave thee unsung, Liber bold in battles, and thee O Maid, the savage wild-beasts' foe, nor thee O Phœbus, dreadful with thine unerring

That nook of the world has charms for me beyond all other retreats, where the honey yields not to Mount Hymettus, and the olive-berry vies with green Venafrum; where Jove grants lingering Spring and Winters mild; and Aulon's slope, friendly to fruitful Bacchus, envies not a whit the grapes of Falerii.

That spot and those blessed heights summon you and me together; there you shall sprinkle with a duteous tear the glowing ashes of your friend the bard.

VII.

An ode of congratulation to Pompeius Varus, once the poet's comrade in the army of Brutus, on his restoration to civil rights.

You that oft with me have been brought to the hour of extremity, when Brutus was commander of the field, who has given you back, a Roman, to your country's gods and the Italian sky, Pompey, the chiefest of my comrades? with whom I oft have worn away the creeping hours with wine, with garland on my hair that shone with Syrian balm.

With you Philippi's fray and headlong flight I proved, my target not with honour cast away; when bravery was crushed, and threatening fronts pressed with their chin the ignominious ground.

But me, all trembling, fleet Mercurius wafted away in thick mist through the foe; you back into the war the billow sucked, and bore along on its tumultuous tides.

Then pay to Jove the feast you are bound to give, and lay beneath my laurel-tree your body wearied with a length of warfare, and spare not the casks that are designed for you.

With oblivious Massic fill high the polished tankards; pour forth the perfumes from capacious shells! Who makes it his task with speed to twine our wreaths of pliant parsley or of myrtle? Whom will Venus appoint to be lord of our drinking? Not less madly than Edonians will I revel; to rave's a pleasure, now my friend's regained.

VIII.

Barine's utter faithlessness, which Heaven will not punish; indeed, her beauty and fascination are ever increasing.

If any punishment for faith forsworn, at any time had wrought you harm, Barine; if you were made less fair by one black tooth, or one discoloured nail, I would believe you. But you, so soon as with vows you have bound your faithless self, flash forth in beauty far more bright than ever, and come abroad, the general interest of our youth.

It profits you to cheat your mother's inurned ashes, and the silent stars of night with all the sky, and the gods who are exempt from cold death. 'Tis at this, I say, that even Venus laughs, at this the guileless Nymphs laugh, and ruthless Cupid, who ever on his gory stone makes keen the fiery shafts.

Think too, that the whole generation is growing up for you, for you is growing a new throng of slaves; and former servants leave not the dwelling of their impious mistress, though they have threatened again and again.

You mothers fear for their youthful sons, you thrifty old men fear, and hapless damsels lately married, lest your fascination make faint their bridegrooms' love.

IX.

To C. Valgius Rufus on the death of Mystes. Since all troubles have their natural end, do not mourn overmuch. Rather let us celebrate the latest victories of Augustus.

Not for ever do showers pour from the clouds upon the squalid plains, or fitful blasts trouble the Caspian sea unceasingly, nor in the regions of Armenia does lifeless ice stand fixed through all the months, Valgius my friend, or are Garganus' woods of oak always groaning beneath the Northern gales, and the mountain-ashes being widowed of their leaves.

You ever in tearful strains dwell upon your Mystes taken from you; and the sorrows of your love fail not when the Morning-star is rising, nor when he flies before the coursing Sun.

But the sire, who had thrice fulfilled the term of life, lamented not through all his years the lovely Antilochus; nor did his parents or his Phrygian sisters weep for the boyhood of their Troilus ever.

Cease at last from weak repinings; and rather let us sing of the newly-won trophies of Augustus Cæsar, and of icebound Niphates, and how the river of Media, added to the conquered nations, rolls along its humbled rapids; and how the Gelonians, within the bound assigned them, career in narrowed plains.

X.

To L. Licinius Murena. The moderate life is the perfect life.

Licinius, you will live more perfectly, by neither always keeping out to sea, nor, while you warily shrink from the storm, too closely pressing on the treacherous shore.

The man who makes the golden mean his choice, in his security is far from the squalor of a ruinous dwelling, in his temperance is far from a palace which envy haunts.

The mighty pine is oftenest tossed by winds, and lofty towers fall with heaviest crash, and lightnings strike the mountain's topmost peak.

A heart well trained beforehand hopes for, when the times are contrary, fears, when they favour, the opposite estate. 'Tis Jove who brings again unsightly Winters, 'tis he who sweeps them away. If 'tis ill now, it will not also be so hereafter; sometimes Apollo with the lyre awakes the silent Muse, and does not always bend his bow.

Show yourself bold and brave when perils press; wisely likewise take in your sails when they swell with too fair a breeze.

shaft. Of Alcides also will I tell, and of the boys of Leda, the one renowned for overcoming with the steed, the other with the fist; and when once upon the mariner has glittered their fair star, down from the rocks the troubled water flows, the winds drop down, and the clouds flee away, and the threatening wave reposes on the deep, for they have willed it so.

I doubt whether after these to tell of Romulus first, or the peaceful reign of Pompilius, or Tarquin's haughty fasces, or Cato's glorious death. Regulus, and the Scauri, and Paullus that flung away his noble soul when the Carthaginian was prevailing, I will gratefully record in an illustrious strain, and Fabricius too. Him, and Curius with the unkempt locks, a soldier good in war, and Camillus, stern penury produced, and an ancestral farm with fitting home.

As a tree by growth unmarked, increases the fame of Marcellus; shines among all the Julian star, like the moon among the lesser fires.

Father and guardian of the human race, thou child of Saturn, to thee by fate is given the charge of mighty Cæsar; mayest thou reign, with Cæsar thy second in power! He, whether it be that he drive along in proper triumph the Parthians subdued, who now hover over Latium, or the Seres and Indians, who dwell close by the confine of the East, inferior to thee shall rule with equity the wide world; thou with thy ponderous car shalt shake the sky, thou on the sacrilegious groves shalt send thy vengeful bolts.

XIII.

To Lydia. The jealous lover. The praise of constancy.

Lydia, when you extol the rosy neck of Telephus, the waxen arms of Telephus, alas, my glowing liver swells with labouring bile. Then neither my feelings nor my colour abide in settled state, and down my cheeks the secret tear-drop flows, that tells with what long-lingering fires I waste at heart. I feel the flame, whether it chance that brawls distempered by wine have marred the whiteness of your shoulders, or the frantic boy has with his tooth printed on your lips a recording mark. You would not, if you duly listen to me, hope that he will be constant, who barbarously hurts the sweet mouth, whose kisses Venus has imbued with the quintessence of her own nectar.

Thrice happy, and more than thrice are they, whom a link unbroken binds, and whose love, not torn apart by evil rancours, will not loose them sooner than their latest day.

XIV.

To the ship of the state.

Ship, shall new billows bear you back to sea? Alas, what mean you? With vigour press into the haven. See you not how your side is stripped of its oarage, and your mast is wounded by the swooping Africus, and how your sailyards are groaning, and how your hull, not bound with cables, can scarce endure a too tyrannous deep?

You have not sails unrent, you have not gods to call upon, when crushed again with woe. Albeit a Pontic pine, the forest's highborn daughter, you may boast your lineage, and your title, an idle thing. In painted poops the trembling sailor puts no trust. Unless you owe the winds a laughing-stock, be you circumspect.

You that were late my sickening weariness, my yearning now, and care that is not light, shun you the seas that flow between the sparkling Cyclades.

XV.

The prophecy of Nereus.

While in Idæan ships across the deep the shepherd was treacherously bearing away his hostess Helen, Nereus with rest unwelcome whelmed the winds, that he might chant the dreadful destinies:

"With an evil omen are you leading home her, whom Greece with many a soldier will require, confederate to destroy your marriage-tie, and Priam's ancient realm.

"Alas, how steeds, how warriors sweat with toil! Carnage how great are you waking for the Dardan race! Even now Pallas is making ready her helmet and ægis and car and wrath. Vainly bold in the protection of Venus will you comb your tresses, and on the unwarlike lyre accompany your songs, the delight of women: vainly in your bridal-chamber will you shun the ponderous spears, and the point of the Cretan wand, and the din, and Ajax swift to pursue; still, alas, you will, though late, besmear with dust your adulterous locks.

"Observe you not Laertes' son, the bane of your race? Observe you not Pylian Nestor? Dauntlessly press you Teucer of Salamis, and Sthenelus skilful in the fight, or if there be need to govern the steeds, no slothful charioteer: Merion also you will learn to know. Lo, the son of Tydeus, that excels his sire, furiously rages to find you; from him you, like a roe, that, forgetful of his pasture, flees from a wolf which he has seen on the valley's farther side, will flee in your cowardice with deep-drawn panting, though 'twas not this you promised to your love.

"Achilles' angry fleet shall stay the hour of Ilium and the matrons of Phrygia: when the predestined winters are past, Achæan fire shall burn the dwellings of Ilium."

XVI.

An apology. Description of the madness of anger; its origin, and fatal effects.

O daughter fairer than a mother fair, assign to my slanderous iambics whatever end you choose; whether it please you to destroy them by fire, or by the Adrian sea.

Not Dindymene, nor the Pythian god who dwells within his sanctuary, nor Liber, stir so violently the soul of their ministers; the Corybantes clash not so furiously their ringing cymbals, as fits of direful anger: them neither Noric sword can cow, nor wrecking sea, nor fierce flame, nor Jove's self sweeping down with dreadful crash.

Tradition tells that Prometheus was constrained to add to the elemental mud a particle severed from every creature, and that he attached to our stomach the fury of a raging lion.

'Twas anger that in crushing ruin laid Thyestes low, and has proved for lofty cities the consummating cause, why it was that they perished utterly, and that the foe's insulting army printed their walls with the hostile plough.

Hush your passion; myself too the fire within the breast stung in my pleasant youth, and sent me frantic to the iambic's rush: now I would fain exchange my wrath for kindness, if only you will become my friend, when my taunts are retracted, and give me back your heart.

XVII.

The poet invites Tyndaris to his Sabine villa near mount Lucretilis.

Oft for the pleasant Lucretilis fleet Faunus exchanges Lycæus, and ever from my she-goats keeps away the fiery summer and the rainy blasts.

Unharmed amid the safety of the grove, the mates of the noisome lord roam in search of lurking arbute trees and beds of thyme, and fear not green adders, nor the wolves of Mars which haunt Hædilia; whene'er, my Tyndaris, low Ustica's vales and polished rocks have echoed with the tuneful flute.

Me Heaven protects; to Heaven my piety and Muse are dear. Here plenty, rich in the glories of the country, shall flow to the full for you from bounteous horn.

Here in a secluded dell you shall shun the heat of the dog-star, and sing with the Teian lute of those who were love-sick for one, Penelope and Circe crystal-fair: here beneath the shade you shall quaff cups of harmless Lesbian; and Thyoneus child of Semele shall not mingle the fray with Mars, nor shall you dread the suspicion of headstrong Cyrus, lest he cast his intemperate hands on one too weak to encounter him, and rend the garland fastened to your hair, and your guiltless dress.

XVIII.

The praise of wine. The pernicious effects of intemperance.

My Varus, plant no tree before the hallowed vine, round Tibur's kindly soil and Catilus' walls. For to them that drink not Heaven has presented all things as difficulties; and gnawing anxieties thus only flee away. Who croaks of irksome warfare, or of penury, after wine? Who sings not rather of thee, O father Bacchus, and of thee, fair Venus?

But that no man may o'erpass what temperate Liber gives, the brawl of Centaurs with Lapithæ, fought to the death over their wine, gives us warning, Evius warns us, no gentle Power to the Thracians, when in ravenous frenzy they separate right and wrong by passion's narrow line.

I would not wake thee, if thou will it not, bright Bassareus, nor drag beneath the open sky what is wrapt in varied foliage. Restrain the terrific cymbals, and the Berecynthian horn withal; for blinded Self-love follows close upon them, and Boast, that lifts too high his empty head, and an Honour who flings abroad his secret, and becomes more transparent than glass.

XIX.

The poet's love for Glycera. He designs a propitiatory sacrifice to Venus.

The Loves' cruel mother, and Theban Semele's boy, and frolic Freedom, bid me give back my heart to the passions that were ended.

'Tis Glycera's radiance that fires me, she who gleams fairer than the Parian marble; her charming perversity fires me, and her face, too dazzling-dangerous to behold.

Venus, with all her power rushing on me, has forsaken Cyprus, and suffers me not to sing of the Scythians, and the Parthian, whose courage lies in his retreating steeds, and of themes that are irrelevant.

Here place living turf, here place vervain, ye boys, and incense with a bowl of two-years' wine; her approach will be gentler when a victim has been slain.

XX.

An invitation to Mæcenas.

You'll drink in modest bowls poor Sabine wine, which in a Grecian jar my own hands stored and sealed, when in the theatre such applause was given you, dear knight Mæcenas, that all at once the banks of your ancestral river, and the sportive echo of the Vatican hill sounded back your praises.

Cæcuban you may drink, and the grape the press of Cales has subdued; my cups the vines of Falerii mix not, nor the hills of Formiæ.

XXI.

Hymn to Diana and Apollo.

Sing of Diana, blooming maidens; boys, sing of Cynthius with the unshorn locks, and of Latona deeply loved by sovereign Jove.

Extol ye her who delights in streams and the foliage of the groves, whatever the leafage be that stands forth either on cool Algidus, or on the dark forests of Erymanth, or of Cragus green;

O youths, extol ye, with not fewer praises, Delos, the native island of Apollo, and himself, with shoulder adorned with the quiver, and the lyre, his brother's gift. 'Tis he who will drive away tearful war, he will drive away woeful dearth and plague, from the people, and from Cæsar our prince, against the Parthians and Britons, prevailed upon by your prayer.

XXII.

To Aristius Fuscus. The good man, wherever he be, is safe from harm.

The man of faultless life, and clear from crime, my Fuscus, needs not the Moorish javelins, nor bow, nor quiver with its brood of poisoned shafts;

Whether o'er the burning Syrtes he choose to make his way, or o'er inhospitable Caucasus, or the regions which Hydaspes washes, the river of romance.

For in the Sabine wood, while I sing of my Lalage, and wander o'er the bound with troubles cleared away, a wolf fled from me though unarmed; such a monster as Daunias, home of warriors, rears not in her spacious groves of oak, nor Juba's land begets, the lions' parching nurse.

Set me amid the plains of lethargy, where not one tree is fanned by summer gale, that quarter of the world which fogs oppress, and the malice of the sky;

Set me beneath the sun's too neighbouring car, in a land where dwellings may not be: I'll love my sweetly smiling, sweetly speaking Lalage.

XXIII.

To Chloe.

You shun me, Chloe, like a fawn, that seeks o'er pathless hills his timorous dam, with vague alarm at gales and rustling wood.

For whether the approach of Spring chance to quiver on the dancing leaves, or the green lizards brush through the brake, he quakes in heart and knees at once.

But I pursue you not to mangle you, like savage tiger or Gætulian lion: cease to follow your mother at last, since now you are ripe for a lover.

XXIV.

To Virgil. A lament for the death of Quinctilius.

What shame or bound can there be to our regret for a life so loved? Prompt the mournful strains, Melpomene, thou to whom the Sire has given with the harp a voice crystal-clear.

Does then an endless sleep o'erwhelm Quinctilius? When shall Reverence, and the sister of Justice, untainted Honour, and naked Truth, ever find one to be his peer?

He fell bewept by many a good man; wept for by no one, Virgil, more than you; you vainly pious, alas! require Quinctilius of the gods, entrusted not to them for such an end.

But if more winningly than Thracian Orpheus you played a lyre to which the trees would listen, blood would return not to the bodiless ghost, which with his awful wand Mercurius, not gentle to dissolve the fates for prayer, has driven once to join his gloomy flock.

'Tis hard! But patience makes the woe more light, whatever 'tis forbidden to amend.

XXV.

Horace taunts Lydia with her approaching old age.

More seldom do the saucy youths shake your closed casements with their frequent knocks, and they rob you not of your sleep; and that door loves the lintel, which once its hinges moved full easily; you hear less and less now: "While I your lover pine the long nights through, Lydia, are you sleeping?"

In your turn, when an old woman, you will weep for your scornful paramours in the solitude of an alley, a slighted thing; while the Thracian wind more fiercely raves in the time between the moons; when such burning passion and lust as is wont to madden the horse's dam, shall rage around your fevered heart: and you will ever lament because the joyous youths are better pleased with ivy green and myrtle dusk, and consign the sapless leaves to Hebrus, the mate of Winter.

XXVI.

The poet, as the happy friend of the Muses, begs Pimplea to inspire him to sing the praise of Lamia.

I, the Muses' friend, commit sorrow and fear to the wanton winds, to bear them to the Cretan sea; I, who am utterly indifferent by whom the monarch of the region of frost beneath the Northern star is dreaded, or what it is that alarms Tiridates.

O thou who joyest in unsullied springs, twine sunny flowers, twine a garland for my Lamia, delightful Pimplea! Without thee worthless is the praise I give: him with chords untouched before, him with Lesbian quill to immortalize, 'tis meet for thee and thy sisters.

XXVII.

The wine-party. Horace endeavours to restrain his quarrelsome companions.

'Tis like Thracians to fight with goblets created for the purpose of delight: away with the barbarous custom, and keep far from bloody brawls the temperate lord of wine! How monstrously does the Median scimitar disagree with wine and lights! Hush the sacrilegious tumult, my friends, and remain still with elbow at rest.

Wish you that I too take a share of the potent Falernian? Let the brother of Megilla of Opus say with what wound, with what shaft, he is perishing in bliss.

Does he falter in frankness? I will drink for no other reward. Whatever charmer is your mistress, she burns you not with fires that need raise a blush, and you always err with a love of gentle birth. Whatever you have to tell, commit it to trusty ears.

Ah wretch, in what a Charybdis were you struggling, youth worthy of a better flame! What witch, what wizard will have the power to release you by Thessalian drugs? What god? Scarce will Pegasus unloose you entangled in a Chimæra of triple shape.

XXVIII.

Dialogue between a sailor and the spirit of the philosopher Archytas. The universal fate. The duty of giving to the dead the rites of burial.

Sailor.

You, who measured sea and land and the sand that knows no numbering, Archytas, the slight gift of a little dust confines hard by the Matine strand; and nought does it avail you to have explored the mansions of the sky, and with the intellect to have sped through the sphere of heaven; for you were doomed to die.

The sire of Pelops likewise fell, though the guest of the gods, and Tithonus wafted to the air above, and Minos admitted to the secret counsels of Jove; and Tartarus holds the son of Panthûs a second time sent down to Orcus; albeit, since by unfastening his shield from the wall he bore witness to the age of Troy, he had surrendered to black Death nought beyond his sinews and skin; one who is, in your judgment, no mean prophet of Nature and Truth.

But all one night awaits, and the path of death, once to be trodden by all. Some the Furies give to make a show for grisly Mars; the greedy sea is set to be the sailor's bane; the corpses of old and young are blended and crowded together, and ruthless Proserpine never passed one life.

Archytas.

Myself too Notus, the impetuous companion of sloping Orion, whelmed in the Illyrian waves.

But you, sailor, grudge not through unkindness to give to my unburied bones and head a particle of shifting sand; so, with whatever tempest Eurus shall threaten Hesperian waves, may Venusia's woods be smitten, you be spared; and may a rich reward flow down to you from whence it can, from the grace of Jove and from Neptune, the guardian of holy Tarentum!

Reck you not to commit an impiety which hereafter will work woe for your descendants? Perchance too, due judgment and high retribution await your own self; I shall not be left with my prayers unavenged, and no atonements will absolve you.

Although you are in haste, not long need you delay; when you have thrice cast dust upon me, you may speed.

XXIX.

A remonstrance addressed to Iccius on his intention of joining the expedition to Arabia Felix.

Iccius, do you envy now the treasures that make Arabia blest, and are you preparing grim war against the monarchs of Sabæa not subdued before, and weaving fetters for the terrible Mede?

Who from among barbarian virgins shall be your handmaid when her love is slain? What boy from a palace, with glossy perfumed locks, shall be set beside your cup, skilled to aim on his father's bow the Seric shaft?

Who will say that river-currents cannot glide backward up the steep hills, and Tiber reverse his course, when you are purposing to exchange for the Iberian corslet the books you have bought up far and wide, the noble books of Panætius, and the Socratic school, though you promised better things than these?

XXX.

A Prayer to Venus.

Venus, queen of Cnidos and Paphos, desert thy beloved Cyprus, and change thy dwelling to Glycera's shrine, who invites thee with a wealth of incense.

With thee may thy glowing boy, and the Graces with zone unloosed, and the Nymphs, haste hither, and Youth, who without thee is not winning, and Mercury.

XXXI.

Prayer to Apollo on the consecration of his temple. The happiness of contentment.

What asks the bard of his enshrined Apollo? What prays he, as from the bowl he pours the new-made wine?

Not for the rich Sardinia's plenteous crops, not for the hot Calabria's goodly herds, not for gold or Indian ivory, not for the meadows which Liris wears with peaceful flow, a voiceless stream.

Let those to whom Fortune has given the vine restrain it with the knife of Cales; and let the wealthy merchant from golden chalice drain wines for which he has bartered Syrian merchandise, a man beloved by Heaven itself, since, truly, three or four times in the year, he visits the Atlantic deep unharmed. My food is the olive, mine is the endive and the wholesome mallow.

Child of Latona, grant that I may enjoy what I have won, both with health of body and with mind unimpaired; and that I may pass an old age not dishonoured, nor one which lacks the lyre.

XXXII.

To the lute of lyric poetry.

We are summoned. If at ease beneath the shade we have with thee composed a sportive lay, which may live for this year and more, come, prompt, my lute, a song of Latium,

Thou that wert first tuned by the Lesbian citizen; who, though dauntless in war, yet in the midst of arms, or if on the oozy shore he had moored his storm-tossed bark, would sing of Liber, and the Muses, and Venus, and the boy who clings ever to her side, and Lycus in the beauty of his black eyes and black hair.

O shell, that art the ornament of Phœbus and pleasing to the feasts of sovereign Jove, that art the sweet soother of troubles, welcome to me, whene'er I duly call thee.

XXXIII.

To the poet Albius Tibullus. The whims and inconsistencies of Love.

To warn you, Albius, not to grieve more than overmuch in your pining for the ruthless Glycera, nor chant those piteous elegies, because she has broken faith, and a younger rival outshines you:—

Lycoris with the beautiful low brow the love of Cyrus consumes; Cyrus is drawn towards the unkind Pholoë; but she-goats with Apulian wolves will mate, ere for a base love Pholoë is frail.

Such is the will of Venus, whose pleasure it is in cruel sport to drive beneath her brazen yoke forms and minds ill-matched. My own self, though a better mistress wooed me, Myrtale has bound fast with pleasing chain, a freedwoman, less gentle than the tides of Adria, when he hollows the Calabrian creeks.

XXXIV.

The poet's recantation. The power of Jove and of Fortune.

Heaven's niggard and unfrequent worshipper, while versed in Wisdom's foolishness I stray, now backward am I forced to turn my sails, and retrace the course I had forsaken:

For the Father of the sky, who mostly cleaves the clouds with gleaming flash, has driven through the undimmed firmament his thundering steeds and flying car; whereby the ponderous earth and wandering streams, whereby the Styx and grisly site of hateful Tænarus, and the confine of Atlas, are rocked.

To change the highest for the lowest, God has power; and he makes mean the man of high estate, bringing what is hidden into light: from one, with flapping loud, Fortune the spoiler bears away the crest, 'tis her joy to place it on another.

XXXV.

Hymn to Fortune. Her caprices. Description of Necessity her forerunner, and of Honour and faithlessness. The goddess is intreated to preserve Augustus in his expedition to Britain. A lament for the civil wars.

Lady, who rulest Antium thy joy, strong to lift even from the lowliest place our mortal frame, or turn proud triumphs into funerals, thee the poor tiller of the country woos with earnest prayer, thee, the mistress of the main, he woos, whoever with Bithynian keel provokes the Carpathian deep.

Thee the savage Dacian, thee the roving Scythians, and cities and nations, and valiant Latium, and the mothers of barbarian kings, and purple tyrants dread, lest with the foot of outrage thou dash down the standing column, or lest the thronging people arouse the loiterers to arms, to arms! and break the sovereignty.

Thee always fell Necessity precedes, who bears in hand of brass large spikes and wedges, and the stringent clamp is there, and molten lead.

Thee Hope adores, and Honour seldom seen, clad in white robe, and scorns not to be thy mate, whene'er with changed garb thou dost prove a foe, and forsake a mighty house.

But the faithless crowd draws back, and the false harlot, friends fall away when casks are drained to the lees, too treacherous to bear the yoke alike.

Mayest thou guard Cæsar, resolved to travel to the Britons at the limit of the world, and the new-raised swarm of warriors destined to bring terror to the regions of the East and to the Red Sea!

Alas, we blush for our scars, and guilt, and brothers slain! From what deed have we shrunk, we, a hardened age? What have our impious hands left unpolluted? From what, through respect for the gods, has our youth restrained its violence? What altars has it spared? Oh, would that on a new anvil thou wouldest forge the blunted steel into another shape against the Massagetæ and the Arabs!

XXXVI.

An ode of congratulation to Plotius Numida, on his safe return from Spain.

'Tis our joy with incense and the lyre, and the duteous sacrifice of a steer, to soothe the guardian gods of Numida, who, safe from the uttermost parts of the West, gives many a kiss among the friends he loves; yet more to none than to his dearest Lamia, remembering well his boyhood spent beneath the selfsame ruler, and the toga which they changed together.

Let not the fair day lack its mark of chalk, nor be there limit to the unbroached flask, nor rest to feet that bound in Saliar mode. And let not Damalis of the copious cups o'ermaster Bassus in the Thracian draught; nor let the rose be absent from our feast, nor parsley ever green, nor lily frail.

All upon Damalis will set their languishing eyes; yet not from her new love Damalis will be torn, clinging more close than twining ivy-folds.

XXXVII.

An ode of joy for Cæsar's victory at Antium. Cleopatra; her frantic designs, downfall, and brave death.

Now should we drink, now should we beat the ground with merry foot, now, my friends, 'twere meet to adorn with the Saliar feast the couch of the gods.

Ere now it were a sin to draw forth the Cæcuban from our ancestral stores, while the Queen was plotting against the Capitol the wreck her madness dreamed of, and destruction for the empire; with her tainted herd of men degraded by disease; she who was reckless enough to hope for anything, and made drunk by the smiles of Fortune.

But scarce one vessel rescued from the flames lowered her frenzy; and Cæsar recalled to genuine alarms her mind distraught with Mareotic wine, when with the oar he chased her close as she flew away from Italy, (as a hawk pursues the gentle doves, or a fleet huntsman the hare o'er snowy Hæmonia's plains,) to consign to fetters the monster of Fate:

But she, seeking the means of death in nobler mood, shrunk not in womanish terror from the sword, nor with swift fleet essayed to mend her loss by winning secluded shores.

Likewise she dared with countenance serene to visit her fallen palace, and bravely take in hand the fierce snakes, to drink into her frame the deadly venom, become more dauntless when resolved to die; for in truth she scorned to be borne as a subject in the cruel Liburnian galleys to grace the haughty triumph, a woman of no mean spirit.

XXXVIII.

To his page.

Boy, I detest a Persian sumptuousness; wreaths twined with bark of linden are distasteful; care not to search in what spot perchance may linger the late-blowing rose. I ask you not with busy toilsomeness to add aught to simple myrtle; myrtle misbeseems not you my cupbearer, nor myself as I drink beneath the plaited vine.

BOOK II.

I.

To Asinius Pollio, the advocate and writer of tragedy, who is now composing a history of the civil wars. A lament for the carnage caused by the conflicts of Romans with their fellow-citizens.

THE civil strife which took its rise from the year when Metellus was consul, and the causes and faults and measures of the war, and the game of Fortune, and the pernicious leagues of the chiefs, and the arms besmeared with bloodshed not atoned for yet, all this, a labour full of perilous hazard, you make your theme, and tread o'er fires that lurk beneath the treacherous ashes.

For a time let the Muse of solemn Tragedy be absent from the stage; presently, when you have set forth the history of the state, you will resume your majestic part in the Cecropian buskin; you, Pollio, the illustrious safeguard of the sad accused, and of the deliberating senate-house; for whom, by your Dalmatian triumph, the laurel has created endless honours.

Even now with the horns' terrific clang you stun the ear, now the clarions ring, now the flash of arms affrights the flying horse and horseman's eyes. Now I seem to hear of mighty leaders soiled with no dishonourable dust; and all parts of the world subdued, but Cato's dauntless soul.

Juno, and each one of the Gods that was the friend of Africa, who had retreated powerless, and left the land unavenged, have rendered the grandsons of the conquerors to be an offering to Jugurtha's shade.

What plain is not enriched by Latin blood, and by its graves attests not our impicus combats, and the crash of falling Italy, which Media heard? What flood or what streams know not our woeful war? What sea has Daunian carnage not discoloured? What coast is free from stain of our gore?

But do not quit your jests, my froward Muse, to repeat the studies of the Cean dirge: with me beneath a Dionæan grot seek for the measures of a lighter quill.

II.

To Sallustius Crispus. The wise use of money. The love of gain grows by self-indulgence. The moderate man is the genuine king.

No beauty has silver which the hoarding earth conceals, my Sallust, you that are a foe to the metal, unless it shine by moderate use.

Through a length of ages will Proculeius live, famed for the father's heart he bore his brothers; him undying Fame will waft along upon a wing that dare not droop.

More widely would you reign by subduing an avaricious spirit, than if you united Libya to distant Gades, and the Carthaginian on either shore were subject to you alone.

The scourge of dropsy grows by self-indulgence, and does not banish thirst, unless the source of the malady has fled from the veins, and the watery languor from the pallid frame.

Virtue, who differs from the crowd, takes Phraates from the number of the blest, though restored to the throne of Cyrus, and teaches the people to disuse untrue expressions; conferring upon him alone a realm, and crown secure, and lasting laurel-wreath, who views enormous hoards with eye that looks not back.

III.

To Quintus Dellius. The wisdom of moderation; the certainty of death. Let us enjoy our life while we may, for death will soon strip us all alike of our possessions.

Be careful to preserve amid difficulties a tranquil mind; no less in prosperity one restrained from overweening joy, my Dellius, you that are doomed to die, whether you have lived in sorrow all your years, or if, reposing in some grassy nook, you have made yourself happy throughout the holidays of life with a deep-stored cask of Falernian.

Where the mighty pine and the white poplar love to unite their branches' hospitable shade, and the fleeting brook strives to hurry onward down its winding channel,—hither bid them bring wine, and perfumes, and the too short-lived blossoms of the pleasant rose; while circumstances and youth allow us, and the gloomy threads of the three sister-fates.

You will quit all those wooded domains you have purchased, and the mansion, and the villa which yellow Tiber washes; you will quit them, and your heir will enjoy the wealth that you have piled on high.

Whether the rich descendant of ancient Inachus, it matters not, or poor and of the lowliest birth you sojourn beneath the sky, the victim of Orcus who never feels compassion.

We all are driven to the same place; the lot of us all is shaken in the urn, sooner or later sure to come forth, and embark us in the boat for a region of endless exile.

IV.

To Xanthias Phoceus. Horace, by an ironical panegyric, rallies his friend on his love for Phyllis, his slave.

To prove that you need not feel shame for the love you bear your handmaid, Xanthias Phoceus,—the slave Briseis, by her snowy bloom, melted Achilles arrogant before; the beauty of Tecmessa, his captive, melted her lord, Ajax, Telamon's son; Atrides, in the midst of the triumph, was fired with love for a maid among the spoil; after the barbarian squadrons had fallen beneath the conquering Thessalian, and the loss of Hector had delivered to the weary Greeks a Pergamus easier to be overthrown.

You cannot tell that the parents of your yellow-haired Phyllis are not opulent, and give splendour to you as their son-in-law; no doubt she mourns her royal blood, and household-gods unkind.

Be sure that she whom you have made your love is not from the villainous crowd; and that one so constant, one with such a distaste for gain, cannot have been born of a mother that would cause you shame.

Heart-whole I praise her arms, and face, and dainty legs; dream not of suspecting one whose life has hurried on to close its fortieth year.

V.

To a friend on his love for Lalage.

As yet she cannot bear the yoke on a submissive neck, as yet she cannot share her fellow's task, or brook the passion of the bull's impetuous love.

Your heifer's heart is o'er the grassy plains, while now in the streams she lightens the o'erpowering heat, now is all eagerness to play with the calves in the watery willow-copse.

Away with longing for the unripe grape; soon to your wish will many-coloured Autumn streak the dull clusters with a purple hue.

Soon she will follow you; for time speeds fiercely on, and will add to her sum of life the years it takes from you; soon with saucy brow Lalage will woo a bridegroom; she, more beloved than Pholoë the coy, or Chloris, whose white shoulder beams as bright, as shines the unclouded moon on nightly seas, or Cnidian Gyges; whom if you set amid a group of girls, the difference hard to see would wondrously mislead discerning guests, by his flowing tresses and perplexing face.

VI.

To his friend the Roman knight Septimius, who would go with him to the ends of the earth. The poet prays that Tibur may be the resting-place of his old age; or, if that may not be, he will choose the country which lies about Tarentum.

My Septimius, you who with me would visit Gades, and the Cantabrian untaught to bear our yoke, and the savage Syrtes, where the Moorish wave seethes ceaselessly:—

May Tibur, founded by the Argive colonist, be, I pray, my age's resting-place; may it be the goal to one who is weary of voyages and travels and warfare!

If Fate's unkindness bar my journey thither, I will haste to the stream of Galæsus dear to the skin-clad sheep, and to the fields that once were ruled by Phalanthus the Laconian king.

XI.

Horace in a half-playful tone advises his friend Quintius Hirpinus to enjoy life wisely, and not to fret.

What the warlike Cantabrian is plotting, and the Scythian parted from us by the barrier of the Adrian sea, care not to enquire, my Quintius, and fret not for the needs of a life whose wants are few.

Backward flies unwrinkled youth, and grace, while withered grayness banishes playful loves and easy sleep.

Spring flowers keep not always the same charm, nor beams the ruddy Moon with face unchanged: why harass with eternal designs a mind too weak to compass them?

Why not, either beneath a lofty plane-tree or this pine, stretched all carelessly, and our gray locks fragrant with the rose and anointed with Assyrian nard, drink while we may? Evius melts away consuming cares.

What boy with speed will temper in the passing brook our cups of fiery Falernian? Who will entice shy Lyde from her home? Go, bid her hasten with her ivory lute, her tresses bound into a comely knot in the fashion of a Spartan girl.

XII.

Horace pleads the unfitness of his lyric poetry to record the wars of the Romans, or the battles of Mythology. He advises Mæcenas to write in prose the history of Cæsar's campaigns, while he himself will sing the praises of Licymnia.

You would not wish that fierce Numantia's lingering wars, or accursed Hannibal, or the Sicilian sea crimsoned with Carthaginian blood, be fitted to the lyre's tender tones; or the savage Lapithæ, and Hylæus intemperate in wine, and the children of Earth, quelled by the hand of Hercules, at the peril caused by whom the shining mansion of old Saturn quaked: and you, Mæcenas, in prose annals will better record the battles of Cæsar, and the necks of threatening kings led through our streets.

For myself, 'tis the Muse's will that I record the sweet songs of my Lady Licymnia, that I record her lustrous flashing eyes, and her heart so true in its deeply mutual love.

Her it misbeseems not to tread a measure in the dance, nor to vie in the jest, nor playfully to throw her arms around the brilliant maidens on the sacred day of Dian's crowded festival.

Would you choose, for all that rich Achæmenes possessed, or fruitful Phrygia's wealth that Mygdon owned, or the Arabians' opulent homes, to barter a lock of Licymnia's hair?

While she bends her neck to meet your fiery kisses, or with a gentle cruelty withholds them, which she would rather should be snatched than asked for, and would sometimes be the first to snatch them.

XIII.

The poet's imprecations on the planter of a tree which had nearly caused his death. Man can never guard against his fate. The charm of lyric song prevails even in the lower world.

That man, whoever did it at the first, both planted you upon an evil day, and reared you with sacrilegious hand, O tree, to be his children's bane and the hamlet's reproach.

I could believe that that man broke his father's neck, and bespattered his inmost chamber with the blood of a guest by night; that man practised Colchian poisons, and every foul crime that is anywhere compassed, who in my field set up you, pestilent stock, you, destined to fall upon your master's guiltless head.

What each should shun is never duly guarded against by man from hour to hour: the Carthaginian mariner shudders at the Bosphorus, and beyond that dreads no hidden fate from another source; the soldier fears the arrows and nimble flight of the Parthian, the Parthian the fetters and dungeon of Italy; but the unforeseen might of Death has swept away nations, and still will sweep them away.

How nearly have we beheld the realms of dusky Proserpine, and Æolus on his judgment-seat, and the far-removed abodes of the pious, and Sappho complaining on her Æolian strings of the girls of her native land; and you, Alcæus, in fuller tone sounding with your golden quill the hardships of voyage, the hardships of exile, the hardships of war!

The shades admire either bard giving utterance to words which merit a holy silence; but the crowd with thronging shoulders more gladly drink in with their ears the tale of battles and of tyrants banished.

What wonder, since, entranced by those lays, the hundred-headed monster droops his sable ears, and the serpents are charmed, entwined in the Furies' locks?

Nay, both Prometheus and the sire of Pelops are beguiled from their labours by the delicious sound; and Orion cares not to rouse the lion or the timorous lynx.

XIV.

Nothing can stay the advance of decay and death, the common doom of all on earth; and men pile up wealth, only for another to waste it.

Alas, the fleeting years, my Postumus, my Postumus, the fleeting years glide away; and piety will never bring a check to wrinkles, and Old Age's stern advance, and unconquerable Death.

No, my friend, not if with three hundred bulls, each day that passes, you strive to pacify the mind of Pluto whom tears may not move; he who imprisons with his gloomy flood Geryon's triple bulk, and Tityos,—the flood, you know, we all must sail across, all we who live upon the gifts of earth; whether it chance that we be kings, or needy tillers of the soil.

'Twill be all in vain that we live safe from gory War, and breaking billows of the hoarse Adrian sea; in vain that through the Autumn times we timorously shield our bodies from the hurtful southern wind.

Go we must, and view that black Cocytus with its sluggish wandering stream, and the accursed children of Danaus, and Sisyphus, son of Æolus, condemned to an endless toil.

Land, mansion, gentle wife, must all be left; and of these trees that you are rearing, (except the hateful cypresses,) not one will follow you, their short-lived lord.

Your worthier heir will waste the Cæcuban, which you have guarded with a hundred keys; and stain the floor with that magnificent wine, choicer than any quaffed at pontiffs' feasts.

XV.

Horace describes the extravagant luxury prevalent among the rich, and praises the simple manner of living of the old Romans.

Soon will regal piles leave but few acres for the plough; on all sides ponds will be viewed spreading more widely than the Lucrine lake, and the bachelor plane will displace the elm; then violet-beds, and myrtles, and all the profusion of fragrance, will throw a perfume on the olive-yards that were fruitful for the former lord; then with its boughs the tangled laurel-grove will shut out the assaults of the heat.

Not so was it ordained by the precepts of Romulus and unshorn Cato, and the rule of the men of old. With them the income of a subject was small, the public revenue large; no colonnade, marked out with long measuring-rods for a subject, caught the gale of the shaded North; and the laws allowed them not to scorn the turf which chance supplied, but bade them at the public expense adorn with fresh-hewn stone their towns, and the temples of the gods.

XVI.

All mankind long for rest, which riches cannot buy. Contentment, not wealth, makes genuine happiness.

For rest he prays the gods who is surprised on the broad Ægæan, when all at once a black cloud hides the moon, and the stars beam not clear upon the mariners; for rest Thrace the furious in war, for rest the Medes adorned with the quiver; for rest, my Grosphus, which cannot be bought with gems or purple or gold.

For it is not treasure, nor the consul's lictor, that clears away the mind's unhappy turmoils, and cares which flit around the fretted vault.

He lives on little well, upon whose modest board his father's salt-cellar gleams; nor does fear or low passion rob him of his light repose.

Why in a narrow life aim we at many a mark? Why change we to lands that are warmed by another sun? What exile from his country has fled from himself as well?

Marring Care climbs ships with brazen beak, and never drops behind a troop of horse; fleeter than stags, and fleeter than the East wind, who drives along the stormy clouds.

A mind that views with joy its present lot, will shrink from caring for what lies beyond, and with an easy smile will soften the bitters of life; nought is there that is blest in every point.

A swift death carried off renowned Achilles; a length of years wore away Tithonus; and perhaps to me the hour will extend that which it has denied to you.

Around you a hundred flocks bleat, and cows of Sicily low; for you the mare trained for the chariot raises its neighing, you fleeces clothe, twice dipped in the purple dye of Africa: to me the Fate who cannot be false has granted a small domain, and the delicate spirit of the Grecian Muse, and power to scorn the envious crowd.

XVII.

To Mæcenas on his recovery from illness. Horace says that the same day must of necessity bring death to them both. Besides, their horoscopes are wonderfully alike; and they have both been saved from extreme peril.

Why rob me of my life with your complaints? 'Tis neither Heaven's pleasure, nor my own, for you, Mæcenas, to depart before me, my fortunes' chiefest glory and support.

Ah, if too swift a stroke bear you away, the one half of my soul, why do I linger still, the other half, not now so prized, nor a complete survivor? That day shall bring the downfall of us both.

I have sworn no false allegiance: we will go, we will go, whene'er you lead the way, prepared in company to take our latest journey.

For myself, neither fiery Chimæra's breath, nor hundred-handed Gyas, should he rise again, shall ever tear me from you; so mighty Justice and the Fates have willed.

Whether Libra looks upon me, or the terrible Scorpion, the more prevailing element of my natal hour, or Capricorn, despot of the Western wave, the star of both of us agrees in a marvellous way.

You Jove's shielding planet, with its opposite radiance, rescued from baleful Saturn, and stayed the wings of flying Fate, when the crowded people in the theatre thrice clapped their hands with joyful noise.

Myself the tree which fell upon my head had carried away, had not Faunus with his right-hand warded off the blow, the guard of men beloved by Mercury.

Forget not to offer victims and a votive shrine; I will sacrifice a humble lamb.

XVIII.

The poet, content with his own moderate fortune, inveighs against the blindness of avarice: for the same end awaits all men.

Within my dwelling ivory does not gleam, nor roof of fretted gold; beams from Hymettus rest not upon columns hewn in the uttermost parts of Africa; nor have I, a stranger heir, taken possession of the palace of an Attalus; nor do client maids of gentle birth spin for me textures of Laconian purple: but honour is mine, and a generous vein of wit; and poor though I be, the rich man courts me; for nought beyond do I solicit Heaven, or crave a powerful friend for ampler gifts, blessed enough in my one Sabine farm.

Day displaces day, and new moons hasten onward but to fade. You, on the verge of death, contract for blocks of marble to be hewn, and, unmindful of the grave, are rearing mansions, and are all eagerness to thrust backward the shores of the sea that roars against Baiæ; for not enough does the bound of the mainland enrich you.

Nay, why you, ever encroaching, pluck up the neighbouring landmarks of the field, and leap across your clients' borders in your covetousness. Both wife and husband are driven forth, bearing in their bosom their ancestral gods and squalid children.

Yet no palace more surely awaits the wealthy heir than the ordained confine of Orcus. Why farther press? Impartial Earth unlocks herself to receive the poor man and the youthful sons of kings; nor was the guard of Orcus tempted by gold to bear back the crafty Prometheus.

'Tis he who confines proud Tantalus and Tantalus' line; he hears, when invoked and not invoked to ease the poor man who has fulfilled his toils.

XIX.

A hymn to Bacchus: his attributes and exploits.

Bacchus I've seen amid retired rocks, dictating hymns, (posterity believe me!) and the Nymphs his pupils, and the ears of the goat-footed Satyrs pricked up to listen.

Evoe! my heart is thrilled with newly-felt alarm, and wildly exults in a breast that is filled with Bacchus. Evoe! forbear, O Liber, forbear, thou that art terrible with thy resistless thyrsus!

'Tis my privilege to sing of the untiring Thyiades, and the fount that flows with wine, and the rivulets with their wealth of milk, and to picture the streams of honey that gush from hollow trees.

'Tis my privilege too to sing of the adornment of thy blessed consort, which is placed among the stars, and of the halls of Pentheus, dashed down with pitiless wreck, and the destruction of Thracian Lycurgus.

Thou dost sway the courses of rivers, thou dost sway the barbarian sea; thou, dewy with wine upon secluded heights, dost harmlessly bind up with a twine of vipers the tresses of the Thracian Bacchanals.

Thou, when the Giants' sacrilegious troop strove up the steep of heaven to scale the kingdoms of thy sire, didst hurl back Rhœtus with thy lion-claws and terrific fangs:

And yet, since reputed to be fitter for dance and jest and sport, thou wast said to be little suited for the fight: but thou wast the soul of peace and of war as well.

Thee, decked with thy golden horn, Cerberus saw and harmed

not; while he gently brushed thee with his tail, and fondled, as thou didst depart, thy feet and legs with his triple tongue.

XX.

The poet predicts his metamorphosis and immortality.

On no common or puny wing shall I be borne through the lucid air, a bard of double shape, and no more shall I sojourn upon earth, and, superior to envy, I shall forsake the cities of men.

Never shall I, the offspring of poor parents, never shall I, whom you call to be your friend, perish, my beloved Mæcenas, or be confined by the Stygian flood.

Even now rough folds of skin are settling on my legs, and I am changing into a white bird above, and downy feathers are springing along my fingers and shoulders.

Soon shall I, a melodious bird, more fleet than Icarus, child of Dædalus, visit the coasts of the roaring Bosphorus, and the Gætulian Syrtes, and the Hyperborean plains.

Me the Colchian, and the Dacian who would fain disguise his dread of the Marsian cohort, and the remote Geloni, will study, me the Iberian scholar will learn, and he who drinks the Rhone.

Far from my unreal funeral be dirges, and unsightly mournings and lamentations; hush the wail, and omit the superfluous honours of the grave.

BOOK III.

I.

Philosophy is a religious mystery which the vulgar cannot understand. The worthlessness of riches and rank. The praise of contentment. Care cannot be banished by change of scene.

I HATE the uninitiated crowd, and drive them from me. Preserve a holy silence! I, the priest of the Muses, sing to maidens and boys strains not heard before.

The sway of awful kings is over their own flocks; over kings themselves is the sway of Jove, made famous by his conquest of the Giants, Jove, who shakes the universe with his nod.

It may be that one man more widely than another arranges in furrows the trees of his vineyard; that one descends into the Plain, a candidate of nobler birth, that one competes as being superior in character and reputation, that another possesses a larger throng of clients: Necessity by impartial law draws the lot of the exalted and the humblest; the capacious urn is shaking every name.

For him, above whose impious neck hangs a drawn sword, Sicilian banquets will not yield the exquisiteness of their delicious taste; the melodies of birds and of the lyre will not bring back his sleep. The gentle sleep of rustic men disdains not lowly homes and shaded bank, disdains not Tempe which the Zephyrs fan.

Him who requires what is sufficient neither the tumultuous sea makes anxious, nor the fierce swoop of setting Arcturus, or the rising Kid, nor vineyards lashed by hail, and the farm that belies his hopes, while the tree blames now the showers, now the stars that parch the fields, now the inclement winters.

The fish feel the waters straitened by the piles that are thrown into the deep; hither contractors in crowds, attended by their servants, and the lord who disdains the mainland, pour down their heaps of rubble. But Fear and the threatenings of the Conscience climb to the same height as the lord; and black Care quits not the brazen trireme, and sits behind the horseman.

But if neither Phrygian marble, nor the wearing of purple robes more brilliant than a star, soothe to rest the troubled mind, nor do the vine of Falerii and the nard of the land of Achæmenes, why should I pile up a stately hall, with gates which Envy haunts, and built in a novel style? Why should I exchange my Sabine dell for wealth more burdensome?

II.

Horace extols the virtue of endurance and valour in fighting for our country, of integrity in politics, and of religious honour.

Let the strong youth thoroughly learn by sharp warfare cheerfully to endure pinching penury, and let him, a horseman of formidable lance, trouble the savage Parthians, and pass his life beneath the sky and in perilous times. At their view of him from the enemy's battlements, the consort of the warring monarch, and the ripe maiden, would sigh, alas! lest the royal lover, unversed in battle-fields, provoke the lion terrible to rouse, whom bloodthirsty anger speeds through the midst of the carnage.

To die for fatherland is sweet and seemly: death likewise overtakes the man who flees, nor spares the loins and coward back of the unwarlike youth.

Virtue, who knows not the disgrace of defeat, gleams with unsullied honours; and does not take or lay aside the axes according to the whim of the popular breeze. Virtue, unfolding heaven to those who deserve not to die, explores the way by a path denied to others; and spurns with soaring wing the vulgar rabbles and the misty earth.

For faithful silence too there is a sure reward: I will forbid him who has divulged the mystery of secret Ceres to be beneath the same roof, or with me to unmoor the frail pinnace: often the Father of the sky, when slighted, is wont to blend the faultless with the sinful; seldom does Punishment, though lame of foot, quit the criminal who goes before.

III.

The merit of integrity and resolution: the examples of Pollux, Hercules, and Romulus. Juno's speech to the gods on the destinies of Rome. Troy may not be rebuilt.

The man that is upright and fixed in his design, not the passion of citizens commanding wrongful acts, not the glance of the imperious tyrant, shake from his firm resolve; nor Auster, restless Adria's stormy lord, nor the mighty hand of Jove when he wields the thunderbolt: if the shattered sphere fall down, the wreck will strike him undismayed.

'Twas by this course that Pollux and roving Hercules with many an effort gained the fiery heights; among them Augustus, reclining at the feast, drinks the nectar with rosy lip. 'Twas by this thou didst earn the prize, O father Bacchus, when thy tigers bore thee to the sky, drawing the yoke with neck untamed; 'twas by this Quirinus escaped Acheron, caught away by the steeds of Mars; when Juno had discoursed in words that were pleasing to the gods in council.

"Ilium, Ilium, a predestined and impure judge and a foreign woman have o'erthrown into the dust, since that day when Laomedon defrauded the gods of their covenanted reward, a city surrendered to me and chaste Minerva, together with its people and guileful chief. Now neither does her shameful guest have charms for the Spartan adulteress, nor does Priam's perjured house by the aid of Hector's might beat back the gallant Achæans; and the war that was prolonged by our feuds has settled into peace.

"Straightway I will resign to Mars my deep wrath and the grandson I hated, whom the Trojan priestess bore. Him I will allow to enter the abodes of light, to quaff the juices of nectar, and to be enrolled among the tranquil ranks of the gods.

"Provided that a breadth of sea rage betwixt Ilium and Rome, let the exiles in any quarter reign in blessedness; provided that upon the tomb of Priam and Paris cattle trample, and wild beasts undisturbed conceal their whelps, let the Capitol stand in splendour, and valiant Rome be able to impose laws on the vanquished Medes. Dreadful far and wide, let her spread her name to the remotest shores, where the central flood sunders Europe from the African, where swelling Nile waters the cornfields; while she shows her courage more by scorning undiscovered gold, (then better placed when earth conceals it still,) than by forcing it to serve for the uses of men, with a hand that plunders every sacred thing. Whatever boundary is set to be the barrier of the world, it she shall reach with her hosts, exulting to visit the region where the fires fiercely revel, the region where revel the mists and rainy dews.

"But with this condition I declare the fates of the warlike Quirites, that they do not, through excessive affection, and overmuch trust in their power, essay to build again the dwellings of their ancestral Troy. The fortune of Troy, springing again to life under a woeful omen, shall be repeated with grisly carnage, while I, the consort and sister of Jove, lead on the conquering battalions. If thrice the wall of brass should rise again by the creation of Phœbus, thrice it should be hewn down and destroyed by my Argives; thrice the captive wife should mourn her husband and her sons."

This subject suits not with the playful lyre: whither art thou speeding, O my Muse? Cease to repeat in thy presumption the discourses of gods, and to enfeeble a mighty theme by puny strains.

IV.

The invocation of Calliope. A miracle in his childhood proved that Horace was protected by the Muses, and they have guarded him since, and will do so, wherever he goes. They are also the friends of Cæsar, and prompt him to clemency and kindness. The evils of violence and arrogant presumption, on the other hand, are exemplified by the attempts of the Titans and Giants, of Gyas, Orion, and others.

Descend from heaven, queen Calliope, and utter, I pray thee, on the flute a lengthened melody, or, if thou choosest now, with ringing voice, or the chords and lyre of Phœbus.

Do ye hear? Or does a charming frenzy beguile me? I seem to hear and roam 'mid hallowed groves, through which delicious streams and breezes steal.

Myself on Apulian Vultur, beyond the threshold of my nurse Apulia, when wearied out with play and overcome with sleep, the ring-doves of romance covered with fresh leaves; which would be a miracle to all, whosoever inhabit high Acherontia's nest and Bantia's glades and low Forentum's wealthy field; how I slept with body safe from deadly vipers and from bears, how I was overspread with sacred laurel and collected myrtle, a daring infant by the grace of Heaven.

Your own, O Muses, still your own, am I lifted to the Sabine steeps, or if cool Præneste chance to attract me, or the slope of Tibur, or limpid Baiæ. Because a friend to your springs and choirs, the rout of the army at Philippi destroyed me not, the accursed tree destroyed me not, nor Palinurus on the Sicilian flood.

Whenever ye will be with me, I, a mariner, will cheerfully explore the raving Bosphorus, and the burning sands of the Assyrian shore, a traveller by land; I will visit the Britons cruel to strangers, and the Concan who delights in horses' blood; I will visit the quivered Geloni and the Scythian river, unharmed.

Ye in Pierian grot refresh exalted Cæsar, so soon as he has assigned to the towns his weary cohorts, and seeks to end his toils.

Ye both give gentle counsel, gracious Powers, and, when 'tis given, rejoice. We know how he with swooping thunderbolt quelled the impious Titans and their monstrous crew; he who governs the ponderous earth, who governs the breezy sea, and the cities of men, and the grisly realms, and rules the gods and mortal throngs with sole impartial sway.

Deep dread had those o'erweening youths, bristling with their forest of arms, struck into the mind of Jove, and so had the brothers who strove to pile up Pelion on dusk Olympus. But what could Typhœus and stout Mimas do, or what Porphyrion with his threatening mien, what could Rhœtus do, and Enceladus, a hurler bold of trees torn from the roots, as they rushed against the ringing ægis of Pallas? In one place stood Vulcan, eager for the fray, in another matron Juno, and he who will never put down his bow from off his shoulders, who in Castalia's crystal dew bathes his flowing locks, who Lycia's thickets haunts, and his native wood, Apollo of Delos and of Patara.

Force void of reason by its own bulk falls down: force regulated even the gods advance to greater might; they likewise hate the power, which in its heart is bent on every crime.

Hundred-handed Gyas is a witness to the truth of my maxims, and Orion, the well-known assailer of spotless Diana, vanquished by her maiden arrow. Earth grieves to be piled upon her monstrous brood, and mourns her children driven by the thunderbolt to lurid Orcus; and the devouring flame has never gnawed through Ætna piled above, nor the vulture, set to be the warder over wickedness, quitted the liver of incontinent Tityos; three hundred fetters keep down the lustful Pirithous.

V.

This ode was probably written before the surrender by the Parthians, (B. C. 23) *of the surviving prisoners who had belonged to the army of Crassus. If so, it was the emperor's design to recover these prisoners which recalled to Horace the story of Regulus. His speech to the senate, and voluntary return to Carthage.*

When Jove is thundering in the sky, we are wont to believe that he is monarch there: Augustus will be accounted a visible deity, when the Britons are united to the empire, and the formidable Parthians.

Has the soldier of Crassus passed his days a degraded husband with a barbarian wife, and beneath a Median king have Marsians and Apulians grown old in the armour of fathers-in-law that were their foes, (Oh, shame on the Senate and our perverted principles!) forgetful of the sacred shields, and of his name, and of the toga, and of undying Vesta, while Jove is yet standing safe, and the city of Rome?

The far-seeing mind of Regulus had guarded against this, when he opposed the shameful terms, and proved that by the precedent destruction would be drawn down upon the coming age, if the captive men did not perish unpitied.

"I have seen," he said, "our standards fastened to Carthaginian shrines, and weapons wrung from our soldiers without bloodshed; I have seen the arms of citizens bound behind them on a free back, and the gates not shut, and fields being tilled which had been laid waste by our warriors.

"The soldier redeemed with gold will come back more brave, no doubt. To disgrace you are adding loss: neither does wool, when dressed with dye, regain the hues that are gone, nor does true valour, when once it has fallen from the heart, care to be restored in the degraded. If the hind fights, when disentangled from the closely-woven toils, that man will be valiant, who has yielded himself to the faith of treacherous foes, and he will crush the Carthaginians in a second campaign, who like a dastard has felt the thongs upon his arms drawn behind his back, and has feared death! He, since he knew not how to win his life, has mingled peace with war. Oh, ignominy! O mighty Carthage, exalted higher by Italy's shameful ruins!"

He is said to have put away from him, as one whose rights were lost, the lips of his chaste wife, and his little children, and to have sternly fixed upon the ground his manly face; until by his influence he made resolute the wavering senators with counsel given at no other time, and amid his sorrowing friends hastened away, an illustrious exile.

And still he knew what the barbarian tormentor was preparing for him; yet he put aside his kinsmen who fain would stop him, and the people who sought to delay his return, just as if he were leaving his clients' tedious business when a suit had been decided, speeding to the fields of Venafrum, or to Tarentum the Spartan town.

VI.

To the Romans. Regard for the national religion should be restored, for neglect of it has brought us many misfortunes. The decay of private morality has been the source of public licentiousness. The simple and hardy life of the old Romans was the cause of their great victories. Now, each successive generation is worse than the one before it.

O Roman, you, though guiltless, will expiate the offences of your forefathers, until you have repaired the temples and falling shrines of the gods, and the statues sullied with blackening smoke.

'Tis because you own yourself lower than the gods, that you rule the world. From them is every beginning, to them ascribe every ending. Many a misfortune have the gods, when slighted, imposed upon afflicted Hesperia. Twice already have Monæses and the host of Pacorus crushed our unblest assaults, and gaily smile to have added the booty to their collars of little price. Almost have the Dacian and Æthiopian destroyed the City when absorbed in civil feuds; the latter striking terror by his fleet, the former more skilled in shooting arrows.

Our times prolific in sin have first polluted marriage, and offspring, and homes; from this fountain sprung the calamity, which has flowed upon the country and the people.

The ripened virgin makes it her delight to be taught Ionian movements, and is fashioned by the modes of art; even now too from her inmost soul she designs unhallowed loves. Next, she seeks for younger paramours amid her husband's banquet, and does not select one, upon whom she is to bestow with stealthy haste forbidden joys, when the lights have been removed; but she rises, when summoned, in the presence of her husband and not without his knowledge, whether the factor calls her, or the captain of a Spanish ship, the munificent purchaser of her dishonour.

Not sprung from parents such as these were the youths who dyed the sea with Carthaginian blood, and struck down Pyrrhus and great Antiochus and accursed Hannibal; but the manly offspring of rustic warriors, trained to turn up the clods with Sabine hoes, and to carry logs hewn according to the will of an austere mother, when the sun was changing the shadows of the hills, and taking off the yoke from the weary oxen, as he brought with parting car the welcome hour.

What is there wasting Time does not impair? The age of our parents, worse than our grandsires, has borne us yet more wicked, who in our turn are destined to beget a progeny more sinful still.

VII.

Horace assures Asterie of the safe return of her lover Gyges, and of his constancy to her, in spite of all temptations. He hints that there is too much fear, that Asterie herself will prove unfaithful.

Why weep for Gyges, O Asterie, whom in the opening spring the fair Zephyrs will restore to you, enriched with Thynian merchandise, a youth of faithful constancy? He by the South winds driven to Oricum, after the season of the Goat's mad stars, sleepless, with many a tear, passes the cold nights.

But the messenger of his anxious hostess, saying that Chloe sighs for him and is miserably burning for your lover, craftily tempts him in a thousand ways. He repeats how the treacherous woman, by false accusations, induced the credulous Prœtus to contrive a speedy death for too chaste Bellerophon. He tells of Peleus almost consigned to Tartarus, while he flees in his continence from Magnessian Hippolyte; and guilefully touches upon stories which prompt men to sin. In vain! for deafer than the waves of the Icarian sea, he hears the words with heart unshaken still.

But be you careful, lest your neighbour Enipeus please you more than is right; albeit no other skilled to rule the steed is so distinguished as he on the turf of the Plain of Mars, and not one so swiftly as he swims down the channel of the Tuscan stream.

At nightfall shut your house, and look not down into the streets at the note of the plaintive fife; and though he often call you cruel, still obdurate remain.

VIII.

Horace invites Mæcenas to dinner on the first of March, the Feast of the Matrons. He says that he will always keep this day as a holiday, because it is the anniversary of his escape from a sudden death. Besides, the prosperous state of the empire is a further reason for festivity.

You wonder what I, a bachelor, am doing on the Kalends of March, what mean the flowers, and the box full of incense, and the charcoal placed upon the living turf, you that are learned in the literature of either tongue.

I had vowed to Liber a pleasant feast and a white he-goat, when almost done to death by the blow of the falling tree. This day of festival, as the year comes round, shall remove the pitch-bound cork from a wine-jar which was trained to drink the smoke in Tullus' consulate.

Take, Mæcenas, a hundred cups in honour of your friend's deliverance, and prolong till break of day the wakeful lamps; let all clamour and passion be far away.

Dismiss your politic cares for the City's weal; the host of Dacian Cotiso has fallen; the Mede, a foe to himself, is distracted by a woeful warfare; our ancient enemy of the Spanish coast, the Cantabrian, is our slave, subdued by a chain at last imposed; now the Scythians, with bow unstrung, are resolving to withdraw from the plains.

Carelessly, as a man not in place, refrain from guarding overmuch that the people in no way suffer; snatch joyfully the gifts of the present hour, and abandon serious thoughts.

IX.

A dialogue between Horace and Lydia. The lovers' reconciliation.

H. So long as I was dear to you, and no more favoured youth was wont to throw his arms about your spotless neck, I throve more blessed than the Persians' king.

L. So long as you burned for no one more than me, and Lydia was not valued less than Chloe, I, Lydia, of high renown, throve more illustrious than Rome's Ilia.

H. 'Tis Thracian Chloe that now governs me, learned in measures sweet, and skilled to play the lyre; for whom I would not fear to die, if Fate would spare that life surviving me.

L. 'Tis Calais, son of Ornytus of Thurium, who is consuming me with mutual torch; for whom I would endure twice to die, if Fate would spare the boy surviving me.

H. What if our ancient love return, and clasp our parted selves with yoke of brass? If Chloe with the auburn hair is spurned, and the door ope to Lydia scorned before?

L. Albeit he is fairer than a star, you more light than cork, and more passionate than the frantic Adrian sea, with you I'd love to live, with you I'd gladly die!

X.

Horace warns Lyce that he cannot put up with her unkindness for ever.

Though you drank of the far distant Tanais, Lyce, wedded to a savage husband, still you would grieve to expose me, stretched before your unkind portals, to the North-winds of the land.

Hear you how loudly the door, how loudly the grove planted within your fair abode groans beneath the blast, and how Jove with his clear influence turns to ice the fallen snows?

Renounce the pride which Venus hates; lest as the wheel speeds round, the rope run back; 'twas not to be a Penelope unyielding to suitors that your Etruscan sire begot you.

Oh, albeit neither gifts nor prayers, nor lovers' paleness with its violet hue, nor your husband smitten with a Macedonian mistress, sway your mind, yet spare your suppliants, though not more pliant than the unbending oak, and not gentler in heart than Moorish snakes. This body of mine will not for ever endure your threshold or the water of the sky.

XI.

To Mercury. Horace begs the god to teach him such melody as will overcome the unkindness of Lydè. Music has power even over hell itself, as is proved by the story of Orpheus. The ode concludes with the tale of the daughters of Danaus, and their doom in the lower world.

O Mercury, (for by thy teaching it was that apt Amphion moved the stones with his song,) and thou, O Shell, skilled to utter ringing music from the seven strings, not vocal once, nor pleasing, now a friend to rich men's tables and the temples too, speak measures to which Lydè will lend her obdurate ears. For she, like a filly three years old upon the spacious plains, sports boundingly, and shrinks from being touched, unversed in marriage, and as yet not ripe for a playful husband.

Thou hast power to draw tigers and forests to attend thee, and to stay the rapid streams; to thy fascination Cerberus yielded, the monstrous doorkeeper of the palace, albeit a hundred snakes fence round his fury-like head, and noisome breath and foul gore flow from his three-tongued mouth. Nay, even Ixion and Tityos smiled with unwilling countenance; the vessel for a time stood dry, while with a welcome strain thou dost soothe the daughters of Danaus.

Let Lydè hear of the maidens' crime and well-known punishment, and of the jar void of water which runs through at the very bottom, and the late-inflicted doom which awaits offences even beneath Orcus. In their impiety, (for what greater sin could they have had the heart to do?) in their impiety they had the heart to destroy their bridegrooms with the cruel steel!

One out of many, worthy of the marriage torch, was nobly false towards her perjured sire, and a maid illustrious to all time; who to her youthful husband said, "Arise, arise, lest a long sleep be given you from whence you fear it not; elude your father-in-law and my wicked sisters, who, like lionesses that have lighted upon calves, mangle them one by one, alas! I, gentler than they, will neither strike you, nor keep you shut within the bars. Myself let my father load with cruel chains, because in pity I have spared my hapless husband; or myself let him banish in his fleet to the uttermost plains of Numidia! Go, whither your feet and the breezes speed you, while night and Venus are propitious; go with a happy omen, and engrave upon my tomb a lament in memory of me."

XII.

Joyless is the life of girls like Neobule, who are ever under the eye of a strict guardian. Neobule, charmed by the accomplishments of Hebrus, forgets her tedious work.

'Tis the lot of hapless girls neither to give free play to love nor wash away their woes with pleasant wine, or to faint through dread of the lashes of an uncle's tongue.

From you Cytherea's winged boy steals your wool-basket; from you, Neobule, the bright beauty of Hebrus of Lipara steals your web and your diligence in the toilsome craft; whene'er he chance in Tiber's waves to bathe his anointed shoulders, he, a better horseman than Bellerophon himself, and never conquered through slackness of fist or foot; skilled too to shoot the stags as they flee o'er the open plain when the herd is roused, and quick to intercept the boar who makes his lair in the depth of the thicket.

XIII.

To the fountain of Bandusia.

Spring of Bandusia, more clear than glass, worthy of pleasant wine and flowers withal, to-morrow shalt thou be presented with a kid, whose brow that heaves with budding horns designs both love and battles. In vain! for to honour thee he shall with crimson blood dye thy cold streams, he, the offspring of the playful herd.

The blazing dog-star's scorching season knows not what it is to light on thee; thou to oxen wearied with the ploughshare, and to the wandering herd, dost afford a delicious coolness.

Thou also shalt become one of the ennobled fountains, when I sing of the ilex-tree set upon the hollow crags, from whence thy babbling brooks dance down.

XIV.

Horace prepares to celebrate as a holiday the return of Augustus from Spain about the beginning of the year 24 B.C.

O people, Cæsar who but lately was said to have sought in the manner of Hercules to win the laurel whose price is death, revisits his household gods, a conqueror from the Spanish strand.

Let the matron who rejoices in her peerless lord go forth to sacrifice with proper rites; and the sister of the illustrious chief, and the mothers of our maidens and of the youths lately delivered from peril, adorned with suppliant wreath. Ye, O young men, and girls who have lately entered upon wedlock, refrain from ill-omened words.

This day, for me a genuine holiday, shall banish gloomy cares; I will fear neither rebellion, nor death by violence of the foe, while Cæsar rules the world.

Go, search for perfume, boy, and garlands, and a cask which recollects the Marsian war, if a crock has any way been able to elude the roving Spartacus. And bid melodious Neæra haste to bind up in a knot her tresses sweet with myrrh; if delay is caused by the odious doorkeeper, come away.

Whitening hair makes mild those spirits which once were eager for brawls and headstrong quarrel; I would not have endured this in the glow of youth, in Plancus' consulate.

XV.

The poet taunts Chloris with her attempts to appear young, and with her frivolous life, while she is really an old woman. The tone of this ode is similar to that of the thirteenth of the fourth book.

Wife of penniless Ibycus, at last set a limit to your viciousness, and to your notorious tasks: since quite near to a seasonable death, cease to play among the maidens, and to throw a cloud upon the brilliant stars.

If aught becomes Pholoë well enough, it does not likewise become you, Chloris; your daughter more properly storms the young men's homes, like a Thyiad when roused by the beat of the timbrel. She by love for Nothus is constrained to sport like a playful kid: to you, an old creature, wool shorn near famed Luceria is becoming; not lutes, nor the rose's crimson flower, nor casks drunk down to the lees.

XVI.

The explanation of the fable of Danaë: the omnipotence of money; the superior blessedness of moderation. Contentment is genuine wealth.

Immured Danaë a wall of brass and massive doors and the grim watching of wakeful dogs had fenced in well enough from nightly lovers, if at Acrisius, the anxious keeper of the secluded maid, Jupiter and Venus had not laughed; for they knew that the way would be safe and open to the god when transformed into a bribe.

Gold loves to travel through the midst of guards, and to burst through rocks with greater might than the shock of the thunderbolt; down fell the house of the Argive augur, plunged deep in ruin, through the love of gain; the man of Macedon clove the gates of cities and undermined his royal rivals by presents; presents ensnare rough navy captains.

Care follows money as it grows, and so does the hunger for riches greater still. With reason have I shrunk from raising aloft a crest conspicuous far and wide, O Mæcenas, glory of the knights.

The more that each man has denied himself, the more he will receive from Heaven: naked I haste to the camp of those who desire nought, and am eager to leave as a deserter the side of the wealthy, the grander lord of a despised estate, than if whate'er the stout Apulian ploughs I were said to hide away in my granaries, amid great riches unenriched myself.

A stream of clear water, and a wood of a few acres, and the unfailing promise of my cornfield, in blessedness of lot surpass (though he knows it not,) him who is splendid in the sway of fruitful Africa. Although for me neither Calabrian bees bring honey, nor wine is mellowing in Læstrygonian jar, nor goodly fleeces grow on Gallic pastures, yet vexing penury is far away, and if I wished for more, you would not refuse to give it me.

By narrowing my desire I shall better extend my tiny revenues, than if with the plains of Mygdonia I were to unite the realm of Alyattes. They who crave many gifts have many wants: 'tis well for him upon whom God with sparing hand has bestowed that which is sufficient.

XVII.

Horace advises his friend of noble descent, L. Ælius Lamia, to beguile by festivity the tempestuous weather which is imminent.

Ælius, nobly sprung from ancient Lamus, since they tell that from him both all the elder Lamias drew their name, and the whole race of their descendants along the recording annals; you from that founder trace your origin, who is said to have been the first who possessed the walls of Formiæ, and Liris drifting on Marica's shores, a monarch of extended sway:—to-morrow a storm driven downward by the East wind will strew the grove with many a leaf, and the strand with worthless seaweed, unless the aged crow, the presager of rain, deceive me. While you may, pile up the seasoned wood; to-morrow you will soothe your Genius with wine and a pig two months old, together with your household released from toils.

XVIII.

Hymn to Faunus on his feast-day, the fifth of December.

O Faunus, wooer of the flying Nymphs, over my borders and my sunny fields gently mayest thou tread, and depart propitious to my little nurslings; if falls a tender kid in the fulness of the year, and the bowl that is the partner of Venus lacks not wine in plenty; if the ancient altar smokes with a wealth of incense.

All the flock sports upon the grassy plain, when December's Nones come round for thee; the hamlet making holiday takes its ease in the meadows, together with the reposing steer: the wolf is wandering 'mid the fearless lambs; the forest showers its wild leaves down for thee; the ditcher rejoices thrice with his foot to beat the hateful ground.

XIX.

Horace invites Telephus to give up for a time his historical researches, and join him at a banquet in honour of Murena.

How far Codrus, who feared not to die for his country, is removed from Inachus, you discourse, and of the line of Æacus, and of the wars that were waged beneath hallowed Ilium; as to the price at which we can purchase a cask of Chian, who with fire will temper the water's chill, who is to afford a house, and at what hour I shall be freed from a Pelignian coldness, you are dumb.

Boy, give with speed a cup in honour of the New Moon, give one in honour of Midnight, give one in honour of the augur Murena; with three or nine fair cups our goblets are mixed. The ecstatic bard, who loves the Muses of unequal number, will thrice three cups demand; to venture on more than three the Grace that shrinks from quarrels forbids, who clasps her naked sisters.

'Tis my joy to play the madman! why stay the blasts of the Berecynthian pipe? Why silent hangs the flute and lyre withal? Niggard hands I hate! Scatter the roses! Let envious Lycus hear the frantic din, and our neighbour not well-matched with Lycus old.

You, all glossy with your clustering hair, you like the brilliant Hesper, Telephus, Rhodé is wooing, she who fits your bloom; myself a wasting love consumes for Glycera my charmer.

XX.

To Pyrrhus.

See you not, Pyrrhus, at how great a risk you would bear away the whelps of the Gætulian lioness? Full soon will you flee the fierceness of the fray, a spiritless ravisher; when she, through the companies of youths that would thwart her, shall make her way to claim the peerless Nearchus; a mighty conflict, whether the greater booty shall pass to you or her.

Meantime, while you draw forth your rapid shafts, while she whets her formidable teeth, the umpire of the fight is said to have placed the palm beneath his naked foot, and to fan with the gentle breeze his shoulder overrun with fragrant tresses, like either Nireus was, or he who was caught away from Ida, the hill of waters.

XXI.

To a wine-jar. Horace, preparing to entertain his friend the orator M. Valerius Messala Corvinus, sings of the manifold virtues of wine.

Born with myself in Manlius' cousulate, whether complaints you bring, or jokes, or brawls and fits of frantic love, or gentle sleep, my gracious jar; in whatever quality it be that you store your exquisite Massic, you that deserve to be moved from your place on a happy day, come down at the bidding of Corvinus, to unseal your well-ripened vintage.

He, though steeped in the Socratic dialogues, is not so austere that he will be indifferent to you; 'tis told that even the virtue of antique Cato often gathered warmth from wine.

You to a temperament at other times stern apply an engine of gentle force; you with the blithe juice of the liberal god disclose the business of the wise, and their deep designs; you bring back hope and strength to troubled minds, and give the poor man horns of might; for he dreads not, after he has felt your influence, the angry crests of kings, or warriors' arms.

You Liber shall prolong, and Venus too, if she come to us with smiles, and the Graces, ever loth to loose their bond, and the living lamps, until returning Phœbus chase away the stars.

XXII.

This ode appears to be an inscription for a tablet to be placed on a pine consecrated to Diana.

O Virgin, guardian of the hills and groves, who, when thrice invoked, dost hear the girls that labour in the travail of birth, and dost rescue them from death, goddess of threefold shape; o'erlooking my cottage let thy pine-tree stand, for me with joy on each completed year to present it with the blood of a boar that as yet but meditates his side-long thrust.

XXIII.

To Phidyle. An innocent heart is the most acceptable sacrifice.

If it shall prove that you have raised to Heaven your upturned palms at each birth of the Moon, my rustic Phidyle, and that with incense and this year's corn and a greedy sow you have appeased your household gods, neither will your prolific vine feel the destroying Sirocco, nor your harvest the barrenness of blight, or your pleasant nurslings the deadly season in the fruit-time of the year.

For the doomed creature that is feeding on snowy Algidus amid the oaks and ilex-trees, or growing up on Alba's lawns, will be a victim to stain with the blood of its neck the pontiffs' axes; you are in no way bounden to solicit the gods with the slaughter of many a ewe, if you wreathe their images with rosemary and brittle myrtle-sprigs.

If clear from guilt your hand is wont to touch the altar, it softens the displeasure of the Penates with holy meal and crackling salt, and would not be more persuasive with a costly victim.

XXIV.

Boundless riches cannot banish fear or avert death. A simple life like that of the Scythians is the healthiest and best. Stringent laws are needed to curb the present luxury and licentiousness, which spring from our excessive opulence. The training of our young has become frivolous and effeminate, and like that of the degenerate Greeks. The desire for wealth is never satisfied.

Although, possessed of greater wealth than the untouched treasuries of the Arabs and opulent India, you were to overspread with your piles of rubble all the Etruscan and Apulian sea, still, since fell Necessity fixes on the loftiest tops her spikes of adamant, you will not loose your mind from fear, nor your head from the snares of death.

Better live the Scythians of the plain, whose wains are wont to draw their roving homes, and the austere Getæ, for whom the acres unallotted bear fruit and corn that is free to every one, and tillage lasting longer than a year is not practised, and a successor, taking his turn on the same condition, relieves him that has fulfilled his toil. There the guileless matron refrains from harming her step-children that are without a mother, nor does the dowried wife command her lord, nor does she trust a sleek adulterer. There parents' virtue is a mighty dowry, and chastity, which never breaks its compact and shrinks from another man; and frailty they hold a crime, or else the price is death.

Oh, whoso shall resolve to put away our impious slaughters and civil frenzy, if he shall seek to have his name inscribed at the foot of his statues as Father of Cities, let him dare to curb our wild licentiousness, sure to win fame from posterity; inasmuch as (alas, how foul a sin!) we in our envy hate virtue while she still lives with us, miss her when removed from our eyes.

What do sorrowful lamentations avail, if offence is not cut down by punishment? What without morals do idle laws avail, if neither that quarter of the world which burning heats enclose, nor the side that is close by the North-wind, and the snows grown hard upon the ground, drive away the merchant, and cunning mariners quell the savage deep; if poverty, that deep disgrace, bids us do and suffer anything, and forsakes the path of Virtue's steep ascent? Let us either into the Capitol, whither the applause invites us, and the throng of them that support us, or let us into the nearest sea send the gems and pearls and vile gold, the substance of our chiefest ill, if we truly repent of our crimes.

We must extirpate the principles of vicious covetousness, and mould with rougher training the minds that are now too soft. The free-born boy, all unpractised, knows not how to keep his seat on horseback, and is afraid to hunt, being more skilled to play, either with the Greek hoop, if you desire him, or, if you prefer it, at gaming which the laws forbid; while the father's broken faith defrauds the partner of his capital, and his friend, and hastes to pile up money for his unworthy heir. 'Tis true the riches grow to monstrous bulk; yet there is something ever wanting to complete the imperfect sum.

XXV.

To Bacchus. Horace, as one possessed with the frantic inspiration of the god, foretells that he will sing in glorious verse the praises of Augustus. This is the only one of Horace's odes which may be said to be written in the dithyrambic manner.

Whither, O Bacchus, art thou speeding me filled with thyself? To what groves or what caverns am I driven in the swiftness of my strange inspiration? Within what grots shall I be heard, essaying to plant among the stars and the council of Jove the everlasting glory of illustrious Cæsar? I will utter something peerless, something fresh, as yet unuttered by another mouth. Even so the sleepless Eviad on the hills is amazed, as she gazes upon Hebrus, and Thrace all white with snow, and Rhodope traversed by barbarian foot, as 'tis a joy to me, while I roam, to view the river-banks and solitary grove!

O thou that art lord of the Naiads, and of the Bacchanals strong to o'erthrow with their hands high-towering ash-trees, nothing mean or in lowly strain, nothing mortal will I speak! Delightful is the peril, O king of the wine-press, to follow the god that wreathes his brow with vine-leaves' greenery!

XXVI.

The poet, as a retiring veteran, dedicates to Venus the arms of a lover, while at the same time he begs her to punish the cruelty of Chloe.

I've passed my life of late as the girls' effective soldier, and not inglorious has been my warfare; now my arms and lute discharged from service this wall shall hold, which guards the left side of the sea-born Venus.

Here, here place the shining torches, and the crow-bars, and the bows which threatened the confronting doors.

Lady, who dost govern blissful Cyprus, and Memphis exempt from Sithonian snow, O queen, with uplifted scourge touch once the disdainful Chloe.

XXVII.

The poet prays that good omens may attend Galatea on her voyage; at the same time he warns her that the weather is not to be trusted in the late autumn, that the sea is then especially dangerous, and that great caution is needed. It was by want of caution that Europa was carried away across the sea. Her story concludes the ode.

May the omen of the screech-owl's oft-repeated note, and the bitch in whelp, or a dun she-wolf running down from the country of Lanuvium, and a fox that has cubs, start upon their way the impious; and may a snake cut short their journey when begun, as, darting like an arrow across the path, it chance to affright the nags: I, a far-seeing diviner in her behalf for whom I fear, ere the bird that forbodes impending showers revisit the stagnant pools, will call up from the rising of the sun the raven of prophetic note.

May you be happy, ('tis my wish,) wherever you choose to be, and live with me in memory, my Galatea; and may neither a magpie on the left forbid you to go forth, nor a wandering crow! But you see with what a turmoil sloping Orion is troubled. I know well what the dark gulf of Adria is, and what misdeeds the fair Iapyx works. May the wives and children of our foes feel the unforeseen commotions of the rising South-wind, and the roar of the blackening deep, and the coasts that shudder beneath the lashing of the waves!

So too Europa to the treacherous bull entrusted her snowy side, and turned pale at the sea with its brood of monsters, and at the perils lurking all around her, though fearless before. But lately in the meadows, intent upon the flowers, and the maker of a garland due to the Nymphs, in the glimmering night she discerned nothing except the stars and billows.

And so soon as she reached Crete mighty in her hundred towns, "O my father," she said, "a name abandoned by your daughter, and affection overcome by frenzy! Whence, whither have I come? Too slight is but one death for maidens' fault! Do I, awake, lament the shameful act, or does an unsubstantial phantom, which flying forth from the ivory gate conveys a dream, beguile me though void of offence? Was it better to travel through a length of waves, or to gather fresh flowers? If some one will now give up to me that detested bull, I will strive to the utmost to mangle with the steel and break the horns of the monster, lately much beloved. Shamelessly I left my father's home, shamelessly I shrink from Orcus. Oh, if thou dost hear these words, any one of the gods, grant that I may wander naked among lions! Before disfiguring leanness overruns my comely cheeks, and the juices waste from off the blooming prey, I long, while fair to view, to furnish food for tigers. Worthless Europa, your father though absent presses you: why hesitate to die? You have the power, with the girdle that has usefully come with you, to wound your neck suspended from this mountain-ash. Or if the rocks and crags with points of death attract you, come, commit yourself to the whirling blast; unless you choose to perform the task of spinning set by a mistress, you, of royal birth, and to be a concubine, and be handed over to a barbarian dame."

As she bewailed herself, Venus stood by perfidiously smiling, and her son with bow unstrung. Presently, when she had jested enough; "Refrain," she said, "from wrath and heated quarrel, when the hateful bull shall surrender his horns for you to mangle them. You know not that you are the bride of unconquerable Jove: hush your sobs: study to bear aright your mighty fortune; half the divided world shall take your name."

XXVIII.

An invitation to Lyde to visit the poet on the feast of Neptune, probably the twenty-third of July.

What better can I do on Neptune's festal day? Bring forth the treasured Cæcuban, my active Lydè, and apply violence to the fortress of wisdom. You mark the noonday sloping towards the eve, and yet, as if the winged day stood still, you pause to pluck down from the store-room the long-lingering wine-jar of Bibulus' consulate.

We in turn will sing of Neptune, and the Nereids' green tresses; you with curving lyre shall celebrate Latona, and rapid Cynthia's darts. In our final lay she shall be sung of, who possesses Cnidos and the sparkling Cyclades, and visits Paphos with her team of swans; Night also shall be praised in a hymn she well deserves.

XXIX.

Horace invites Mæcenas to leave Rome for a time, in the midst of the hot season, and come to visit him at his Sabine cottage. Mæcenas was at this time prefect of the City. Horace takes the opportunity of deprecating excessive anxiety about the future, which we cannot control. He represents himself as the philosopher of contentment.

Mæcenas, scion of Etruscan kings, I long have had in store for you well-ripened wine in a cask not broached before, together with the blossom of roses, and balsam expressed for your hair. Tear yourself away from impediments; do not always survey well-watered Tibur, and Æsula's sloping corn-land, and the heights of parricide Telegonus. Forsake your palling sumptuousness, and your pile, the neighbour of the lofty clouds; cease to admire the smoke and splendour and din of opulent Rome! Changes are mostly welcome to the rich; and suppers of neat simplicity, beneath the humble roof of the poor, without canopy and purple, are wont to smooth away the wrinkles of an anxious brow.

Now the bright father of Andromeda displays his fire which lay hid before, now Procyon rages, and the star of the rampant lion, as the sun brings again the parching days. Now with his languid flock the weary shepherd seeks the shade and stream, and the brakes which shaggy Silvan haunts, and the voiceless river-bank is without the wandering winds.

You ponder what position best becomes the state, and for the sake of the City anxiously fear what the Seres are plotting, and Bactra, once the realm of Cyrus, and Tanais distracted by feuds.

God in his providence shrouds in the darkness of night the issue of future time, and smiles if a mortal flutter to pierce farther than he may. Be careful to regulate serenely what is present with you; all else is swept along in the fashion of the stream, which at one time, within the heart of its channel, peacefully glides down to the Tuscan sea; at another, whirls along worn stones and uprooted trees and flocks and houses all together, amid the roaring of the hills and neighbouring wood, whene'er a furious deluge chafes the quiet rills.

He will live master of himself, and cheerful, who has the power to say from day to day, "I have lived! to-morrow let the Sire overspread the sky either with cloudy gloom or with unsullied light; yet he will not render of no effect aught that lies behind, nor shape anew and make a thing not done, what once the flying hour has borne away."

Fortune, delighting in her cruel work, and perversely bent on playing her capricious game, shifts to and fro her unstable honours, kind now to me, now to another. I praise her while she stays: if she flaps her nimble wings, I surrender what she has given, and wrap myself up in my own virtue, and woo undowried honest poverty.

'Tis not for me, if the mast is groaning beneath the stormy Africus, to resort to piteous prayers, and strive to bargain with vows that my Cyprian and Tyrian wares may not add riches to the grasping sea. Then myself, under the protection of a two-oared skiff, safe through the Ægæan's brawls the breeze will waft, and Pollux with his twin brother.

XXX.

The Poet's monument.

I have reared a monument more enduring than brass, and loftier than the pyramids' royal structure; which not the wasting shower, not the raving North-wind can have power to overthrow, or the countless succession of years, and the ages' flight.

I shall not wholly die, and a large portion of my being will escape the Queen of death; ceaselessly shall I grow, and be fresh in the praise of posterity, so long as with the silent virgin the pontiff shall ascend the Capitol.

I shall be told of, how that where brawls impetuous Aufidus, and where Daunus, poor in his store of water, reigned over rustic tribes, I, rising from a low estate to greatness, was the first who adapted to Italian measures the Æolian lay.

Assume, my Melpomene, the pride of place your merits have won, and with the Delphic laurel graciously bind my hair.

BOOK IV.

I.

Horace begs Venus not to renew her war against him, now that he is growing old; he says that she would do better to make his younger friend Paullus Maximus her champion. But unawares he feels himself possessed by love.

O VENUS, dost thou wake the warfare that long has paused? Forbear, I pray thee, I pray thee! I am not the man that I was beneath kind Cinara's sway. Cease, cruel mother of the gentle Loves, near my tenth lustre's close to bend to thy soft behests one now too hard to feel them.

Away, whither winning prayers of young men call thee back. More seasonably to the house of Paullus Maximus wilt thou speed, wafted on the wings of shining swans, and revel there, if thou dost seek to fire a heart that is meet for thy influence.

For he, high-born and beautiful withal, and one who lacks not speech in behalf of the anxious arraigned, and a youth of a hundred accomplishments, will carry far and wide the banners of thy command; and whene'er, as he prevails, he chance to laugh to scorn his rival's lavish gifts, near Alba's meres he will set thee up of marble beneath a citron roof.

There will thy nostrils breathe a wealth of incense, and thou wilt be charmed with the blended notes of the lyre and Berecynthian pipe, not without the flute; there twice each day boys joined with blooming maids, as they adore thy divinity, thrice with fair foot shall shake the ground according to the Salian measure.

Myself not damsel now nor youth delights, nor fond hope of a sympathising soul, nor to contend in cups of wine, nor to entwine my brows with fresh-plucked flowers.

But why alas, my Ligurine, oh why flows down my cheeks the slowly-dropping tear? Why, in the midst of fluent words, with an uncomely silence fails my tongue? In the dreams of night I now have caught and hold you; now 'tis you I follow o'er the lawn of the Plain of Mars; you, hard-hearted one, I follow through the rolling waters.

II.

To Iulus Antonius, the son of M. Antonius the triumvir. It is a hopeless task to attempt to rival Pindar. His dithyrambics, pæans, encomia, epinicia, and dirges. Horace contrasts with Pindar's genius his own studied poetry. The triumph of Augustus over the German tribe of the Sygambri.

Whoe'er, Iulus, essays to rival Pindar, supports himself on wings waxened by the art of Dædalus, and is doomed to give his name to the glassy sea.

As a torrent rushing from a mountain-top, which rains have fed beyond its wonted banks, so surges Pindar, and in boundless force with deep mouth pours along; worthy to win Apollo's laurel-wreath, whether through his bold dithyrambics he rolls new phrases forth, and onward sweeps on measures freed from law; or whether he sings of gods, or of kings the offspring of gods, beneath whose hands the Centaurs fell by a deserved death, beneath whom fell the flame of the dreadful Chimæra; or whether he records those whom the palm of Elis brings back home exalted to the sky, or the boxer or the steed, and presents them with a gift more precious than a hundred effigies; or whether he laments the youthful lover snatched away from his weeping maiden, and extols to the stars his might and spirit and golden virtues, and withholds him from the gloom of Orcus.

Strong is the gale that wafts the swan of Dirce, whene'er, Antonius, he spreads his wings into the high spaces of the clouds. I in the mood and manner of a Matine bee, (which culls the pleasant thyme with ceaseless toil about the wood and slopes of dewy Tibur,) a tiny minstrel, mould my studied verse.

You, a poet of a nobler quill, shall sing of Cæsar, whene'er, adorned with the well-earned laurel leaf, he shall lead captive along the sacred slope the fierce Sygambri: nothing more great or good than him have Fate and Heaven's grace bestowed on earth, nor will they ever give, albeit the ages return to the primeval gold.

And you shall sing of our joyous days and the City's public game for the return of Cæsar which has been granted us, and of the forum bereft of its lawsuits.

Then, if I shall speak aught worthy to be heard, the best power of my voice shall bear its part; and blest in the regaining of Cæsar I will sing of thee, O fair daylight, of thee that art worthy to be praised!

And while he moves along, we, all the citizens, will utter not once alone thy name, Io Triumphe! Io Triumphe! and will offer gifts of incense to the gracious gods.

Ten bulls and as many cows will pay your vow; my own a tender calf will pay, which has left its dam, and is growing to youth amid the abundant herbage; reflecting on its brow the crescent fires of the moon when bringing round her third rising; where it has received the mark, snow-white to view, all else a tawny red.

III.

To Melpomene. The reward of her favourite. To her it is due that I am now acknowledged to be the lyric poet of Rome.

The man whom at his birth with gentle glance thou, O Melpomene, once hast looked upon, him the Isthmian toils shall not ennoble as a boxer, him the fleet courser shall not bear along a conqueror in Achæan car, nor shall the business of war exhibit him to the Capitol, a chief adorned with the foliage of Delos, because he has beaten down the swelling threats of kings:—

But the streams that flow beside the fruitful Tibur, and the tangled leafage of the groves, shall fashion him to be of high estate in the Æolian lay.

The children of Rome, the princess of cities, deign to set me among the lovely companies of the bards; and now I am bitten less by Envy's tooth.

Thou that dost sway the golden shell's sweet ringing, Pierian Lady, thou that canst give even to dumb fishes, if it please thee, the music of the swan;

'Tis to thy bounty that all this belongs, that I am pointed out by the finger of passers-by as the minstrel of the Roman lyre: that I draw a poet's breath and please, if I do please, is thine.

IV.

This ode is on the victory of Claudius Drusus Nero, the younger son of the Empress Livia, over the Vindelici. Drusus is compared to a young eagle and lion. His stepfather Augustus is praised, as having trained him to greatness. The influence of birth and of education on the character. The battle of the Metaurus is recalled, as having been won by an ancestor of Drusus. Hannibal is made to extol the valour and resolution of Rome.

Like the winged minister of the thunderbolt, to whom the monarch of the gods committed the dominion over roving birds, when he had proved him faithful in the matter of yellow-haired Ganymede:—

Erewhile his youth and ancestral spirit has driven him forth from the nest, all ignorant of toils, and soon the gales of Spring, when the clouds are swept away, have taught him, still trembling, unwonted efforts; next, a vigorous impulse has sent him as a foe upon the sheepfolds, now the passion for feast and fray has spurred him on against the wrestling serpents:—

Or like a lion just weaned from the milk of his tawny mother's teat, whom a roe has seen when absorbed upon the smiling pastures, doomed to die beneath his unfleshed tooth:—

Such the Vindelici saw Drusus waging war beneath the Rhætian Alps; (whence they derived the custom which throughout all time arms their right hand with the Amazonian battle-axe, I stay not to inquire; and all things 'tis not permitted us to know;) but hordes victorious long and widely, in their turn vanquished by the strategy of a youth, felt what was the power of an intellect, what was the power of a genius duly nurtured beneath the sanctuary of an auspicious roof, what was the power of the fatherly spirit borne by Augustus towards the Neros in their boyhood.

Brave men by brave and good men are engendered; there is in steers, there is in horses the merit of their sires; nor do fierce eagles beget the unwarlike dove.

But teaching furthers inbred energy, and genuine modes of culture nerve the soul; whenever morals chance to fail, defects disfigure minds whose birth is good.

What debt, O Rome, thou owest to the Neros, the river Metaurus is witness, and Hasdrubal put to rout, and that bright day when gloom was chased away from Latium, the day which smiled the first with fair success, since the fiend of Africa, as flame through firebrands, or Eurus through Sicilian waves, careered through the towns of Italy.

Henceforth the Roman manhood grew in an unbroken course of prosperous toils, and the shrines, laid waste by the Carthaginians' sacrilegious outbreak, held gods that stood erect;

And thus at last spoke treacherous Hannibal: "We stags, the prey of ravening wolves, are still perversely pursuing those whom 'tis our splendid triumph to foil and flee.

"The race, which valiantly from Ilium burnt conveyed its sacred things tossed on the Etruscan seas, and its children and aged sires to Ausonian towns, that race, as an ilex-tree lopped with the sturdy axe on Algidus that teems with shadowy bowers, through losses, through carnage, draws means and spirit from the steel itself. Not with greater vigour, when its body had been cleft, did the hydra grow up against Hercules incensed at the defeat; nor have the Colchians reared a mightier prodigy, or Thebes, Echion's town.

"Plunge it in the deep,—it will come forth more fair: grapple with it,—'twill throw to earth with high renown the unscathed conqueror, and wage wars for its matrons to tell of.

"No more to Carthage shall I send proud messengers: fallen, fallen is all hope, and the fortune of our line, now that Hasdrubal is slain.

"There's nought that Claudian hands will not achieve; for them both Jove protects with gracious power, and skilful diligence speeds through the perilous points of war.

V.

A prayer for the speedy return of Augustus, who, after his victories over the Germans, remained some time in settling affairs in the western provinces. He actually returned to Rome at the beginning of the year 13 B.C.

You that were born by the kindness of the gods, most excellent protector of the race of Romulus, too long have you now been absent; return, since it was a speedy return which you promised to the Fathers' holy conclave. Restore, good chief, the light to your country: for when your countenance, like the spring, has beamed upon the people, more pleasantly passes the day, and fairer shine the suns.

As with vows and omens and prayers a mother calls her boy, whom the South wind's envious breath keeps sundered from his sweet home, while he tarries across the waters of the Carpathian sea longer than the term of a year, and never does she turn her face away from the winding shore;—so, smitten with the yearnings of constancy, our fatherland asks for Cæsar.

For the steer in safety ranges through the fields; Ceres nourishes the fields, and bounteous Prosperity; the mariners ever are flying across a pacified main; Honour shrinks from giving cause for reproach; by not one outrage is the pure household stained; morality and a law have quelled the tainted sin; mothers are commended by the likeness of their children; punishment, a close companion, follows guilt.

Who would dread the Parthian, who would dread the icy Scythian, who would dread the brood which savage Germany engenders, while Cæsar is preserved? Who would heed the warfare of fierce Iberia?

On his own hills each man passes through the day, and weds the vine to the unmarried trees; after this, he joyfully returns to his cups, and to the second course invites you as a god; you with many a prayer, you with wine poured forth from the bowl he worships, and your divinity he mingles with his household-gods, as did Greece, in her regard for Castor and mighty Hercules.

Oh, that you may, good chief, grant to Hesperia a length of holidays! So pray we sober in the morning, when the day is all before us; so pray we bedewed with wine, when the sun is sinking down beneath the Ocean.

VI.

Hymn to Apollo. This ode forms a kind of introduction to the Secular Hymn.

God, whose might to punish a boastful tongue the offspring of Niobe felt, and which Tityos the ravisher felt, and Phthian Achilles, almost the conqueror of lofty Troy, a warrior greater than all the rest, yet not a match for thee; albeit he, the son of ocean Thetis, as he fought with his terrific spear, shook the Dardan battlements. He, like a pine struck by the biting steel, or a cypress beneath the East wind's shock, fell down extended far and wide, and laid his neck in Trojan dust.

He would not, shut up in the horse which counterfeited an offering to Minerva, have ensnared the Trojans in their ill-timed revelling, and Priam's palace in the gaiety of its dances: but openly dreadful to the captured, (alas, foul crime! alas!) he would have burnt with Achæan flames the children that could not speak, even him who was still hidden within his mother's womb; had not the sire of the gods, vanquished by thy prayers and those of sweet Venus, granted to the fortunes of Æneas a circle of walls built with a fairer omen.

Minstrel, teacher of Thalia with the ringing voice, Phœbus, who dost bathe thy hair in Xanthus' stream, defend the honour of the Daunian Muse, Agyieus ever young! 'Tis Phœbus who has given me inspiration, Phœbus has given me the art of song and the name of poet.

Flower of our maidens, and boys born of noble parents, you that are the wards of the Delian goddess who with her bow stops the flight of lynxes and stags, observe the Lesbian measure and the note my finger strikes, while you duly hymn Latona's youthful son, and duly hymn the Shiner of the Night with her growing torch, her who is gracious to the crops, and swift to roll along the current of the months.

Presently, as a bride, you will say: "I, when the cycle brought round its festal days, rendered a hymn that was pleasing to Heaven, well taught in the measures of Horace the bard."

VII.

To his noble friend the eloquent advocate Torquatus, on the return of Spring. Though the earth renews itself, and the waning moon waxes afresh, yet death is the ending of human life. Let us then make the best of our days while they last.

The snows have fled away; now grass to the plains comes back, and foliage to the trees; Earth changes her phase, and streams subsiding glide within their banks; the Grace, with the Nymphs and her twin sisters, ventures unclad to lead along the dance.

Not to hope for immortality the year warns you, and the hour that whirls along the kindly day. The cold grows mild beneath the western gales, Summer treads on the steps of Spring, doomed itself to perish, so soon as fruit-bearing Autumn has poured forth his store, and lifeless Winter next speeds back again.

Yet the swift moons make good their losses in the sky; we, when we have fallen to that place whither fell father Æneas, whither fell wealthy Tullus, and Ancus, are but dust and shadow.

Who knows whether the gods in heaven will add to-morrow's hours to the sum to-day completes? All that you shall chance to have bestowed on your own dear heart will escape the covetous hands of your heir.

When once you have met your doom, and Minos has pronounced upon you his august decree, not your birth, Torquatus, not your eloquence, not your piety will restore you to life: for neither does Diana release from the darkness of hell her chaste Hippolytus, nor has Theseus power to break off the fetters of Lethe from his beloved Pirithous.

VIII.

To C. Marcius Censorinus. The poet's gift is an immortality of fame. It was usual for friends to exchange presents called strenæ, "étrennes," on the Kalends of March and at the Saturnalia, towards the end of December.

Censorinus, I would munificently bestow on my familiar friends bowls and pleasing vases of bronze; I would bestow tripods, that were the prizes won by gallant Greeks; and you would bear away not the meanest of my gifts, if I in truth were rich in works of art, which either Parrhasius or Scopas produced, the latter skilful to present in stone, the former in limpid colours, at one time a mortal, at another a god. But the means to do this I possess not; nor does your fortune or your choice need toys like these.

In verse is your delight; verse we are able to bestow, and to set its value on the gift. Not marble statues graved with a people's inscriptions, whereby soul and life after death come back to valiant leaders, not Hannibal's hurried flight, and threats flung back upon himself, not the burning of impious Carthage, blazon more plainly the exploits of him, who, when he came back home, had earned a name from Africa subdued, than do the Calabrian Muses; and if paper holds its peace, you will never bear away the guerdon of what you have excellently done. What would the son of Mars and Ilia be, if jealous Silence suppressed the deserts of Romulus? Æacus, rescued from the Stygian waves, the genius and goodwill and tongue of mighty poets commit enshrined to the isles of wealth.

'Tis the Muse who forbids to die the man that is worthy of renown; 'tis the Muse who blesses him with a place in heaven. Thus the vigorous Hercules is a guest at the coveted banquets of Jove. The sons of Tyndarus, a bright constellation, rescue from the depth of the waters the shattered ships; Liber, with fresh vine-leaves decked, to happy issues brings the vows of men.

IX.

To M. Lollius, who was consul 21 B.C. *The immortality of poetry. Many heroes of old have become forgotten because they had no poet to sing their exploits. Horace will immortalize the feats and the virtue of Lollius.*

Lest perchance you may deem that the words will perish, which I, born beside Aufidus who echoes afar, utter by arts not made known before, words to be wedded to the strings of the lyre;—think how, if Mæonian Homer possess the higher seat, the Muse of Pindar does not lie unfamed, and the songs of Ceos, and the threatening verses of Alcæus, and Stesichorus' stately lays; and whate'er of yore Anacreon playfully sung, time has not destroyed; still breathes the love, and still live the ardours, that were committed to the lute of the Æolian girl.

Not Laconian Helen alone has been fired with love for an adulterer's glossy dressed locks, and admired his robes o'erspread with gold, and his regal array and retinue; nor was Teucer the first to point shafts on a Cydonian bow; not once only was Ilium assailed; 'twas not Idomeneus or Sthenelus alone who fought battles meet for the Muses to rehearse; not the first was dauntless Hector or valiant Deiphobus to sustain wounds for the sake of their chaste wives and their children. Many a brave man lived ere Agamemnon; but they all, unwept and unknown, are o'erwhelmed by eternal night, because they are without a sacred bard.

Worth hidden is not far from buried sloth. I will not pass you by unsung and unpraised by my pages, and will not, O my Lollius, suffer envious Forgetfulness undisturbed to prey on your feats so manifold. You have a mind that is both sagacious in action, and steady in prosperous and perilous times; one that punishes greedy fraud, and abstains from money which draws the world to follow it; and your mind is a consul not only for a single year, but so often as it, a good and faithful judge, sets the honourable before the expedient, flings back with lofty mien the bribes of the guilty, and through opposing battalions victoriously opens a way for its arms.

You would not rightly call "blest" the man who has great possessions; more rightly does he assume the title of "blest," who has learned how to use wisely the gifts of Heaven, and to endure stern penury, and who fears disgrace worse than death; he for his dear friends or fatherland is not afraid to perish.

X.

To Ligurine.

You that are cruel as yet, and mighty in the gifts of Venus, when the unexpected down shall come upon your pride, and the locks that now float upon your shoulders shall have fallen away, and the hue, that now surpasses the blossom of the bright-red rose, shall be changed, and transform Ligurine into a shaggy visage; you will say, alas, whene'er you chance to see yourself in the mirror, a different form:—"The mind I have to-day, why as a boy did I have it not? Or why to these feelings return not my unblemished cheeks?"

XI.

Horace invites Phyllis to visit him on the thirteenth of April, the birth-day of Maecenas.

I have a cask well filled with Alban wine which is passing its ninth year; I have in my garden, Phyllis, parsley for weaving garlands; I have a large abundance of ivy, wherewith you bind your hair and brightly shine. The house is smiling with silver; the altar, twined with wreaths of holy vervain, longs to be sprinkled with the sacrifice of a lamb; the whole band is hurrying; boys mixed with girls are running to and fro; the flames are flickering, as through the roof they whirl the sooty smoke.

Yet, that you may know to what delights you are summoned, you have to keep the Ides, that day which divides April, the month of sea-born Venus; that day which is with me rightly a high day, and holier almost than my own birthday, because from this dawn my Mæcenas reckons his flowing tide of years.

Telephus, whom you desire to win, that youth not of your condition, a girl wealthy and wanton has already enthralled, and keeps him bound with pleasing chain. Phaëthon scathed by the thunderbolt affrights ambitious hopes; and winged Pegasus affords you a solemn warning, (he who would not brook his earthly rider Bellerophon,) always to aim at what is meet for you, and, by deeming it a sin to hope for more than is lawful, to avoid an ill-assorted lover.

Come now, latest of my loves, (for henceforth I will never feel the flame for any other woman,) truly learn measures to render with your lovely voice; by song the gloom of care will be diminished.

XII.

This ode, written in the early spring, is addressed to Virgil; though perhaps not to the poet. It is an invitation to a feast: but Horace playfully tells his friend that he must pay for his wine by bringing with him a box of perfume.

Now Spring's companions, they who soothe the main, the Thracian breezes, drive along the sails; now neither meads are stiff nor rivers roar swollen with winter snow.

The bird is building her nest, while she sadly mourns for Itys,—the bird unhappy, and the eternal shame of Cecrops' house, because she sinfully avenged the barbarous lusts of kings.

Amid the velvet grass the guardians of the goodly sheep are playing lays upon the pipe, and charm the god to whom the flocks are pleasant and Arcadia's dusky hills.

The season, O my Virgil, has brought thirst; but if you yearn to quaff the vintage which was pressed at Cales, you that are the client of our youthful nobles, with nard you must purchase your wine. A tiny alabaster box of nard will draw forth a cask of wine, which now reposes in the stores of Sulpicius, a cask of bounteous power to grant fresh hopes, and of prevailing force to wash away the bitters of care.

If you are eager to approach these joys, come quickly with your merchandise; I design not to steep you in my cups exempt from cost, like a rich man in a plenteous mansion.

But fling aside delays and thoughts of gain; and mindful, while it may be, of the dark fires, mix with your meditations a brief folly: 'tis sweet at fitting time to lose our wisdom.

XIII.

The poet taunts Lyce, now growing old, with her desperate attempts still to seem young and fascinating. This ode is perhaps intended to form a contrast to the tenth of the third Book.

Lyce, the gods have heard my prayers, the gods have heard them, Lyce; you are growing an old woman, and yet would fain seem fair, and you shamelessly sport and drink, and in your cups with quavering note essay to wake regardless Love. He keeps his watch on Chia's beauteous cheeks, Chia in youthful bloom, and skilled to play the lute. For all disdainful he flies by the withered oaks, and shrinks from you, because those yellow teeth disfigure you, because wrinkles disfigure you, and the snows of the head.

Not robes of Coan purple now, nor brilliant pearls, bring back to you the times which once the flying day has stored and shut up in the public annals.

Whither has fled your charm, alas! or whither your bloom? Whither your graceful motion! What have you of her, of her, who used to breathe the spirit of love, who had stolen me from myself away; she, blessed after Cinara, a form well-loved, and full of winning wiles?

But Fate to Cinara granted fleeting years, while she resolved to preserve Lyce to be a match for the date of the beldame crow; so that glowing youths might be able to view with many a laugh the torch sunk away into the ashes.

XIV.

The praise of Tiberius Claudius Nero, the step-son of Augustus, on his victories over the tribes of the Rhaetian Alps. His brother Drusus is the hero of the fourth ode of this Book. But the present ode is so framed as to be in the main a panegyric of the emperor.

What zeal of the Fathers, or what zeal of the Quirites, with ample awards of honours, can for ever immortalise your virtues, O Augustus, by inscriptions and recording annals, O mightiest of all princes, wherever the sun sheds light on shores where man may dwell? You the Vindelici, free before from Latin law, lately learned to know, what was your might in war.

For with your soldiers Drusus fiercely struck to earth with more than a single requital the Genauni, a restless tribe, and the nimble Breuni, and the castles set upon the dreadful Alps: next, the elder of the Neros engaged in an obstinate conflict, and by the favouring grace of Heaven routed the savage Rhæti; he, glorious to view in the struggle of Mars, with what havoc he beat down the breasts that were vowed to a free death, much as the South wind troubles the wild waves, when the group of the Pleiades is piercing through the clouds; he, swift to overthrow the enemy's squadrons, and drive the neighing charger through the midst of the fires.

So bull-shaped Aufidus is whirled along, who flows beside Apulian Daunus' realm, when he begins to rage, and against the well-tilled fields designs a terrible deluge,—as Claudius with overwhelming rush swept away the iron ranks of the barbarians, and, by mowing down the foremost and the last, strewed the ground, a conqueror without disaster; while you supplied troops, while you supplied strategy, and the gods that are your friends.

For on the same day on which Alexandria humbly opened wide to you her havens and deserted palace, propitious Fortune, after the space of three lustres, rendered successful the issues of war, and conferred upon your accomplished commands the glory and the honour that we yearned for.

You the Cantabrian reveres, unconquerable ere now, and the Mede and the Indians; you the roving Scythian reveres, O unfailing guardian of Italy and sovereign Rome! You Nile obeys, who hides his fountains' sources, and Ister; you rushing Tigris obeys, you the monster-haunted Ocean obeys, which roars against the distant Britons. You the land of Gaul obeys, she who quakes not at death, and the land of hardy Iberia; to you the Sygambri, who delight in carnage, do homage with arms laid down.

XV.

This epilogue to the fourth Book contains a panegyric of Augustus, as the restorer of peace, the reformer of morals, the guardian of the state, and the dread of foreign enemies.

Phœbus, when I would sing of battles and conquered cities, sharply warned me with the note of his lyre, not to spread my tiny sails across the Tuscan main.

Your age, O Cæsar, has both given back to the fields abundant crops, and restored to Jove, our country's god, the standards torn down from the Parthians' haughty portals, and closed the gate of Quirine Janus freed from wars, and imposed the regular rule of order to be a curb on wild-wandering lawlessness, and put away our faults, and recalled the ancient virtues, whereby the glory of Latium and the might of Italy grew, and the renown and majesty of the empire was extended to the rising of the sun, from his chamber in the West.

While Cæsar is guardian of the state, no frenzy among the citizens, or violence, shall drive away our repose; no passion, which forges swords and embroils unhappy towns.

Never shall they who drink the deep Danube break the Julian decrees; never shall the Getæ, never shall the Seres or the faithless Parthians; never they who are born beside the stream of Tanais.

And we, on common days and holy days as well, while we enjoy the gifts of playful Liber, together with our children and our matrons, having first duly made our prayer to Heaven, will sing, after the manner of our forefathers, in strain blended with Lydian flutes, of chieftains who fulfilled all Virtue's work, and of Troy and Anchises and the offspring of bounteous Venus.

INTRODUCTION TO THE SECULAR HYMN.

According to an oracle in Greek Hexameters preserved by Zosimus, the Sibylline books divided time into "secles" of a hundred and ten years each; and Horace in this hymn follows the same method of division. But Valerius Antias says that the term of a secle was one hundred years. Others have thought that the secle was not of any specific length, but that its duration was bounded by portents and signs given by the gods. So the haruspex Vulcatius announced that the comet which appeared shortly after the assassination of Julius Cæsar indicated the end of the ninth secle and the beginning of the tenth. For according to the belief of the Etruscans the secles were ten in number; and Servius says that the Cumæan Sibyl divided the secles by the names of different metals, and that she also declared what divinity was the lord of each secle, the tenth secle belonging to the Sun. Perhaps the secle immediately before the last was sacred to Diana the sister of Apollo the god of light, as November, the last but one of the months, was sacred to the goddess by the tradition of the civil year.

Virgil speaks of the computation of time by secles at the beginning of his fourth Eclogue: "Now has come the latest age of the Cumæan (Sibylline) hymn; the mighty line of cycles begins its round anew." And soon after, addressing Diana, he says "Thine own Apollo now is king." Virgil seems to identify the system of secles with that of the "Great Year" of the world, which was also called the "Platonic Year," because the doctrine was especially cultivated by the Platonists and Stoics. This "year" was supposed to be completed when all the heavenly bodies should return to the same position that they were in at the beginning of the world. When this should happen, it was said that every part of the universe, including man, would repeat its past history. It appears that Virgil looks upon the secles of the Sibylline books as corresponding to the "months" of the Great Year. Ten or twelve secles of a hundred and ten years each would not, however, by any means make up the shortest of the enormous periods of time of which the Great Year has been variously computed to consist; but on such a subject anything like accuracy is certainly not to be expected. The idea which lies at the root of the system of secles and that of the Great Year seems to be the same; namely, that all the universe is passing through a perpetual series of revolutions, and repeats itself at settled periods.

It is clear that the Romans were by no means certain or agreed as to when the end of a secle was really completed. The emperor Claudius said that Augustus had anticipated the time, and that the term was really ended in his own reign. Domitian also celebrated Secular games. These games in many points bore a resemblance to those called during the republic the Tarentine or Taurian games, but in other points they seem to be greatly different; and it does not appear likely that that these two festivals were actually identical.

The Secular hymn was sung on the last of the three days during which the feast continued, by a chorus of twenty-seven boys and the same number of maidens, each of whom had both parents still living.

In this poem Horace appears as a kind of poet laureate, writing by the direction of Augustus. It was written in the forty-ninth year of the poet's life. The hymn does not possess a great measure of the genius and spirit which mark many of the odes: but it has a solemnity and dignity which are well suited to the subject of religion. For Horace is here a religious poet, singing by the command of the chief of the state, and according to the admonition of the Sibylline verses, which were made known to the Roman people, when the Senate ordered the "Fifteen Men," who were the keepers of these books, to consult the holy oracles. Anything like fervour or excitement would have been out of place in the hymn of the orthodox poet of the City. The religion of Rome was very different from that of Greece. It was unimaginative and formal. It was a strictly national religion, with the advantages and disadvantages of established forms.

The Romans were singularly averse to change in the minutest points of their rites and ceremonies. To the scrupulous observance of these they attributed the successful growth of their empire. In later times the decline and disasters of the state were imputed to the spread of Christianity, and the consequent neglect of the orthodox gods. This hymn, so grave and majestic, is quite in keeping with this feeling. If we may say so, it is almost Virgilian in character. Horace is hardly like himself here. He is as the minister of Church and State. When he prays to the Sun, it is to the effect that the Sun in all his course may gaze on nought that is greater than the city of Rome. Ilithyia is entreated to bless marriage and to prosper the decrees of the senate, so that Rome may never want a numerous race of men. May Ceres bless the crops! May the Fates grant that the future of Rome may be as great and glorious as her past!

Of this feeling the emperor himself, the head of Church and State at once, offering a sacrifice of white oxen, the lineal descendant of Anchises and Venus, is an emblem and sign. All the world is subject to Rome. The Saturnian age of Truth, Peace, and Honour is about to return. Rome will conquer that she may be clement to the conquered.

The variation of the cæsura, according to the Greek usage, adopted so often in this hymn, impairs the liveliness and easy flow of the lines: in other odes it would have marred the grace and beauty of the verse; but here it suits the solemnity and formality of the subject. The praise which the elder Scaliger gives the hymn, that it is "learned, full, terse, elaborate, happy," is well deserved. At the conclusion the poet, speaking by the chorus, expresses a confident hope that the people may return to their homes with the full assurance of the favour of all the assembled gods of the Roman empire.

THE SECULAR HYMN.

The opening address to Apollo and Diana, first together, then separately: prayers to other divinities. The two Powers are intreated to bless the Roman people, and Augustus. Description of the happy state of the empire under Caesar's rule. The final invocation of Apollo and Diana. The conclusion.

Phœbus, and Diana mistress of the woods, ye that are the shining beauty of the sky, ye that are ever adorable and adored, grant the blessings we pray for at a hallowed season; at which the verses of the Sibyl have counselled that chosen maidens and chaste youths recite a hymn to the gods who take pleasure in the Seven Hills.

Kindly Sun, who with thy glittering car dost draw forth and hide away the daylight, and dost rise to life, another and the same, mayest thou be able to gaze on nought that is greater than the city of Rome.

Ilithyia, who dost give thy grace duly to bring forth at their full time the offspring, protect our matrons, whether thou deemest it meet to be invoked as Lucina or as Genitalis.

Goddess, rear the young to ripeness, and further the decrees of the Fathers on the marrying of women and on the law of matrimony, that is to be fruitful in the birth of a new generation: so that the settled round, which runs through years eleven times ten, may bring again the hymns and games with their attending crowds, thrice in the bright day, and as often in the pleasant night.

And ye, O Fates, that have the power truly to predict that which has been uttered once for all, and which the ordained issue of events keeps sure, add propitious destinies to those that are now accomplished.

May Earth, prolific in fruits and flocks, present Ceres with her garland of ears of corn; may the healthful showers and gales of Jove nurse the springing plants.

Gracious and gentle with thy shaft laid by, Apollo, hear the boys who pray to thee; hear the girls, O Luna, crescented queen of the stars.

If Rome is your workmanship, and bands from Ilium reached the Tuscan shore, a number bidden to change, by a prosperous voyage, their household gods and city; for whom, unharmed, through burning Troy, holy Æneas, outliving his country, opened a free path, he, destined to give them more than they had left;—ye gods, grant morals fair to docile youth; ye gods, to quiet old age grant repose; grant to the people of Romulus wealth and progeny and every glory!

And may the illustrious descendant of Anchises and Venus obtain the blessings for which he worships ye with the homage of white oxen, still superior to his enemy, still merciful to the prostrate foe!

Now by sea and land the Median fears our mighty forces and the Alban axes; now the Scythians beg replies from us, though lately haughty, and the Indians too.

Now Faith, and Peace, and Honour, and antique Modesty, and neglected Virtue dares to return, and Plenty appears to view, rich with her o'erflowing horn.

And may Augur Apollo, adorned with flashing bow, and dear to the Muses nine, he who raises up by his health-giving art the body's exhausted limbs, if he graciously beholds the heights of the Palatine hill, ever prolong the Roman state, and Latium in happiness, to another lustre and a better age.

And may Diana, who possesses Aventinus and Algidus, hearken to the supplications of the Fifteen Men, and lend propitious ears to the children's prayers.

That Jove and all the gods confirm these vows, I bear back home a good and stedfast hope, I, a chorister trained to rehearse the praises of Phœbus and Diana.

INTRODUCTION TO THE EPODES.

An Epode is defined to be the third part of an ode; and again, as the short line following an iambic verse, used by Archilochus and Horace: but the name "Epode" was not, we may be sure, used by Horace himself. The Delphin Editor professes his ignorance of the reason of the name; he thinks that perhaps the Epodes were so called by some later grammarian, as being placed, in the editions of Horace, next to the Odes. Horace himself calls them in his Epistles "Parian Iambics;" that is, Iambics after the manner of Archilochus of Paros. In the 16th Ode of the first book he is thought by some to allude to them under the name of "swift Iambics," which he had written in the fervour of pleasant youth, and for which in jest he professes his repentance. From his boast that he was the first to introduce them into Latium, it would seem that Horace published them in his lifetime, rather than that they were collected and published after his death, as Walckenaer says. Orelli and others have fixed 30 B. C. for the date of their publication, when Horace was thirty five years old. Probably by this positive assertion no more is meant than that none of these Epodes have any internal evidence of a later date. They were all, like the Odes, written on particular occasions, addressed to particular friends, or were attacks on certain enemies; thus they would become more or less known one by one; that these Epodes were the poems which the necessities of "a bold poverty" drove Horace to write, it is impossible to say for certain.

However, that they were written by Horace while still young cannot be doubted. If Horace alludes to them in the Odes under the name of "swift Iambics", then he expressly says that he tried his hand on their composition in the vehemence of his impetuous youth. The date of several of them is more or less evident from the nature of the subject. Thus the 1st Epode refers either to the expedition against Sextus Pompeius, B. C. 35, or to the preparations against Antony before the battle of Actium, five years later. Earlier still would be the date of the 7th and the famous 16th Epode, perhaps the most beautiful of all the Epodes, if, as has been usually thought, they allude to the Perusian war, which followed almost directly after the battle of Philippi. Horace was then only 24 or 25 years old. After the battle of Cannæ, some of the Romans, considering that all was lost, proposed that Italy should be abandoned: so Horace, lamenting that the civil wars had brought that to pass which no foreign enemies could do, declares in this 16th Epode that the time was now come for all true-hearted Romans to seek another and better home. The description of the beauty of the Fortunate Islands is very poetical; but the effect of the whole Epode is spoilt by the disproportionate length of this part of the poem; if the account of the peace and fertility of the distant islands had been more carefully contrasted with the wars and troubles of Italy, the Epode would have been finer. We can hardly doubt that, if this poem had been written later by Horace, he would have given it that polish and compression to which he afterwards attached so high, perhaps too high a value. The same diffuseness of description appears in the 2nd Epode. But diffuseness was no fault of Horace in his later days. When Niebuhr says that the most poetical time of Horace was in his youth, it is hard to know what he means; certainly, if happiness and finish of expression are important elements of the Horatian poetry, it is impossible to agree with the historian of Rome. About the same time that he wrote the above-mentioned Epodes, Horace wrote the 4th Epode against Menas, a freedman and lieutenant of Sextus Pompeius, who was a double traitor. Augustus rewarded his treachery, so that Horace appears to show much courage in attacking him. It is true, as Wieland and Niebuhr say, that Horace deserves the reproach of a flatterer less than Virgil. In the flattery of Horace there is always a certain amount of independence. The date of the 9th Epode cannot be mistaken. With it we may of course compare the 37th Ode of the 1st book, a much finer poem. This Epode alludes clearly to the defeat of Sextus Pompeius, the so-called son of Neptune, to Cleopatra and her court, to the battle of Actium, and the retreat of the hostile ships. It was was written when Horace was 34 years old. The 14th Epode is supposed to allude to Terentia the wife of Mæcenas, to whom she was afterwards the cause of so much unhappiness. Whether it does so or not, it proves that the friendship between the poet and his patron was by this time intimate. To fix the date of some of the Epodes, as that for instance which upbraids Neæra with her want of faith, would seem to be quite arbitrary. But none of the Epodes have any allusions which refer to the later years of Horace's life. And perhaps we may say that they are all marked by a style of comparative youth. Hardly any of them have that terseness and refinement which characterise the Odes and Epistles. And many of them, as those about Canidia, Mævius, Cassius, are marked by a virulence of expression, not unnatural at a time when Horace's prospects were gloomy, on his return to Rome after the battle of Philippi; but from which he freed himself in his later writings, as a prosperous and contented man of the world, still more as one taught by divine philosophy to become gentler and better with the advance of old age. The Epodes are chiefly written in Iambic verses, the metre used by Archilochus in his satires. The Iambics are not always of the same number of feet, and are diversified by being sometimes joined to hexameter or to half-elegiac verses.

Lord Lytton rightly considers the Epodes as a link between the earlier Satires and the Odes. Some of them approach nearer to Satires, some are more akin to Odes. Thus the 6th is an Epode of which it cannot be said that it is free from the spirit of Archilochus. The 11th on the other hand is an Ode of great beauty, probably taken pretty closely from some Greek original, now no longer extant. The 13th Epode is one of the same character. Again, some of the Epodes have a mixture of poetry and satire in them. Thus, when Horace sings of the charms of the country which he loved so well, in tones evidently genuine, not ironical, the expression of a true affection, not of a passing fancy, he is pleased to give a touch of satire at the end, by pretending that the speaker is an usurer, whose real interest in life is gain. The least pleasing of the Epodes are those connected with Canidia. Horace appears in them as a second Archilochus, in a temper and spirit alien from his own kindly nature, armed by rage with suitable Iambics. The 8th Satire, inferior to the other Satires, is also an attack on the same person, whose real name, as the scholiasts tell us, was Gratidia, a seller of perfumes at Naples. After all, we are unable to tell what so moved the anger of the kindly poet, or indeed, how much of his wrath was real. The last mention of Canidia is indirect, at the close of the Satires.

Generally, no doubt, the Epodes are the least agreeable and the least striking of the writings of Horace; compared with his other productions they are almost rough and unpolished; the Satiric parts of them are very inferior to the Satires, almost in a different style and tone altogether; the lyric parts fall far short of the excellence of the odes; still, they give a picture of the times in which they were written; they illustrate a particular portion of the life of the poet, the dark days of poverty and obscurity, and the time when he came into the notice of the great, and first obtained competency and fame; they breathe the spirit of patriotism and independence; in places they have many touches of beauty, are as vigorous as any of his writings, and are interesting as containing the signs of those gifts which have made the name of Horace dear to many a reader.

THE EPODES.

I.

Horace expresses his readiness to accompany Maecenas to any part of the world, and especially on the expedition here spoken of. He is influenced by the disinterested feeling of gratitude to his benefactor.

You will go, my friend, with the Liburnian galleys amidst the tall turreted ships, prepared, Mæcenas, to undergo every danger of Cæsar, and make it all your own. What am I to do, I to whom life is sweet while you live, otherwise a burden? Shall I, as bidden, follow the path of ease not pleasant save in your company, or shall I endure this toil with the spirit that becomes a manly soul? Yes, endure it I will, and you either o'er the Alpine summits, and the inhospitable Caucasus, or even to the furthest bay of the West will I follow with brave spirit. You may ask, how can I lighten your toil by mine, I who lack strength for wars? I reply, my alarms in your society will be less, for fear possesses us more in absence; even as the bird, that tends her brood of unfledged young, dreads the stealthy approach of the serpent more if she has left them, not that, though she were in the nest, she could give more aid by her presence. Right gladly will I serve in this and every war for the hope of your favour, not that more oxen may be yoked to my laborious ploughs, nor that my cattle may change Calabrian for Lucanian pastures before the rising of the scorching dog-star, nor that my bright marble villa may reach the Circæan walls of Tusculum on the hill. Enough and more than enough has your bounty enriched me; I care not to amass stores that I may bury them, like the miser Chremes, in the earth, or waste them, as a thriftless prodigal.

II.

The usurer Alphius praises the charms of country life, its freedom from alarms and cares, its humble duties, simple fare, pleasant sights. But after all his love of money is too strong for his sentimental feelings.

"Blest is the man who far away from business, as the antique race of mortals, tills his paternal farm with his own oxen, from all usurious dealings free: he is not startled by the fierce notes of the martial trump, nor shudders at the raging sea; he shuns the forum and the insolent thresholds of citizens raised to high estate. So then, either he weds the full-grown shoots of the vine to the tall poplar, or in some retired dell gazes at the winding herds of lowing cattle, or, pruning with his hook unfruitful boughs, grafts in others more productive, or stores in clean jars the honey strained from the comb, or shears the tender sheep: or else, when Autumn lifts o'er the fields his head with a goodly crown of mellow fruit, how does he joy to pluck the pears he has grafted, or grape that vies with purple in its hue, meet present for thee, Priapus, or thee, Silvanus, guardian of his bounds! As Fancy bids, he lies either beneath an ancient oak, or at times in the close grass; meanwhile, within deep banks glide on the streams, the birds make their plaint in woods, and fountains splash with jets of water clear; all sounds to invite light slumbers. But when the wintry season of thundering Jove gathers its rains and snows, then with his pack of hounds he drives from either side the fierce boars into the nets that stop their course, or on smooth pole stretches the fine-meshed nets, snares to entrap the greedy thrush, and captures in the noose the timorous hare or foreign crane, the pleasant prizes of the chase. Midst scenes like these who does not forget the painful cares attendant on love? But should a chaste wife give her share of help to bless his home and dear children, true as Sabine matron, or sunburnt wife of industrious Apulian swain, as she piles up on the holy hearth logs of seasoned wood to greet the return of the tired master, or as she pens up within the close-woven hurdles the joyous flock, milking their full udders, or, bringing forth from the sweet cask this year's wine, prepares the unbought meal: then the Lucrine fish would not please me more, nor turbot, nor scar, that storm roaring upon the Eastern waves may drive to our sea; the African bird is not more pleasant to my palate, nor the Ionian moor-fowl, than olive picked from the choicest boughs of the trees, or herb of sorrel that loves the meadow, or mallow that gives health to the oppressed body, or lamb slain at the feast of the god of bounds, or kid saved from the fangs of the wolf. During these repasts, how joyous the sight of well-fed sheep hastening home, of tired oxen bringing the inverted plough-share on their drooping necks, and the home-born slaves of the wealthy house, like a swarm of bees, ranged round the Lares shining in the fire-light!" Such were the words of the usurer Alphius; he was just on the point of turning rustic; he got in all his money on the Ides; when the Calends come, he wants to put it out again.

III.

Horace in this epode addressed to Maecenas expresses his humorous horror of garlic.

May the man, whoe'er he be, that with unnatural hand has strangled his aged father, eat garlic, herb more noxious than hemlock! Ye reapers, oh how tough are your stomachs! What is this poison raging in my entrails? Was blood of vipers boiled in these herbs, and I knew it not? or did Canidia's hand dress this cursed dish? When Medea admired beauteous Jason above all the Argonauts, with the juice of garlic she anointed all his body, as he went to yoke the untried oxen; in garlic her gift was steeped, when on her rival she took her vengeance, and then fled on car of winged snakes. Ne'er yet on thirsty Apulia settled such heat of dog-star, nor did the present sent to Hercules the doer burn with greater fury on his shoulders. But you, Mæcenas, full of your jokes, if e'er you fancy such a herb as this, may your mistress put up her hand to stop your lip, and lie at the end of the couch!

IV.

An attack upon a man of low birth, who gave himself great airs on account of his having been made military tribune.

As is the natural antipathy between wolves and lambs, such is mine to you, with your back galled by Iberian cords, and your legs by hard fetters. Strut insolent in your wealth: money changes not birth. As with measured gait you walk in the Sacred Way, clad in toga six ells broad, can you not see how that all passing either way turn their faces in undisguised indignation? "Why! this is the man lashed by the triumvirs' rods even to the disgust of the common crier, but now he ploughs a thousand acres of Falernian land, and with his nags wears the Appian way, and sits in the front rows, magnificent knight, braving Otho's law. What boots it then that so many ships, pointed with beaks of ponderous weight, should sail against pirates and bands of slaves, when this man, even this, is tribune of the soldiers?"

V.

The piteous lamentation of a boy of noble birth, doomed to die by a lingering death, that thence may be made a love potion to be administered to Varus, who had been faithless to Canidia. She is held up at once to ridicule and execration. Compare Epode 17 *and Satire* 8 *in Book* I, *probably both written about the same time.*

"But, oh ye Powers of heaven, ruling the earth and race of man, what bodes this scene tumultuous? Or why are all your faces turned so fiercely on me alone? I pray you by your children, if ever Lucina came to your call at real birth-pains, by this my purple stripe which graces me for nought, by Jove who will surely rebuke deeds like these, why on me do you gaze, as a stepmother, or as wild beast assailed by iron weapons?" Uttering such wailings from the quivering mouth, stood there the boy stripped of his ornaments, a tender frame, such as might soften the impious hearts of Thracians; meanwhile Canidia, her locks entwined with short snakes, and head dishevelled, bids burn in magic flames wild fig-trees torn from graves, and cypresses, funereal trees, and eggs smeared with blood of hideous toad, and feathers of screech-owl, bird of night, and herbs Iolcos sends, and Iberia fruitful in drugs, and bones snatched from the teeth of starving bitch. Then Sagana, with vest tucked up, sprinkles o'er all the house waters of lake Avernus, her hair erect, as the sea-urchin bristles rough, or running boar. But Veia checked by no remorse began to throw up the ground with sturdy mattock, that in a pit the boy might pine away, gazing on the food changed twice or thrice during the weary day; with face prominent as far as bodies poised upon the chin rise above the water; for his dried marrow and shrivelled liver were to make a love potion, so soon as his eyeballs had withered away, fixed on the forbidden food. That Folia of Ariminum was not absent then is the belief of Naples, city of leisure, and of each neighbouring town; she by Thessalian song plucks from the sky the enchanted stars and moon. Then savagely Canidia gnaws with her yellow tooth the uncut nail of her thumb; what said she then? or what forbore to say? "Hail each of you," she cried, "no unfaithful arbitresses to my deeds, thou, Night, and thou, Hecate, queen of silence during the sacred mysteries; now, e'en now be here, now on this hostile house your wrath and power direct. Whilst in the awful woods the beasts lie hid, relaxed in pleasant sleep, may the dogs of the Subura howl at the adulterous old man, that all may laugh at him smeared with such spikenard, so that more perfect never my hands prepared.—But what has happened? why have my poisons, worthy of Colchian Medea, lost their power? With drugs such as these she vengeance took on her haughty rival, child of great Creon, then fled: that day the robe, a gift in venom steeped, destroyed the bride in a sheet of fire. Surely no herb or root concealed in savage haunts has escaped my search! He sleeps on couches smeared with oblivion of all my rivals. But ah! he walks at large, free through the charm of some more learned sorceress. Yet by no common potion, Varus, O soul doomed to suffer much, shall you come hastening back to me; no Marsian enchantments shall recall your reason: a draught more potent I will prepare, and mix it stronger for your disdainful heart; and sooner shall the heavens sink beneath the sea, while the earth is spread above, than you not burn with my love, as this bitumen burns in black fires." Hereupon the boy no more, as he had done, essays to soothe the impious hags with gentle prayer, but, at a loss how to break silence, yet uttered Thyestean curse: "Magic drugs," he cried, "can confound the power of right and wrong, they cannot avert the retribution due to mortal deeds; with curses I will pursue you, the curses of hate no victims will atone. Nay when, as you ordain, I have breathed forth my life, I will, as a spirit of Frenzy, haunt you in the night; in ghostly form I will attack your faces with crooked talons; such is the power of the Manes, those gods below; as nightmare sitting on your restless breasts I will with panic scare away your sleep. From street to street on all sides the crowd pursuing will stone you to death, ye unclean hags, and last of all your unburied limbs shall be torn by wolves and birds of the Esquiline hill. My parents alas! survive my death, but surely shall be witnesses of this sight."

VI.

Addressed to one who slandered the defenceless. Horace assures him that he can and will defend himself.

Why trouble innocent strangers, like a dog cowardly against the wolf? Why not turn on me, if you dare, your idle menaces, and attack one ready to bite in return? I will pursue you, even as Molossian hounds, or tawny dogs of Sparta's breed, a power that befriends the shepherds, prick up their ears, and drive through the deep snow whatever beast runs before them: you with tremendous bayings fill the wood, then snuff the food thrown to you. Beware, beware: against the bad I am all roughness, and ready with uplifted horn, like him rejected as son-in-law by faithless Lycambes, or as Bupalus' fierce foe. What! shall I, attacked by the tooth of malice, weep like a helpless boy?

VII.

The blood of Remus slain by his brother is atoned for by the blood of his descendants in civil war.

"Whither, whither rush ye, a guilty race? Why do your hands grasp swords but lately sheathed? Has then too little Latin blood been shed on the plains and o'er Neptune's realms, not that Rome might burn the haughty towers of rival Carthage, or that the Briton as yet untouched by war might walk in chains along the Sacred Slope; but that, as Parthians would pray, our city should fall by its own act? E'en wolves and lions have not such a nature, savage indeed, but not against their kind. Is it blind frenzy, or some fiercer power, or sin that drives you on? Reply." Speechless are they, and a sickly pallor discolours their countenance, and their minds are stricken with stupor. E'en so it is: Rome is pursued by bitter fates, and the guilt of a brother's murder, from the day there was shed upon the ground the blood of innocent Remus bringing a curse upon his descendants.

IX.

Addressed to Maecenas, as is supposed, after the news of the battle of Actium had reached Rome, B.C. 31.

When shall I quaff in joy for Cæsar's victory the Cæcuban wine reserved for holyday repasts, with you, O blest Mæcenas, beneath your lofty roof; a duty Jove accepts; while sounds the lyre in unison with the flutes, as they give the Phrygian, it the Dorian strain? E'en as of late, when driven from the straits fled Neptune's son, the Captain, after his ships were burnt, and he had threatened Rome with those bonds, which, friend of faithless slaves, he had taken from their hands. A Roman soldier alas! (but ye, posterity, will refuse belief,) sold into slavery to a woman, carries stakes and arms, and stoops to serve wrinkled eunuchs, and midst war's standards the sun beholds the disgrace of an awning. Then to our side two thousand Gauls wheeled their neighing steeds, in chorus singing Cæsar; and the sterns of the hostile ships, rowed backwards to the left, lie hidden in the harbour. Io Triumphe! Why delayest thou the car of gold, and heifers never yoked? Io Triumphe! So great a captain thou didst not bring back from the Jugurthine war, not so great returned Africanus, to whom upon the ruins of Carthage Valour raised a monument. By land and sea the enemy defeated has doffed his purple cloak, and now is clad in mourning; he is carried either to Crete, isle famed for a hundred towns, by gales that bless him not, or sails for the Syrtes troubled by Notus, or is borne by capricious waves. Bring hither, boy, cups of a larger size, and wine of Chios or Lesbos, or mix for us Cæcuban to stay our qualmish sickness. I joy to drown my care and fear for Cæsar's fortunes in sweet cups of the god who frees the soul.

X.

In this Epode, the opposite of Ode 3, Book 1, Horace expresses his hope that a storm may overtake Maevius and drown him in the sea.

With evil omens from its mooring sails the ship freighted with noisome Mævius: forget not, Auster, to lash either side of the vessel with rough billows! Let black Eurus upheave the main, and tear the rigging and scatter the shivered oars; let Aquilo rise as mighty as when are snapped the quivering oaks on the high mountains; nor any friendly star appear on the dark night, when sets the grisly Orion; and may he be borne o'er waters as tumultuous, as those which troubled the victorious Grecian host, when Pallas turned her wrath from the ashes of Troy on the ship of impious Ajax! How soon shall your mariners be bathed in sweat, and how sickly shall be your pallor! Unmanly are your wailing cries, and prayers from which Jove turns his face, when the Ionian bay shall roar with the rainy Notus, and break your keel. But if your body lies on the winding shore, a rich prey to gladden the birds of the sea, then to the Tempests I will offer a lusty goat and lamb.

XI.

Horace tells his friend Pettius he cannot write verses, as once, for Love's hand is upon him, and the remedies of love are uncertain.

I feel no heart, as once, friend Pettius, to write tender verses, smitten as I am by grievous love, by love, who singles me out of all for his flames to burn me. This is the third December, which shakes the glory from the woods, since my mad passion for Inachia ceased. Woe is me, throughout the city—I am ashamed of such ill-doing—was I the talk of all. And for those banquets I must grieve, where dull spirits, and silence, and sighs drawn deep betrayed the lover. "Is the honest genius of a poor man no match for gold?" So used I to make my appeal to your sympathy, when I was heated with more generous wine, and the god who knows not reserve had drawn my secrets forth. "But now that anger surges in my soul so free, that to the winds it scatters these thankless remedies, which bring no relief to my sore wound, my shame is gone, and I shall cease to vie with unworthy rivals." Such was the course I praised with virtuous words when in your presence: you bid me go back home; but my wavering feet bore me to doors alas! unfriendly, and to thresholds, woe is me!, how hard! against which I bruised my loins and side.

XIII.

While nature is stormy without, let friends be joyous within. Life is short and full of troubles, but has its pleasures and alleviations.

The heavens frown with rough weather, and Jove is downward drawn with rain and snow; now seas, then woods war with the Thracian blasts; let us, my friends, snatch our opportunity from the present day, and whilst our limbs are vigorous still, and joy becomes us, let age be cleared from off our clouded brow. Bring you forth the wine made when Torquatus was consul in my natal year. Care not to speak of aught beside: God perchance will settle back in peace our lot by kindly change. To-day right joyously I bedew myself with Achæmenian nard, and on the lyre of Mercury lighten my heart of dreaded cares; even as the noble Centaur sang to his tall pupil: "Mortal child of immortal Thetis, for you, destined to be invincible, waits the land of Assaracus, which the cool streams of little Scamander and rolling Simois divide; unalterable is the woof by which the Fates have cut off your return; never shall your azure mother bear you home; when there, you must lighten every toil by wine and song, the two sweet comforters of unsightly sorrow."

XIV.

Addressed to Maecenas to excuse himself for not having completed a long-promised poem.

Mæcenas, true friend, you will be the death of me, if you ask so often, why a soft indolence has spread itself into my inmost soul, as though with thirsty throat I had drained cups inducing Lethæan slumbers: a god, yes, a god forbids my bringing to the finishing point the iambics I began, my long promised poem. Not otherwise, 'tis said, Anacreon of Teos loved Samian Bathyllus, and oft on hollow shell mourned for his passion, in measures freely flowing. You yourself are burning woefully; but if no brighter beauty kindled with fire beleaguered Troy, rejoice in your lot: I am racked by love of Phryne, a freedwoman, a mistress not content with a single admirer.

XV.

Horace complains of the broken faith of one Neaera, who had abandoned him for a wealthier rival, and he warns him that he will meet with the same perfidy.

'Twas night, in cloudless sky the moon was shining amid the lesser stars, when you, fearing not to profane the divinity of the great gods, swore to the oath that I dictated; and clinging to me with twining arms, closer than tall oak is embraced by ivy, vowed that whilst wolves are the enemies of sheep, and Orion, the disturber of the stormy sea, is the dread of sailors, whilst wave in the breeze the flowing locks of Apollo, so long my love should be returned. But ah!

Neæra, destined are you to grieve through my resolution; for if in Flaccus there be aught of manhood, he will not brook that you ever to a rival give your hours, and, angry with you, will look for one who will return his love. Nor will his resolve give way to your beauty which has once displeased him, if settled wrath has passed into his soul. And you, whoe'er you be, happier now, who shew yourself so proud at my expense, rich you may be in flocks and many an acre, for you Pactolus may flow with gold, and known to you perhaps are the mysteries of Pythagoras, the seer born to many a life, in beauty you may surpass Nireus; yet with sighs shall you mourn her love transferred elsewhere, and I in turn shall laugh.

XVI.

1—13. *Describes the threatened ruin of Rome by civil wars.*

A second age is now wearing away in civil wars, and Rome by her own act is falling through her own strength. The city, which neither the neighbouring Marsians had power to destroy, nor Tuscan troops of menacing Porsena, nor the rival valour of Capua, nor Spartacus fierce in war, nor the Allobroges faithless in days of change; the city unsubdued by wild Germany with its blue-eyed warriors, or by Hannibal, name abhorred by parents; this city we shall ourselves destroy, an impious age whose blood is doomed, and again wild beasts shall be the lords of the soil. A conquerer and barbarian, alas! shall trample on our ashes, and the horsemen strike our city's streets with echoing hoof; and insolently scatter (oh unholy sight!) the bones of Quirinus, sheltered now from wind and sun.

15—40. *An exhortation to his countrymen to bind themselves by oath to a voluntary and perpetual exile.*

Perchance all in common, or at least the better-minded part of you, are consulting how best to escape from woeful troubles. Let no opinion be preferred to this; even as the state of Phocæa's people fled into exile, bound by a solemn curse; as they left their fields and own sacred homes and their shrines to be a dwelling-place for wild boars and ravening wolves; to go whither feet can carry, whither o'er the billows Notus invites or wanton Africus. Is this your pleasure? or has any one better advice to give? Why delay at once to embark with propitious omens? But let this be our form of oath: "As soon as stones lifted from the lowest depths swim on the surface, then to return may not be a sin; that we need not repent setting our sails homeward on the day that the Po washes Matinum's peaks, or the lofty Apennine juts into the sea, and a wondrous love forms monstrous unions with strange passion, so that tigers may gladly pair with stags, and the dove mate with the kite, and trusting cattle lose their dread of glaring lions, and the he-goat, now smooth, haunt the briny main." To such oaths as these, and others like them, that may cut off a return to dear home let us bind ourselves, and go, the whole state, or the part wiser than the crowd who will not learn; let the craven and despairing still press their ill-starred beds; but you of a manly spirit away with womanish sorrow, and wing your voyage beyond the Tuscan shores.

41—66. *A full description of the happy isles.*

Us Ocean waits, that wanders round the world; let us speed to the fields, the blessed fields, and to the isles of wealth, where Earth unploughed supplies her corn each year, and ever flourishes the unpruned vine, and the topmost bough of the olive shoots and never disappoints, and the dusky fig adorns its proper tree; from hollow oak flows honey, lightly the rill with tinkling foot bounds down the mountain heights. There the unbidden goats come to the pails, and the kindly flock brings back distended udders; nor roars around the fold the evening bear, nor does the deep soil heave with vipers. More too in our bliss we shall admire; how that watery Eurus ne'er sweeps the fields with drenching showers, nor are the seeds rich in promise scorched in the arid earth, as the king of the heavenly Powers tempers either extreme. Hither sped not the ship Argo with her rowers, the shameless Medea set not foot here, nor did sailors of Sidon turn sail-yards hitherward, nor Ulysses' toilsome crew. No ill contagion hurts the cattle, the burning violence of no star scorches the flock. Jove set apart those shores for a pious race, when he debased the days of gold with brass; when he hardened the ages with brass, and then with iron; from which an auspicious flight is granted to the pious, with me for their seer.

XVII.

1—52. *Horace represents himself as entreating Canidia for mercy. He retracts the charges he had made against her, in an ironical recantation.*

Now, now to witchcraft's workings I surrender, and humbly beseech by Proserpine's realms, by Hecate's powers not lightly to be provoked, and by the magic books able to unfix the stars and call them down from heaven, Canidia, forbear at last your charms of imprecation, and unroll backwards, unroll your rapid wheel. Telephus to pity moved the grandson of Nereus, though in his pride he had marshalled against him the Mysian lines, and hurled his pointed spears. The matrons of Troy anointed the body of Hector the slayer of heroes, when doomed to wild birds and dogs, after that the king went forth from the city, and threw himself, sad sight, at the feet of the obstinate Achilles. The toilsome mariners of Ulysses stripped their limbs of rough bristling hides, for so consented Circe; then reason and speech returned to them gradually, and the familiar grace of the human countenance. Enough and more than enough is the atonement I have paid to you, sweetheart of many a boatman and huckster. My youthful look is gone, the hue of modesty has left my bones clad now with yellow skin; my hair is grey through your ointments, no ease succeeds my toil to give me rest; night follows close on day, and day on night, nor can I relieve the tightened breathing of my chest. So then, wretched man that I am, I am forced to believe a truth I once denied, that Sabine enchantments can trouble the heart, and Marsian chants can split the head. What would you more? O sea! O earth! I burn, as ne'er burned Hercules smeared with the poisoned blood of Nessus, nor the undying Sicilian flame in glowing Ætna; but till I am reduced to dry cinders and borne by insulting winds, you glow like crucible with Colchian drugs. What end awaits me now? what payment can I make? Declare; impose your penalty, with good faith will I pay it, ready to make atonement should you name a hecatomb of bullocks, or from my lying lute demand a song, how chaste you are, yes you, how honest; so shall you range among the stars, a golden constellation. Castor and the brother of great Castor, offended on account of Helen defamed, yet, overcome by prayer, restored the bard his eyesight taken from him. And you, (for you have power,) free me from my frenzy, you, a woman disgraced by no shame of father, you, no hag skilled to scatter the ashes on the ninth day among the graves of the poor. You surely have a heart kind to strangers, your hands are pure, Pactumeius is your true son, and of your childbirth there is no doubt, whenever you come forth strong after your travail.

53—81. *Canidia is made to speak as one who is deaf to Horace's prayers.*

Why do you pour forth prayers to stopped ears? The rocks are not deafer to the naked sailors, when wintry Neptune buffets them with dashing surge. What! are you with impunity to divulge and deride the mysteries of Cotytto, the rites of Cupid unchecked by law, and unpunished to fill the city with my name, as though you were high-priest of witchcraft on the Esquiline hill? what then would be the good to have enriched Pelignian hags, and to have mingled poison full swift in its effects? But no, a death more lingering than you pray for awaits you, and you must prolong a wretched thankless life only for this, that you may ever survive to bear fresh pains. So longs for rest the father of faithless Pelops, Tantalus craving ever for the bounteous repast; so longs Prometheus to a vulture bound; so longs Sisyphus to set the stone on the summit; but Jove's laws forbid. At times you will wish to spring from lofty towers, anon to lay your breast bare with the Noric sword; in vain will you bind a noose around your throat in the despair of your sickening grief. Then shall I ride mounted on your hated shoulders, and the earth shall yield to my arrogance. I can give motion to images of wax, as your own prying eyes have seen, and from the sky my charms can pluck the moon, I can wake the dead from their ashes, and mix cups of pining love, and am I to lament the issue of my craft as unavailing against you?

INTRODUCTION TO THE SATIRES.

MANY have written more or less fully on Roman satire, its origin, and history; as the elder Scaliger, Casaubon, Heinsius, Dacier, the learned husband of a more learned lady, Dryden, the Delphin editor of Juvenal, Ruperti, Gerlach, Walckenaer, and others. The origin of Satire, even if so many learned men had not fully discussed the subject, could hardly be doubtful or obscure. Satire arose, as poetry in general arose, from the rude devotion and festive revels of the rustics in days of old. The Greek plays, tragic and comic alike, had the same origin. Ceres and Bacchus were the teachers and inspirers of these rough and unlettered poets. Often have been quoted the standard passages of Virgil, Horace, and Tibullus, in which is described the worship of the stout swains of old, their rural songs, their alternate strains and boisterous raillery. It seems indeed a long way from the uncouth and extemporaneous effusions of these husbandmen at the end of harvest to the highly-polished satires of Boileau and Pope; but it is a way easily followed; and, after all, the difference is more one of form and style than of real feeling. In the unshapen poetry of an early and uncivilized people, all styles and kinds are found mixed together, as yet undistinguished, in what may be called a formless and confused chaos; presently the various parts of poetry separate from one another, just as is the case in all things, in nature, in language, in society; from the rustic gibe poured forth in alternate verse came the farces, then the plays of Livius Andronicus; whilst Ennius, amongst his other works, and after him Pacuvius, wrote compositions which they called Satires. These satires embraced all varieties of subjects, serious and gay, were composed in metres mingled together in the same poems, were like a dish laden with a medley of all sorts of food, (whence came the name "satire,") and contained fables, dialogues, allegories, precepts, description, eulogy, censure, all thrown together. They could not then have been altogether unlike the satires of Horace.

And yet Lucilius passes for the inventor of Satire. In what particular points Lucilius differed from Ennius, and how he deserves the honourable name of "the inventor of Satire," it is hard to say. Indeed Quintilian only says that in Satire Lucilius first obtained distinguished praise. Probably Lucilius first gave a regular form to Satire. It is likely, too, that his satires were a great advance in excellence on those of Ennius. He used chiefly the hexameter verse, and did not mingle together different metres in the same book, as Ennius did. Probably, too, his books had greater unity than those of Ennius, and less variety of incongruous matter. If so, his Satires would be a step forward, and less according to the original meaning of the name, but would approach nearer to the notion which the word Satire now conveys.

Quintilian claims Satire as entirely Roman, and Horace speaks of it as a kind of writing untouched by the Greeks; and yet in another place he says that Lucilius owes all to writers of the old Greek comedy. There is no contradiction in these statements. In form no doubt Satire is not Greek. The Greeks have nothing exactly like the Roman Satire. There is no Greek Horace, or Greek Juvenal. The writings of Archilochus, bitterer than gall, which are said to have driven those attacked by them to suicide, whatever may have really been their force and power, were doubtless more like lampoons than satires. They were attacks on particular persons, like some of the Epodes of Horace, and some of the less pleasing poems of Catullus. Whilst the Roman comedies of Terence were formed on the model of the new Greek comedy, the satires of Rome were like the old Greek comedy, in personality, wit, vigour, freedom.

Horace appears to have given much offence by his remarks on the defects of Lucilius. Either it was orthodox to admire Lucilius, or the detractors of Horace were glad of a handle for attacking him. Quintilian says that some were such devoted admirers of Lucilius as to prefer him not only to other satirists, but to all other poets. He says that he holds a middle judgment between such admirers and the depreciator Horace, who compares Lucilius to a muddy river. "For," says Quintilian, "there is in him an admirable erudition, freedom too, and an abundance of salt." Cicero long before had often mentioned Lucilius as erudite and polished, as one who wrote neither for the most learned, nor for the illiterate, as witty and free-spoken and ready. However, if we can judge at all by the fragments of Lucilius still preserved (which, though numerous, are all of them very short, and probably very corrupt), we should say that what Horace says of him is true, and in fact short of the truth.

Like indeed to Horace was Lucilius in many points. Both served in wars in their early youth. As Horace lived on familiar and intimate terms with Augustus and Mæcenas, so did Lucilius with Scipio and Lælius. Both poets were men of a free and independent character. It is, however, probable that Lucilius was much the severer and sharper critic of the two. Macrobius speaks of him as a keen and violent writer. Lactantius mentions him in conjunction with Lucian. Persius and Juvenal both speak of the way in which he scourged the vices of his times, whilst the same Persius describes Horace as moving laughter, and by his playful satire stealing into the hearts of his readers. Still Lucilius and Horace had many points in common. Horace was his own biographer, so was Lucilius. Both met with envy and jealousy, and defended themselves with vigour. Both set themselves up to criticize the writings of other authors. Horace's satires are full of dialogues. The same appears to have been the case with those of Lucilius. Avarice and extravagance were the vices which either satirist especially attacked. Both condemned the luxury that prevailed in their times, and themselves preferred a quiet and rural simplicity. Lucilius is supposed to have laughed at the pedantry of philosophers, as Horace afterwards did. Lucilius' journey to the shores of the Sicilian strait is said to be the model of Horace's journey to Brundusium. The journey of the earlier poet appears not to have been to accompany any great man, as Horace accompanied Mæcenas, but to have been a tour of pleasure, after the same simple fashion in which Horace tells us he liked to travel.

Yet in one point the two satirists were utterly different. Lucilius, as Horace tells us, and as we cannot help judging from the fragments of his verses still extant, was a rapid and careless writer, not so very far removed from the rude vine-dressers and early husbandmen of Italy. He regarded quality less than quantity, and, as though it were a great feat, would dictate two hundred verses in an hour, standing on one foot. Horace was careful and exact, never diffuse, considering and weighing each line; he was, as Keightley says, the most elliptic of writers, in a language which is the most elliptic of languages. Lucilius was a clumsy and harsh writer; but, if his thirty books of satires had come down to us, we should no doubt have had a faithful, if rough picture of the troublous and restless times in which he lived, of the advance of luxury in the republic, of the character of Scipio, and of the manners of Lælius, much truer than that given in the dialogue of Cicero. We, who have the eighteen satires of Horace, know what we should have lost, if time had robbed us of them. They are far better to us than the pages of regular history. They let us into a thousand little things, of which history is ignorant or disdainful. However minutely Lucilius may have described the society of his times, he could hardly have excelled Horace in this point, while the charm of Horace's style is his own and unrivalled. Finish and care are apt to make writings dull, as Massillon is said to have taken the life out of his sermons by continually retouching them. The finish of Boileau's writings gives them a certain tameness. But the marvel of Horace is, that, though he is so finished, he is never dull. All comes as fresh from him as if he spoke the utterances of a child of nature.

"Satires," he calls these writings sometimes; at other times he calls them "Discourses" (Sermones). And indeed they by no means answer to the idea of satires, as we now understand the word, but are more like easy conversations with himself and others. They are free from ill-will and malice. He has faithfully kept the promise he has made about this. They are good-natured. They contain a variety which is admirable. At times they are satires, direct or indirect, on particular persons, or in general, on avarice, ambition, profligacy, luxury, superstition, on the follies and foibles of mankind. But mingled with these attacks are all kinds of subjects. Thus, for instance, in his journey to Brundusium there is scarcely any satire, as we should call it. Up and down the satires he has plenty to say about his friends. He is no niggard of praise towards them. Dryden says of him, "Folly is his quarry, not vice." He is no set philosopher, as Persius was, no declaimer like Juvenal. He has much salt, little gall. His metaphors and figures are not strained, as those of Persius are. He has turns, sudden and unexpected, and never wearies by dwelling too long on one subject. He enlivens his writings by dialogues inserted abruptly. He has little fables and similes and tales introduced quite naturally. He never speaks of himself as of a great author, and disarms criticism by the way in which he confesses his own faults and weaknesses. He appears to be writing easily, and as one who plays with literature, and for all that he is a consummate artist. If aught were omitted or transposed, the effect would be much marred. Many of his lines, from their point and brevity, have passed into proverbs. He takes care to end nearly every satire with a light jest, and lets himself fall gently before he closes. When he describes his good father, the education he had received, his daily life, the little troubles and inconveniences which ruffled the surface of a comfortable and contented existence, he is more charming than ever.

Some satires, as the 9th of the 1st book, give a complete picture of a single event. The 2nd book is on the whole more powerful, but less easy and natural than the 1st, and one can see that Horace writes in the 2nd book with a certain amount of authority, and there is in it more satire, strictly so called, than in the 1st book. And yet the 6th satire in the 2nd book, which describes his simple happiness in the country, his bores and interruptions in the city, his easy conversation with his patron, and which ends with the story of the two mice, has hardly a word of satire in it. As Walckenaer says, in the sense which we now attach to satire, but which was not yet attached to it by the Romans even in the days of Augustus, it seems strange to give the name of Satire to a piece so full of elegance and gentleness, with no malice or ill-nature in it, no indignation or severity. In this satire we have the picture of a man modest, content, grateful, free from ambition, enjoying a happiness much more secure than that of the country mouse, (who is here the type of Horace,) when drawn against his better judgment from the country to town. The mouse living on the hill-side with its grove of trees represents to us the poet in his villa in the deep valley under the hill Lucretilis.

Juvenal, the other great satirist of Rome, has often been compared with Horace. A great poet has compared them. Dryden, in his famous "Letter to the Earl of Dorset," called also "a Discourse on Satire," at great length and in brilliant language has given the reasons why he prefers Juvenal. He calls Horace more general and various, more copious in his instructions, one who insinuates virtue by familiar examples: but Juvenal, he says, is more vigorous and masculine, his expressions are more sonorous, his verse more numerous, his indignation more vehement, his spirit has more of the commonwealth of genius. A man of Dryden's turn of mind would be sure to prefer Juvenal. A man like Boileau or Pope would be sure to set more store on Horace. Dryden himself, with much good sense and ingenuousness, allows that he prefers Juvenal, because he suits his own taste better. There can hardly be a greater contrast than that between the man of a delicately playful wit and gentle humour, and the man of fierce invective and rhetorical morality. Juvenal owes nothing to Horace. He is one of the most original of writers. What is said of the want of originality in Latin poets certainly does not apply to Juvenal. His own indignation, and the depravity of the times in which his lot was cast, no study of any other writer, made him a satirist. He lived in days "bad for the man, good for the satirist." But he never can be a companion or familiar friend, as Horace is. For one edition of Juvenal it would be curious to know how many there have been of Horace.

A more natural comparison is that between Horace's own satires and epistles. Now his satires are not altogether unlike letters, and his epistles are not quite unlike satires, at any rate satires in the sense in which Horace uses the word. Still there are contrasts. His satires were written in his earlier days, the epistles in his declining years. In the epistles he writes with greater authority than he ventures to assume in most of the satires. There is more spirit, life, vigour, versatility in the satires; in the epistles there is a more soft and gentle tone. The satires are more about his detractors, the epistles more about his friends. In the epistles there is less to offend modern notions of taste and feeling. The satires are written in a joyous spirit, which is tinged with melancholy in the epistles. The satires give us on the whole more pictures of life in general, of the state of Rome, of society, its habits, feasts and amusements, its jokes and rivalries: in the epistles we have more of a calm spirit. The epistles are nobler than the satires, and mark an improvement in the character of the poet. They have a more perfect finish, and are more refined and thoughtful. The sentences are shorter and rounder in their compass. Horace may be regarded, as Keightley says, as the inventor of the Poetic Epistle. If he had never written anything after the satires, we might have thought that nothing could have surpassed their characteristic charm; but when we read the epistles, we may say that Horace has surpassed not others only, but himself also.

SATIRES. BOOK I.

I.

1—22. *The general discontent of mankind is unreal, and might well irritate the good-natured gods.*

HOW comes it to pass, Mæcenas, that no one lives contented with the lot which either choice has given him, or chance thrown in his way, while he admires the fortune of those who follow a different profession? "O ye happy traders!" says the soldier laden with the weight of years, whose strength is broken with hard toil. On the other hand the trader, as the south winds toss his ship, says: "A soldier's life is better; for how stands the case? the armies clash in battle; in the turning-point of a short hour comes swift death, or victory and joy." The farmer's life is admired by him who is learned in the law and statutes, when at early cock-crowing his client comes knocking at his doors. The other, when having given bail he is dragged from the country to the town, loudly declares none to be happy but those living in town. Other instances of the same kind are so numerous, that they could tire out even loquacious Fabius. Not to delay you, hear the point of my argument. If some god were to say: "Lo, here I am to do what you want: you, sir, who a minute ago were a soldier, are to be a trader; you, who just now were a lawyer, see, you are now a farmer; there, change sides and characters as on the stage: away with you: but why do you stand still? Can they be unwilling to change? And yet they might be as happy as they fondly wish." What reason is there to prevent Jove in his anger puffing out his cheeks against them, and declaring that he will not be so weak for the future as to listen to their prayers?

23—40. *A discontented avarice is reproved even by the brute creation.*

Further, that I may not, like a jester, joke as I go through the subject; (and yet a man while joking may surely tell the truth, as often schoolmasters give cakes to boys to wheedle them into willingness to learn their alphabet;) however, let us put aside jokes and turn to serious things. Yon farmer, that turns up the earth with strong plough, this cheating landlord here, soldiers and sailors that boldly scour o'er every sea, declare that this is the meaning of their enduring such toil; when they are old, they will retire into ease and security, having collected for themselves a small pittance; just as the ant (for this is their example), a creature little, but great in industry, drags with its mouth all it can, and adds to the heap it raises, an animal not ignorant or improvident of the future; but she, as soon as Aquarius saddens the inverted year, creeps out in no direction, but uses her store, a wise creature: whereas, neither by torrid heat, nor by winter, fire, water, sword, can you be turned aside from gain, finding no obstacle to stop you, if only your neighbour be not richer than you.

41—60. *What is the use of unemployed money? Enough is a feast. Great wealth is useless, and dangerous too.*

What pleasure is there so stealthily deep in a hole of the earth timorously to hide an immense weight of gold and silver? "Ah," says the miser, "because, if I lessen it, it will at last be reduced to a worthless penny." "But unless," I reply, "you do so lessen it, what is the charm of this heap piled so high? Suppose your floor has threshed out a hundred thousand bushels of corn, will your stomach on that account hold more than mine? just as if it so happened that you among the slaves carried the bag full of loaves on your laden shoulder, you would not therefore receive more than he who carried nothing. Or say, what odds does it make to him who lives within the bounds of nature, whether he farms a hundred or a thousand acres? But you will say, 'Ah, 'tis pleasant to take from a large heap.' Nay, but so long as you let us take as much from our little, why should you praise your granaries more than our tiny bins? It is as if you wanted a pitcher-full or a glass-full of water, and were to say: 'I had rather take this quantity from a great river, than from this little well;' the natural result is, that those who take delight in an unreasonable quantity are carried off with the bank, and hurried down by the impetuous Aufidus; whilst he who wants just as little as is needful neither draws up muddy water, nor loses his life in the swollen stream."

61—91. *The miser has a wretched kind of self-applause; but he, like Tantalus, is never satisfied; he knows not the real use of money, lives in dread, is lonely in sickness, meets with no love, even from relations.*

But a large part of mankind are deceived by a vain covetousness, and say one never can have enough, for that money is the measure of worth. Now what can you do with such a man, but bid him go and be wretched, since he has a fancy so to be? As of a certain man at Athens it is told that he, being rich and mean, used to despise the hootings of the people thus: "The people, they hiss me, but I, I applaud myself at home, as soon as I contemplate my coins in my chest." Thirsty Tantalus catches at the streams as they fly from his lips. You laugh; why so? change but the name, and of you the tale is told: you heap up money-bags collected from all quarters, you sleep on them, gape over them, you are compelled to spare them, as though they were holy, or to take the pleasure in them that you would in pictures. Do you not know the good of money, the end it serves? Why, buy bread with it, vegetables, a pint of wine, in addition, such things as nature suffers pain, if bereaved of. What, to be wide awake half dead through fear, night and day to live in dread of rascally thieves, fire, your slaves, lest they plunder you and run away, is this so delightful? Of such goods as these may I ever be utterly destitute! But if your body, attacked by a chill, becomes full of pain, or any accident confines you to your bed, have you any one to sit by you, get your fomentations ready, entreat the doctor to raise you up, and restore you to your children and affectionate relations? No, your wife does not want you to get well, nor does your son; all hate you, even your acquaintance, boys and girls alike. Can you wonder, when you put money above all else, that no one shews you the affection you deserve not? What, if you choose to retain and keep the affection of those relatives given you by nature with no trouble of your own, would you then be so unlucky as to lose your labour? Would not that be like training a donkey to run as a racer on the Campus Martius, obedient to the bit?

92—100. *Set bounds to your desires. There are other evils besides poverty, as Ummidius found.*

In short, put bounds to your pursuit of wealth, and, as you have amassed more, so dread poverty less, lest your end be that of a certain Ummidius—it is a short story—so rich was he, that he measured, not counted his money; so mean was he, that he dressed no better than a slave, to his last hour he lived in perpetual dread of actual starvation: not so came his end, for his freed-woman cleft him through with an axe; she was as brave as any Clytemnestra.

101—107. *Do you, then, advise me to be a spendthrift? No, not so; surely in all things there is a mean.*

What then, sir, is your advice? to live like spendthrift Mænius, or the gourmand Nomentanus? Not so: why, you proceed to set contraries against contraries face to face: when I say, Be not a miser, I do not say, Be a worthless prodigal. There is a mean between Tanais and the father-in-law of Visellius. There is a mean in all things; in short there are fixed limits, beyond which on either side truth and right cannot be found.

108—120. *The miser is never contented, always envious, thinks only of those richer than himself, can never say, no, not when dying, I have had enough.*

I return to the point whence I digressed, how that no miser is ever content, but envies those who have followed another line of life, pining with envy, if his neighbour's goat gives more milk, forgetting to compare himself with the crowd of poorer men, ever striving to surpass this or that wealthy man. Thus, in his haste to be rich, ever before him stands a richer man: it is as when chariots start from the barrier, the running horses bear them swiftly on, then hard on the steeds that beat his own presses the charioteer, making small account of him whom he has passed, and who slowly goes amongst the hindmost. Thus rarely can we find the man who says he has had a happy life, and who, contented with his portion of days, leaves the banquet like one who has had his fill. But enough; you will think that I have been pilfering the desks of blear-eyed Crispinus; so I will not add a word more.

II.

1—24. *Men fall into one of two extremes, avarice or prodigality, and think to escape from one fault by running into its opposite.*

The guilds of singing girls, the vendors of drugs, beggars, actresses in farces, buffoons, all that sort of people, are sad and troubled at the death of the singer Tigellius: no wonder, for he was generous to them. The man of the opposite character dreads the name of spendthrift, and grudges a poor friend as much as would ward off from him cold and pinching poverty. If you ask another why so lavishly he wastes the noble property of his grandfather and father on his thankless appetite, buying up every dainty with borrowed money, he answers that he should not like to be thought mean and narrow-minded. One set praises him, another condemns him. Fufidius rich in lands, rich in money put out to interest, dreads the character of a worthless prodigal; he cuts away sixty per cent from the principal, and the more deeply in debt the ruined man is, the more hardly he presses him; he is ever on the look-out for bonds of minors who have just put on their toga, and whose fathers keep them tight. "Great Jupiter!" we exclaim, as soon as we hear of this extortion: "but then surely he lives in a style proportionate to his gains?" Not so: you would hardly believe how severe he is to himself, so that the father in the play, whom Terence brings on the stage as leading a miserable life after he has driven away his son, does not torture himself worse than Fufidius does. Now, if you ask me what I am driving at, I reply, This is what I want to shew, that while fools avoid one vice, they run into its opposite.

III.

1—19. *The account of Tigellius, the most inconsistent of men.*

It is a general fault of all singers, that, when among their friends, they never can make up their mind to sing, however much pressed; when no one asks them, they never stop singing. This was a characteristic of Tigellius, a worthy child of Sardinia: Cæsar, who might have compelled him, could not persuade him, though he intreated him by the friendship he and his father had for him: if the whim took him, then he would chant "Io Bacche!" from the first course to the dessert, one minute in the highest key, then in the lowest on the tetrachord. There was no consistency in the man: he would often run as one fleeing from an enemy, very often walk as solemnly as one bearing the sacred basket of Juno: often he kept two hundred slaves, then only ten; sometimes his talk was of kings and tetrarchs, all in the magnificent style; anon his language was, "Give me a three-legged table, a shell of clean salt, a coat, never mind how coarse, to keep off the cold." Supposing you presented this thrifty contented man with a million sesterces, in a few days he had not a farthing in his pockets. He would sit up all night till the morning appeared, then all day he snored. Never was such an inconsistent creature.

19—37. *It is easy to see other people's faults. Self-love is foolish and wrong; let us examine ourselves.*

But now perhaps some one may say to me: "You, sir, have you no faults?" To be sure I have, but of another sort, and perchance not so bad. Whilst Mænius was carping at Novius behind his back, "You there," says one present, "do you not know yourself, or as one unknown do you think to impose on us?" "I for my part," says Mænius, "make allowances for myself." This love is foolish and extravagant, and deserves the brand of censure. Whilst you look at your own failings, much as a blear-eyed man might whose eyes are unanointed, why is your sight of your friend's faults as keen as that of eagle or Epidaurian serpent? Then to you in your turn it comes to pass, that your acquaintance peer into your faults. Here is a man a little quick-tempered, ill able to bear the sharp criticism of our modern wits; no doubt he is open to ridicule, as one is who is shorn in country style, whose toga hangs loosely, whose badly fastened shoe fits his foot ill; and yet he is a good man, so that you will not find a better; a friend to you, and under a rough exterior is concealed a great genius. In short, sift and examine yourself, whether any faults are not implanted in you, either by nature, or by bad habits: for in the neglected field grows the fern whose end is to be burnt.

38—42. *It were well, if friends, like lovers, could be blind.*

Now, let us first look at the fact that a lover either sees not the ugly blemishes of his mistress, or is even charmed with them, as Balbinus was with the polypus in Hagna's nose. Would to heaven we could make the like mistakes in friendship, and that such errors had a fair name given them by right feeling!

43—66. *We should do as parents do, give gentle names to the faults of our friends: but now their very virtues have the names of vices given to them.*

We should not be offended at any fault of a friend, more than a parent is with the defects of a child; a boy squints, his father talks of the cast of his eye; or he calls him a little dear, when he is quite a dwarf, like that abortion Sisyphus not long ago; another child with misshapen legs is called a Varus; or if he can barely balance himself on his crooked ancles, then his father with a lisp speaks of him as a true Scaurus. So, if a friend lives rather nearly, let us call him a thrifty man. Another is rather wanting in tact, and somewhat vain; he expects to appear complacent to his friends; or, if he be rather rough and too free, let him pass for an honest blunt man; if rather hot-tempered, let him take his place among men of spirit. As I imagine, such charity would make and keep friends. But we invert even virtues, and, when a vessel is pure, desire to smear it. There lives amongst us an honest soul; "Ah," say we, "a poor creature:" to the cautious man we give the name of dull. Another avoids every snare set for him, and never exposes himself to attack, as he lives in the present age, where keen envy and calumnies are so rife; he is a sober-minded careful man, but we call him false and sly. Or is there one of character too undisguised (just as I at times have thrust myself on you, Mæcenas), one who, when his friend is reading or meditating, interrupts and annoys him with trifling talk; then we say, "Plainly this man has no common tact."

66—98. *We all have our faults, so we must pardon one another, and not condemn little failings as we would great sins. The Stoic dogma that all transgressions are equal is against sense, right feeling, and expediency.*

Alas, how ready we are to sanction a law that presses hard on ourselves! For no man by nature is faultless; the best man is he whose soul is troubled with fewest faults. A pleasant friend, as is but fair, will balance my faults by my good qualities, and incline the weight of his judgment to the latter, if they be more numerous, in case he desires my love; on this condition I too will weigh him in the same scales. He who expects not to offend his friend by his own lumps, must pardon that friend's warts: it is a fair rule, if one looks for allowance to failings, to give like measure in return. In short, inasmuch as it is impossible utterly to eradicate the fault of a passionate temper, and other defects that cling to us who are no philosophers, why does not right reason use its own weights and measures, and correct each offence with a suitable punishment? Were a master to crucify a slave, because, when told to remove a dish, he licked up the half-cold sauce of the half-eaten fish, men in their senses would count him madder than Labeo. How much more outrageous and great is your sin, when a friend has committed a little offence, for resenting which you are regarded as unamiable, if then you with bitter feeling hate and avoid him, as Ruso was shunned by his debtor! to the poor man came the black Calends, then, if he could not raise somehow or another the principal and interest, with outstretched neck he had to listen, like a captive, while his creditor read his wearying histories. My friend, suppose, has knocked off the table a dish that old Evander often held in his hands; for this, or because, being hungry, he took before me a chicken that was placed in my share of the dish, should I regard him as a less agreeable friend? What am I to do, if he is guilty of theft, or breach of trust, or disowns his covenant? Those who hold all sins to be equal are hard pressed, when brought to the test of real life; feelings and habits make against them, and expediency itself, which is pretty nearly the source of justice and equity.

99—124. *The Epicurean doctrine touching the first state of man, and the origin of law. This doctrine is agreeable to common sense.*

When men like animals crawled forth upon the early earth, as dumb and low as brute beasts, for acorns and beds of leaves they used to fight with nails and fists, and presently with clubs, and so in order of time with the arms that necessity invented, until they discovered words and names to express their utterances and feelings; afterwards they began to desist from war, to fortify towns and enact laws against theft and robbery and adultery. For before the age of Helen, woman was the most pernicious source of war; but by obscure deaths fell they, whom he who was superior in might struck down, as a bull does in the herd. That laws were introduced through dread of injuries one must needs confess, if one would search into the annals and records of the world. Nor can nature put such a separation between right and wrong as it does between advantages and their opposites, things to be avoided and things to be desired; nor will true reason ever prove that the sin is as great and the same, for a man to gather the young cabbages of his neighbour's garden, and to filch away by night the sacred vessels of the gods: let us adopt a rule appointing suitable punishments to each case, so that you may not cut one deserving only the whip with the horrible scourge. For as to your striking one with a switch who deserves a severer lashing, I confess I am not afraid, though you say theft is as bad as robbery with violence, and threaten to cut down with the same hook tall and short shrubs alike, if men entrusted you with royal power.

124—142. *Horace laughs at the doctrine of the Stoics that the philosopher of that school is not wise only, but knows all arts, is beautiful, a king.*

If the philosopher is rich and a good cobbler, and the only beautiful one, and a king, why wish for what you already have? "Ah," says the Stoic, "you do not see the meaning of father Chrysippus. The philosopher never made himself a pair of shoes or sandals, and yet he is an excellent shoemaker." "How so?" I ask. "Why, as Hermogenes, albeit he opens not his mouth, is yet an excellent singer and musician, as Alfenus is a good workman, though he laid aside all his tools, and closed his shop, so the philosopher is the best workman of every work, yes he alone, yea and king too." "What!" say I; "why, the mischievous boys pluck you by the beard, and unless you keep them in order with your club, the surrounding crowd press and throng you, and you, poor wretch, burst with anger and howl like a dog, O mightiest of mighty monarchs! To be short, whilst your royal highness goes to a penny bath, and no body-guard attends you except that bore Crispinus, my kind friends will pardon my peccadillos, for I am no philosopher, and I in my turn will gladly bear with their shortcomings, and, though a subject, live happier than your Majesty."

IV.

1—13. *The merits and defects of Lucilius the satirist.*

Eupolis and Cratinus and Aristophanes the poets, and other authors of the Old Comedy, if any one deserved to be portrayed as a rogue and a thief, an adulterer, an assassin, or was for other reasons infamous, without reserve used to brand him as such. Lucilius in all points adheres to them, them he follows, he has changed only the feet of the verse and metre, a writer not inelegant, of quick discernment, but harsh in the composition of his lines, for in this point he was faulty: within the hour he would often dictate two hundred verses, as though it were a mighty exploit, standing on one foot. As he flowed on like a muddy stream, one would have been glad to remove a good deal; a verbose author, too lazy to endure the labour of writing, correct writing, I mean, for as to quantity, I do not regard that.

13—38. *Horace is unlike Crispinus in facility of composition, and unlike Fannius in fondness for public recitation: and besides, he knows how unpopular is his sort of writing.*

See, here is Crispinus, he challenges me, giving me long odds. "Take," says he, "if you please, writing tablets, so will I; name your place, hour, umpires; let us see which of us two can compose most." "No," say I, "I thank Heaven for having given me a poor and humble genius, that speaks but seldom and very little; whilst do you, if so you please, imitate the air enclosed in bellows of goat-skin, puffing hard till the fire softens the iron. Fannius was fond of his own writings; without any one asking him he brought his desks and bust; whilst my writings no one reads, as I fear to recite in public, because there are persons not at all fond of this sort of literature, as is natural, when most of them deserve censure. Draw any one you please out of the middle of the crowd: he is troubled either with avarice or wretched ambition; or he is maddened with adulterous passion; or he is dazzled by the brightness of plate; or, as Albius, has a stupid admiration for vessels of bronze: another barters merchandise from the quarter of the rising sun to the region warmed by its evening rays, nay through all dangers headlong he is borne, like a cloud of dust by a whirlwind, dreading lest he should lose a farthing of his property, or not increase it. All these people fear verses, hate poets. "See," say they, "the wisp of hay on his horn; give him a wide berth; if he can but raise a laugh for himself, there is not a friend he would spare; whatever he has once scribbled on his paper, he longs for all to know as they return from the bakeries and reservoirs, boys and old women, all alike."

38—62. *Horace does not pretend to be a poet; indeed comedy, and satire, the daughter of comedy, are hardly poetry at all.*

Now come awhile, and hear a little in answer. In the first place I will except myself from the list of those whom I allow to be poets; for you surely would not consider it enough to write lines of the proper number of feet, nor would you regard as a poet one who, like me, composes what is akin to common prose. The honoured name of poet you would give to the man of genius, to one inspired in soul, to the tongue that is to utter noble things. For this reason some have made it a question whether comedy be poetry at all, for there is no inspiration and vigour either in the diction or the subjects; except so far as by a certain scansion it differs from prose, it is mere prose. Perhaps you will object, "See, how the angry father rages, because his prodigal son, madly in love with a mistress, refuses a wife with a large dowry, and utterly disgraces himself by walking drunken in the streets, torch in hand, in the daylight." "But," I reply, "would not profligate Pomponius hear language as strong as this, if his father were alive?" So then it is not enough to make a mere verse of plain words; for if you broke the line up, then any father would storm in the same fashion as the father on the stage. And if from my present writings, or those of old Lucilius you were to take the regular scansion and measures, placing the first word last, and inverting the order, the case would be quite different from breaking up the following:

"After that Discord grim
Burst wide War's posts and portals bound with steel."

Here would you still find the pieces of the dismembered poet.

63—93. *Horace hopes he is not ill-natured, nor vain, nor malignant, but only fond of a harmless banter.*

But enough of this: on some other occasion I will enquire whether comedy is true poetry or not; now all I ask is, whether you are reasonable in disliking this sort of composition. Keen Sulcius and Caprius, wretchedly hoarse, walk up and down with their bills of indictment, both of them a great terror to robbers: but he that leads a good life, whose hands are clean, need fear neither. However like you are to Cælius and Birrus the robbers, I am not like Caprius and Sulcius: why dread me? I do not wish my works to appear in any shop or at any columns, that the hands of the people and of Hermogenes Tigellius may sweat over them: I do not recite to any one but friends, and that upon compulsion, not anywhere, nor before anybody. Many recite their writings in the middle of the forum, or in the bath; they say the voice sounds sweetly in the enclosed place. Vain people may be pleased with this, as they stay not to enquire, whether thus they do not behave without tact, and out of season. "You take delight," says he, "in annoying, and do this from malice prepense." I reply, "Whence have you picked up this stone to cast it at me? Is your authority for this actually one of those with whom I have passed my life? He who backbites an absent friend; who does not defend him when another blames him; who tries to raise the horse-laughter of the company and to get the name of a wit; who can make up a story about what he has never seen; who cannot keep a secret entrusted to him; that man is a black sheep, of him, Roman, you must beware. Often may you see four at dinner on each of the three couches; one of these will sprinkle his banter on all except the host, on him too, when he has well drunken, and when the truth-speaking god of liberty opens the seals of the heart with wine. Now such an one appears agreeable and polite and free-hearted to you who are an enemy to malice. And I, if I have had my laugh at vain Rufillus who smells like a scent-box, and at Gorgonius stinking like a he-goat, do I seem to you a spiteful backbiter?"

94—103. *A sample of real malignity.*

If any mention of the thefts of Petillius Capitolinus arises in your presence, you would defend him after that way of yours, saying: "I have been a comrade and friend of Capitolinus since we were boys, and at my request he has done much for my sake, and I am glad he lives in our city uncondemned; but yet I do wonder how he was acquitted on that trial." Now this is as the juice of the black cuttle-fish, this is like very verdigris: that such ill-nature shall be far from my writings and from my heart first, I promise as truly as I can promise anything.

103—129. *Horace says if he is a little too free, it is to be attributed to the education he had from his worthy father.*

If my language is ever too free, too playful, such an amount of liberty you will grant me in your courtesy: for to this my good father trained me, to avoid each vice by setting a mark on it by examples. Whenever he would exhort me to live a thrifty, frugal life, contented with what he had saved for me, he would say, "Do you not see how hard it is for the son of Albius to live, and how needy Barrus is, a signal warning, to prevent any one from wasting his inheritance." If he would deter me from dishonourable love, he would say, "Do not be like Sectanus:" to save me from an adulterous passion, when I might enjoy an unforbidden love, he used to say, "Trebonius' exposure was not creditable. A philosopher will give you the right reasons for shunning or choosing things; I am contented, if I can maintain the custom handed down from our ancestors, and, so long as you need a guardian, preserve your life and character from ruin; when mature age has strengthened your body and soul, then you will swim without a cork." Thus he moulded my boyhood by these words, and if he advised me to any course of conduct, he would say, "You have an authority for so acting," and put before me one of the select judges; or if he would forbid me, then said he, "Can you possibly doubt, whether this is disreputable and injurious, when this man and that man are notorious for an evil report. As the funeral of a neighbour frightens to death the intemperate when sick, and, through dread of their own end, makes them careful, so minds still docile are often deterred from vice by the disgrace of others."

129—143. *The result of this training, as Horace hopes, is that he is free from gross vices, and has a desire to improve himself.*

Through this education I am sound from all ruinous vices, though I am troubled with moderate and pardonable failings; perhaps, too, a large deduction even from these has been made by advancing years, free-spoken friends, my own reflections; for I am not wanting to myself, whenever my little couch or arcade receives me. "This, I think, would be more correct; acting so, I shall do better: so will my friends find me pleasant. A certain one in this did not so well: am I to be so heedless, as to behave like him?" Such are my silent meditations; when I have a little leisure, I amuse myself by my writings; now this is one of those moderate faults of mine, and if you will not pardon it, a great band of poets will come to succour me, (for indeed we are a clear majority,) and, like the Jews, we will make a proselyte of you, and force you to join our company.

V.

1—26. *Horace with Heliodorus travels to Forum Appii. Then by a canal during the night to Feronia, and so to Anxur on the hill.*

After my departure from great Rome, Aricia received me in a poor inn; my companion was Heliodorus, by far the most learned of all the Greeks; then on we went to Forum Appii, a town crammed full of boatmen and extortionate tavern-keepers. This journey we were so indolent as to divide into two; it is only one to the more active; the Appian Way is less tiresome to the leisurely traveller. Here I, on account of the utter badness of the water, proclaim war against my stomach, and have to wait for my companions at dinner with impatient temper. And now night began to draw its shades over the earth, and to dot the sky with stars: then the slaves bantered the boatmen, and the boatmen the slaves: "Bring to here," cries one: "why you are putting in hundreds; stay, that's enough." Whilst the fare is demanded, and the mule fastened, a whole hour is gone. Troublesome musquitoes and marsh frogs keep sleep from our eyes, while the boatman drenched with much sour wine sings of his absent mistress, and a passenger rivals his song; at last the weary traveller drops asleep, and the lazy boatman fastens to a stone the halter of the mule, and turns it out to graze, and snores on his back. And now day was dawning, and we find that the boat is not going on;

till up springs a choleric fellow, and belabours with willow cudgel the head and ribs of mule and boatman; so it is the fourth hour, and we are hardly landed. Then our faces and hands we bathe in thy fair water, Feronia: and after breakfast crawl on three miles, and go under the gate of Anxur, a town built on rocks that shine white from afar.

27—51. *From Anxur they travel though Fundi, Formiae, Sinuessa, over the Campanian bridge, through Capua, to Cocceius' villa at Caudium. Horace meets with Maecenas, Virgil, and Varius, his dear friends, and with others.*

Here we expected good Mæcenas, and Cocceius, both sent as envoys on important matters, whose habit it was to mediate between estranged friends. And here I put on my sore eyes black ointment; meanwhile Mæcenas arrives, and Cocceius with him, and at the same time Capito Fonteius, that accomplished gentleman; Antony had not a greater friend than him. We are only too glad to leave Fundi under the prætorship of Aufidius Luscus, where we laugh at the badges of office worn by the crazy scribe, his prætexta and laticlave, and pan of live coals. Next, being tired, we pass the night in the city of the Mamurra family, where Murena lends us a house, Capito entertains us at dinner. The following day shines upon us, as much the pleasantest day in our journey; for at Sinuessa there meet us Plotius, Virgil and Varius; the world cannot show souls freer from stain, or more devoted friends to me. Oh, what embraces there were! oh, how great was our joy! As long as I have my senses, I would compare nothing to a delightful friend. Then the little villa next to the Campanian bridge gave us a roof over our heads, and the purveyors, what they are bound to supply, all necessaries. Leaving this place, our sumpter mules are eased of their pack-saddles early in the day at Capua; Mæcenas goes to play at ball, Virgil and I to sleep; for it is bad for the sore-eyed and dyspeptic to play at ball. At the end of the next stage we are received in Cocceius' well-stored villa situated above the taverns at Caudium.

51—70. *A jocular description of a contest of words between two parasites of Maecenas.*

And now, O Muse, be so kind as briefly to record for me the battle of words between Sarmentus the buffoon and Messius the game-cock; and sing to me who were the parents of either combatant. Messius was of the glorious stock of the Osci; as to Sarmentus, his mistress still lives; such were the ancestors of these who met in fight. Sarmentus began the action thus: "I say you are like a wild horse." We all laugh; and Messius says, "I accept your simile," and fiercely shakes his head. Then says the other: "Ah, if the horn had not been cut out of your forehead, what would you not do, seeing, though mutilated, you thus threaten?" For an ugly scar disfigured the left side of his shaggy forehead. He had many a joke too on his Campanian disease, and on his face, asking him to dance the Cyclops' pastoral dance; no need had such as he of mask or tragic buskin. Much had Messius the game-cock to say to this, asking him, whether, according to his vow, he had yet dedicated his chain to the Lares; if he was a scribe, yet this did not one whit abate his mistress' claim upon him; then he enquired why he had ever run away at all, one pound of meal was enough for such a lean pigmy. Thus very pleasantly our dinner passed.

71—93. *The fire at the inn at Beneventum. They cross the hills familiar to Horace, pass Equotutium, and reach Canusium.*

From hence we go straight on to Beneventum, where our bustling landlord nearly burnt his house down, whilst roasting lean thrushes; for the wandering tongue of flame, as the fire-god glided up the old kitchen, hastened to lick the top of the roof; then might you see the hungry guests and frightened slaves all eager to save the dinner and extinguish the fire. From that point Apulia begins to show to my eyes its familiar mountains scorched by the Altino; these mountains we had never got over, had not a neighbouring villa at Trivicum welcomed us; there the fire drew tears from my eyes, as on the hearth was burning green wood with the leaves on. Thence onward we are whirled in carriages twenty-four miles, to reach at night a little town with a name I may not speak in verse; however, I can very easily describe it; here is sold water, the commonest of all things; but the bread is most excellent, so that the traveller, who knows the road, carries it on his shoulders a stage further; for the bread at Canusium is gritty; the town is no better supplied with water; brave Diomede of old was its founder. Here Varius sorrowfully leaves his weeping friends.

94—104. *He then travels from Rubi to Brundusium; at Egnatia he is, as a philosopher, sceptical about a miracle.*

Thence we arrived at Rubi quite fatigued, as was to be expected, the stage being long and the road broken up by the rain. Next day's weather was better, but the road still worse, even to the walls of Barium, a fishing town: then Egnatia, a place built when the Nymphs were angry, gave us theme for laughter and joke, where they try to persuade us that frankincense melts without fire in the entrance of the temple. The Jew Apella may believe it, not I; for I have been taught that the gods lead a life free from care, and that if nature works wonders, it is not that the gods trouble themselves to send them down from the roof of heaven. Brundusium is the end of my long narrative and long journey.

VI.

1—17. *Maecenas, though himself as nobly born as any one, yet never attached too much value to high birth.*

There is none in all the inhabitants of Lydian Etruria more nobly born than you, Mæcenas; and your ancestors, maternal and paternal alike, commanded in the days of old mighty legions; and yet you do not, like most, turn up your nose at men of lowly origin, such as me, the son of a freedman. When you say that it makes no difference who a man's father is, provided he himself be free-born, you are right in your persuasion that even before the reign of Servius, the king so lowly born, often many, sprung from ancestors of no account, have yet lived lives of probity, and risen to high honours; on the other hand that Lævinus, though descended from that Valerius, by whom Tarquinius Superbus was driven forth and fled from his regal power, was never valued at more than a single farthing in the judgment even of that people who set a mark of censure on him: you know that people well, how in their folly they often give honours to the unworthy, and are the vainglorious slaves of fame, and stare awe-struck at inscriptions and busts. How then ought we to act, we so far, so very far removed from the vulgar?

18—44. *A man should keep in the station he was born in, if he would avoid a thousand troubles and annoyances, for the people cannot endure these upstarts.*

For, granted that the people at the elections should prefer Lævinus to Decius, a new man, and that the censor Appius should remove me from the senate as the son of a freedman: well, it would only be what I deserved for not being content to remain in my own skin. But the truth is, Vanity draws all bound to her glittering car, low-born and high-born alike. How did it benefit you, Tullius, to resume the laticlave you had laid aside, and to become a tribune? Envy fastened closer on you: in your private station it had been less. For as soon as any foolish man binds round his leg the four black straps of leather, and wears the laticlave down his breast, straightway he hears it said: "Who is this man? who is his father?" Just as if one is disordered with that vanity of Barrus, desiring to be thought handsome, then, wherever he goes, he makes the girls curious on each point, his face, his calf, his foot, teeth, hair; so he, who offers to take care of the citizens, the city, the empire, Italy and the shrines of the gods, forces all men curiously to enquire who is his father, and whether he is dishonoured by birth from an unknown mother. "What! do you, the son of some slave, a Syrus, or a Dama, or a Dionysius, do you dare to throw down Roman citizens from the Tarpeian rock, or hand them over to Cadmus?" "But," says he, "my colleague Novius sits one row behind me, for he is what my father was." On this account do you imagine yourself a Paullus or Messala? and then this Novius, if two hundred wagons and three funerals meet in the forum, will shout with a voice able to drown horns and trumpets; and this at any rate impresses us people.

45—64. *An account of Horace's introduction to Maecenas.*

Now to return to myself, the son of a freedman, whom all carp at as the son of a freedman, at present, because I am intimate with you, Mæcenas; formerly, because I was a tribune in command of a Roman legion. The two cases are unlike; the first honour might perhaps with reason be envied, but not your friendship, the less so, as you are cautious to admit none but the worthy to your intimacy, and keep far from you base flattery. Neither in this can I call myself lucky, as though by chance I had got your friendship, for it was no luck that brought me to your notice: the good Virgil first, then Varius, told you my character. The day I came to see you, I spoke but little, and that nervously; silent shame stopped me from speaking more. I tell you no tale of an illustrious father, or of my riding about my farm on a nag of Saturium, but the plain truth of myself. You answer, such is your way, but little; I left you; then, nine months after, you send for me again, and bid me be in the number of your friends. I account it a great honour that I pleased you, for you can distinguish between a true gentleman and one that is base, not judging by the distinction of the father, but by a life and heart unsullied.

65—88. *Whatever I am, I owe it to my good father, who spared no expense or care on my education.*

And yet, if the faults and defects of my nature are moderate ones, and with their exception my life is upright, (just as if one were to censure blemishes found here and there on a handsome body,) if no one can truly lay to my charge avarice, meanness, or frequenting vicious haunts, if (that I may praise myself) my life is pure and innocent, and my friends love me, I owe it all to my father; he, though not rich, for his farm was a poor one, would not send me to the school of Flavius, to which the first youths of the town, the sons of the centurions, the great men there, used to go, with their bags and slates on their left arm, taking the teacher's fee on the Ides of eight months in the year: but he had the spirit to carry me, when a boy, to Rome, there to learn the liberal arts which any knight or senator would have his own sons taught. Had any one seen my dress, and the attendant servants, so far as would be observed in a populous city, he would have thought that such expense was defrayed from an old hereditary estate. He himself was ever present, a guardian incorruptible, at all my studies. Why say more? My modesty, that first grace of virtue, he preserved untainted, not only by an actual stain, but by the very rumour of it; not fearing that any one hereafter should make this a reproach, if as auctioneer, or collector, like himself, I should follow a trade of petty gains; nor should I have grumbled at my lot; but as the case is now, to him more praise is due, I owe him greater thanks.

89—111. *Horace would not change his father or his lot, if he could. Many are the advantages of his present easy and humble life.*

So long as I have my senses, I trust I never shall be sorry of having had such a father; and may I never defend myself as so many do, who say it is no fault of theirs, that their parents were not free-born and illustrious. Utterly different is my language and my sentiments from theirs: indeed, if nature bid us resume the journey of life from a certain year, and choose such parents as each would prefer to suit his ambitious longings, I should be content with mine, and unwilling to select those distinguished by the fasces and chairs of office: the people would count me mad, but you perchance would think me sound-minded, for being unwilling to carry an irksome burden to which I have never been accustomed. For then directly I should have to make my fortune larger, then I should have more visitors, I should have to take with me two or three clients, lest forsooth I go to the country or travel abroad alone; I should have to keep more grooms and horses, and to take carriages with me. But now on dumpy mule I may go, if so I fancy, as far as Tarentum, whilst the weight of the saddle-bags chafes its loins, the rider its shoulders: so no one will taunt me with meanness, as they do you, Tillius, when, on the road to Tibur, you, the prætor, are attended by five slaves bearing your kitchen utensils and case of wine. So far do I live in greater comfort than you, illustrious senator, and a thousand others.

111—131. *An account of the manner in which Horace spent his day.*

Wherever the whim takes me, I walk leisurely alone, I enquire the price of vegetables and flour, and often in the evening take a turn through the cheating Circus and Forum; I stop and listen to the fortune-tellers, and then home I return to my dish of leeks, chick-peas and pancake. My dinner is served by three servants, my marble side-table holds two cups with a ladle; close at hand is a common vessel, a jug with a bowl, all Campanian earthenware. Then I go to bed, not troubled with the thought that to-morrow I shall have to rise early and meet Marsyas, who says that he cannot stand the cheek of the younger Novius. I lie till the fourth hour, then I take a stroll, or, after reading or writing in quiet as much as is agreeable, I anoint myself with oil, unlike that which dirty Natta robs the lamps of. But when I am tired, and the sun's increasing heat has warned me to go to the bath, I shun the Plain of Mars and the game at ball. Having taken a sparing luncheon, such as just will prevent my passing the day on an empty stomach, I take my ease at home. This is the life of those who are free from the wretched burdens of intrigue; thus I comfort myself with the thought that I shall live more pleasantly, than if my grandfather, father, and uncle had all been quæstors.

VII.

1—20. *A contest between Rupilius Rex of Praeneste and Persius, supposed to have taken place while Horace was serving in the army of Brutus.*

On the proscription list was Rupilius Rex, the king, a man all slime and venom; him the Hybrid Persius took vengeance on; a story, I imagine, known to all sore-eyed men and all barbers. This Persius was a rich man, and had very large business at Clazomenæ; also a troublesome lawsuit with the king: Persius was a hard man, in power of annoyance he could beat the king, confident was he and swelling with passion, so foul-mouthed as to distance the Sisennæ and the Barri with the fleetness of white coursers. To return to the king: these two men could come to no terms; and indeed all men are contentious in proportion to their courage, when they go to war with one another; thus between Priam's son Hector and the spirited Achilles deadly was the anger, so that death alone could part them, the reason being only this, that either chieftain was of the highest courage: whereas, if discord troubles two cowards, or if the combatants are unequally matched, as were Diomede and Lycian Glaucus, then let the less valiant be only too glad to get off, and tender presents besides: however, when Brutus was prætor of the wealthy province of Asia, then engaged Rupilius and Persius, such a pair that Bacchius was not more fairly matched with Bithus. Fiercely they rush forward to the trial; a fine exhibition, both of them.

21—35. *The account of the contest.*

Persius opens his case; a laugh is raised by all in court; he praises Brutus, he praises his retinue; as to Brutus, he calls him the sun of the province; his officers are stars of salubrious influence; except the king, who had risen like the dog-star, the farmers' enemy: on rushed Persius like a winter torrent through a forest, where the axe seldom comes. Then the man of Præneste, in answer to his adversary's full stream of bitter words, retorts with abuse taken from the vineyard, like a vine-dresser stout and unconquered, to whom often has to yield a passer-by with mighty voice crying to him, "Cuckoo!" But Persius, a Greek, being steeped besides in Italian vinegar, shouts aloud: "In the name of the great gods, Brutus, I entreat you, for it is your habit to rid us of kings, why not cut the throat of this king also? This, believe me, is one of your proper works."

VIII.

1—22. *Priapus, set up by Maecenas in his newly-made gardens, is introduced as contrasting the former state of the site with the present.*

Once I was the stem of a fig tree, a good-for-nothing log of wood, when the carpenter, doubting whether to make of me a bench or a Priapus, thought it best to make me a god. So a god am I, of thieves and birds the special terror, for my right hand keeps thieves off, whilst the crown of reeds fixed on my head scares the troublesome birds, and prevents their lighting in the new gardens. To this ground formerly any fellow-slave would hire bearers to carry on a poor bier the bodies thrown out of their narrow cells. Here was a common burying-place for wretched paupers, for Pantolabus the buffoon and the spendthrift Nomentanus. Here a stone marked out a thousand feet in front, and three hundred in depth, with the inscription upon it, that the monument might not pass to the heirs. Now one may live on the Esquiline, for it is a healthy spot, and one may take a walk on the sunny terrace, whence but lately with sad thoughts men looked on the ground hideous with bleaching bones; whilst to me it is not so much the birds and beasts wont to infest the spot that give me distress and trouble, as the witches who with charms and poisons torture the souls of men: these women I cannot destroy, nor anyhow stop them from gathering bones and noxious herbs, as soon as the wandering moon shows her beauteous face.

23—50. *Priapus was a witness of the abominable proceedings of Canidia and Sagana, and gave them a good fright.*

I myself saw Canidia stalking along with her sable robe tucked up, naked were her feet, dishevelled her hair, she howled in company with the elder Sagana: their ghastly colour made them both horrible to look on. Then they began to scrape the earth with their nails, and to tear with their teeth a black lamb; the blood was all poured into a trench, that from it they might entice the spirits of the dead, the souls that were to give responses. There was an image of wool there with another of wax; the larger was that of wool; it was to punish the smaller form; for the waxen one seemed, as in suppliant guise, just about to perish, as by a slave's death. One of the witches calls on Hecate, the other on fierce Tisiphone; then might you see serpents and hell-hounds roaming about, and the moon blushing and hiding herself behind the tall sepulchres, that she might not witness such deeds. Why need I describe the details? how the ghosts in converse with Sagana made the place echo to their sad shrill cries, and how they buried in the ground the beard of a wolf, with the teeth of a spotted snake, and how the fire blazed more freely, fed by the effigy of wax, and how I shuddered at the words and deeds of the two witches, I, a witness, but not unavenged; for as loud as the noise of a bursting bladder was the crack of my fig wood; off ran the two into the city; then might you see not without laughing much and much amusement, the false teeth of Canidia fall out, and the lofty head-dress of Sagana tumble down, and the herbs and enchanted bonds of their arms fly about.

IX.

1—20. *Horace is beset by an impertinent man.*

I happened to be walking along the Sacred Street, as is my wont; I was thinking of some trifle or another, quite lost in it: up runs to me a man I only knew by name, and, seizing my hand, says, "How do you do, my dearest friend?" "Pretty well," say I, "as times go, and am quite at your service." As he kept sticking close to me, I anticipate him by saying, "Have you any further commands?" But he to me: "You must know me, I am a scholar." Then say I, "On that account I shall esteem you more." I was wretchedly anxious to get away from him; so at one moment I quickened my pace, at times I came to a stop, I whispered anything in my servant's ear, whilst the perspiration was trickling down to my very ancles. "O Bolanus, how I envy you your hot temper," said I to myself; he meanwhile went on chattering about anything, praising the streets, the city. As I did not answer him a word, he says, "You are dying to get away, I have seen it from the first; but it is no good, I shall stick to you, and accompany you all the way you are going." Then said I, "There is no need for you to take such a long round, I want to visit some one you do not know; it is across the Tiber, a long way off, he is ill in bed, it is near Cæsar's gardens." He answers, "I have nothing particular to do, and I am a good walker; I will go with you all the way." Down go my ears, like those of a sulky donkey, when it feels the weight too heavy for its back.

21—34. *The man praises himself. Horace's humorous despair.*

Then he begins: "Unless I deceive myself, you would not esteem Viscus or Varius as friends more than me: for who is a better or readier poet than I am? who can dance with more ease than I? Hermogenes himself might envy my singing." Here was an opportunity of putting in a word: "Is your mother alive? have you relations to whom your life and health are important?" "No," says he, "I have not one; I have laid them all at rest." "Happy people!" say I, "now I am left; so despatch me at once; for my sad fate is now at hand, predicted to me, when a boy, by a Sabine old woman, after she had shaken her divining urn: 'This boy will neither poisons dire, nor hostile sword destroy, nor pleurisy, nor cough, nor gout that makes men limp; on some future day a chatterbox will end his life; wherefore all great talkers let him, if wise, avoid, as soon as he has grown to man's estate.'"

35—48. *The object of the persecutor now appeared, which was to get, through Horace, an introduction to Maecenas.*

So we had reached Vesta's temple, and a fourth part of the day was gone, and it chanced he was bound to appear to answer to one to whom he had given bail, or, if he failed, to lose his cause. "If you love me," says he, "give me your aid in court." I answered, "May I perish, if I can appear before a prætor, or know aught of common law; and I am in a hurry to get you know where." "I am doubtful," says he, "what to do, to leave you or my case." "Me, I pray!" said I. "No, I won't," said he; and then went on before me: I, for it is hard work to contend with one's conqueror, even follow. Then he resumes his attack: "On what terms are you with Mæcenas? he is select in his friendship, being a man of sense; no one ever made a more adroit use of his fortune. You would have in me a powerful backer, able to play the second part, if you would but introduce me; may I utterly perish, if you would not make for yourself a clear stage!"

48—60. *Horace pays Maecenas an indirect compliment.*

I replied: "We do not live on the terms that you imagine; there is not a house more honest than that, or more free from such intrigues; it never annoys me, if another there is richer or more learned than I am; each has his own position there." "What you tell me," said he, "is wonderful, almost incredible." "But," say I, "it is the truth." "Well," said he, "you increase my desire for his intimacy." I reply, "You have only to wish for it; such is your virtue, you will take him by storm; he is one that may be won, and this is the reason why he is so hard to approach at first." "I will not be wanting to myself," said he: "I will bribe the servants; if the door be shut in my face to day, I will not give up; I will watch my opportunities; I will meet him at the corners of the streets; I will attend him to his home. Life nothing grants to man, save through great toil."

60—74. *The appearance of Aristius Fuscus on the scene.*

While he is thus busy in his talk, lo, Fuscus Aristius meets us, a dear friend of mine, and one who knew the man right well. We stop; we exchange salutations. I begin to pull and pinch his arms that are as dead, I nod, I wink to him to deliver me. The mischievous wit laughs, pretending not to know what I mean; I begin to wax warm with anger, observing to him, "Surely you did say you had something secret to speak to me of." Fuscus says, "Yes, I remember well; but I will talk to you of it at a more convenient season; to day is the thirtieth sabbath; you would not, surely, scandalize the circumcised Jews." "Oh," say I, "I have no such scruples." "But I have," said he; "I am a weaker brother, one of the many; so pardon me; I will speak to you at another time." "Alas!" I exclaimed, "Oh this day, how black it has arisen for me!" Off goes the wicked wag, and leaves me like a victim with the knife at my throat.

74—78. *Horace's unexpected delivery.*

By chance the plaintiff meets him face to face, who with loud voice shouts to him, "Whither, thou basest of men?" Then thus to me, "May I make you a witness?" I give my ear to be touched. He hurries the man off to trial; on either part a shout was raised; people rush together from all sides; so was I saved by Apollo.

X.

Lucilius is amended by Cato.

[Lucilius, how full of your faults you are, I can clearly prove by the witness of Cato, your own advocate, for he tries to improve your ill-composed verses. This, as he was a better man, he did much more gently, and with a much nicer taste than that other critic, who, when a boy, was much encouraged by the whip and green rope, that so he might arise to help the ancient poets against modern fastidiousness, he, the most learned of grammarian knights. But to return.]

1—19. *Horace blames the roughness of Lucilius.*

Yes, I did say that rough was the measure of the verses of Lucilius: who is such an unreasonable partisan of Lucilius as not to allow this? And yet he is praised in the same satire for having rubbed the city down with so much Attic salt. However, though I allow this, I am not prepared to allow other points; for so I should admire even Laberius' farces, as though they were fine poems. For it is not enough to make the hearer's jaw open wide with laughter; although there is a certain merit even in this; but conciseness is required, that the thoughts may run on, unembarrassed by words loading the wearied ears: we need, too, language sometimes severe, often gay, maintaining the character sometimes of an orator or poet, then awhile of a polished wit, who puts not forth his strength, but husbands it on purpose. A joke often decides weighty matters more powerfully and better than does severity. Those famous writers of the old comedy took their stand on this point, in this are worthy of all imitation; though that coxcomb Hermogenes never reads them, nor that monkey, whose only skill is in singing the verses of Calvus and Catullus.

20—39. *Lucilius' much-praised medley of Greek and Latin words is not worth much, and is unnatural, and does not suit Horace's own unpretending ways.*

But it is said: "Lucilius did well in his medley of Greek and Latin words." "Ah, backward are ye in your learning, for how can ye think that to be difficult and admirable, which Pitholeon of Rhodes attained?" But you say: "A style neatly set in words of either language is charming, just as when one mixes a cask of Falernian wine with Chian." "Is this so," I ask you, "only when you write verses, or would you do it, if you had to undertake the difficult defence of Petillus? While the brothers Poplicolæ, Pedius and Corvinus, plead with energy in the Latin tongue, would you, forsooth, forgetting your fatherland and father, prefer to mix words fetched from abroad with those of your own country, like the native of Canusium with his mongrel talk? And indeed I, born on this side the sea, tried once to write Greek verses: then Quirinus appeared to me in a vision after midnight, when dreams are true, and forbad me in these words: "'Twere as mad to carry logs of wood into a forest, as to desire to fill up the numerous ranks of the Grecian host.' Bombastic Alpinus murders Memnon, and by his fictions muddles the source of the Rhine; meanwhile I amuse myself with my writings not intended to contend for a prize in the temple with Tarpa for judge, nor to be brought out over and over again on the stage."

40—49. *Horace's contemporaries excelled in various branches of poetry; he himself ventured on Satire.*

Of all men living, Fundanius, you are the one to write pleasant chatty comedies, in which the cunning courtesan and Davus cheat old Chremes; in trimeter iambics Pollio sings of regal feats; spirited Varius draws forth the vigorous epic, as no one else can; delicacy and grace is Virgil's gift from the Muses, whose joy is in the country. My kind of composition, attempted by Varro Atacinus and by some others without success, perhaps I can write better than they; inferior am I to the inventor, nor would I venture to pluck from his brows the crown that is fixed there with so much glory.

50—71. *His censure of Lucilius' faults does not imply he thought himself his superior; Lucilius himself, if now alive, would try to improve his own verses.*

No doubt I did liken Lucilius to a muddy stream, which often bears in its channel more that should be removed than left. Come now, prithee, do you, a scholar, find no fault in great Homer? Would courteous Lucilius desire no change in the tragedies of Accius? Does he not laugh at Ennius' verses as wanting in dignity, though he speaks of himself as not greater than those he censures? And why should not I, while reading the writings of Lucilius, raise the question, whether it was his own fault, or the impracticable nature of his subject, which denied to him verses more polished and with a softer flow than could be looked for from one who, contented with the mere making of an hexameter verse, was pleased to have written two hundred lines before dinner, two hundred after? Such was the genius of Etrurian Cassius, like the torrent of a rapid river: fame tells that the author's own works and writing-cases made his funeral pile. Granted, say I, Lucilius was a pleasant polished writer, more finished than the author of the rough kind of poetry untouched by the Greeks, and than the crowd of earlier poets: yet he also, had fate put off his days to our age, would rub out many a line, and prune all that exceeded a perfect finish, and, as he made his verse, would often scratch his pate, and bite his nails to the quick.

72—92. *Horace, though he disregards a vain popularity, yet would be much grieved if his writings did not please the circle of his own accomplished friends.*

Often must you erase, if you mean to write verses worthy of a second perusal; labour not for the admiration of the vulgar, be content with a few readers. Can you be so foolish as to desire your poems to be dictated in common schools? "I desire it not, satisfied if the knights applaud me," to use the words of bold Arbuscula, who despised the rest of the spectators, when hissed off the stage. Am I to be disturbed by that offensive Pantilius, or troubled if Demetrius pulls my verses to pieces behind my back, or if that impertinent Fannius, the parasite of Hermogenes Tigellius, depreciates me? Only may my writings meet with the approval of Plotius and Varius, Mæcenas and Virgil, of Valgius and excellent Octavius and Fuscus; and may either Viscus praise them. Apart from vanity, I may name you, Pollio, and you, Messala, with your brother; and you too, Bibulus, and Servius, and you likewise, blameless Furnius; very many others, learned friends of mine, purposely I omit, hoping they may smile on my lines, be their merit what it may, for grieved should I be, if their pleasure fell short of my hopes. But you, Demetrius, and you, Tigellius, I bid you go and wail amidst the chairs of your female scholars. Haste, my boy, and quickly add these words to my book of satires.

BOOK II.

I.

1—23. *A dialogue between Horace and the lawyer Trebatius, who advises Horace not to write Satires, but to write Caesar's praise. Horace professes his inability for such ambitious poetry.*

HORACE.

To some my satire seems too keen, and my work strained beyond its proper sphere; others think all my compositions weak, and that a thousand verses as good as mine could be spun in a day. I come to consult you, Trebatius.

TREBATIUS.

Keep quiet.

HORACE.

Do you mean, I am not to write verses at all?

TREBATIUS.

I say so.

HORACE.

May I perish utterly, if your advice is not the best: but the truth is, I cannot sleep.

TREBATIUS.

I say that those who cannot sleep soundly should anoint themselves and thrice swim across the Tiber, and, as night draws on, soak themselves well with strong wine; or, if such a mighty passion for writing possesses you, venture to sing the exploits of invincible Cæsar; you will gain many a reward for your labours.

HORACE.

That were my ambition, excellent father, but I lack the ability; for it takes more than a common writer to sing of ranks which bristle rough with darts, or Gauls who fall, the spear-head breaking short, or wounded Parthian sinking from his horse.

TREBATIUS.

But still you might write of Cæsar, just and firm of purpose, as wise Lucilius did of Scipio.

HORACE.

I will not be wanting to the occasion, when a fit one offers: but only at a lucky moment will the words of Flaccus find Cæsar's ear attentive: he is like a horse, which if you stroke clumsily, out he kicks, guarded on every side.

TREBATIUS.

But better is this, than in stinging verse to wound Pantolabus the buffoon, and Nomentanus the spendthrift, when each one fears for himself, though you touch him not, and hates you.

24—34. *Horace's taste is for satire.*

HORACE.

What would you have me do? Milonius dances, as soon as the fumes of wine reach and affect his head, and the lustres double; Castor delights in steeds, Pollux, sprung from the same egg, in boxing; as many men alive, so many thousand tastes; my pleasure is to get my words into lines in the style of Lucilius, a better man than either of us. He in days of old would trust his secrets to his books as to faithful companions; let things turn out ill or well, to them he had recourse; so that all the life of the old poet is open to our view, as though painted on votive tablet.

34—60. *Horace will not begin the attack on others, but will defend himself. The instinct of self-preservation bids him do this.*

Him I follow, I half Lucanian, half Apulian; for the colony of Venusia ploughs close up to the boundaries of the two countries; old tradition tells how that, when the Samnites were driven out, they were sent thither to prevent the enemy's incursions on Rome through an open frontier, were it Apulia or Lucania that made violent attacks in war; now this pen of mine shall not wantonly attack any living wight, and shall guard me, as sword kept close in sheath; for why should I try to draw it, while safe from the attack of robbers? My prayer is this: "O Jove, father and king, my unused weapon would that rust may eat, nor any one injure me a lover of peace!" But he who troubles me—Better not touch me, I cry—he shall rue it, and be a marked man, and the talk of the whole town. Cervius, when angry, menaces us with laws and the judicial urn; Canidia threatens her enemies with the poison Albutius used; Turius speaks of a mighty mischief, if you go to law when he is a judge: now that each terrifies his foes by that in which lies his power, and that this is in obedience to the strong law of nature, you may follow me in inferring from the fact that the wolf attacks with fangs, and the ox with horns, so taught only by instinct. Scæva was a spendthrift; his mother would not die; trust her to him, for his right hand is too dutiful to commit any crime: strange, aye about as strange as that wolf does not attack with heel, or ox with tooth: but the deadly hemlock will carry off his old mother in the poisoned honey. Not to delay you, I will only say that whether a calm old age awaits me, or death around me hovers with black wings, be I rich or poor, at Rome, or, should fortune so ordain, in exile, whate'er my life's complexion, write I will.

60—79. *Trebatius cautions Horace: he replies that Lucilius, though a keen satirist, was safe, and acceptable to the great men of his day.*

TREBATIUS.

Young man, I fear, your days can ne'er be long; some of your great friends will strike you with a chill.

HORACE.

How so? Lucilius first of all men ventured to write in this style; he plucked off the hide, in which men walked so fair before the public view, while inwardly so foul; were Lælius or he who drew from the overthrow of Carthage a title fairly won, offended by his satiric genius, or were they angry because Metellus was attacked, and Lupus overwhelmed by verses that brand with infamy? And yet he fastened on the chief men of the state, and on the people tribe by tribe; for of a surety he favoured virtue only and her friends. Nay, when from the crowd and stage of life withdrew into retirement the virtue of Scipio, and the gentle wisdom of Lælius, they would trifle with him, and at their ease amuse themselves, until the herbs were dressed for dinner. Be I what I may, though far below Lucilius in station and genius, yet, that I have lived with the great, Envy can never deny, though fain she would, and while seeking to fix her tooth on something fragile, will meet with what is solid—unless, learned counsellor, you take some exception.

79—86.

TREBATIUS.

Indeed I can propose no amendment here. But yet would I warn you to beware, lest ignorance of our sacred laws perchance bring you into trouble: there is a right of action and suit, if any one compose against another ill-natured libels.

HORACE.

Ill-written, if you please, sir; but if one compose well-written verses, and Cæsar's judgment approve them; if one, whose life is blameless, has his bark at one who deserves disgrace; why then, the prosecution will break down amidst laughter; and you will leave scot-free.

II.

1—22. *The excellencies of a simple fare and of plenty of exercise.*

What and how great the virtue to live on little (nor is this my own doctrine, but these are the precepts of Ofellus, a rustic sage, wise without rules, a man of home-spun wit), learn, my friends, not amongst dishes and polished tables, where the eye is dazzled by senseless splendours, and the mind, staying itself on a lie, refuses the better part; but here, before we dine, let us discuss the point. Why so? I will explain, if I can. Badly is the truth weighed by any corrupt judge. Go, hunt the hare, and tire yourself by riding on an unbroken horse, or if Roman exercises exhaust you who have adopted Grecian fashions, and if the swift-flying ball or the quoit is your pleasure, your interest in which gently beguiles the severity of the toil, go, I say, strike the yielding air with the quoit; then, when the toil has beaten out of you your daintiness, then, when you are dry and empty, despise, if you can, plain food, and refuse to drink any mead, unless made of the best wine and best honey. The butler is not at home, and stormy is the dark sea, and the fish are safe; bread with salt will appease your growling stomach. How do you suppose this end is obtained? The height of the enjoyment is not, in the savour that costs so dear, but in yourself. Therefore earn you your sauce by hard exercise; the man bloated and sickly-pale with gluttony, no oyster, or scar, or foreign lagoïs will delight.

23—38. *There are all kinds of fancies about what we eat.*

However, I shall hardly get out of you the desire of tickling your palate with a peacock on your table rather than a chicken; vain appearances mislead you; just because the peacock is a rare bird, and a gold coin must buy it, and on its painted tail a gaudy show is spread to view; as if that were aught to the point. For do you eat those admired feathers? When the bird is dressed, where is its beauteous plumage? Yet though there is no difference, you prefer one meat to the other: it is plain you are deceived by the difference of the appearance. But grant this is so: yet what sense tells you whether this fish was a river pike or caught out at sea, nay, whether it had been tossed among the bridges or at the mouth of the Tuscan river? In your folly you praise a three-pound mullet; and yet you must cut it in pieces to eat it with your bread. Your eye is your guide, I see; wherefore then dislike large pikes? Because forsooth nature made these large, the others light of weight. A hungry stomach seldom scorns plain food.

39—52. *Luxury so excessive did not always prevail; and there are still the remnants at our dinners of former simplicity.*

"Ah would that I could gaze on a lordly mullet stretched on lordly dish!" so says the gourmand's throat that would not have disgraced the devouring Harpies. But come from heaven, ye siroccos, and cook these men their dainties! Though without your breath the boar and fresh turbot are tainted, when a surfeiting plenty troubles the sickened stomach, which sated prefers turnips and acid elecampane. There still is left some old simplicity in the feasts of our great men, where cheap eggs and black olives yet find a place. It is not so very long ago that the table of Gallonius the auctioneer was infamous for a sturgeon. What! did the sea produce no turbots in those days? Safe was the turbot then, safe in its nest the stork, until you epicures were taught by an authority, a would-be prætor. And now if any one issued an edict that roasted sea-gulls were delicious, the Roman youths, apt pupils in depravity, would yield obedience.

53—69. *Yet we should avoid the opposite fault of meanness.*

A mean style of living will differ from a moderate one in Ofellus' judgment; indeed, in vain have you avoided one fault, only to turn aside perversely to its opposite. Avidienus, to whom the name of 'dog' clings, drawn from his nature, eats olives five years old, and the fruit of the wild cornel tree, and is too stingy to draw his wine till it is turned; as to his oil, its smell is intolerable, though he is celebrating the day that follows a wedding, or a birthday, or some other holyday, in robe whitened by the fuller; from a horn of two pints' size with his own hand he drops this oil on the cabbage, liberal enough of his old vinegar. What manner of living then will a wise man adopt, and which of these two will he follow? "On one side a wolf attacks, on another a dog worries you," as they say. His mode of life is decent, who does not offend by meanness, and neither on this side nor on that is unfortunate in his style of living. For he will neither be like old Albutius, savage to his slaves, while apportioning to them their duties; nor, as easy-natured Nævius, will give his guests greasy water; this too is a great fault.

70—93. *The disadvantages of excess, the advantages of a frugal diet; the praise of the men of old.*

Now hear the great blessings of a frugal diet. In the first place good health; how injurious variety of food is to a man, you may well believe by remembering how at times a simple fare has settled on your stomach; whereas as soon as you mix boiled and roast, shell fish and thrushes, sweets into bile will turn, and the thick phlegm will cause intestine war. See how pale rises each guest from a dinner distracting by its variety! Nay, the body laden with yesterday's excess weighs down its companion the soul, and fastens to the earth that particle of the divine Essence. But the temperate man in an instant consigns to sleep his refreshed body, then rises all fresh to his appointed duties. And yet he too now and then can pass to more generous fare, when the returning year shall bring some holy time, or he would invigorate his weakened frame, when too years advance, and the infirmity of age looks for kinder treatment; but what can you add to that indulgence anticipated by you in the days of youth and strength, if ill-health comes upon you, or sluggish age? Our fathers praised a high boar; not, I suppose, because they had no nose, but this was their meaning, that a friend, arriving late, would eat it when tainted with more comfort than the greedy master of the house would dine on it though still fresh. Oh, that the early world had produced myself among heroes such as those!

94—111. *Luxury brings disgrace and ruin. If we are ever so rich, could not we spend our money better? The future too is uncertain for all.*

Do you not allow something to the voice of fame? Sweeter than song it fills the human ear. Great turbots on great dishes bring huge discredit and loss. Then angry is your uncle, all your neighbours, you condemn yourself, in vain you long for death, for in your need you lack a penny to buy a halter with. "Right is it," says the wealthy man, "for Trausius to be reproved by your words: but I have a noble revenue, and wealth ample for three monarchs." Be it so: is there nothing better on which to spend your superfluity?

Why is any worthy man so poor, and you so rich? Why are the ancient temples of the gods in ruins? Why, worthless man, do you not measure out a portion of that great heap to your country? Ah, you alone of all, I suppose, can never meet with mishap! Some day your enemies will have a great laugh at you. For which of the two can trust himself best to meet the accidents of chance, he who to superfluities accustoms his soul and pampered body, or he who, blessed with little and cautious for the future, in peace, as a wise man, provides fit arms for war?

112—136. *Ofellus describes his life; he was thrifty in former days, and so has been able courageously to meet unlooked-for misfortunes.*

To induce you to believe my words, I will tell you how, when a little boy, I remember Ofellus using his means then undiminished as moderately as now, when impaired. You may see him in the allotted farm with his cattle and his sons, a stalwart tenant-farmer, telling thus his tale: "It was no wont of mine on a working day to dine on more than vegetables, and a smoked ham. And if a friend I had not seen for long should visit me, or if to me when at ease some neighbour, a welcome guest, came walking through the rain, then we enjoyed ourselves, not with fish fetched from town, but on a chicken or kid; presently raisins and walnuts with dried figs graced our second course. After that, our amusement was to drink, with the law of forfeits for the master of our feast; and Ceres, whom we honoured on condition that so with lofty stem she would deign to rise, cleared from our wrinkled brow with wine our serious cares. Let fortune raging stir new civil turmoils; how much from my means will she take? Have I, or you, my boys, been less sleek since this new landlord came? Nature has established neither him, nor me, nor any one, lord of this land in perpetuity; he ejected me; some villainy, or ignorance of tricky law, at any rate in the end an heir, who longer lives, will eject him. The farm is now Umbrenus'; once it was called Ofellus'; of no man is it the absolute property; but passes to the use, now of me, now of a successor. Wherefore with courage live, and with courageous breasts stem adverse fate."

III.

1—16. *Damasippus, a new convert to Stoicism, taunts Horace with his Epicurean indolence.*

DAMASIPPUS.

So seldom do you write, that not four times in a whole year do you call for your parchment, while you retouch your writings, and are out of temper with yourself, because, so freely indulging in wine and sleep, you give us no poems worthy of the talk of men. What will you produce now? For we look for something, as from the midst of the Saturnalia you have taken refuge here. In your retirement from the revels give us something worthy of your professions. Begin. Why, there is nothing. In vain you blame your pens. and make the innocent wall suffer, born in an hour when gods were angry, aye and poets too. And yet yours was the countenance of one who threatened many glorious poems, if your little villa once received you at your leisure under its cosy roof. What did you mean by packing up Plato and Menander, and taking with you into the country such illustrious attendants as Eupolis and Archilochus? Are you trying to appease envy by the abandonment of virtue? You will be despised, wretched man. Avoid that wicked Siren, sloth; or else, whatever you have made your own in better days, you must be prepared now to resign.

16—42. *An account of Damasippus' bankruptcy, his idle life as a virtuoso, his intended suicide, his changed life.*

HORACE.

May the gods and goddesses present you, Damasippus, with a barber in return for your good advice! But how come you to know me so well?

DAMASIPPUS.

After the shipwreck of all my fortunes at the middle Janus, I have attended to other people's business, having been dashed by the storm out of my own. There was a time when I was fond of looking out for bronze vessels in which old Sisyphus, that man of craft, might have washed his feet; I judged what was sculptured unskilfully, what cast roughly; as a connoisseur I valued this or that statue at a hundred thousand sesterces; gardens and fine houses I, above all other men, knew how to buy at a profit; whence the crowded streets gave me the name of the very god of gain.

HORACE.

Oh, I know, and wonder to find you cured of that disease.

DAMASIPPUS.

And yet the old disease was driven out in a strange way by a new one, as happens, when into the stomach passes the pain of the foot, side, or head; or as from a lethargy up starts a man as a pugilist, and pounds his doctor.

HORACE.

Provided anything like this does not happen to me, let it be as you like.

DAMASIPPUS.

My friend, not to deceive yourself, know that you are mad and nearly all fools, if there be one word of truth in Stertinius' talk; from his mouth I, an apt pupil, wrote down these admirable precepts on the day that he comforted me, and bid me nurse my philosophic beard, and return from the Fabrician bridge, no longer despondent. For after my bankruptcy I was going to throw myself with veiled head into the Tiber; then he, as my lucky genius, stood by me, and said: "Beware of doing anything unworthy of yourself; false shame," quoth he, "troubles you, who fear to be thought mad in the midst of madmen. For in the first place I will enquire what frenzy is; and if it shall be found in you alone, I will not say a word more to stop you from dying bravely."

43—63. *The Stoic dogma that all the world is mad except the Stoics; though madness assumes different and even opposite forms.*

Him, whom perverse folly and ignorance of the truth blind and hurry onward, the Stoic Porch and school pronounce insane. This definition comprises nations and mighty monarchs, all men, saving only the philosopher. Now hear, why men who have put on you the name of madman, are all as demented as you are. It is as in a forest, where men stray in every direction, their error takes them out of the right path; one wanders away to the left, another to the right; each is equally in error, but they are misled by different ways: so believe yourself to be insane only so far, that the man who laughs at you is quite as mad with his own tail hanging behind him. One set of fools fear when there is no danger, complaining that fire, rocks, rivers are in their way on a level plain; another set diverse from this, but not a whit more sensible, rush through fire and rivers; there shout to them affectionate mothers, respectable sisters, relations, fathers, wives: "Look out," they bawl, "here is a deep pit, here a huge rock." But they are as deaf, as was drunken Fufius once; he acted slumbering Ilione, and remained sound asleep, though two hundred thousand Catienuses shouted, "Mother, on you I call." Now I will prove to you that the mass of mankind are mad after a similar pattern.

64—76. *The extravagant man is insane; but it is a question, whether the money-lender is not equally so.*

Mad is Damasippus, the purchaser of old statues: sane, I suppose, is Damasippus' creditor; well, be it so: but if I say to you, "Accept some money that you need never return to me," are you mad, if you accept it, or would you not rather be so, if you refused the gain offered to you by propitious Mercury? Draw up ten obligations as strong as Nerius can draw them; if that is not enough, add a hundred after the model of Cicuta, that knotty man of the law, add a thousand bonds; yet from all will slip this scamp, this modern Proteus. When you drag him off to court, he will laugh immoderately, he will transform himself into a boar, bird, rock, or, if he pleases, a tree. A madman manages his affairs ill, a man in his senses well; then, believe me, Perillus is much more addle-pated, who gives you a security to sign, from which he can never recover the debt.

77—81. *The world is as one great asylum. There are four great classes of madmen.*

Attend and arrange your toga, all ye that are pale with the disease of perverse ambition, or avarice, of luxury, or gloomy superstition, or have any other fever of the mind: come near me all in order, and I will prove that you are mad, every one of you.

82—103. *The avaricious are as numerous a class as any, of whom Staberius was a notable instance, yet Aristippus his opposite was nearly as bad.*

By far the largest quantity of hellebore should be administered to misers; indeed, perhaps, sound reason would assign to them all the crops of Anticyra. The epitaph of Staberius was the sum total of his property: this his heirs had to engrave on his monument, being bound by the penalty of exhibiting to the people a hundred pairs of gladiators, and a banquet at the discretion of Arrius, and as much corn as the province of Africa reaps. "This is my will," wrote Staberius; "as to whether it is a perverse one or a right one, do not attempt to lecture me." Now, I suppose, this was a proof of the foresight of Staberius. For what was his meaning, when he directed his heirs to put on the stone of his grave the sum total of his property? This, surely, that all his life long he considered poverty a shocking vice, and guarded against nothing so carefully; if he had perchance died poorer by a single farthing, so much a worse man would he have thought himself; for all things, virtue, character, honour, things celestial and terrestrial alike, are the servants of fair wealth: and he who amasses it, he is illustrious, valiant, just. What, and wise too? Even so, and a king too, and whatever he has a fancy to be. This his wealth, earned by his virtue, he believed would redound to his glory. In no ways like him was the Greek, Aristippus, who bid his servants throw away his gold in the midst of Africa, because, forsooth, the weight of it delayed their journey. Which of the two is the greater madman? Nothing is proved by an instance which solves one hard case by another.

104—123. *The love of hoarding money is perfectly unreasonable, but so common that we do not see its utter folly.*

If a man were to buy up lyres, and store them together when bought, being a person without any taste for music or any accomplishment; if knives and lasts, he who was no shoemaker; sails, he who was set against a merchant's life; all would with reason pronounce such men crazy and demented. How differs from them the man who amasses golden coins, ignorant how to use his stores, fearing to touch them, as though it would be sacrilege? One stretched at full length watches by the side of a great heap of corn, continually, with a big club in his hand; he, the hungry owner of it all, does not dare to touch a single grain, and would rather eat bitter leaves, so stingy is he; in his cellar are casks of Chian and old Falernian, a thousand of them, nay, that is a mere nothing, three hundred thousand; and yet he drinks sour vinegar; see, he sleeps on straw, he, a man in his eightieth year, while coverlets, on which feast chafers and moths, lie spoiling in his chests: still, I suppose, few would count this miser insane, because a large majority of mankind are troubled with the same malady. That a son, or perhaps a freedman, may inherit and waste all this property, do you so guard it, you old dotard, Heaven's enemy? Is it that you dread want? Little will each day dock from your savings, if you begin to dip your cabbage in better oil, and to anoint your scurfy pate. Why, if almost anything is enough for you, do you perjure, steal, plunder from every where? Is a man like you sane?

128—141. *The madness of Orestes preceded, not followed, the murder of his mother.*

Supposing you were to take to killing with stones the public, and your own servants bought with your own money, all would cry out against you as a madman, boys and girls alike: when you strangle your wife, or poison your mother, are you sane? Why not? for you do not the deed at Argos, nor is it with the sword that you kill your mother, as did Orestes, who was mad. But now do you think that it was only after the murder of his mother that Orestes went mad? Was he not rather driven into frenzy by those wicked Furies, before he pierced his mother's throat with the reeking point of his sword? Nay, from the time that Orestes passed for being unsound of mind, he did nothing in any way to be condemned; he never dared wound with his sword either his friend Pylades, or his sister Electra; he merely abused both, calling one a Fury, the other some other name suggested by his magnificent anger.

142—157. *The story of Opimius, in whom the ruling passion was strong in death.*

Poor was Opimius, for all his stores of silver and gold; wine of Veii was his beverage on holidays out of a cup of Campanian earthenware, on working-days he drank wine turned sour; once he fell into a deep lethargy; and round about his coffers and locks his heir was running in extravagant joy. But he had a doctor very prompt and trusty, who roused him in the following way: he ordered a table to be set, on it to be poured sacks of coin, and sent for many to count the money; in this way he wakens up the dying man; then says to him: "Unless you guard your property, a greedy heir will presently carry it off." "What, in my lifetime?" says Opimius. "Be on your watch then, that you do not die; give your mind to this." "What would you have me to do?" says the sick man. "Your blood is poor, and your powers will fail you, unless a great stay from food supports your sinking stomach. Do you hesitate? Come now, take this little cup of rice-gruel." "What did it cost?" says he. "Oh! very little." "But how much?" "Eight pence." "Alas," says the sick man, "what odds, whether I die by disease, or by theft and robbery?"

158—167. *As in the body, so in the soul freedom from one evil does not imply freedom from all.*

Who then, after all, is sane? "He who is free from folly." What, as to the miser? "He is fool and madman." But if a man is not a miser, does it follow he is sane? "Certainly not." How so, Sir Stoic? "I will explain. 'The patient has no disease of the stomach,' imagine Craterus to be the speaker: 'is he therefore well, and may he get up?' 'No,' says that eminent physician; 'his ribs or his kidneys are attacked by acute disease.' So this man is not perjured, he is no mean miser: let him offer his pig to the propitious Lares: not so, for he is ambitious and rash; therefore let him take ship for Anticyra. It is all the same, whether you present all your substance to a greedy gulf, or never use your savings."

168—186. *Oppidius on his death-bed warned his two sons, each of an opposite folly.*

Servius Oppidius had two farms at Canusium, he was possessed of an ancestral fortune, and 'tis said that he divided them between his two sons, and on his death-bed gave them this advice: "I have observed you, Aulus, carrying carelessly in the folds of your toga your dice and walnuts, giving them away, throwing them about in play; you, Tiberius, gloomily counting them, hiding them in holes; I am greatly frightened, lest opposite kinds of madness should possess you; and one follow the steps of Nomentanus, the other of Cicuta. Wherefore I entreat you both by our household-gods, one not to lessen, the other not to increase the property your father thinks sufficient, and nature sets as a limit. Further, that vainglory may not tickle you, I will bind you both by this oath: whichever of you shall be elected an ædile or prætor, let him be as one outlawed, and accursed. Are you going to waste your substance on vetches, beans, and lupines, that with broad toga you may strut in the circus, or have a bronze statue set up to your honour, stripped of your lands, stripped of the money of your inheritance, you madman; that, forsooth, you may get the applause which Agrippa gets, like a cunning fox mimicking a noble lion."

187—223. *Ambition is madness, as is shown by the instance of Agamemnon, told in the form of a dialogue.*

"Son of Atreus, why do you forbid any one to think of burying Ajax?" "I am a king." "I ask no more, being but one of the common people." "And just also are my commands; but if I seem to any one unrighteous, I allow him with impunity to say what he thinks." "Mightiest of monarchs, may the gods grant to you to take Troy, and bring your fleet safe home! Am I really allowed to ask for an opinion, and give one in my turn?" "Yes, ask what you please." "Well then, I ask, why rots the body of Ajax, a hero second to Achilles alone, often the illustrious saviour of the Greeks, so that Priam and Priam's people rejoice at his having no burial, by whose valour so many of their youths lost a sepulchre in their native soil?" "Because in his madness he slaughtered a thousand sheep, crying out that he was killing renowned Ulysses, and Menelaus, and myself." "But you, when before the altar you place your darling daughter at Aulis in the stead of a heifer, and sprinkle her head with meal and salt, you wicked man, are you not deranged?" "How so, sirrah?" "Mad as he was, when he laid the cattle low with his sword, what did Ajax do? He did no violence to wife or son; he uttered many a curse on the Atridæ, but Teucer and even Ulysses he never injured." "But I, that I might start on their way the ships fastened to the unfriendly shore, knowing full what I did, appeased Heaven with blood." "Yes with your own blood, you raving madman." "My blood certainly, but no madman am I." "He who entertains imaginations opposed to truth, and bewildered by the confusion of crime, he will be considered insane, and, whether it be through folly or passion that he errs, it makes no difference. Ajax slew innocent lambs, and was insane; you, knowing what you were doing, committed a crime for vain renown, and are you in your senses, and is your mind, so swollen with ambition, free from fault? Supposing a man was fond of carrying about in a litter a pretty lamb, was to treat it as a daughter, provide for it dress, maids, gold, call it by endearing names, betroth it to a gallant gentleman; would not the prætor interfere, and take from him every legal right? And so the care of him would pass to his sane relations. And if one sacrifices a daughter as though she were a dumb lamb, is he in his senses? you cannot say he is. Thus, where there is depravity and folly, there is the very height of madness; the criminal is raving mad, and he who is dazzled by the glitter of glory, has thundering round him Bellona, goddess who delights in blood-stained votaries."

224—246. *Extravagance is a third form of insanity. The instances of Nomentanus, of Clodius, and the sons of Arrius.*

Come now, let us together attack extravagance, and extravagant Nomentanus: for right reason will demonstrate that spendthrifts are fools and madmen. No sooner had he inherited a thousand talents, than prætor-like he issues his decree for fishmonger, fruiterer, poulterer, perfumer, all the ungodly set of the Tuscan street, fowl-fattener, parasites, all the market, and all Velabrum, to come to his house next morning. Naturally, they came in crowds; the spokesman was the pander: "Whatever I have, whatever each of these have at home, is, believe us, at your service; send for it to-day or to-morrow." Now hear the reply of this considerate young man: "In Lucanian snows you sleep booted, that I may have a boar for dinner; you again sweep the stormy seas for fish. Idle man am I, unworthy of such possessions; take it; receive a million sesterces; you, three million, from whose house comes running your wife, when called at the dead of night." The son of Æsopus took from the ear of Metella a famous pearl, and with the idea, as I suppose, of swallowing a million sesterces in one gulp, diluted it in vinegar; how was he less mad than if he had thrown it into the rapid river or the sewer? The children of Quintus Arrius, a precious pair, twins in profligacy, in childish folly and depraved fancies used to lunch on nightingales, a most costly dish. How would you set them down? Would you mark them with white chalk or black charcoal?

247—280. *Love is as silly as any childish game, it is inconsistent, superstitious, doting, and often leads to crime.*

If a man with a beard found delight in building baby-houses, in yoking mice to a toy-cart, in playing at odd and even, in riding on a long stick, one would say that madness possessed him. But if right reason demonstrates that love is something still more childish, and that it makes no difference, whether you are busy with raising your toy-houses in the sand, as you did when three years old, or whether you maunder troubled with love, I demand of you, Will you do as Polemo did, when he became a changed man? Will you lay aside the livery of your mental malady, the bandages, cushions, neck-wrappers; as 'tis said that he, after his drinking bout, stealthily plucked the chaplets from his neck, as soon as he heard the reproving voice of his fasting tutor? You offer fruit to a sulky child: he refuses it; you say "Take it, darling:" he says he will not: if you do not offer it, he longs for it: how differs from the child the lover, when the door is shut in his face, and he deliberates, shall he go or not, and yet is sure to return, even if not sent for, and hates the doors, and yet cannot tear himself from them? "What, shall I not go, now that she makes the advances? Or rather, shall I not resolve to put an end to my pains? She has turned me out of the house: now she calls me back: shall I return? No, not if she entreats me." Now hear what says the slave, a deal wiser than his master: "Sir, things without method and sense cannot be dealt with on any system or method. Such is the evil nature of love; it means war, then peace: it is as changeable as the weather, it floats as if by blind chance; and if any one tries to make it regular in his own case, he will manage about as well as if he were to endeavour to be mad on a regular system and method." What! you pick out the pips of Picenian fruit, and rejoice, if you happen to hit the ceiling with them; are you in your senses? On your old palate you strike out lisping words: are you less silly than the child that builds card-houses? Add blood to folly, and stir up the fire with a sword. To take a late instance, Marius stabbed Hellas, and then threw himself down; was he not a lunatic? or would you acquit the man of madness, to find him guilty of a crime, applying, according to usage, cognate terms to things?

281—299. *Superstition is a fourth kind of madness.*

There was a freedman, he was old and sober, in the morning he would wash his hands, then would run to the places where streets meet, and there would he pray, "Deliver me, yes, me alone from death: what so much to ask? 'Tis a light thing for the gods to do:" the man was sound in both his ears and eyes; but if he were a slave in the slave-market, his master, unless fond of a lawsuit, would not have warranted his reason. Now Chrysippus places this class also in the house of Menenius so fruitful in madmen. "Thou, Jove, givest great pains of body, then takest them away;" so says the mother of a boy who has been ill in bed for five long months, "If the chilly quartan ague leaves my child on the morning of the day of thy appointed feast, naked shall he stand in Tiber's stream." Good luck or the doctor raises the sick boy from imminent danger; but the crazy mother will be the murderer of her child, by sticking him up on the cold bank, and so bringing back the fever. Now with what malady is her mind disordered? With superstition. These were the arms which my friend Stertinius, the eighth wise man, put in my hands; hereafter no one can call me madman with impunity, for he who so names me, shall hear as much in reply, and shall be told to look behind on what hangs from his own back, though he sees it not.

300—326. *Dialogue between Horace and Damasippus, in which Horace playfully alludes to his own foibles, his airs, his poetry, his hot temper, his many loves.*

HORACE.

Sir Stoic, enlighten me, and so may you after your losses sell all your property at an advantage! Since there are so many kinds of folly, what is my particular one? To myself I seem sane.

DAMASIPPUS.

No wonder: when mad Agave was carrying the head of her unhappy son torn from the trunk, did she think herself mad?

HORACE.

Well, I confess my folly; one must needs yield to the force of truth; I allow that I am mad; only do you declare to me, what you consider to be my besetting malady.

DAMASIPPUS.

Hear: in the first place you are building, which means that you imitate the tall, you, a man who from top to toe measure about two feet; and yet you laugh at the airs and gait of Turbo in his armour, a man with a soul too big for his body: how are you less ridiculous than he? Is it right that you should do all that Mæcenas does, you who are so unlike him, and so inferior in a rivalry with so great a man? A frog was absent when its young ones were crushed by the foot of a calf; one only escaped, and told its mother the whole tale, how a huge beast had squeezed to death its brothers and sisters. The parent asked "How big was the monster?" Puffing herself out she said, "Could it have been as big as this?" "Bigger by half," said the young one. "What, as big as this?" said the old one. As she kept puffing herself more and more, the young one said, "If you burst yourself you will never be as big." Now this little simile suits you very well. To this add your poetry, which is as if one said, "Throw oil on fire:" if any man is in his senses who composes poetry, then you are. I say nothing of your dreadful temper.

HORACE.

Enough, stop.

DAMASIPPUS.

Or your style beyond your means.

HORACE.

Damasippus, mind your own business.

DAMASIPPUS.

Or your thousand ravings for a thousand loves.

HORACE.

O greater madman, be merciful at last to your inferior in madness!

IV.

1—11. *An ironical glorification of the precepts of gastronomy, which are as follows.*

HORACE.

Whence and whither, Catius?

CATIUS.

I have no time to stop, being eager to commit to memory by my method precepts which throw into the shade those of Pythagoras, and of him whom Anytus prosecuted, and of learned Plato.

HORACE.

I confess my fault in interrupting you at such an unlucky moment; but kindly pardon me, I pray. If anything slips your memory, you will presently recover it; be this a gift of nature, or the result of art, anyhow you are admirable.

CATIUS.

Nay, this was what I was thinking of, how to retain all the points, the subject being so delicate, and expressed so delicately.

HORACE.

Tell me the name of the author. Was he a Roman or a foreigner?

CATIUS.

I will myself repeat to you the precepts, but must withhold the name of the author.

12—34. *Precepts touching eggs, cabbages, mushrooms, mead, shell-fish, and other points.*

Remember to put on your table eggs of a tapering shape, as having more taste, and whiter than round ones; being thick too, they contain the yolk of a male chicken. Cabbages grown in dry soil are sweeter than those that come from the market grounds near Rome; nothing is more insipid than the produce of a wet garden. If suddenly in the evening a friend looks in upon you, to prevent the hen just killed from being tough, I advise you to dip it still alive into mead made of Falernian wine; so will it be tender. The best sort of mushrooms are those gathered from meadows; others one can ill trust. That man will pass his summers in health, who ends his morning meal with black mulberries picked from the tree before the sun is oppressive. Aufidius had a way of making his mead of strong Falernian; it was a great fault, because nothing but what is mild should be put into the empty stomach; mild should be the mead with which the stomach is washed. If your sluggish bowels refuse to act, limpet and common shell-fish will remove the obstacle, or the low-growing herb of sorrel with a cup of white Coan wine. With increasing moons increase the slippery shell-fish; but every sea does not produce the finest sort. The peloris of the Lucrine lake is better than the murex of Baiæ, oyster-beds are at Circeii, from Misenum come sea-urchins: the broad scallop is the glory of luxurious Tarentum.

35—62. *More precepts about dinners, wines, and other points. Money will not do every thing. The excellence of the art tested by its power of provoking appetite.*

Let no ordinary man lightly take to himself the science of dinner-parties, unless he has first duly considered the delicate question of taste. For it is not enough to have cleared the fishmonger's board at a great cost, unless one knows which fish should be done in sauce, and which, when fried, will tempt the sated guest to raise himself on his elbow. An Umbrian boar fed on holm-oak acorns weighs down the dishes of the host who eschews insipid meat; as to the Laurentian, he is a bad beast, fattened on sedge and reeds. Roes reared in a vineyard are not always eatable. The professed epicure chooses the wings of a hare fruitful in young. Touching the nature and proper age of fish and birds, no palate before mine had considered and revealed the truth. Some men's genius is poor, only equal to the invention of new pastry. But it is by no means enough to spend all one's care on a single point; as if one only tried to give good wine, and then were indifferent as to the oil in which the fish was dressed. Expose Massic wine to a cloudless sky; all the thickness in it will be cleared away by the night air, and the bouquet that affects the brain will pass off; the same wine strained through linen will lose its full flavour. He who skilfully mixes wine of Surrentum with the dregs of Falernian, thoroughly collects the sediment with a pigeon's egg, for the yolk sinks to the bottom, carrying with it all foreign substances. To the drinker, if he flags, give fresh spirit by fried prawns and African snails: lettuce rises on the acid stomach after wine; more and more by ham and sausages does it crave to be stimulated and restored; nay, prefers any thing brought smoking-hot from dirty eating-houses.

63—75. *The rules about sauce; directions about the fruit.*

It is worth while thoroughly to master the qualities of compound sauce. The simple consists of sweet olive oil; this ought to be mixed with rich wine, and with the same pickle of which the Byzantine jar smells so strongly. When this has been made to boil with a mixture of chopped herbs, and has stood to cool, after Cilician saffron has been sprinkled over it; then do you add besides the oil of the pressed berry of the olive of Venafrum. The fruit of Tibur is inferior in juice to that of Picenum, but superior in appearance. The grape of Venucula is good for preserving in jars; the Alban is best when thoroughly smoked. On enquiry, you will find that I the first of all men placed round the table on clean dishes this kind of grape together with apples, lees, and fish-pickle, white pepper sprinkled through a sieve, and black salt.

76—87. *Little things make all the difference in a dinner.*

It is a monstrous sin, after you have spent three thousand sesterces at the market, then to cramp the fish, that once swam freely through the sea, in a narrow dish. It gives quite a turn to the stomach, if a servant, after licking the stolen bits, soils the cup with his greasy hands, or if nasty dirt sticks to an ancient goblet. On common brooms, napkins, sawdust, how little need be spent! But if these things be neglected, scandalous is the crime. What! will you sweep tesselated pavement with a dirty palm-broom, and put unwashed coverlets over cushions bright with Tyrian dye? Do you forget that as such details need less care and expense, so to neglect them is more culpable, than to omit such luxuries as are granted to the tables of the rich alone?

88—95. *Horace implores Catius to take him with him to the next lectures.*

HORACE.

Learned Catius, in the name of Heaven and of our friendship, remember to take me with you, whenever you go to such lectures. Strong is your memory, and accurately you repeat all; and yet as a mere reporter you cannot give me so much delight. There is too the look and bearing of the great man; blest were you in the sight of him, yet for that very reason you prize it not to the worth: but I feel no slight desire to approach the hidden sources, and to quaff draughts of the wisdom of such a blessed life.

V.

1—8. *Opening dialogue between Ulysses and Teiresias.*

ULYSSES.

Answer me still another question, Teiresias, besides all you have told me. By what ways and means can I repair my broken fortunes? You laugh: why so?

TEIRESIAS.

What! you man of wiles, are you not content with the promise of a return to Ithaca, and of a sight of your household gods?

ULYSSES.

O seer, that ne'er did lie to mortal man, you see how I am to return home, according to your prophecy, naked and needy, and to find there neither my store-room of wine, nor my flock untouched by the suitors; and well you know that without money both birth and virtue are as worthless as sea-weed.

9—22. *Ulysses, says the seer, must make up his mind to be a fortune-hunter, or poor he will remain.*

TEIRESIAS.

Since, coming straight to the point, you say that your dread is poverty, hear by what method you can become rich. A thrush, we will suppose, or some other delicacy comes as a present to you; let the bird wing its way to some rich and splendid house, where the master is old: or your well-cultivated farm bears sweet fruit, or other produce meet for offerings; even before the household god let the rich man enjoy this, the rich man deserves your veneration most. Now, be he ever so perjured, ever so low-born, stained with a brother's blood, nay a runaway slave, for all that, if walking with him at his request, never decline to give him the inside.

ULYSSES.

Do you mean that I am to give the wall to that filthy Dama? Not so at Troy did I bear myself, but ever vied with better men than myself.

TEIRESIAS.

Ah well, you will be a poor man.

ULYSSES.

I'll bid my stalwart soul endure e'en this. Already worse I've borne. Continue then, and tell me whence I may draw wealth and stores of brass.

23—44. *The arts of the fortune-hunter, who will support the rich in their lawsuits, and to curry favour with them will endure any toil and indignity.*

TEIRESIAS.

Well, I have told you, and again I tell you; everywhere craftily fish for legacies from old gentlemen; perhaps one or two shrewd ones will nibble the bait off the hook, and then escape from your snares, but do not you give up hope, or abandon your art, because once baffled. If on any occasion there is a lawsuit in the forum, of greater or less importance, do you see whether one of the two be rich and childless, and though he be a rascal, who with wanton audacity brings an action against a better man, yet do you be the advocate of the scoundrel, making no account of the opponent, however superior in character and the justice of his cause, if he has a son at home, or a fruitful wife. Address the rich man, "Quintus" for instance, or "Publius," (the prænomen tickles the delicate ear,) "your merit has attached me to you; I know the quibbles of law; I can defend a cause; I would let any one put out my own eyes rather than slight you, or rob you of a rotten nut; my chief care is that you should not lose a farthing, or be the laughingstock of any man." So bid him go home, and take care of his dear self; do you become his pleader. Endure still and persevere, whether the flaming red dog-star is splitting the mute statues, or Furius, distended with rich tripe, spits hoary snow all over the wintry Alps. Then will some one nudge another standing near with his elbow, and say: "Do you not see how untiring he is, how useful to his friends, how keen in their service?" So will more tunnies swim up, and your fishpools be better stocked.

45—57. *Observe when a rich man's only child is sickly. Be careful not to overdo your trade.*

If any one's son, the heir of his great fortune, be in poor health, lest transparent attentions to a bachelor or widower betray you, do you creep gently by assiduous court into the hope of being put in the will as heir in remainder, and should any chance remove the child to the regions below, of taking the vacant place: this game seldom disappoints. Perhaps the will is handed to you to read, forget not to decline this, and to push it aside, yet so as by side-glance to catch the contents of the second line of the first page; swiftly run your eye across to see whether you are sole heir or coheir with many. Often will a shrewd man, once a quinquevir, now recast as a notary, baffle the gaping crow, and the fortune-hunter Nasica will be the laughingstock of Coranus.

58—83. *The story of Nasica. The legacy-hunter must be prepared to flatter and oblige his rich friend.*

ULYSSES.

Are you frenzied, or purposely do you mock me with obscure prophecies?

TEIRESIAS.

O son of Laertes, whatsoever I say will happen, or it will not: divination is a gift to me from great Apollo.

ULYSSES.

However, declare the meaning of the story just alluded to, if it is lawful so to do.

TEIRESIAS.

In the days when shall live the young hero, the terror of Parthia, a child of the race of the noble Æneas, and shall be mighty by land and sea, the gallant Coranus shall marry the tall daughter of Nasica, a man who will object to pay in full. Then the son-in-law will act thus; he will hand his father-in-law the will, and beg him to read it: Nasica will often decline, but at last will take it, and read it by himself, and will then find for himself and his family a legacy of disappointment and grief. I have this further advice to give you; perhaps an artful woman or a freedman manages the old dotard, do you make common cause with him or her; praise them, so will you be praised yourself when absent. This helps, no doubt, but it is far the best to take by storm the citadel in the person of the old man himself. If he writes wretched verses, as madmen often do, you must praise them. If he is a libertine, do not wait for his demands, but, before he asks, obligingly hand over Penelope to your better.

ULYSSES.

What say you? do you think Penelope could be induced, that good and virtuous lady, whom the suitors could not tempt to leave the paths of rectitude?

TEIRESIAS.

Ah, well; but this was because those young gentlemen, who visited your house, did not like giving, their minds were set on eating more than on love; in these circumstances Penelope was virtuous, no doubt; but let her once get the taste of gain in partnership with you from one old rich man, she will be like the hound, which nothing can drive from the greased hide.

84—98. *The story of the old lady at Thebes. Caution is needed for the fortune-hunter. He must persevere even to the end.*

I will tell you what happened when I was an old man. There was at Thebes a roguish old woman: she, according to directions in her will, was buried as follows: her body was anointed with plenty of oil, and her heir had to carry it on his bare shoulders; this was to see whether she could slip out of his hands after her death: no doubt, because he never let her go during her lifetime. You must be wary in your approaches, neither deficient in attentions, nor excessive beyond measure. The peevish and morose are offended by one obtrusively garrulous: but then neither will silence do. You must be the Davus of the play, standing with head bent forward, much like one struck with awe. Make your advances most obsequiously; if the breeze freshens, warn him, "Be careful, sir, cover your precious head;" get him out of a crowd by pushing for him; lend your ear to his babbling. Or if he is ridiculously fond of praise, then until he shall lift up his hands to heaven, and say, "Hold, enough," do you with praises press him, and fill his swelling vanity with empty words, as skin with air.

99—110. *After your success, still keep up appearances, and look out for fresh windfalls.*

And now his death relieves you from your long attention and servitude, and wide awake you hear read: "I bequeath to Ulysses a fourth part:" then do you drop in such words as these: "And is my old comrade Dama really gone? Ah, where shall I find so true, so honest a friend?" If you can manage it, shed a tear or two: the countenance betrays joy, but do you disguise it. If the monument is left to your discretion, be liberal in the raising of it; let the neighbourhood praise the handsome funeral. Perhaps one of your coheirs is elderly and has a bad cough, then say to him, that if he would like to be a purchaser of a farm or house in your share, you would gladly convey it to him for a nominal consideration. But me imperious Proserpine drags away; farewell and live prosperous.

VI.

1—15. *Horace's contentment; his prayer to Heaven.*

Often did I pray that I had a piece of land, not so very large, with a garden, and near the house a perennial spring of water, and a little wood besides. Heaven has done more and better for me than my wishes. It is well; son of Maia, I ask nothing further, save that thou wilt continue to me these blessings. I trust that I have not increased my property by any evil arts, and that I am not going to diminish it by vice, or negligence: I offer no such foolish prayers as these; "O would that mine were the corner, which now spoils the shape of my little farm!" or, "Would that some lucky chance would discover for me a pot of money, as once to him, who was a tenant-farmer, and, finding a treasure, bought the very farm which he had tilled, for Hercules proved a friend and enriched him!" I trust what I have makes me thankful and content; if this be so, then thus I pray, "O make for me, Heaven, my cattle fat, and all I have heavy, except my wit, and as thou usest to be, still be my best guardian."

16—39. *The happiness of his placid life in the country contrasted with his troubles and plagues at Rome.*

So when I have retreated from the city into the mountains, and my country citadel, shall not my retirement be the favourite subject of my satires, and of my prosaic muse? There evil ambition cannot hurt me, nor the leaden sirocco, nor unhealthy autumn, that brings gain to Death by the funerals of the young. Thou father of the dawn, or Janus, if so thou hadst rather be addressed, from whom is the beginning to mortals of work and toils of life, for such is Heaven's will, do thou be the first subject of my song. At Rome I am hurried away by thee to be security. Bestir yourself, thou sayest to me, lest another do his duty to a friend before you. So let the North wind sweep the earth, let winter whirl the snowy day in shorter circle, go I must. There must I speak in clear and distinct voice words for which I may have afterwards to smart, and then I have to push through the crowd, and hurt those who get in my way. With bitter curses angrily plies me some one: "Madman, what do you want, what mean you that you so strike all that stop you, as you hasten back to Mæcenas with something on your mind?" Now that this is my delight, yea, and as honey to me, I deny not. And yet, as soon as I get to the Esquiline hill, once the abode of gloom, other peoples' affairs jump round my head and side in hundreds. "Remember that Roscius entreated you to be at the Puteal before eight in the morning to-morrow, to be a witness for him." "The notaries begged you, Quintus, not to forget to return to-day touching that fresh and important matter of common interest." "Manage to get Mæcenas to set his seal to that document." If I say, I will try my best, then he says urgently, "You can, if you please."

40—58. *Horace describes his intimacy with Maecenas, and the envy and idle curiosity of others.*

Seven years and more have flown, 'tis nearly eight, since Mæcenas first chose me for one of his friends, just that he might have some one to take in his carriage on a journey, to whom he might confide such trifles as these: "What o'clock is it? Is the Thracian Gallina a match for Syrus? If people are not careful, now begins the cold morning air to nip them:" and other remarks safely to be trusted to a leaky ear. Meantime our friend is more and more exposed to envy every day and hour. "Why, he went to the public spectacles with Mæcenas; he played at ball with him in the Plain of Mars; a child of fortune," all exclaim. There flies a chilling report from the Rostra through the streets: every man that meets me, consults me: "My good friend, you must needs know, for you have access to the great, is there any news about the Dacians?" "Oh I, I know nothing." "How you ever love to jest!" "But may all the gods trouble me, if I know anything." "What, does Cæsar mean to give the estates he promised to the veterans in Sicily or on Italian soil?" When I swear I know nothing, they are amazed, and think me without doubt the very closest and most taciturn of all mortals.

59—76. *Horace longs for the country, his quiet evenings, and cheerful dinners with his friends, and conversations not without profit.*

In such things as these my day is lost, while I keep wishing to myself thus: "O country, when shall I behold you, and when will it be granted to me, at one time reading the writings of the ancients, at another taking my siesta, and spending my hours in indolence, to quaff at my ease the sweet forgetfulness of anxious life? O when shall beans, the relations of Pythagoras, and other vegetables made savoury with fat bacon, be served on my table? O feasts and nights divine, when I and my friends dine before my own Lar, when I give to the saucy household-slaves the dishes I have first tasted!" Each guest follows his own fancy; for there the guests are free from unreasonable laws, and different is the strength of the cups, according as one is able to bear stronger wine, or prefers to grow mellow with draughts of moderate strength. So then we begin to talk, not of our neighbours' villas and houses, nor whether Lepos dances well or ill: but we discuss what concerns us nearer, and it is evil to be ignorant of; as, "Are men made happy through riches or virtue?" "What attracts us to friendship, interest or probity?" "What is the nature of the chief good?"

77—117. *The fable of the two mice.*

Between-whiles my neighbour Cervius pleasantly tells us old tales bearing on the case in hand. For instance, if any one ignorantly praises the wealth of Arellius which brings him so much care, thus my friend begins: "Once on a time (so runs the tale) a country-mouse received a town-mouse in his poor little hole, hospitably welcoming his old friend. Rough was the country-mouse, and attentive to his gains, and yet could open his close soul to hospitality. To be short, he grudged neither his hoarded chick-pea, nor his long oats, and, carrying in his mouth raisins, and half-eaten bits of bacon, strove by the variety of the food to overcome the daintiness of his guest, who hardly deigned to touch each piece with squeamish tooth: whilst the master of the house, stretched on this year's straw, was eating spelt and darnel, leaving for his friend the best of the feast. At length says the city-mouse, 'Why, my friend, are you content to live so patiently on the slope of a hanging wood? How can you prefer the wild country to the city and the world? Take my advice, and set out at once, since all earthly creatures have mortal souls, and neither high nor low escape death; wherefore, my good friend, enjoy yourself in pleasure, and forget not the shortness of life.' With such words was roused the rustic, and lightly he jumps out of his hole; then both perform their intended journey, wishing to creep under the walls of the city at night. And now night held the heaven's middle space, when the two mice set foot within a wealthy mansion, where covers dyed in scarlet looked bright on ivory couches, and many viands remained from yesterday's great dinner-party, in piled-up baskets hard by. There lay at ease on purple covers the rustic, while up and down runs his active host, bringing up one dish after another, and exactly performs the duties of a servant, tasting first all he offers his guest. The other, reclining, enjoys his improved fortunes, and amid the good cheer is a happy visitor, when suddenly a terrible noise of opening doors drives both the mice from their seats. Frightened they both ran through the dining-room, and still more were they terrified out of their wits, when the lofty house resounded with the barking of mastiffs. Then said the country-mouse: 'I have no taste for a life of this kind, so good bye; my wood and hole by its safety from danger will content me with humble vetches.'"

VII.

1—20. *Dialogue during the Saturnalia between Horace and his slave Davus, who gives instances of the inconsistency of mankind.*

DAVUS.

I have been listening to all your remarks, and desire to say a little to you, but, being only a slave, do not venture.

HORACE.

Is it Davus?

DAVUS.

Yes, Davus, a servant attached to his master, and tolerably honest, yet not such a paragon as to be likely to die soon.

HORACE.

Come, use the freedom of the month of December, sanctioned by our ancestors. Tell your tale.

DAVUS.

Some men are consistent in the love of their vices, and follow out their purposes; but many more waver between the pursuit of right and their inclination to depravity. Thus Priscus, for instance, was observed frequently wearing three rings, then again he had not one on his left hand: he lived inconsistently, changing the stripe of his tunic every hour; he would walk out of a noble house, and then suddenly hide himself in a place, from which a decent freedman could hardly be seen coming out without losing his character; sometimes he lived a profligate life at Rome; then he would be a scholar at Athens; all the Vertumni one can imagine must have been angry on his birthday. The opposite was Volanerius the buffoon; a richly-deserved gout crippled the joints of his hands; so he paid a boy every day to put into and take out of the box the dice; at any rate he was consistent in vice, and, so far, less wretched and a better man than the other, who was as one pulling uneasily sometimes with a tight, sometimes with a loose cord.

21—45. *Davus applies this to his master Horace, the most inconsistent of mortals.*

HORACE.

Tell me at once, you rogue, the point of this wretched stuff.

DAVUS.

It applies to yourself.

HORACE.

How so, you rascal?

DAVUS.

Why, you praise the condition and habits of our people of olden days, and yet, if some god were suddenly to take you back to the days gone by, you would obstinately refuse, either because you do not really believe in the truth of your confident assertions, or else because you are unstable in your defence of what is right, for you are like a man sticking in the mire, vainly wishing to pluck his foot out. At Rome you pine for the country, in the country you glorify the distant city, you fickle creature. If it so happens that no one invites you to dinner, then you praise your quiet dish of herbs, as though you were carried to dinner parties bound hand and foot, and bless yourself, and hug yourself in your happiness, because, forsooth, you have not to go out anywhere to dinner. But let Mæcenas invite you late in the evening, when the lamps are just lighted, then loud are your shouts and bawling, and you are frantic: "Make haste, bring the oil; are you all deaf?" and off you go. Mulvius and the other parasites depart cursing you with curses we must not repeat. One of them says perhaps: "I do not deny that I am easily led by my stomach, I snuff a savoury smell; weak am I and lazy; if you please, a glutton too. You being such a one as I, nay, perhaps more worthless, yet wantonly attack me, as though you were a better man, and disguise your vices under a cloak of fine names." What, are you not found to be a greater fool than I, whose price was five hundred drachmas? Remove the terrors of your countenance, restrain your angry hand, while I deliver the lessons taught me by the porter of Crispinus.

46—82. *The porter's lecture to show that real slavery consists not in the outward state of life, but in the condition of the will.*

Your neighbour's wife has charms for you; a low courtesan for Davus: which of us commits a sin that most deserves the cross? When you have cast aside your badges, and the ring you wear as a knight, and your Roman citizen's dress, and come forth transformed from a judge into a common slave, with a cloak disguising your perfumed head, are you not what you pretend to be? Full of fear you are let into the house, and you tremble in your very heart in alternate fits of terror and lust. What matters it, whither you go away, surrendered to be branded, to be slain with rods and with the sword, or whether, shut up shamefully in a chest, you touch with your knees your crouching head? Has not the husband of the offending matron a rightful power over both? Over the seducer a power still more rightful. Although too the woman is afraid of you, and does not trust her lover, you with your eyes open will pass beneath the yoke, and hand over to a furious master all your property, and your life, and body, and character.

Well, you have escaped: so, I suppose, you will fear for the future, and having had a warning, will be careful: not so: you are looking out for fresh opportunities of terror and ruin, a slave not once, but often. Yet what wild beast, having burst its bonds and escaped, perversely returns to them again? You say, "I am no adulterer." Very likely; but neither am I a thief, when wisely I keep my hands off your plate. Remove danger, take away restraint; then forward nature springs, as free to err. A pretty master, you, to be over me, you, a slave to the lordship of so many men and things; three or four times the prætor's rod may touch you, but this never frees you from your wretched fears. Add another remark more of no less weight; for whether the slave of a slave is called a substitute, as your custom names him, or a fellow-slave, what am I to be called in respect of you? Why, you, my master, are the wretched slave of others, pulled about by your passions, as a puppet is by strings which another jerks.

83—89. *The wise man alone is free.*

Who then is free? He who is wise, over himself true lord, unterrified by want and death and bonds, who can his passions stem, and glory scorn: in himself complete, like a sphere, perfectly round; so that no external object can rest on the polished surface: against such a one Fortune's assault is broken.

89—101. *Love is one kind of slavery; the insane admiration of the fine arts is another.*

Now can you recognise any of these marks as belonging to you? A sweetheart demands of you five talents, insults you, shuts the door in your face, throws cold water over you; then calls you back. Now loose your neck from the shameful yoke; come say, "I am free, yes, free." You cannot; for your soul is troubled by no gentle master, and sharp are the spurs which prick your weary spirit, and on you are driven, though you would fain refuse. Or again, when you stand amazed at a picture by Pausias, how are you less in error than I, the admirer of the battles of Fulvius, Rutuba, and Placideianus, drawn with stiffly-stretched leg, scenes painted with red chalk or charcoal, as true to life as if the men brandishing their weapons were really fighting, striking, parrying? Knave and loiterer are Davus' names then: you, sir, are styled a nice and experienced connoisseur of antiques.

102—118. *The glutton is a slave, and will suffer for his gluttony, be he who he may: slaves are all who cannot bear their own society; these things apply to Horace himself.*

I am worthless, if attracted by a smoking cake: does your wonderful virtue and temperance resist the temptation of a rich dinner? Compliance with my stomach's craving proves more fatal to me: why so? because my back pays for it: but will you escape punishment, if you seek for dainties which cannot be cheaply got? No: for bitter turn luxuries indulged in without restraint, and your staggering feet refuse to support your diseased body. Is the slave a sinner, who at nightfall exchanges a stolen body-scraper for a bunch of grapes; and is there nothing servile in him, who, in obedience to his belly, parts with his estates? Again, you cannot bear to be alone for an hour, nor can you employ your leisure time aright; you avoid yourself, like a runaway and truant slave, while you strive, now with wine, now with sleep, to baffle Care. In vain; for the gloomy partner pursues and follows your flight.

HORACE.

Where can I find a stone?

DAVUS.

What for?

HORACE.

Where can I find some arrows?

DAVUS.

The man is mad, or else he is writing verses.

HORACE.

Unless you are off in a minute, you shall join the eight labourers on my Sabine farm.

VIII.

1—17. *The description of a dinner-party given by Nasidienus, a man remarkable for his wealth and vanity.*

HORACE.

How did you enjoy yourself at the dinner of Nasidienus the wealthy? For when I sent to invite you, I was told you went there to dine early in the afternoon.

FUNDANIUS.

So much, that I never spent a pleasanter evening in my life.

HORACE.

Tell me, if you do not object, what dish first appeased the anger of your appetite.

FUNDANIUS.

First was served a Lucanian boar, caught while the soft South wind blew, as the father of the feast assured us; it was garnished with pungent rapes, lettuces, radishes, all things suited to rouse the sated stomach, skirret, fish-pickle, lees of Coan wine. Then, on the removal of this course, a servant with loins girded began to wipe the maple table with a purple napkin, while another cleared away all that ought to be removed, as likely to offend the company: next in walks a dusky slave, Hydaspes, as solemnly as an Athenian maiden carrying the sacred basket of Ceres; he brought Cæcuban wine; Alcon, another servant, brought home-made Chian. Then said the master: "If you, Mæcenas, prefer Alban or Falernian to those on the table, we have both."

18—33. *The names and places of the company on the triclinium.*

HORACE.

Oh the miseries of wealth! But now I am anxious to know, who were the company with whom you, Fundanius, were so happy?

FUNDANIUS.

On the highest couch I reclined, and next to me Viscus of Thurii, and beyond him, if I remember right, Varius; in the middle row was Mæcenas, with Servilius Balatro and Vibidius, the friends he had introduced; on the lowest couch was the master of the feast, with Nomentanus above, Porcius below him; Porcius amused us by swallowing whole cakes at a mouthful; Nomentanus' duty was to point out with his forefinger any delicacy that might have been overlooked; for as to the rest of us, not such connoisseurs, we dined on birds, shell and other fish, which had a lurking flavour quite unlike the usual taste: as appeared directly, when he handed me the livers of a plaice and turbot, such as I had never tasted before. Then he instructed me how that honey-apples are more rosy, if picked when the moon wanes; what difference this makes, he can tell you better than I can.

33—41. *The account of the drinking.*

Then said Vibidius to Balatro: "Unless we drink ruinously, we shall die unavenged:" and he calls for larger cups. Pale turned the face of our host, for there was nothing he dreaded so much as hard drinkers, either because they do not restrain their tongues, or because strong wines make dull the delicacy of the taste. Vibidius and Balatro emptied into their large cups whole bowls of wine; all followed their lead, except the two guests on the lowest couch; they spared the flagons.

42—53. *The continuation of the dinner. Nasidienus explains various points, important for giving a good dinner.*

Then is brought in a sea-eel; its full length was seen on the dish, round it were the prawns swimming in sauce. Upon this spoke the master of the feast: "The fish was caught before it spawned; if taken later, it would have been less delicate. These fish are dressed in sauce, made of oil from the very best press of Venafrum; of pickle from the Spanish mackerel; of wine five years old, this must be Italian wine, and put in while it is being boiled; for after it has stood to cool, Chian wine suits it best of all; forget not white pepper and vinegar made of Lesbian wine when turned sour. I first taught men to boil in this sauce green rockets and bitter elecampane; but Curtillus bid them boil sea-urchins not washed in fresh water, as superior to the pickle which the shell-fish yields."

54—78. *The falling of the tapestry. The sorrow of the host, and the sarcasm of Balatro, mistaken by Nasidienus for a compliment.*

While thus he lectured, the hanging tapestry fell heavily on the dish, bringing down more dirty dust than the North wind raises on the fields of Campania. We fear some grave disaster; but finding there is no danger, recover our spirits. Rufus buried his head, and wept, as though his son had been cut off by an early death. When he would have stopped no one knows, had not philosophic Nomentanus thus comforted his friend: "Alas, O Fortune, what god is more cruel towards us than thou? How sad is it that thou ever delightest to mock the fortunes of man!" As to Varius, he could hardly hide his laughter with his napkin: while Balatro, sneering at everything, said: "Such is the condition of our life; thus never will your industry meet with the fitting meed of glory. That I forsooth may dine sumptuously, are you to be tortured and distracted with sundry cares, lest the bread be burnt, or sauce served up with the wrong seasoning, or your servants wait ill-girt and untidy? Then there are the misfortunes of the tapestry falling, as just now, of a groom stumbling and breaking a dish. But a host is like a general; prosperity hides his genius, adversity best discovers it." Nasidienus said to this: "May Heaven grant you every blessing you desire! So kind a man are you, so courteous a guest." Which said, he calls for his slippers. Then on each couch you might have heard the sound of separate whispers buzzing in each ear.

79—95. *The renewed energy of the host. He bores his guests; their cruel vengeance.*

HORACE.

Why, I should have preferred this to any play: but please tell me what next gave you cause for laughter.

FUNDANIUS.

Vibidius asked the servants, whether the flagon also is broken, since he calls for cups, and none are brought; we laugh for various pretences, whilst Balatro supplies the jokes: then, you return, O Nasidienus, with countenance quite cheery, as one who meant to mend his fortune by his skill: him followed servants bearing on mighty dish crane already cut up, and plentifully sprinkled with salt, and meal besides; also the liver of a white goose fattened on rich figs, and hares' wings torn off and served by themselves; "For thus," said he, "they are a much greater delicacy than if you eat them with the loins:" next we beheld placed on the table blackbirds with their breasts browned, and pigeons without their hinder parts. All these were delicacies; but the master of the feast would tell us the history of their natures and qualities; and we escaped from him, and our vengeance was not to taste a bit of them, just as if Canidia had tainted them with breath more venomous than that of the serpents of Africa.

INTRODUCTION TO THE EPISTLES.

HORACE'S Epistles may be said to be a continuation of his Satires in the form of letters. As many of the Satires contain little that can be called satirical in the modern sense of the word, so too but few of the Epistles are letters except in form. They do indeed comprise one excellent specimen of a letter of introduction, the ninth of the first Book; one, the fourteenth of the same Book, is a piece of playful banter; the third, fourth, and fifth are in the light style of friendly correspondence; while the twentieth, which is inscribed "To his Book," forms a sort of epilogue to the Epistles he had then written; but, as a rule, they are compositions like those which Pope, following the manner of Horace, has made familiar to us as Moral Essays.

In the first of all these Epistles, which possesses many points in common with most of its successors in the same Book, Horace begs his friend Mæcenas not to press him to write more odes, since he has abandoned poetry now that he is growing old, and means to devote himself entirely to the study of philosophy. For, compared with the Odes, Horace does not look upon the Epistles as poetry at all; just as he had spoken of "the prosaic Muse" of satire. The rhythm of the Epistles is, however, considerably more harmonious than that of the Satires, and the thoughts are generally expressed in a more poetical style. Though the writer does not affect to aim at anything like the grandeur and varied music of the Epic hexameter, or of such a poem as the Georgics, yet there is a mellowness and evenness in the flow of the verse, which accords well with the more sedate manner of the poet as he is now advancing in years, and with the terseness and felicity of the form in which he conveys his thoughts.

The main principle of the philosophy which Horace preaches in this first Epistle (as he does in the others, and elsewhere in his writings) is this: "Moderation is wisdom." Horace professes with truth not to attach himself implicitly to any particular school of philosophy. This principle, however, he probably adopted from a well-known passage in the second book of Aristotle's Ethics, where it is said that virtue is midway between the vices of excess and defect. Cicero in his work on Orators, entitled "Brutus," tells us that it was a maxim of the old Academy that virtue is a mean. Horace reproduces this maxim in the eighteenth Epistle of the first Book, where he says: "Virtue is a mean between vices." But indeed the principle colours the whole of his writings, and he is never tired of returning to it. Whether he pronounces that a miser is ever in want, or exhorts us to wonder at nothing, or sings of the happiness of him who makes the golden mean his choice, or proclaims that the moderate man is the genuine king, the feeling is ever the same. There is little enthusiasm in Horace's moral philosophy. And yet his love and admiration of virtue are evidently sincere and strong, as also is his patriotism. There is much earnestness in the tone of the second ode of the third Book, where the poet declares that "to die for fatherland is sweet and seemly;" and the same spirit is equally shewn in the sixth and twenty-fourth odes of the same Book, and in many other passages. So too the morality taught by Horace in the Epistles sometimes rises almost to enthusiasm, as in the fine passage in the first of the Epistles, where he exclaims: "Be this our wall of brass; to feel no guilt within, no fault to turn us pale:" and in the sixteenth Epistle: "Through love of virtue good men shrink from sin." But, for the most part, Horace maintains in his precepts a practical and moderate tone, and gently exposes and rebukes the weakness and folly, rather than the wickedness of vice. In this, as has often been observed, his manner forms a strong contrast to the indignant declamation of Juvenal. If Juvenal is the opposite of Horace in his vehemence, so too is Juvenal's energy unlike Horace's pensiveness. For throughout the writings of Horace, notwithstanding all his humour and wit, an almost sorrowful tone may not unfrequently be traced. Pensiveness has indeed always formed a feature in the characters of humorous men; and perhaps in the case of Horace the constitutional feebleness of his health may have also been one of the causes of this occasional depression of spirits. The passages in which he speaks of death are gloomy, and not relieved by hopefulness. Though the fear of death is mentioned, in the charming verses that conclude the last of the Epistles (which are very successfully paraphrased by Pope), as a frailty from which the wise should be free, yet the poet fails in his own case to exemplify this ideal wisdom. His lament addressed to Virgil on the death of Quinctilius[1], his condolence with his friend Valgius[2], his famous lines addressed to Postumus[3], and the ode of tender sympathy in which he assures Mæcenas of his devoted faithfulness[4], all alike breathe the spirit of dreary mournfulness. Juvenal, on the contrary, in the well-known lines at the end of his tenth Satire, which have been translated by Dryden into verses which perhaps surpass his original in excellence, speaks hopefully and cheerfully of the end of life. Of the gods he says,

"In goodness, as in greatness, they excel;
Ah, that we loved ourselves but half so well!"

[1] I. 24. [2] II. 9. [3] II. 14. [4] II. 17.

And presently he mentions, as the highest blessing for which we can pray to Heaven,

"A soul that can securely death defy,
And count it Nature's privilege to die."

At the same time, there is no doubt that the tinge of sadness which now and then pervades the poems, and indeed some of the most popular poems, of Horace, has added not a little to the fascination of his writings, and especially of his Odes.

"Our sweetest songs are those which tell of saddest thought."

In the two Epistles of the second Book, and also in the Art of Poetry, which is written in the form of a letter, and should properly have been included among the Epistles, Horace appears as a literary critic, a character in which he had appeared on other occasions before, as in the tenth Satire of the first Book. In the first of the two Epistles which form the second book, Horace compares the older Latin poets with those of his own time. He gives the praise of superior merit to the later writers, and assigns the more complete knowledge of Greek literature as the principal cause of this superiority. He evidently thinks that the earlier poets of Rome may fairly be charged with a want of polish and refinement, a fault which he had in his satires more particularly imputed to Lucilius. At the same time, he complains that praise is given to authors of a past age on account of their antiquity only, and without a due consideration of their actual merits.

Lucretius and Catullus are undoubtedly the two foremost of the poets of Rome who wrote previously to the time of Horace. Yet Horace never mentions Lucretius at all; and his single allusion to Catullus (in the 10th Satire of the 1st Book) is almost contemptuous, as of a writer of trifling pieces, to be sung by third-rate musicians. It seems wonderful that Horace should have been unable to discern, not only the splendid genius of Catullus, but also his distinguished skill as an artist. It is possible that Horace may have felt some jealousy of the poetical merit and fame of Catullus, as of one who had, in fact, before himself "adapted to Italian measures the Æolian lay;" but, most probably, the marked difference in the schools of poetry, to which they may be said to have severally attached themselves, was that which, most of all, made Horace blind to the genuine excellence of both Catullus and Lucretius. For although these two poets resembled Virgil and Horace, in so far as they drew from the Greek the sources of their poetry, and often closely imitated their originals, yet in the form and style of their compositions they both differ greatly. Lucretius is most plainly a writer whose verses are generally rough and unpolished; and Catullus, though a real artist, and one who sometimes manages his metre with dexterity, (as he does in a high degree indeed in his Atys,) yet is he more often careless and diffuse; he will not spend the time and trouble which must have been spent by Virgil and Horace in giving to their verses that subtle and exquisite variety, that conciseness and happiness of expression. Authors who possess this latter excellence, "correctness of style," as it is sometimes called, have always been intolerant of its absence in other writers. It was not without a certain self-complacence that Pope wrote the couplet,

"Ev'n copious Dryden wanted, or forgot,
The last and greatest art, the art to blot."

This intolerance has extended to the admirers of "correct" poets: so Lord Byron (though he certainly did not himself follow the style of that school which he deeply venerated,) was so extravagant in his admiration of Pope that he evidently thought him a greater poet than Shakespeare, though he does not venture actually to say so; however, he goes so far as to call Shakespeare, on account of his want of correctness, "the barbarian;" and he constantly reviles and disparages the poets of his own day for their deficiency in those merits of style which are characteristic of the so-called "Augustan" age of English poetry. "Depend upon it," he says, "it is all Horace then, and Claudian now, among us." In Roman literature too, and at Rome in the time of Horace, there existed two schools of poetry; that of the severe, restrained, and finished style of Virgil and Horace, and that of the florid and grandiloquent versification which Horace so often blames. It is abundantly clear in the satires of Persius, that these two opposite schools of poetry existed at the time he wrote.

The second Epistle is in some points like the first Epistle of the first Book. Horace says that he has now resigned the functions of a poet, and devoted himself to philosophy; he takes the opportunity of attacking the superficial and showy compositions of many poets of his own day, and lays down more correct and true principles of the art of poetry.

Horace in his Epistles fascinates us more than in his Satires, possibly even more than in his Odes. Though the Odes contain most of the poetry, strictly speaking, which Horace has left us, yet the Epistles perhaps give us a more complete idea of those points in his character which have made him the familiar friend of so many generations. We can realise, as we read these Epistles, the warmth and sincerity of his friendship, the good-natured humour and delicate sympathy which he shows as an observer of the characters of men, the unfailing tact and tenderness with which he hints at the faults of his friends, and the undoubted genuineness and earnest tone of his morality. Horace is certainly the author who has been chiefly followed by the didactic writers of later times; and it is not extravagant to say that the Epistles, the most mature and excellent of his didactic works, have exercised, in no small degree, a beneficial influence on the manners and civilization of modern Europe.

EPISTLES. BOOK I.

I.

1—19. *Horace excuses himself to Maecenas for giving up the composition of lyric poetry. Philosophy is better suited to him as he grows older. But he is not bound to any particular school.*

You, Mæcenas, who were the subject of my earliest lay, who shall be the subject of my latest, would fain shut me up in the old training-school, though a gladiator publicly approved enough, and already presented with the wand of freedom. My age is not the same; no more is my inclination. Veianius, having fastened up his arms to the door-post of Hercules' temple, lies hidden in his country retreat, that he may not so often on the edge of the arena have to implore the people for his freedom. There is one whose voice is often ringing in my unobstructed ear: "Sensibly set free betimes the horse that is growing old, lest he laughably fail in the end, and strain his panting flanks."

So now I lay down verses and every other toy; what is true and becoming I study and inquire, and am all absorbed in this; I amass and arrange my stores, so that afterwards I may be able to bring them forth. And lest you ask, perchance, under what leader I am, beneath what roof I shelter myself; not bound to swear as any one master dictates, wheresoever the tempest drives me, thither am I borne as a guest. Now I turn practical, and am plunged in the waves of politics, true Virtue's guard and rigid sentinel; now unawares I slide back into the maxims of Aristippus, and endeavour to subject things to myself, not myself to things.

20—40. *Wisdom is the true business of life; yet most of us must be content with but a moderate share of it: wisdom too is the only power which can tame our passions.*

As the night is long to them whose mistress plays them false, and as the day is long to them who work for debt; as the year is sluggish to wards, whom their mother's strict supervision restrains; so, slow and joyless flow to me the hours, that delay my hope and purpose to do with diligence that which is profitable alike to the poor, alike to the wealthy, which, when neglected, will be injurious to boys and to old men alike.

It remains that with these rudiments I govern and comfort my own self. You may not be able with your sight to discern as far as Lynceus; yet you would not on that account disdain to be anointed when your eyes are sore; nor, because you may despair of gaining the limbs of unconquered Glycon, would you refuse to keep your body free from the knotty gout in the hand. You may advance up to a certain point, if it is not granted you to go beyond. Your bosom boils with avarice and torturing desire: there are spells and words, wherewith you may be able to allay this pain, and to rid yourself of a large portion of the malady. You are swollen with the passion for renown: there are sure purificatory rites, which will have power to relieve you, when with sincere faith the formula has thrice been read. The envious, passionate, slothful, drunken, lewd, no man is so utterly savage that he cannot become civilised, if only he lend to culture an attentive ear.

41—69. *Men will do and suffer anything to avoid poverty, but nothing to gain virtue, which is more precious than gold. A clear conscience makes a man truly a king.*

'Tis the beginning of virtue to escape from vice, and the beginning of wisdom to be free from folly. You see with what distress of mind and body you strive to avoid those ills which you believe to be the greatest, a narrow fortune, and the ignominy of defeat in competition for office. With speed as a merchant you run to the ends of India, flying from poverty through sea, through rocks, through flames: are you not willing to learn and listen and trust a better man, so that you may not care for those things, which in your folly you admire and yearn for?

What combatant about the hamlets and cross-ways would disdain to be crowned at the great Olympian games, if he had the hope, if he had the warrant of the pleasant palm of victory without the dust? Silver is meaner than gold, gold is meaner than virtues. "O citizens, citizens, we must seek for money first; virtue after cash!" These precepts Janus proclaims from his highest to his lowest arcade; these precepts youths and old men ever repeat, with satchels and tablet hung from their left arm. You have spirit, you have character, and eloquence, and credit; but if six or seven thousand sesterces are wanting to make up the four hundred thousand, you will be a plebeian. But boys at their games say, "If you act aright you shall be king." Be this our wall of brass: to feel no guilt within, no fault to turn us pale.

Tell me, I pray, is the Roscian law the better, or the children's ditty, which confers the realm on those who do aright, a ditty that was chanted by the manly Curii and Camilli? Does he advise you better, who bids you "make your fortune, make your fortune; fairly if you can; if not, by any method make your fortune:"—so that you may have a closer view of Pupius' lamentable pieces; or he, who, ever at your side, exhorts and trains you to confront disdainful Chance, independent and erect?

70—93. *I cannot follow the popular ideas, because I see that they all tend one way, namely, to money-making. Besides, not only do men differ from one another in their pursuits, but no man is ever consistent with himself.*

But if the Roman people chance to ask me, why I am not pleased with the same opinions as they, as I enjoy the same colonnades, I shall answer as once the wary fox replied to the lion when sick: "Because the foot-prints frighten me, since they all look towards your den, and none back from it." You are a many-headed monster: for what shall I follow, or whom? A part of mankind is eager to farm the revenues; some there are who with cakes and apples hunt for hoarding widows, and catch old men, to send into their preserves; the wealth of many grows by secret usury.

But let it be that different men are attracted by different objects and pursuits: are the same men able to maintain for an hour their approval of the same things? "No bay in all the world outshines delightful Baiæ!" If so the rich man chance to say, the lake and sea feel the passion of the impetuous master; if unreasoning caprice chance to make auspices to lead him: "To-morrow, workmen, you will carry your tools to Teanum." The marriage-bed is in his hall: he says there is nothing superior to, nothing better than a single life: if 'tis not, he swears that happiness is possessed by husbands alone. With what noose shall I hold this Proteus who is ever changing his form? How does the poor man act? Why, laugh! He changes his garrets, his couches, his baths, his barbers; in his hired boat he is just as sea-sick as the opulent man who sails in his private trireme.

94—108. *External inconsistencies are noticed at once, while those of life and practice are passed over. The epistle ends with a joke on the Stoic doctrine of the perfect man.*

If I chance to meet you with my hair unevenly dressed by the barber, you laugh; if perchance I have a threadbare vest beneath a glossy tunic, or if my toga hang unequally and awry, you laugh: what do you, when my judgment is at war with itself, when it disdains what it sought for, and seeks again what it lately abandoned, when it is in a turmoil, and incoherent in the whole system of life, when it pulls down, builds up, exchanges squares and circles? You think that I am mad like other folks, and neither laugh at me, nor consider that I need a physician, or a committee appointed by the prætor, although you are the safeguard of my fortunes, and get angry about an ill-pared nail of your friend who hangs upon you, who looks to you!

To conclude; the wise man's less than Jove alone; rich, free, ennobled, fair; in short, a king of kings; above all things sound,—except when a cold in the head annoys him.

II.

1—31. *This epistle appears to be written to the elder son of M. Lollius, to whom is addressed the ninth ode of the fourth book. Horace begins by demonstrating, in the manner of the Stoic philosophers, the merit of Homer as a teacher of morals.*

Elder son of Lollius, I have read afresh at Præneste, while you are practising elocution at Rome, the writer of the Trojan war; who tells us what is fair, what is foul, what is expedient, what is not, more clearly and better than Chrysippus and Crantor. Listen to the reasons why I have formed this belief, if there be nothing which prevents you.

The story, in which it is told how Greece in lingering war was dashed against the land of the barbarians on account of the love of Paris, contains the broils of foolish kings and peoples. Antenor deems it best to cut away the cause of the war. What does Paris say? He declares that he cannot be forced to reign in safety and live in prosperity. Nestor is anxious to settle the disputes between Pelides and Atrides; love burns the one; anger, however, burns them both together. Whatever folly the kings commit, the Achæans suffer for it. By faction, by deceits, by crime, by lust, and by anger, they offend within and without the walls of Ilium. On the other hand, he has set before us Ulysses, as a notable instance of what is the power of valour and what is the power of wisdom; that wary man, the conqueror of Troy, who examined the cities and customs of many men; and who, in his efforts to contrive for himself and for his comrades a way to return across the spreading deep, endured many a hardship; he, a man who would not be overwhelmed by the contrary waves of circumstance. You know the Sirens' lays, and Circe's cups; if with his companions he had in folly and greediness drunk of them, he would have become a being hideous and soulless, beneath a harlot mistress, would have lived the life of an unclean hound, or a hog that loves the mud. We are mere cyphers, and born to consume the fruits of the earth, Penelope's suitors, spendthrifts, and the young courtiers of Alcinous, who employed themselves more than was proper in attending to their bodily pleasures; who thought it seemly to slumber till noon, and to charm their care to sink to rest at the music of the lyre.

32—71. *Men will take more trouble for bad deeds than for good, and more for the body than the mind. Yet, without contentment and peace of mind, material acquisitions cannot be enjoyed. Avarice and envy are always beggars, and remorse follows anger. Youth is the time to learn self-control. Whether you drop behind or outrun my principles, I shall still adhere to my philosophy of moderation.*

Robbers arise by night to cut the throats of men: do you not wake from sleep to save yourself? But if you will not do it when in health, you will have to run when dropsical; and unless before daybreak you call for a book and a light, if you do not vigorously apply your mind to honourable pursuits and objects, you will be kept awake, and tortured, by envy or love. For why do you hasten to remove those things which hurt the eye;—but, if aught consumes the mind, put off the time of cure from year to year? He who begins, possesses half the act; dare to be wise; begin. He who defers the hour for living aright, is waiting like the clown until the brook run out; but it glides and will glide on to every age with rolling flood.

We make money the object of our aims, and a wealthy wife to bear our children, and wild woods are tamed by the ploughshare: let him to whose lot there falls what is sufficient yearn for nought beyond. 'Tis not a mansion and estate, 'tis not a pile of bronze and gold, that is wont to remove fevers from its master's diseased body, to remove cares from his mind. It must needs be that the owner is in health, if he designs to use aright the riches he has amassed. The man who desires or fears, mansion and fortune delight him just as painted panels delight sore eyes, warm applications the gout, the music of the lute those ears which are troubled with collected dirt. Unless the vessel is clean, whatever you pour into it turns sour.

Scorn pleasures; pleasure bought with pain is hurtful. A miser is ever in want; let your desire aim at a fixed mark. Envy pines away at the sight of her neighbour's flourishing fortunes; Sicilian tyrants never discovered a torture more intense than envy. He who does not curb his anger will wish that thing undone which irritation and impulse have prompted him to do, in his hurry to inflict a violent punishment to gratify his animosity. Anger is short-lived frenzy: govern the temper; for unless it obeys, it commands; be sure you keep down it with bits, keep down it with a chain.

The breaker trains the horse while apt to learn, and with neck still pliable, to go on its way as the rider directs; the hunting hound, from the time when it first bayed at a deer-skin in the kennels, begins its service in the woods. Now, while a boy, drink in my words with heart still clear, now commit yourself to better men. The jar will long preserve the odour of wine with which it has once been saturated. But if you lag behind or vigorously outpace me, I neither wait for him that is slow of foot, nor strive to overtake those who run before me.

III.

To Julius Florus, who is serving on the staff of Claudius Tiberius Nero. The letter consists mainly of inquiries and observations as to the literary pursuits of members of the staff; and concludes with a hope that the quarrel between Florus and Munatius has ended in a reconciliation.

Julius Florus, I am anxious to know in what regions of the world Claudius, the step-son of Augustus, is serving. Does Thrace detain you, and Hebrus bound with snowy fetter, or the straits which run between the neighbouring towers, or Asia's wealthy plains and hills?

What description of works is the diligent staff composing? This also I desire to know. Who is taking upon himself to record the exploits of Augustus? Who is spreading to a distant age his wars and treaties of peace? What is Titius doing, he who soon will come to be on the Romans' lips; he who has not shrunk from quaffing draughts of the Pindaric spring, daring to scorn the common pools and streams? How is his health? How is his regard for me? Is he essaying, at the prompting of the Muse, to fit to Latin chords the Theban measures; or does he wildly rave and mouth in the tragic art? Pray what is Celsus doing; he who has been and must be often warned to search for resources of his own, and to refrain from laying hands on any writings which Apollo on the Palatine has admitted; lest if, perchance, the tribe of birds some day shall come to claim the plumage which is their own, he provoke laughter, like the wretched crow when stripped of her stolen hues. What are you venturing on yourself? About what beds of thyme are you nimbly flitting? Not puny is your genius, not untilled and of an uncomely roughness. Whether you are whetting your tongue for pleading, or studying to give opinions in the common law, or composing an attractive lay, you will win the foremost prize of the conqueror's ivy. But if you could abandon those cold applications which nourish cares, you would advance whither heavenly Wisdom led you. This practice, this pursuit, let us all earnestly follow, both the humble and the exalted, if we wish to pass our life, beloved by our country and by ourselves.

This too you ought to say in your reply, whether Munatius is as dear to you as is meet, or whether your goodwill, badly sewn together, ineffectually unites, and is bursting asunder again. But whether hot blood or a misunderstanding of the facts chafe you in the wildness of your untamed necks, in whatever region you are living, you that are not such as should dissolve your brotherly alliance, a votive heifer is being fattened to grace your return.

IV.

To his friend Albius Tibullus, the elegiac poet. Horace here professes himself to be entirely a disciple of Epicurus.

Albius, gentle critic of my satires, what shall I say that you are doing now in the district of Pedum? Writing something to surpass the pieces of Cassius of Parma, or sauntering silent amid healthy woods, musing whate'er is worthy of one that is wise and good? You never were a body without mind. The gods have given you beauty, the gods have given you wealth, and the skill to enjoy it. What more could a fond nurse pray for her darling charge, who, like you, has the power to think aright, and to utter what he feels, and to whose lot there falls abundantly favour, fame, health, and decent means, with a purse that does not fail?

'Twixt hope and care, 'twixt fears and fits of passion, believe each day has dawned to be your last: welcome will steal upon you the hour that is not hoped for. Myself you will find plump and sleek, in high condition, when you wish to laugh at a hog from the sty of Epicurus.

V.

Horace invites to dinner the advocate Torquatus, to whom he wrote the seventh ode of the fourth Book. He tells his friend that to-morrow is a holiday, so that he may well forget his occupations for a time. The poet extols the virtues of wine, as in the twenty-first ode of the third Book; and describes the preparations he is making for the banquet.

If you can recline at my table on couches made by Archias, and shrink not from dining on a miscellaneous salad in a modest dish, I will expect you, Torquatus, at my house at sunset. You will drink wine which was drawn off into jars, between marshy Minturnæ and Petrinum the hill of Sinuessa, in Taurus' second consulate. If you possess aught better, send it; or else obey my orders at the feast. Long has the hearth been brightly polished and the furniture made neat in honour of you. Dismiss visionary hopes, and the competition for wealth, and Moschus' case: to-morrow being Cæsar's birthday, the festal hours grant indulgence and slumber; you will be able without loss to pass in genial conversation the length of the summer night.

Wherefore have I wealth, if I am not allowed to use it? He that is sparing and overmuch austere through regard for his heir is next door to a madman; I will begin to drink and scatter flowers, and will even submit to be accounted indiscreet. What is there tipsiness does not effect? It unlocks hidden secrets, it bids hopes be realised, it impels the coward to the field, it lifts the load from off the anxious mind, it teaches new accomplishments! Whom have not flowing cups made eloquent? Whom have they not made free in pinching penury?

These matters I am bound to provide for efficiently, and not against my will withal; that no soiled coverlet, no dirty napkin, make you turn up your nose; that both tankard and plate display you to yourself; that there be not among trusty friends one who would carry our words beyond the threshold; that like may unite and be linked with like.

I will engage to meet you Butra and Septicius, and Sabinus, unless an earlier invitation and a girl whose company he prefers keep him away; there is also room for more introductions by the guests: but the noisome goat oppresses crowded feasts. Only write back how many you would like to bring; lay business aside, and by the back-door elude the client who is keeping watch in the hall.

VI.

Equanimity is happiness: fear and desire alike disturb our peace of mind. You will find my maxim true, if you seek the chief good in any other pursuit; (1) *in riches,* (2) *in political honours,* (3) *in sumptuous living, or* (4) *in love aud trifling. The person to whom this epistle is addressed, Numicius, or, perhaps, Minucius, is not elsewhere mentioned by Horace, or by other writers.*

To wonder at nothing is about the one and only thing, Numicius, which can make a man happy, and keep him so. This sun and stars and seasons which depart at regular periods, some there are who view, not infected with any dread: what deem you of the bounties of the earth, what of the gifts of the sea which enriches the far-distant Arabs and Indians; what of the shows, the plaudits, and the favours of the partial Roman? In what measure, with what feeling and eyes, do you consider that they should be viewed? He who dreads the opposites of these, wonders much in the same manner as he who feels desire; the trepidation on either side is painful, so soon as an unexpected object startles one or the other. Whether he joys or grieves, desires or fears, what is it to the point, if, whatsoe'er he chance to see better or worse than his expectation, he is stunned with eyes fast fixed, and mind and body too? Let the wise man receive the name of the fool, the just of the unjust, if he follow after Virtue herself farther than is sufficient.

Go now, adore old plate and sculptured marble, and vessels of bronze, and works of art; wonder at the hues of Tyrian purple and gems withal; rejoice because a thousand eyes gaze on you as you speak; in your diligence go to the forum at daybreak, and in the evening to your home, lest Mutus reap more corn from the fields that were the dowry of his wife, and (which is a shameful thing, since he is sprung from meaner ancestors,) he be rather an object of admiration to you, than you to him.

Whatever is beneath the earth, time will bring forth into the sunshine; it will bury and hide away things which now are glittering. Though Agrippa's colonnade and Appius' way have beheld you as a well-known visitor, it still remains for you to go to that place to which Numa has passed and Ancus too.

If your chest or reins are tortured by a sharp disease, search for means to escape from that disease. You wish to live aright: what man does not? If virtue only can bestow this blessing, bravely give up all toys, and study her.

You think virtue to be words, and a forest fagots: beware lest your rival get into harbour before you, lest you miss the market for your Cibyratic and Bithynian merchandise: let the circle of a thousand talents be completed; then as many more, and further let a third thousand follow, and the quantity which makes the heap a square. No doubt our Lady Money bestows a dowried wife, and credit, and friends, and high birth, and beauty; and Persuasion and Venus adorn the man of cash. The king of the Cappadocians, though opulent in slaves, is destitute of coin: be not you such as he. Lucullus, as they say, when asked if he could supply for the stage a hundred purple cloaks, says, "How can I lend so many? Yet I will search, and then send all that I find I have." So after, he writes to say that he has at his house five thousand purple cloaks; and that the prætor might take some or all of them. Meagre is the household, where there are not many things superfluous, which escape the notice of the master, and are a profit to his knaves. So then, if wealth alone can make a man happy, and keep him so, be the first to go back to this work, the last to leave it off.

If display and popularity create blessedness, let us purchase a slave, to tell us the names of the people, to nudge our left side, and compel us to stretch the hand of greeting across the tradesman's scales. "This man possesses much influence in the Fabian tribe, that man in the Veline; this other will confer the fasces, and in his malice snatch away the ivory curule chair from whomsoever he pleases." Introduce the words, "Brother," "Father;" according to each man's age, pleasantly adopt each man.

If he who dines well, lives well,—it is daybreak, let us go whither the palate guides us; let us fish, let us hunt, as Gargilius used to do, who was wont to order that his toils, hunting-spears, and slaves, should in the early morning pass through the crowded forum and the people, that one mule out of many might bring home before the eyes of the people a purchased boar. With our food undigested, and swollen with the feast, let us bathe, heedless of what is becoming and what is not, worthy to be classed among the Cærites, a graceless crew of Ithacan Ulysses, to whom forbidden pleasure was dearer than their fatherland.

If, as Mimnermus deems, nothing be pleasant without love and jests, then pass your life in love and jests. Live long, farewell; if aught you know more true than these precepts which you read, frankly impart them to me; if not, like me, use these.

VII.

1—24. *Horace excuses himself to Maecenas for not keeping his promise to come to Rome, on the ground that it would be dangerous to his health. He feels that this reason will satisfy Maecenas, as being a friend who has always had a sincere regard for his welfare.*

Though I gave you my word that I would stay in the country only five days, I have been looked for, liar as I am, all through the month of August. But if you wish me to live in sound and perfect health, Mæcenas, you will grant me when I fear sickness the indulgence you grant me when sick, so long as the early figs and the heat adorn the undertaker with his guard of sable lictors, so long as every father and fond mother are pale with anxiety for their children; and diligence in courtesies, and the routine of the law-courts, bring on fevers and unseal wills. But when winter spreads its sheet of snows over the Alban fields, your poet will go down to the sea, and spare himself, and read, crouching in a corner; yourself, sweet friend, he will visit again with the Zephyrs, if you allow him, and the first swallow.

'Twas not in the way a Calabrian host bids you eat pears, that you made me opulent. "Eat, pray." "That's enough." "But take away as much as you like." "You are very kind." "You will carry with you little presents not displeasing to your young children." "I am as much obliged by the gift, as if I were sent away laden with the pears." "As you please; you leave them for the pigs to eat up to-day." The spendthrift and fool gives away those things which he disdains and hates; this seed produces ingratitude, and will produce it throughout all years. An honest and wise man professes himself ready to grant favours to the deserving; and yet knows well how coins differ from counters: I will also show myself deserving, in proportion to the merit of my benefactor.

25—45. *If you would have me always at Rome, you must give me back my health and youth. I must be free, even if my freedom cost me the loss of all your favours. I would give back all, as Telemachus refused the horses which were unsuited to his poor and rocky island.*

But if you are to be unwilling that I leave you for any place, you must give me back my strength of chest, the jet-black locks upon my slender brow;—you must give back my winning words, you must give back my engaging smile, and the mood to lament over the wine-cup the flight of saucy Cinara.

It chanced that a slender little fox through a narrow chink had crept into a corn-bin; and when she had eaten her fill, she was struggling in vain to get out again with her body plump: to her quoth a weazel at a distance, "If you wish to escape from that bin, you must be lean when you go back to the strait gap, which you passed through when lean." If I am challenged by this allegory, I give up all; I neither praise the poor man's sleep when surfeited myself with fattened fowls, nor for the riches of the Arabs do I barter the perfect freedom of my leisure. Often have you praised my modesty, and received from me before your face the names of "king" and "father," and not a word less generous in your absence; examine whether I have the power cheerfully to restore your gifts. Not ill spoke Telemachus, the offspring of enduring Ulysses: "Ithaca is not a region suited for horses, since it is neither spread out in level tracts nor lavish in a wealth of herbage; Atrides, to yourself I will leave your gifts, because they are more fitted for you." Him that is little, little things become; 'tis not imperial Rome that charms me now, but Tibur free from crowds, and peaceful Tarentum.

46—95. *The story of Volteius Mena and his patron L. Marcius Philippus, with an implied allusion to the relationship between Horace and Maecenas. The attainment of our wishes does not always make us happy.*

Philippus, diligent and vigorous and renowned as a pleader, when he was returning from business about the eighth hour, and complaining, since he was then advanced in life, that the Carinæ was too far from the Forum, observed, as they say, a certain man, just shaved, standing in the shadow of a barber's shop then empty, and deliberately cleaning with a pocket-knife his own nails. "Demetrius," (this boy was wont to receive not awkwardly the orders of Philippus,) "go, inquire, and bring me word, what place that man comes from, who he is, what is his condition, who is his father, or who is his patron." He goes, returns, and tells, that his name is Volteius Mena, an auctioneer, of slender fortune, known to be of unblamed character, one whose pleasure it is to bestir himself on occasion, and to take his ease, and to earn and spend, a man possessed of humble friends and a home of his own, and fond of the shows, and a game in the Plain of Mars when his duties are dispatched. "I should like to inquire from the man himself all that you tell me; bid him come to dinner." Mena does not quite believe the invitation; he silently wonders in his mind. Why say more? "Your master is very kind," he replies. "Can it be that he sends me a refusal?" "He does, the rascal; and cares not for you, or is afraid of you."

In the morning Philippus accosts Volteius while selling shabby second-hand goods to a crowd of the poor that lack the toga; and, unsaluted, bids him good-day. He begins to plead to Philippus his work and the ties of his trade, as an excuse for not having come in the morning to his house, and, lastly, for not having seen him first. "Consider that I have pardoned you on this condition, that you dine with me to-day." "As you please." "Then you will come after the ninth hour; now go, diligently increase your fortune." When he came to dinner, after he had said things meet and unmeet to be uttered, he is at length sent away to bed. He, when he had oft been seen to run to the house as a fish to the concealed hook, a morning client, and now a settled guest, was bidden to go with his patron into the country that lies near the city, on the proclamation of the Latin Holidays. When mounted on the carriage drawn by nags, he ceases not to praise the Sabine country and climate. Philippus observes and laughs, and as he seeks to gain by every means matter for recreation and laughter, between giving him seven thousand sesterces and promising to lend him seven thousand, he persuades him to buy a small farm. So he does. Not to detain you with rambling talk beyond what is sufficient, he changes from a spruce man to a clown, and prates of nothing else but furrows and vineyards, makes ready the elm to receive the vine, half kills himself over his pursuits, and ages through his passion for gain. But when his sheep were lost by theft, his goats by sickness, when his crop disappointed his hope, and his ox was worn to death with ploughing, exasperated at his losses, in the middle of the night he seizes his cob, and betakes himself in a rage to the mansion of Philippus. When Philippus sees him all squalid and unshorn, he says, "You seem to me, Volteius, to be too strict and bent on your work." "By Pollux, my patron, 'wretched' is what you would call me, if you wanted to give me my real name! Wherefore by your Genius and right hand and household gods I beseech and conjure you, give me back to my former life."

96—98. *The moral of the tale.*

Let him who has once observed how far the fortune he has given up excels that which he has aimed at, return betimes, and resume the things he has resigned. It is meet that every man should measure himself by his own rule and foot.

VIII.

To Celsus Albinovanus, who is serving on the staff of Tiberius in the province of Asia. This letter seems to be a reply. Horace speaks of his own fickleness and discontent, and gently recommends moderation to Celsus in prosperity.

To Celsus Albinovanus joy and success! Muse, at my request, bear back this wish to the comrade and secretary of Nero. If he asks you what I am doing, tell him that though many and grand are the things I threaten to do, my life is neither perfect nor pleasant; not because the hail has beaten down my vines, or the heat withered my olives, or my flock is sickening on distant pastures; but because, less healthy in mind than in all my body, I will listen to and learn no lessons to alleviate the malady; because I am offended with my honest physicians, and angry with my friends, since they endeavour to shield me from my fatal lethargy; because I follow what has injured me, avoid what I believe will benefit me, am as fickle as the wind, loving Tibur when at Rome, and Rome when at Tibur.

This done, ask him, Muse, of his health, how he manages his affairs and himself, how he stands in favour with his youthful patron and the staff. If he says "All is well," first wish him joy; then forget not to drop this warning into his delicate ears: "As you bear your fortune, Celsus, so shall we bear with you."

IX.

A letter of introduction written to Tiberius Claudius Nero, the future Emperor Tiberius, in behalf of Titius Septimius, to whom is addressed the sixth ode of the second book.

Claudius, 'tis evident that Septimius alone understands how highly you esteem me; for when he begs and constrains me with intreaty, actually to endeavour to praise and commend him to you, as one who is worthy of the mind and house of Nero who chooses only what is honourable, when he deems that I enjoy the privileges of an intimate friend, he sees and knows what power I possess more clearly than I do myself. Indeed, I mentioned many reasons why I should go excused; but I feared that I might be thought to have feigned my resources to be weaker than they are, as a dissembler of my real influence, and profitable to myself alone. So I, in escaping the disgrace of a heavier fault, have stooped to win the prize which belongs to an unabashed brow of the town. But if you commend me for doffing my modesty at the bidding of a friend, enroll this friend among your flock, and believe him brave and good.

X.

This Epistle is addressed to Aristius Fuscus, as also is the twenty-second ode of the first Book. It begins with contrasting Horace's own love of the country with his friend's fondness for the town; then follows the praise of Nature; and finally the poet dwells on the superior happiness that moderate means and contentment afford, compared with riches and ambition.

I, a lover of the country, bid Fuscus hail, a lover of the town; for we are in fact on this point alone utterly unlike, though almost twins in everything beside; since, in the spirit of a brother, whatever one denies the other denies, and we assent together, like old and well-known doves.

You keep within the nest; I extol the brooks of the pleasant country, and the rocks overgrown with moss, and the grove. Do you ask why? I live and am a king, so soon as I have left those things which you exalt to heaven with loud applause; and, like the priest's runaway slave, I shrink from sweet wafers; 'tis bread that I need, which now to me is choicer than honey-cakes.

If it is proper to live agreeably to Nature, and a flat of ground to build a house upon must first be sought for, know you any place which surpasses the happy country? Is there a region where the winters are milder, where a more refreshing breeze allays both the raging of the Dog-star and the influence of the Lion, when full of fury he has received the stinging Sun? Is there a region where envious Care less distracts our slumbers? Is herbage in scent or sweetness inferior to Libyan mosaics? Is the water which struggles to burst the leaden pipes in the streets more limpid than that which dances noisily along its sloping bed? Why, a wood is carefully reared among the columns of various hue, and that mansion is praised, which surveys a length of fields. Should you drive Nature out with a pitch-fork, still she will every time speed back, and victoriously, by stealthy degrees, burst through your morbid squeamishness.

He who knows not how to compare skilfully with Sidonian purple the fleeces which have drunk Aquinum's dye, will not incur a more certain loss, or one that comes closer home to his heart, than he who has not the power to discern falsehood from truth.

The man whom the flow of prosperity has overmuch delighted, will be shaken by a change of fortune. If you chance to admire anything, you will be loth to lay it down. Shun grandeur; beneath a humble roof you may outrun in the course of life kings and the friends of kings. A stag, superior in the fight, was wont to drive away a horse from their common pasture, until the weaker in the lengthened strife besought the aid of man and took the bit; but after he had quitted his foe, an impetuous conqueror, he did not dislodge the rider from his back, nor the bit from his mouth. So, he who through dread of poverty lacks freedom that is more precious than metals, carries in his covetousness a master, and will be a slave for ever, because he knows not how to live upon a little. If the fortune he possesses does not fit a man, it will, like the shoe in the story, trip him up, if it be too large for his foot, pinch him, if too small. If pleased with your lot, you will live wisely, my Aristius, and not let me go unchastised, when I shall appear to be hoarding up more stores than are sufficient, and never to pause. Money amassed is each man's lord or slave; though it deserves rather to follow than to pull the twisted rope. These lines I am dictating for you behind Vacuna's crumbling shrine, blest in all else, except that you are not my companion.

XI.

To Bullatius, who is travelling in Ionia. Change of scene does not alter the mind. If it be tranquil, the meanest and least interesting place is agreeable.

Bullatius, what has been your impression of Chios and far-famed Lesbos? What of pretty Samos? What of Sardis, the palace of Crœsus? What of Smyrna and Colophon? Whether above or below their fame, are they all of no account, compared with the Field of Mars and Tiber's stream? Does it come into your mind to wish for one of the cities of Attalus, or do you extol Lebedus, in your sickness of voyages and travels? You know what Lebedus is; a hamlet more desolate than Gabii and Fidenæ; yet there I could choose to live, and, forgetful of my friends, and by them to be forgotten, to view from the land, at a distance, the turmoil of the deep. But neither will he who is hastening from Capua to Rome, when bespattered with rain and mud, choose to spend his life at an inn; nor does he who has caught a cold extol ovens and baths as fully furnishing a happy life: nor would you, if the driving South-wind chanced to toss you on the deep, on that account sell your ship beyond the Ægæan sea.

For one in perfect soundness, Rhodes and fair Mytilene do the same as a cloak at midsummer, an athlete's dress amid the snowy blasts, Tiber during winter, a stove in the month of August. While it may be, and Fortune keeps her gracious looks, at Rome let Samos be praised, and Chios, and Rhodes, that are far away. Do you with grateful hand take every hour, which Heaven's grace shall chance to bless you with; and put not off your joys from year to year; that in whatever place you shall have been, you may say that you have lived agreeably: for if it be reason and discretion which take away our cares, and not a spot that commands a wide expanse of sea, 'tis the sky, and not the mind, they change who speed across the main. A busy idleness is tiring us; by means of ships and chariots we seek to live aright. What you are seeking for is here; 'tis at Ulubræ, if serenity of spirit fail you not.

XII.

Horace introduces Pompeius Grosphus to Iccius, to whom he addressed the 29th Ode of the first book. He was the steward of Agrippa's property in Sicily. He compliments him, probably ironically, on his philosophy, advising him to be content, recommending Grosphus to him, telling him the news.

Should you make a good use, Iccius, of the Sicilian rents of Agrippa, which you collect, Jove himself could not give you a greater abundance. Stay your complaints: he is not poor who enjoys a sufficiency of the use of things. Your digestion is good, your lungs sound, you are free from gout; well then, the wealth of kings can give you nothing better. If you are as one in the midst of rich dishes living abstemiously on vegetables and nettle-broth, then you will not change your style of life, though fortune's stream should suddenly flow for you with gold: either because riches cannot change your nature, or because you believe all else combined to be inferior to virtue alone. I am astonished at Democritus' cattle eating the crops in his field, whilst his active mind is abroad, absent from the body; yet you, in the very midst of the itch and infection of gain, are the student of no mean philosophy, and still pursue your sublime studies; enquiring what are the causes that curb the sea, what controls the year, whether by their own will move the wandering planets, or in obedience to a law; what buries in gloom, what brings out into light the moon's orb, what is the meaning and power of the discordant concord of the universe; whether Empedocles is wrong, or the acuteness of Stertinius astray. Now whether you dine on fish, or murder only leeks and onions, do you cultivate the friendship of Pompeius Grosphus, and anticipate all his wishes; his desires will never exceed reason and equity. But that you be not ignorant of the state of our republic, know that the Cantabrians have yielded to the valour of Agrippa, the Armenians to Claudius Nero; that Phraates on bended knee has accepted the imperial sway of Cæsar; that golden Plenty has poured forth fruits on Italy from her full horn.

XIII.

Horace had sent his poems to Augustus by Vinius Asella, on whose name he plays, giving him directions suited to the joke on the asinine name.

At your departure, Vinius, many a long lesson I gave you; so do you deliver my sealed volumes to Augustus, only if he be well, in good spirits, only, in short, if he ask for them, lest you err through zeal in my cause, and by an excess of officious service bring dislike on my writings. Perchance the heavy burden of my book may chafe your back; then rather throw it quite away, than rudely dash it down, like panniers, where you were told to take it; for so you would make your paternal name of Asina a jest, and become the talk of the town. Put out your strength up slopes, o'er rivers, through bogs; when, successful in your efforts, you have arrived at the end, keep your burden in such a position that you look not as though you carried the parcel of books under your arm like a clown would a lamb, as drunken Pyrrhia a ball of stolen wool, as a poor tribesman his sandals and little hat to a dinner; see too that you tell not every one how you have perspired in carrying verses that may perhaps interest the eyes and ears of Cæsar: though stopped by many an urgent question, yet push forward still; off with you, fare you well, beware lest you stumble and break what is entrusted to your charge.

XIV.

A letter to his bailiff, who dislikes the country, and longs to return to a city life; while Horace, detained at Rome, has his heart in the country.

Bailiff of my woods and of my farm which makes me my own master again, but which you despise though five households live on it, and it often sends five worthy householders to Varia, let us have a friendly contest, whether you will root the thorns more vigorously from the land, or I from my soul, and whether Horace himself or his farm shall be in a better state. I am detained at Rome by the affectionate grief of Lamia, who sorrows for his brother, who mourns for his lost brother and will not be comforted, and yet my soul's desire ever bears me to my farm, as a steed eager to burst the barrier which is across the course. I call a country life, you a town life, happy: and doubtless he who likes another man's lot must dislike his own. So either in his folly unfairly blames the innocent place, while really in fault is the mind, which can never escape from itself. Once you were a slave of all work; your thoughts, though you spoke not, desired a country life; now you are a bailiff, and you long for the city and public games and baths. You know my consistency and my sorrow in departing, whenever hated business drags me to Rome. Opposite are our tastes, and herein the difference between you and me, that what you think a waste and ungenial wilderness, I and those on my side call pleasant, hating what you consider so beautiful. For the sake of the stews and greasy cook-shops you are smitten with regret for the city; besides, the nook of the world you are now in would bear pepper and frankincense sooner than it would bear grapes, and there is no neighbouring inn to supply you with wine, nor any courtesan flute-player, to whose music you may strike the ground with heavy foot; yet, for all that, with spades you work the fields long untouched, and attend to the unyoked ox, filling him with gathered leaves; then, if you have a lazy fit, the stream gives you more work; for if the rain falls, by many an embankment it must be taught to spare the sunny mead. Come now, hear what causes our want of agreement. Me once became finely-spun dresses and glossy locks; I once, as you know, without a present could please the grasping Cinara; I began to quaff cups of Falernian wine at noon; but now a plain dinner suits me, and a siesta on the grass beside my stream: I am not ashamed of my past follies; but I should be, if now I ended them not. There, where you are now, none with evil eye askance can impair my comforts, no one poisons me with the bite of secret malice. As I move the stones and clods, my neighbours laugh. You would rather munch your daily allowance with the city servants, and in your prayers your fancy flies to join them; whilst my shrewd city-slave envies you the use of wood, cattle, garden. Even so the lazy ox longs for housings, the horse would fain plough. My opinion is, that each should be content to practise the trade he knows best.

XV.

1—25. *Horace is advised by the court doctor to try cold baths rather than hot ones, and makes enquiries of his friend Numonius Vala about Velia and Salernum.*

Write to me, friend Vala, about the winter at Velia and the climate of Salernum, the manners of the people, the state of the roads thither: for Antonius Musa tells me that Baiæ is useless for my health, and has even made me disliked there, now that I bathe in cold water in the middle of winter. Indeed, the town laments the abandonment of its myrtle groves, and the contempt of its sulphur waters famous for driving from the system the lingering disease; it is angry with patients who dare to use for the head-ache and indigestion the waters of Clusium, and who visit Gabii and its cold country. So I must needs change my place, and drive my horse beyond the familiar inn. "Whither so fast, my steed?" says the angry rider, pulling the left rein, "I am not now going to Cumæ or Baiæ;" to a horse a bit is as a voice, its ear is in its mouth. Tell me, Vala, which town is best supplied with corn; do they drink rain-water in tanks, or perennial wells of fresh water? As to the wines of that country, I set no store on them. In my own country retreat I can put up with any wine: when I go to the sea, I require something generous and mellow to drive away care, to make a rich hope flow through my veins and soul, to give me ready speech, and recommend me with renewed youth to a Lucanian mistress. Tell me, my friend, in which country are most hares, most wild-boars, in which seas are found most fish and sea-urchins; my hope is to return home from my visit as plump as any Phæacian; so it is right your letter should tell me this, and I will trust you.

26—46. *Account of Maenius the parasite, which Horace applies to his own case.*

Mænius with spirit spent all his father and all his mother left him; then he would pass for a witty parasite, he dined out anywhere, he had no fixed feeding-place; if he were fasting, citizens and strangers were all alike to him, he would fiercely fasten any amount of abuse on any one, he was a very pest, a whirlwind and bottomless gulf to the market; all he got he made a present to his greedy stomach. If he could obtain little or nothing from those who liked or feared his vices, then he would dine on dishes of tripe, and cheap lamb; three bears could not have eaten more: then he would, forsooth, condemn the stomachs of spendthrifts to be branded with a red-hot iron, quite a censor and a second Bestius. And yet, if he lighted on some better booty, he utterly consumed it all, and then would say, "I am not surprised at those who spend their goods in eating; for there is nothing better than a plump thrush, nothing more beautiful than a rich paunch." Now in truth I, Horace, am this man; when poor, I admire a safe humility, resolute enough in the midst of common things; but let something better and richer come in my way, then I affirm that you alone are wise and live well, whose money is conspicuously invested in handsome country-houses.

XVI.

1—16. *Horace describes to his friend Quinctius his farm, and its charms.*

To prevent your asking, my good Quinctius, about my farm, whether with arable land it supports its master, or enriches him with the berries of the olive, or with orchards, or meadow-land, or the elm clad with vines; I will describe to you its form and situation in easy chatty style. Imagine a line of hills, unbroken, save by one shady valley, whose right side the morning sun illumines; while, departing with its swift car, it warms the left. You may well praise the temperature. Why, as the thorns bear so liberally the cornels and sloes, as the oak and ilex gladden the herds with plenty of acorns, and their master with thick shade, you would say Tarentum was transported there, with all its leafy woods. My fountain too is fit to give a name to a stream, such, that neither is cooler nor purer the Hebrus that flows round Thrace: its waters run beneficial for the head-ache, beneficial for indigestion. This retreat so pleasant, if you will believe me, even delightful, ensures your friend's health at your service in September's days.

17—45. *Advice to his friend, whom he contrasts with the vain man, who loves flattery and vulgar admiration.*

You are living the true life, if you take care to deserve your character. For some time past all we at Rome have pronounced you happy; but I fear that you may rely upon others rather than on yourself, and that you may think that others besides the good and wise can be happy; and so be like a man in a fever, who, because men say he is in good and sound health, conceals his sickness till the hour of dinner, and till his hands are seized with a trembling on the very table. It is the false shame of fools that tries to conceal ulcers not healed. If a man were to talk to you of wars fought by you on land and sea, and were to flatter your idle ears, saying, "May Jove, to whom you and the city are alike dear, keep it doubtful, whether you wish the people's good most, or they yours:" in such words you will recognise praises due to Augustus alone. When you allow yourself to be addressed as wise and faultless, prithee, tell me, have you a right to the name to which you answer? No doubt you and I both are pleased with the name of a good man. But then the people who gave you the name to-day, to-morrow, if they please, will take it from you; even as, having elected to high office an unworthy candidate, they can withdraw the honour from him. Then say they, "Resign this honour, it is ours." Resign it I must, and retire sad at heart. But if this same people declare that I am a thief, one lost to all sense of shame, assert that I strangled my father, am I to be stung by their calumnies, and change colour? For none does undeserved honour delight, or false charges alarm, save the man full of sin, who needs to be reformed. But who is the good man of our people? He, forsooth, who keeps the decrees of the senate, the statutes and laws of the state, before whom as judge are decided many grave suits, who is a sufficient security, whose testimony settles causes. And yet the whole of his family and the neighbourhood know the man, though decked out in a showy hide, yet inwardly to be full of all iniquity.

46—62. *Many a man who seems to be good is actuated by fear, not love; his morality is hollow.*

My slave says to me, "I am no thief, no runaway." I reply, "You have your reward, you are not scourged." He says, "I have not committed murder." I reply, "You shall not be food for carrion-crows on the cross." Once more he says, "I am a good and honest servant." My Sabine bailiff shakes his head to that, and says, "No, no." Even so the wolf is on its guard and dreads a pit, a hawk the suspected snare, the gurnard the baited hook. Through love of virtue good men shrink from sin: you commit no crime, because you fear punishment. Let there be a hope of not being found out, you would treat things sacred and profane alike; and if out of a thousand bushels of beans you steal one, my loss in that way is, as I judge, less, but not your crime. The good man admired by every forum and every tribunal, on the days that he appeases the gods by the offering of a pig or ox, with loud voice says, "O father Janus," with loud voice says, "O Apollo;" then, just moving his lips lest he be overheard, he prays, "Lovely Laverna, grant that no one may suspect me, grant me to pass for a righteous and holy man, cast over my sins and frauds a cloud as thick as night."

63—79. *The miser is a slave. The good man is free and fearless, come what will.*

How better or more free than a slave is a miser, when he stoops down to pick up a penny stuck in the mud at a cross-way, I confess I do not see: and the covetous man must be a coward; and then he who lives the life of a coward, in my judgment never will be free. He has thrown away his arms, he has deserted the post of virtue, being ever busy and overwhelmed with the cares of making money. Now when you can sell a captive in war, it is a pity to kill him; he will be a useful slave; if he be hardy, let him be a shepherd or ploughman, or let him traffic for you at sea in the midst of the wintry waves; let him make grain cheaper by his labour, and bring in corn and all sorts of provisions. A good and wise man will boldly say: "Pentheus, king of Thebes, what do you unrighteously condemn me to bear and endure?" The king says, "I will take away your goods." He replies, "Ah, you mean my cattle, chattels, beds, plate: you are welcome to them." Then says the monarch, "In handcuffs and fetters I will bind you, under the care of a cruel jailer." He replies, "The god, when I please, will himself loose me." By which I suppose he means this: "I will die; death is the final boundary-line of all things."

XVII.

1—12. *Directions to Scaeva, how to live with the great: at the same time, it is not altogether a life of ease.*

Scæva, you are quite wise enough to manage your own affairs, and know the proper way of living with the great; and yet you may learn a lesson from your humble friend, though he needs teaching himself; it is as if a blind man were to show the way; but see, if I too can say anything that you may care to make your own. Should pleasant rest and sleep till day-break delight you, should dust and the noise of wheels or of an inn annoy you, then would I advise you go to Ferentinum. For joys fall not to the lot of the rich alone, and he lives not amiss who from the hour of his birth to his death has met with no notice. But if you would do good to your family, and give yourself a more generous diet, then do you, lean and poor, visit him who can give you a good dinner.

13—32. *The difference between the Cynic and the Cyrenaic, and why Horace prefers the Cyrenaic.*

Diogenes said, "If Aristippus could be content with vegetables, he would not wish to dine with princes." Aristippus replied: "If my censor knew how to associate with princes, he would despise vegetables." Now inform me which of these two philosophers' words and acts you approve, or, as younger than I am, hear why Aristippus' view is to be preferred. For they say he baffled the snarling Cynic thus: "I play the fool for my own sake, but you for the people's: and my conduct is much the more correct and honourable. That I may have a horse to ride, and be maintained by a great man, I pay him attentions: you solicit worthless things, inferior to him who gives them, although you bear yourself as one in want of nothing." Every complexion of life, condition, fortune, became Aristippus, aiming at a higher rank, but usually content with his present lot. But look at the man, whom his contentment clothes with his double coarse wrapper; I shall be surprised if a change in his station would become him. The one will not wait for his purple cloak; in any dress, no matter what, he will walk in the crowded streets, and will gracefully support either character. The other will avoid a mantle of Milesian texture, as worse than a dog or snake, and will starve himself to death, unless you give him back his tatters; so give him them back, and let the man live in his folly.

33—42. *To please great men is not the first of all things, but neither is it the last.*

To achieve great exploits, and to show before our citizens captive foes, is what rises to the throne of Jove, and aims at heavenly glory. But to please the leading men of the state is not the least of merits. 'Tis not any man that can get to Corinth. He who fears not to be successful, remains inactive: well, and what of him who has reached the end? Has he acted like a man? And yet in this effort, or nowhere else, is the point of our enquiry. One shrinks from the burden, as too heavy for his little soul and weak strength: another lifts it and carries it to the end. Either virtue is an empty name, or the man of enterprise rightly aims at honour and reward.

43—62. *Various directions how to live with the great.*

Those who in the presence of their patron say nothing of their poverty will get more than those who beg: it makes a difference, whether you take modestly, or snatch greedily. And yet to get is the beginning and origin of all you do. He who says, "I have a sister without any dowry, a poor unhappy mother, a farm I cannot sell, and which will not maintain my family," really cries aloud, "Give me food." Then chimes in a neighbour: "And I too should have a slice and part of the present." But, now, if the raven in the story could but have fed in quiet, it would have had more meat, and much less strife and envy. He, who, taken as a companion to Brundusium or pleasant Surrentum, complains of ruts and severe cold and rain, of his box being broken open, or his travelling goods being stolen, plays off the well-known tricks of a courtesan often bewailing her loss of a chain or ankle-band, so that at last there is no faith in real losses and grief. Nor does one, who has once been made a fool of, care to raise from the crossings a beggar with a broken leg; many a tear may run down his cheeks, he may swear by the name of holy Osiris, and say "Believe me, I am in earnest; cruel men, lift up a lame man." "Go and get a stranger!" the neighbours shout back till they are hoarse.

XVIII.

1—20. *In living with the great we should aim at the proper mean between obsequiousness and roughness.*

Unless I much mistake you, my free-spoken friend Lollius, you will dislike appearing in the character of a parasite, while you profess to be a friend. As a matron will be unlike and different in look from a courtesan, so, distinct from an insincere parasite will be a friend. There is a vice the very opposite of this, almost worse, a rustic roughness, rude and offensive, recommending itself by a close-shaven skin and black teeth, claiming to pass for simple candour and sterling worth. But virtue is a mean between vices, removed from either extreme. One man is unduly obsequious, the jester of the lowest couch at dinner; with dread he watches the nod of his wealthy entertainer; he so echoes his words, and catches them up as they fall, that one would suppose he was a boy repeating his lessons to a severe master, or an actor in a farce playing an inferior part. Another will often wrangle for any trifle, as for goat's wool, he will fight for it, armed to the teeth: "What," says he, "am I not to be believed above all others? am I not to blurt out as sharply as I please my real thoughts? if so, I would not thank you for a second life." What then is the point of dispute? Just whether Castor or Dolichos is most skilful; which is the best road to Brundusium, the Minucian or Appian.

21—36. *There should be no rivalry in style of living with one's patron. What Eutrapelus did.*

The man whom ruinous love and desperate gambling beggars, whom vanity clothes and anoints beyond his means, who is possessed with a thirst and craving hunger of money, to whom poverty is a shame and a bugbear, has a rich friend furnished with ten times as many vices; this rich friend hates and dreads him, or if he hate him not, then he sets up to guide him, and, like an affectionate mother, would have him wiser and more virtuous than himself, and says what indeed is pretty near the truth: "Rival me not, my wealth allows folly; you are a poor man; a wide toga becomes not a sensible client; cease to contend with me." There was one Eutrapelus, who, if he wanted to do a man a mischief, would send him costly dresses; for he knew that the silly happy fool would, with the new dresses, assume forthwith new notions and new hopes; would sleep to daylight, neglect for a mistress his honourable duty to his patron, borrow at a high rate of interest, and would end by being a gladiator, or hire himself to drive a market-gardener's hack.

37—66. *Neither should there be any prying into a patron's secrets, nor any disregard of his tastes. An allusion to Lollius' amusements.*

Never pry into a patron's secrets, and if he trusts you with one, keep it hidden, though tried by wine or anger. Praise not your own tastes, censure not those of your friend: if he has a mind to hunt, do not be for composing poems. In this way burst the band of brotherly affection between the twins Zethus and Amphion, until the lyre disliked by the graver brother was silenced. As, it is said, Amphion gave way to his brother's tastes, so do you comply with the gentle orders of your great friend: and when he would take into the fields his hounds and his mules laden with Ætolian nets, do you rise and lay aside the crabbed temper of the unsocial muse, that at dinner you may enjoy with him your food with that relish which toil alone can give. Hunting is a national pursuit, gets a man a good name, prolongs life, strengthens the limbs, specially in the days of health, when in fleetness you surpass the hounds, in strength the wild boar. Besides, no one wields manly arms more gracefully than you do: you know how the ring of spectators applauds when you take your part in the reviews on the Plain of Mars; in short, when very young, you served in the fierce war against the Cantabrians under that general, who is now taking down from the Parthian temples our standards, and annexes to the Italian empire all that is as yet unconquered. Further, to prevent your refusing and standing aloof without excuse, remember how, at times, you amuse yourself on your paternal estate, though you always take care to do nothing out of tune and harmony: your mock fleet divides the boats: your servants represent the battle of Actium in sham fight; you are one captain, your brother the other; the lake is the Adriatic: and so you contend, till winged victory crowns one or other of you with the leaves of bay. Now he, who thinks you sympathise with his tastes, will approve and praise your sport with hearty applause.

66—95. *Advice to be cautious, not to introduce others without enquiry, to assimilate oneself to a patron's manners and disposition.*

That I may further advise you, if indeed you need an adviser, often consider what and to whom you speak of any one. Avoid a curious man; he is sure to be a gossip. Ears wide open to hear will not faithfully keep a secret. A word once uttered is gone past recall. Admire no maidservant or boy in the marble hall of your respected friend; lest the master of the pretty boy or dear girl make you foolishly happy with such a trifling present; or, by refusing it, vex you. Consider carefully the character of any one you recommend, lest presently his vices cause you shame. We make mistakes, and introduce an unworthy person: so then, if such an one be found guilty, do you, once deceived, cease to defend him: on the other hand, one you know thoroughly, if he be attacked by calumny, do you protect and uphold him, confident in your patronage: for if he be assailed by Theon's slanderous tooth, do you not feel that the danger will soon reach yourself? Surely your own property is in peril, if the neighbouring wall is in flames; and a fire, if neglected, gathers strength. To those who have never tried, it may be pleasant to court a great friend: he who has tried, dreads the courting. While your vessel is out at sea, look to it, lest the gale shift and bear you back. Serious men dislike a cheerful companion, those who love a joke dislike a serious one, the quick-witted dislike a sedate companion, the careless him who is busy and industrious: hard drinkers of Falernian wine after midnight will not bear you if you refuse the offered cups, however loudly you may declare you fear feverish heats at night. Remove the cloud from your brow: usually a modest man passes for a reserved man, a silent man for a sour-tempered one.

96—112. *But, however occupied, neglect not moral philosophy. This, says Horace, is my meditation in the happy retirement of my country-home.*

Midst all these duties, study, and enquire of learned men how you may calmly pass your days; asking, whether you are still harassed and troubled by desires never satisfied, or by fears and hopes of things indifferent; whether virtue is a lesson to be learnt, or nature's gift; what will stay your cares and make you again a friend to yourself; what gives pure tranquillity, is it honour, or pleasant gain, or a retired path and way of a life unnoticed? Now, when Digentia's cool stream refreshes weary me, Digentia, from which drinks Mandela, a village wrinkled with cold, what suppose you, my friend, are my thoughts and prayers? They are even these: "May I have my present means, or even less; may I live for myself the remainder of my days, if it be Heaven's will still to spare me: may I have a good supply of books and food to last each year; may I not waver, as one hanging on the hopes of an uncertain hour!" But enough, if I pray Jove for what he gives and takes away: may he give me life and means: a contented mind I will secure for myself.

XIX.

1—20. *Horace's edicts about poetry only get him plenty of servile imitators.*

If you believe old Cratinus, my learned friend Mæcenas, no poems written by water-drinkers can long live, or long be popular. As soon as Bacchus enlisted crazy poets among the ranks of his Satyrs and Fauns, the dear Muses generally smelt of wine in the morning. Homer from his praise of wine is convicted of having been given to wine: father Ennius himself never sprang forth to sing of arms, till he was merry with wine. "I assign to the sober the dry business of the Forum and of Libo's hallowed plot, I interdict the grave from poetry." This my decree was no sooner issued, than the poets began to emulate one another in drinking strong wine at night, and reeking of it by day. What then! supposing a man with rough and stern countenance, bare foot, and with the texture of a scanty toga, were to ape Cato, would he therefore reproduce the virtues and morals of Cato? Iarbita heard the voice of Timagenes, and, vying with him, burst a blood-vessel, so anxious was he to be thought a man of wit and eloquence. An example, easily imitated in faults, is apt to mislead: supposing I happened to have a pale face, they would drink cummin that thins the blood. O ye apes of others, ye are a servile herd: how often have your troubled efforts moved either my spleen or my laughter?

21—34. *Horace's claims to originality.*

Through ground as yet unoccupied I freely trod, not in the footsteps of others. The man who has confidence in himself leads the swarm that follows. I first to Latium showed the Parian iambics, following the metre and spirit of Archilochus, but not his subjects, nor the words that drove Lycambes to suicide. And lest you should crown me with leaves more scanty, because I ventured not to alter the metres and art of the poetry, recollect that masculine Sappho tempers her genius by the measures of Archilochus, so does Alcæus too, though in subjects and arrangement of metres he differs, looking for no father-in-law whom to befoul with malignant verses, nor weaving a halter for any bride by defaming lines. Alcæus, celebrated by no Roman tongue before, I first as Latin lyrist have made known: 'tis my pride that I introduced what was till then untried, and that I am read by the eyes and held in the hands of freeborn Romans.

35—49. *Horace did not court publicity, and is therefore abused.*

Perhaps you may like to know why the ungrateful reader, though at home he admires and praises my humble works, yet abroad disparages and censures them. I hunt not for the applause of the fickle public, by gifts of expensive dinners, and presents of cast-off clothing: I will not lower myself by listening to and defending grand writers, so as to curry favour with the cliques and platforms of the grammarians: hence all these expressions of spite. I should be ashamed to read to crowded theatres writings unworthy of such an audience, or to make a fuss about my trifling verses. If I use this language, then says my critic, "You are ironical, sir, reserving your lines for the ear of our Jove: for you are confident that you alone distil poetic honey, fair in your own eyes." These sneers I fear to answer with scorn, and, dreading that I may be torn by the sharp nails of my enemy, I cry aloud that I like not his place, and beg for an interval from this sport. For sport like this brings forth a hurried and passionate contest, whence spring fierce enmities and deadly war.

XX.

1—8. *Horace warns his book of the fate that attends publishing.*

You seem, my book, to be looking wistfully towards Vertumnus and Janus; I suppose you want to be published by the Sosii, neatly polished by their pumice-stone. You hate the locks and seals, which modesty is thankful for; you lament that so few see you; you praise publicity. I did not so educate you. Well then, off with you whither you long to descend from my house. Remember, once started you cannot return. When severely criticized you will say, "Wretched book that I am! what have I done? what did I want?" You know well you will be rolled up tight enough, when your admirer is sated and weary of you.

9—28. *You may be popular for a time, but presently be sent into the provinces, or made a school-book of. However, if you have an opportunity, give the public some account of him who wrote you.*

Now perhaps through hatred of your sin I am a poor prophet; but I think you will be loved at Rome, till the bloom of youth leave you. Then, thumbed by the people, you will become dirty, and in silence will be food for the sluggish moths, or will be banished to Utica, or sent in a bundle to Ilerda. Then your monitor, to whom you will not listen, will have his laugh, being like the man whose donkey was restive, and he pushed him over a precipice in a passion: for who would strive to save another against his will? This too awaits you, that, when overtaken by lisping old age, you will teach boys the rudiments of their learning in the streets of the suburbs. However, if the warm sun collects a few more to listen to you, tell them about me, how, the son of a freedman in narrow circumstances, I spread my wings beyond my nest; what you take from my birth, add to my merits; you may mention how I have pleased the chief men of the state in peace and in war; describe me as short in stature, grey before my time, fond of the sunshine, quick-tempered, soon appeased. Should any one ask my age, inform him that I completed my forty-fourth December, in the year when Lollius received Lepidus as colleague.

EPISTLES. BOOK II.

I.

1—4. *Introductory compliment to Augustus.*

SINCE alone you support the burden of so many great affairs, protecting the Italian state by your arms, gracing it by morals, improving it by laws, I were an offender against the public weal, were I by a long epistle to occupy your time, O Cæsar.

5—17. *Augustus alone has escaped that envy, which has disparaged the virtues of all others.*

Romulus, and father Liber, and the brothers Castor and Pollux, heroes received after great exploits into the celestial mansions, whilst civilizing the world and the human race, settling rough wars, allotting lands, founding cities, lamented that their merits did not meet with the gratitude which they had hoped for: he who crushed the dreadful hydra, and subdued the well-known monsters by the labours which fate ordained, by experience found that envy was a monster not to be conquered till the hour of his death. He who depresses the merits of others who are inferior to himself, blasts them by his own brilliancy; when his light is quenched, his memory will be loved. But to you, while still with us, we give honours betimes, and set up altars on which to swear by your name, and confess that none like you has e'er arisen, none will e'er arise.

18—33. *Horace passes to his subject, namely, that the unreasonable admiration for ancient writers is to be condemned.*

Yet this your people, so wise and just in this one instance of setting you above our national, above the Grecian heroes, in other matters judge by a very different standard and measure, and despise and dislike all except what they see to be removed from earth and to have passed from life; for so bigoted are they in their admiration of the ancients, as to maintain that the twelve tables enacted by the decemvirs, which forbid to sin, the treaties made by the kings either with Gabii or with the sturdy Sabines, the books of the priests, the old tomes of the soothsayers, are all utterances of the Muses on the Alban mount. If, simply because the oldest writings of the

Greeks are also the best, Latin writers are to be weighed in the same balances, there is nothing more to be said; the olive has no stone, the nut has no shell; we have attained the summit of glory; in painting and music we excel the Greeks, and wrestle more skilfully than their athletes anointed with oil.

34—49. *The question may be reduced to a reductio ad absurdum.*

If time improves our poems, as it does our wines, I shall be glad to know, how many years exactly may claim a value for writings. Ought a writer deceased a hundred years ago to be reckoned among the ancient and perfect, or among the modern and worthless? Let a fixed time end our dispute. Well, then, he is an ancient and approved author who has completed his century of years. What then, he who died a month or year short of that time, in which class should we put him, among the ancient poets, or among those whom the present age and posterity should reject with scorn? Well, he may fairly be set among the ancients, who wants a short month or even a whole year. I take advantage of what is allowed me; and, like one who plucks at the hairs of a horse-tail, so I subtract first one year, then another, till, like a sinking heap, he, baffled, fails, who looks in annals, and estimates merit by years, and can admire nothing till the goddess of death has hallowed it.

50—62. *An account of the characteristics of the old poets.*

Ennius, a wise and vigorous writer, and a second Homer, as the critics say, seems to trouble himself but little as to the result of his promises, and of his dreams after the fashion of Pythagoras. Is not Nævius constantly thumbed by us? Does he not cling to our memories as though he were almost an author of to-day? So sacred do we think each ancient poem. When the question arises, which poet is superior, then Pacuvius bears the palm of a learned old writer, Accius of being a sublime one; it is said that Afranius' gown would have suited Menander, that Plautus bustles on in his plays after the pattern of Sicilian Epicharmus, that Cæcilius excels in dignity, Terence in art. These are the authors whom mighty Rome learns by heart; their plays she beholds, crammed in the contracted theatre; these she accounts and ranks as poets, from the age of the writer Livius even to our days.

63—92. *Horace again condemns the undiscriminating admiration of the ancients then in fashion.*

Sometimes the people judge correctly; at other times they err. If they admire, and glorify the old poets so, as to prefer none, nay to compare none to them, they are wrong. But if they allow that these are sometimes too old-fashioned, generally harsh, often slovenly, then the people is sensible, and agrees with me, and Jove sanctions the judgment. When I was little, Orbilius, my master, dictated to me the poems of Livius; he was fond of flogging me, but I am not dead set against those poems, nor think they ought to be destroyed; but that they should be considered faultless and beautiful and almost perfect, does astonish me; in which, if by chance a word should appear not quite ungraceful, or if here and there a verse is found not so inelegant as the rest, unfairly it recommends and sells the whole poem. I lose my patience, when works are censured, not as uncouth, or rough, but as new, and when for the ancient poets men demand, not indulgence, but honour and reward. If I question whether Atta's play is successful amidst the saffron and flowers of the stage, nearly all our fathers would exclaim that shame is lost, seeing that I endeavour to censure a drama acted by dignified Æsopus and learned Roscius: for these men either deem nothing right, except what they approve themselves, or scorn to listen to their youngers, and, when old, to allow that what they learnt when boys is not worth preserving. So, he who extols the song of the Salii written by Numa, and who wishes to be thought the only man who knows that, of which really he is as ignorant as I am, he in truth is no supporter or admirer of the genius of the dead, but the detractor of our writings; us and our writings he maliciously dislikes. If the Greeks had disallowed what then was new, as much as we do, what had been ancient now? Or what had remained to be read and thumbed by the public in general use?

93—117. *The taste of the Greeks contrasted with that of the old Romans; who, however, now are changed, and are a nation of would-be poets.*

When Greeks put wars aside, they took to trifles; and, as fortune smiled, sank into luxury; then did they burn with passion for athletic games or equestrian races; or admired sculpture in marble, ivory, and bronze; or with eyes and souls hung enraptured on pictures; or delighted to listen to players on the flute, and tragic actors; like an infant girl at play under its nurse's care, what eagerly it loved, that soon it, sated, left. For is there anything liked or disliked, that you do not suppose is quickly changed? Such was the character of the good times of peace, and of the gales of prosperity. At Rome 'twas long the delight and fashion to be awake at dawn and open the house; to expound the law to a client, to lend money on good security to solvent debtors, to learn from one's elders or to teach one's juniors how to increase property, how to check wasteful indulgence. Changed is the taste of the fickle people; and now all glow with one poetic passion; boys and grave fathers alike crown their locks with chaplets at their banquets, and dictate verses. I, who declare I am no poet, am found to tell more lies than the Parthians, and, before sun-rise, wake and call for pen, and paper, and writing case. He who was never on board, fears to steer a ship; none but a professional man dares to prescribe southernwood for a patient; physicians undertake physicians' duty; artizans alone handle tools: but, learned and unlearned, we scribble verses, all alike.

118—138. *Yet this poetic madness is innocent; nay, is not without advantages.*

And yet this frenzy, and slight madness, has many good points, as you may thus argue: rarely avarice possesses the poetic mind; verses are the bard's darlings, other passion he has none; as to losses, runaway slaves, fires, he laughs at them; to cheat a friend or ward he never schemes; his diet pods of beans, or brown bread; though an inactive and poor soldier, yet is he useful to the state, for surely you will allow that small things are a help to great. The tender lisping mouth of a child the poet forms; even in their early days he turns the ears of the young from evil words; presently he fashions the heart by kindly precepts, he is the corrector of roughness, of malice, of anger; he tells of virtuous deeds, the dawn of life he furnishes with illustrious examples; the helpless and sad of soul he comforts. Whence could the pious boys and virgins learn their hymns of prayer, had not the Muse granted us a bard? The chorus prays for aid, and Heaven's presence feels, and in set form of persuasive prayer implores rain from above, averts disease, drives away dreaded dangers, obtains peace, and a season rich with its crops: appeased by hymns are gods above, and gods below.

139—167. *The origin of the Roman drama, its licence and restraint; then Grecian literature tamed her rude conqueror.*

Our rural ancestors, content with a little, having housed their grain kept holyday, and refreshed their bodies, yes, and their souls too, patient of labour through the hope of rest; so together with the partners of their work, their boys and faithful wives, they used to propitiate the goddess of the earth with a pig, the god of the woods with milk, with flowers and wine the Genius who forgetteth not how short is life. These holydays introduced the Fescennine licence, which in alternate verse poured forth rustic taunts, when liberty, gladly welcomed each returning year, would sport in pleasing mood, until the jests grew fierce, and began to turn into furious lampoon unrestrained, and, threatening, passed through honourable families, no one forbidding. Stung to the heart were those whom the blood-stained tooth of satire bit; even those as yet untouched took alarm at the common danger; and so a law was passed, and punishment imposed, to forbid that any one should be described by malicious verses: thus they changed their note, compelled through dread of death by cudgelling to use better language and to please. We conquered Greece, and Greece conquered her rude captor, and introduced the arts into rustic Latium; and so that rough Saturnian measure fell into disuse, and wit polite expelled the offensive venom of satire, though for many a day lingered and linger still the traces of our rustic vein. For not till late did the Romans apply their intellect to Greek letters, and only after the Punic wars, when now at rest, began to enquire what lessons Sophocles and Thespis and

Æschylus could teach. They assayed, too, to see if they could properly translate, and were satisfied with their attempts; for gifted are they with sublimity and vigour, and breathe the spirit of tragedy sufficiently, and are not wanting in a happy boldness, but ignorantly consider a blot ugly, and dread to correct.

168—181. *The difficulties of comedy, and its discouragements.*

'Tis thought that comedy, drawing its subjects from humble life, requires less pains; but the truth is, the labour is greater as the indulgence is less. Observe how Plautus supports the characters of the young man in love, of the careful old father, of the tricky pander; how great and grand Dossennus is in greedy parasites, how loose the sock in which he runs o'er the stage; to fill his purse is his desire, if that be done, he cares not whether his play succeeds or fails. If Vanity in her windy chariot bears the poet to the stage, an inattentive spectator takes the breath out of his sails, an attentive one puffs them out again. So light, so small is that, which casts down or revives a soul craving for praise. Farewell the stage! if, as my play fails or thrives, I grow lean or fat.

182—207. *The noise of the theatre, and the vulgar taste for scenery and spectacles, may well discourage a poet.*

Oft, too, even a bold poet is terrified and put to flight, when those superior in number, inferior in worth and rank, an ignorant and stolid crowd, prepared, should the knights object, to fight it out, in the midst of the play call for a bear or boxers; such are the sights the rabble will applaud. But now-a-days even the knights' pleasure has all fled from the ear to the empty joys of the uncertain eyes. For four hours or more the curtain never drops, while troops of horse and files of foot pass swiftly by, unhappy monarchs are dragged across the stage with hands bound behind their back; then Belgic cars, easy carriages, Gallic wagons, ships, speed on, and borne along is ivory, the spoil of war, and captured Corinth's wealth. Could Democritus return to life, he would have a laugh, when the cameleopard, a distinct species, or a white elephant, arrests the gaze of the crowd; Democritus would behold the people more attentively than any play, no actor could give him so good a spectacle as the people themselves; he would suppose the poets were addressing a deaf donkey; for what voice of man can overcome the noise that echoes through our theatres? One would think it was the roaring of the woods of mount Garganus, or of the Tuscan sea. So great the din at the representation of the play, at the spectacle of the arts and wealth of foreign lands; as soon as the actor, covered with his tawdry finery, stands on the stage, then is heard the clapping. But has he spoken? No, not a syllable. What then has met this approval? The robe that vies with purple through its Tarentine dye.

208—213. *Horace hopes he can estimate, as well as any one, the genius of the true poet.*

Yet, lest you think I damn with faint praise that poetry which I decline to try, but others write successfully, I will say that he seems to me as one able to walk on a tight rope, who, a true poet, tortures my breast with his fictions, can enrage, then soothe me, fill me with unreal terrors, and by his magic art set me down either at Thebes or Athens.

214—231. *Horace would now recommend to his patron those who write for readers, though he allows poets are a set of men, that, by their vanity, stand in their own way.*

But some, rather than endure the disdain of the haughty spectator, prefer to trust themselves to the mercy of a reader; to such now do you pay a little attention, if you would fill with books your gift worthy of Apollo, and invite our poets to ascend verdant Helicon with greater enthusiasm. True, we are a set who do ourselves much mischief, ('tis as though I were to destroy my own vineyard) when you are anxious or tired, and we offer you our volume; when a friend ventures to censure a single verse, and we are annoyed; when, unasked, we repeat passages already read; when we lament the want of notice of our labours, and of our poems spun with so fine a thread; or when we expect that so soon as you have heard we are composing verses, you will be so kind as, unasked, to send for us, and place us above want, and force us to write. However, it is worth enquiring, what sort of poets will be the guardians of a virtue tried abroad and at home, and not to be entrusted to any unworthy bard.

232—244. *Alexander the Great was a good judge of painting and sculpture, but not of poetry.*

A favourite of Alexander the Great was that wretched poet Chœrilus; uncouth were his verses, born in an unlucky hour; yet he put down to their credit the Philips he received for them, the king's coin. However, as ink when touched leaves a mark and stain, so, generally, do poets by bad verses disfigure brilliant exploits. And yet that same king, who in his lavishness paid so dearly for that ridiculous poem, by an edict forbad any one except Apelles to paint himself, and any one besides Lysippus to cast a bronze statue representing the countenance of the valiant Alexander. But now transfer that judgment, so nice in viewing these works of art, to books and to the gifts of the Muses, and you would swear that he was born in Bœotia's dull atmosphere.

245—270. *Augustus showed a better taste than Alexander. Horace would gladly sing his praises, but lacked the ability, and wishes to avoid the disgrace of being a poet, whose poems are but waste paper.*

Dear to you were the poets Virgil and Varius, and they do not disgrace your judgment of them, nor the gifts received by them to the great credit of the giver; for not so well by bronze statues is expressed the countenance, as in the works of poets shine forth the character and qualities of illustrious heroes. Nor do I prefer my satires and epistles, that crawl in prose along the ground, to the celebration of exploits, and to the singing of tracts of countries, of rivers, and of forts crowning mountains, and of barbaric realms, and how that wars are ended throughout the whole world under your auspices; for the closed bars now confine Janus the guardian of our peace, and the Parthians dread Rome under your imperial sway: but my power is unequal to my will; and your majesty admits not of a weak poem, nor does my modesty venture to essay a theme beyond my strength to complete. Zeal offends by a foolish love, and, most of all, when it would recommend itself by verses and the poet's art; for we all learn and remember more readily what we deride, than what we admire and venerate. I value not the officious attention which disgusts me, and I do not choose to be represented in bust of wax, if the likeness is to be bad; nor care I to be lauded in ill-written verses, lest I have to blush at the stupid offering, and, together with my chronicler, like a corpse stretched out in an open coffin, be carried down into the street where they sell frankincense and scents and pepper, and all that is wrapped in the pages of the dunce.

II.

1—19. *A playful illustration of Florus' conduct towards himself.*

Florus, honest friend of good and great Nero, supposing some one were to try to sell you a slave, a lad born at Tibur or Gabii, and were to deal with you as follows: "Here, sir, is a boy, fair, and handsome from top to toe, he is your slave for eight thousand sesterces; born in my house, he is quick in his services at his master's beck, has a slight tincture of Greek, is suited for any employment whatever, you may fashion him to what you please like soft clay; he can sing too; untrained is his voice, but pleasant to one drinking his wine. Many recommendations shake confidence, if the seller praises his wares unfairly, to get them off his hands. No difficulties press me; I am not rich, but owe no man anything; none of the slave-dealers would give you such a bargain; nor indeed is it every one who would get it from me. Once, it is true, he played truant, and, as is natural, hid himself under the stairs through dread of the whip that was hanging up. You would pay the money if you can get over his running away, his one fault." The seller, I suppose, may take the money, without fear of any legal penalty. With your eyes open you bought a faulty slave; you had notice of the condition: can you then prosecute the seller, and trouble him with an unjust suit?

20—40. *He had told his friend not to expect a letter, much less any verses, and illustrates the case from the story of a soldier of Lucullus.*

I told you, my friend, when you set out, that I was indolent, I told you I was almost unfit for such duties of friendship, to prevent your so cruelly scolding me, if no letter from me were delivered to you. What good did I then do, if, after all, you attack the laws which are in my favour? Further, too, you complain that the verses you looked for I never sent, false man that I am. In Lucullus' army was a soldier, he had collected money by many a toil; one night he was tired and snored, and lost it all to a farthing: after that, he was as fierce as any wolf, angry with the enemy and himself alike; as a hungry beast that savage shows its teeth, he stormed, so they say, a royal garrison admirably fortified and rich with many stores. By this exploit he became famous, is adorned with honourable gifts; over and above, receives twenty thousand sesterces. It so happened about this time, that the prætor would storm a castle, no matter what; then he began to exhort the man with words that might have roused even a coward's soul, saying: "Go, my friend, where your valour calls you; go, and luck be with you; great rewards your merits will attend. Why stand there?" To this replied the soldier, shrewd, however rustic: "Yes go he will, where you wish, general, he who has lost his purse."

41—54. *He gives a sketch of his life, till poverty drove him to write verses.*

It was my fortune to be bred at Rome; there I read the tale of the mischief wrought to the Greeks by the wrath of Achilles. Kindly Athens gave me a little more learning to this end, that I might be minded to distinguish right from wrong, and to hunt for truth in Academus' groves. But the hard times tore me from that pleasant spot, and the tide of civil war bore me, a novice, into that host, which was fated to prove no match for the strength of Cæsar Augustus. Then Philippi sent me from its field, brought low with clipped wings and stript of my paternal home and farm; and so venturesome poverty drove me to write verses; but now that I have all I can want, no doses of hemlock could ever cure me of madness, if I would scribble rather than sleep in peace.

55—64. *Then, think of my time of life, and of the diversities of taste in poetry, and that no one can please every one.*

The years, as they go, steal from us things one after another; they have robbed me of my jokes, my loves, my feasts, my games; they are now striving to wrest from me my poetry. What would you have me do? Besides, we have not all the same tastes and likes. Odes are your delight, another is pleased with iambics, a third with satires like Bion's, and caustic raillery. I fancy I see three guests, who call for quite different viands as their tastes vary. What am I to offer? what not? You refuse what another orders: what you desire, the other two find distasteful, and detest.

65—86. *And then, is Rome the place for a poet? Learned Athens or the quiet country is the home of a poet, not noisy, busy Rome.*

Besides, do you think I can write verses at Rome, in the midst of so many cares, so many labours? One calls me to be security; another to hear him read, to which I must postpone every duty; one friend is ill in bed on the Quirinal mount, another at the extremity of the Aventine, I must visit both; these distances, you see, are charmingly convenient. Oh! but the streets are clear, so that there is nothing to stop thought. Not quite so; see hurrying along the bustling contractor with his mules and porters; a crane hoists at one moment a stone, then a weighty beam; melancholy funerals jostle sturdy wagons, one way runs a mad dog, another way a filthy sow: go to, now, and meditate musical verses. The whole chorus of bards loves groves, eschews cities; clients, as in duty bound, of Bacchus, the god who delights in sleep and shade: and do you mean that I am to be a poet in the midst of noise by night and by day, and there to follow the path of minstrelsy trodden by few? A genius chooses for his retreat quiet Athens, there he devotes seven years to study, and grows gray over his books and literary cares; usually, when forth he walks, he is more mute than a statue, while the people shake with laughter: and here at Rome should I, in the midst of the billows of business, and the tempests of the city, attempt to compose verses worthy to wake the music of the lyre?

87—105. *Then, the absurd flattery of poets one to another may well make one dislike the trade of verse-writing.*

There were two brothers at Rome, one a lawyer, the other a rhetorician; their compact was, that the one should hear unmixed praises of the other; one was to be a Gracchus in his brother's eyes, the other a Mucius in his turn. This madness possesses our tuneful bards quite as much. I compose lyrics, my friend writes elegiacs. This is our language: "O work admirable to contemplate, engraven by the nine Muses!" Prithee, do you see, with what airs, with what importance, we gaze round Apollo's temple with niches vacant for the Roman bards? Presently too, if you have time, follow, and at a convenient distance listen to what either poet is reciting, and why he weaves for himself a chaplet. We receive blows, and deal as many back on our foe, in a lazy kind of combat, like gladiators when the candles are first lighted. I go home a second Alcæus on the strength of his vote; who is he in my judgment? Why, nothing short of Callimachus; or if that contents him not, he rises to Mimnermus, and waxes greater through the name of his own choosing. Much do I endure to appease the irritable race of bards, while I scribble verses myself, and as a suppliant canvass for the interest of the people: now that I have finished my poetic course, and recovered my wits, I would stop my ears, once open to those who read without requital.

106—125. *Bad poets are happy in their vanity; the real poet is severe upon himself.*

Ridicule attends bad poets; but then they delight in their own writings, and are venerable in their own eyes, and if one is silent, without waiting longer, they praise whatever they have written, a race happy in their own conceits. But he who would compose a poem that will fulfil the laws of his art, when he takes his tablets, will take also the spirit of an upright censor; he will not scruple to remove from their place all fine phrases lacking brilliancy, and regarded as wanting in dignity and as unworthy of honour, though reluctantly they depart, and still linger within the shrine of Vesta; he will kindly for the people's use bring forth words that have long lain in obscurity, once in vogue with ancient Cato and Cethegus, but now sunk in shapeless oblivion and dreary age: he will adopt new names produced by usage, the parent of language: though strong, yet clear, like a transparent stream, he will pour forth a wealth of words, and enrich Latium with the fulness of his eloquence: but what is luxuriant he will prune, what is rough he will refine by a sensible culture, what has no merit he will utterly take away: he will appear like an actor, and turn and twist his limbs, as one who dances now like a Satyr, now like a clownish Cyclops.

126—140. *Yet the self-satisfied poet is the happiest, as may be illustrated by the story of the Argive.*

But yet, better be thought a silly and dull poet, provided my own faults please me, or at least escape me, than to be ever so sensible, and to chafe in one's spirit. There lived one at Argos of no mean rank, who used to fancy that he was listening to admirable tragic actors; he would sit happy, and applaud in the empty theatre; yet meanwhile he could correctly discharge all the duties of life, an excellent neighbour, an amiable friend, civil to his wife; he could command himself so far as to forgive his servants, and was not quite a madman though the seal of a bottle were broken; he could avoid walking against a rock or into an open well. Him his relations with much labour and care cured, expelling the disease and bile by doses of pure hellebore; so he returns to his senses; whereupon he says, "By Pollux, my friends, you have been the death of me, not my deliverers, who have robbed me of my pleasure, and violently taken from me my soul's dearest illusion."

141—157. *There is a time for all things, a time to give up verse-writing, and to learn true wisdom, that we may free ourselves from avarice.*

No doubt it is good to learn wisdom and cast aside trifles, and leave to boys the sport that suits their age, and not to be always hunting after words fit to be set to the music of the Latin lyre, but to master the harmonies and measures of the true life. Wherefore I hold converse with myself, and in meditation ponder such thoughts as these: If no draughts of water assuaged your thirst, you would tell the doctors; dare you not confess to any one, that the more you have acquired, the more you want? If a wound got no better by the use of the prescribed root or herb, you would cease to have it dressed by that which had no efficacy. You have been told, perhaps, that riches, Heaven's gift, deliver their possessor from depravity and folly; though, since you were richer, you find yourself no wiser, you still persist to follow the same counsellors. But if it were true that wealth could give you wisdom, contentment, moral courage, then surely you had reason to blush, if a greater miser than you could be found in the whole world.

158—179. *But what do we mean by property? Is the word, property, applicable at all to such a state of things as is found in man's life?*

If what a man buys by the forms of legal purchase is his property, there are some things, if you believe the lawyers, to which use gives a title. The farm is yours, on the produce of which you live; and Orbius' bailiff, harrowing the cornfields from which you are to get your bread, owns you as his true lord. For money paid you receive raisins, chickens, eggs, your cask of wine: why, this is your way of purchasing bit by bit a farm bought for three hundred thousand sesterces, or perchance for even more. What odds does it make, whether you live on what you paid for lately, or a long time ago? A man bought a farm at Aricia or Veii; he buys the vegetables at his dinner, though he may think he does not, he buys the logs with which he heats his copper pot in the cold evening: yet he calls all his own property, up to the poplar planted at the settled boundary to prevent a dispute with his neighbour: just as if anything were property, which at the point of every passing hour, by prayer, by purchase, by violence, by death the end of all things, changes its masters, and passes to the ownership of another. Thus to none is granted the use in perpetuity; and an heir comes after the heir of him who was heir to one before, as waves follow waves; what then avail rows of houses or granaries, or what avail Lucanian mountain-pastures united to Calabrian, if great things and small alike are mown by the scythe of Death, a god not to be won by gold?

180—204. *Various are the tastes and natures of men, as the Genius of each fashions them. Horace hopes that he may avoid extremes, and live contented with his lot.*

Jewels, marble, ivory, Tuscan images, paintings, plate, garments dyed in African purple, there are who have not, here and there is one who does not care to have. One of two brothers prefers idling, playing, perfuming, to the unctuous palm-groves of Herod; another, rich and restless, from the dawn to the evening-shades reclaims the woodlands with fire and the iron plough; why so, is only known to the Genius-god, who, the companion of our existence, rules our natal star, the god of human nature, destined to die when each man dies, various of face, fair, or dark. I will enjoy my own, and take what need requires, from my moderate sum; I will not fear my heir's judgment of me, because he finds no more than I have bequeathed him: and yet I would not be ignorant how much the cheerful giver differs from the spendthrift, how much the frugal from the miser. 'Tis one thing lavishly to waste, another not to grudge to spend, and not to strive to increase one's store; 'tis better, like a schoolboy in the holidays, to snatch a fleeting enjoyment of life. Far from my home be a mean squalor; let my vessel be large or small, I that sail in it am the same: I am not borne along with swelling sails and prosperous gales, yet I pass not my whole life midst adverse winds; in strength, genius, display, virtue, station, fortune, behind the foremost, ever before the last.

205—216. *Many besides avarice are the faults of our nature. As we grow in years, may we grow in goodness, and be ready to leave life with a good grace.*

So then you are no miser: go your way. What then? Are you free of all vices together with that one? Is your soul delivered from vain ambition? from the fear of death? from anger? Can you laugh at dreams, magic terrors, prodigies, witches, nightly phantoms, Thessalian portents? do you count your birthdays with a thankful mind? can you forgive a friend? do you grow a milder and better man as old age draws near? How are you relieved by pulling out one of many thorns? If you know not how to live aright, give place to the wise. You have played and eaten and drunk your fill; 'tis time you depart; lest, if you drink more deeply than is proper, you be jeered and driven from the feast by an age which is sprightly with a better grace.

INTRODUCTION TO THE ART OF POETRY.

LUCIUS CALPURNIUS PISO, to whom, with his sons, is addressed the last epistle in Horace's works, had gained victories in Thrace: but he is much better known as the friend of Horace. He is praised by Velleius Paterculus, Seneca, and Tacitus, for having executed the duties of the unpopular office of Prefect of the city with remarkable industry, gentleness, and wisdom. He lived to a great age, outliving Horace by thirty-nine years. Horace in this epistle speaks of the elder of the sons as likely to write verses. The epistle is rightly placed next to the epistles to Augustus and Florus. The subject of the three epistles is in the main the same. They are all written upon the literature of Rome and Greece. But the third epistle, being more general and somewhat more systematic, received even in early days the ambitious title of the "Art of Poetry." It is so called twice by Quintilian. Priscian, Terentius Scaurus, Symmachus, and others, give it the same name. This title has contributed at once to the reputation and to the disparagement of the epistle. Such an honourable name placed it almost in the same rank as Aristotle's treatise on poetry. Horace's lively letter has been naturally far more popular than Aristotle's dry discussion, and for one reader of the Poetics there have doubtless been hundreds of Horace's work. The epistle, dignified with such a name, has had several imitations in modern times. On the other hand, students of it, misled by this title, have expected more than they have found. They have forgotten that it was a letter, not a treatise. We may well suppose that no one would have been more surprised than Horace himself to have heard his letter called by so great a name, and may well imagine what a delightful epistle he could have written, disclaiming the doubtful honour. Horace writes for a particular object, his wish being, as it seems, to deter a certain young man from publishing his compositions rashly; and it has been made almost a matter of complaint, that he is as one who seeks to discourage the aspirations of genius. Perhaps Horace had read the youthful attempts of the elder son; he may have found them wanting in originality, or rough and incorrect; it is unreasonable to accuse Horace (as Scaliger, a great critic of an unamiable character, has done,) of dealing with the little points that concern grammar, rather than poetry. Horace writes as ideas occur to him, in the way in which letters are usually written; and he has been reproached with a want of that very order and lucid arrangement on which he himself sets so high a value. He ends his epistle abruptly, in a humorous manner, after his usual happy way, just as we say it is well to leave a friend with a joke at the end of a conversation; and critics have spoken of the treatise as unfinished. Horace would have replied perhaps: "Unfinished, no doubt; but would you have me as long-winded as blear-eyed Crispinus? The gods forbid! I should bore my friends, young or old. For friends I write, not for critics."

Now, if it be true that Horace's friends, like many other young men, wanted warning rather than encouragement, it is natural that the general style of the treatise should be practical rather than enthusiastic. Here we have the "Art of Poetry" rather than the "Science of Poetry." Here are no high-flown rhapsodies, no metaphysical inquiries, no philosophical analysis. Abstract questions are not discussed here, as to the true theory of poetry, and the like; whether, for instance, Aristotle is right when he says that the aim of tragedy is to purify the passions by means of pity and terror, or whether the pleasure that tragedy gives arises "from its awakening in us the feeling of the dignity of human nature, or from the display of the mysteries of Providence and Fate." These questions to some are interesting, to others simply unintelligible. At any rate they have nothing to do with Horace's Art of Poetry. He had no taste for such vague and profound inquiries, little suited to the age he lived in, or to the practical turn of the Roman mind, or to the particular object of his epistle. Those who consider Aristotle's Poetics a shallow book, will be sure to think Horace's Art of Poetry still more shallow. Walckenaer[1] in his account of Horace's treatise speaks of the eleven precepts of Horace on poetry: this division gives an idea of regularity not to be found in this book; and if we are to count precepts, we should find many more than eleven or twelve scattered up and down in the epistle. Horace throws together in a loose and lively way his pleasant pieces of advice to his friends. His Art of Poetry is an "art without an art;" or, if there be art, it is art concealed. He is truly natural throughout. As Pope said of Homer, so may we say of him, "Horace and Nature are the same." He begins with a jest and ends with a jest. He laughs good-naturedly at the pretty patches of a pompous poetry. He recommends modesty and diffidence. He claims liberty for himself, and his illustrious friends Virgil and Varius, to invent new words and expressions, but he does not look that these should have an immortality, which the most splendid material works of the Empire were not destined to enjoy. It is true that in the middle of the epistle the writer is more methodical, and speaks with an authority which he had earned by his success: but even here he is still unassuming, and mixes together various subjects; as of metre, feet, epic poetry, tragedy, comedy and satiric poems, of the characteristics of the various ages

[1] Walckenaer, *Vie d'Horace.* Paris, 2nd edition, 1858.

of life, of the office of the chorus, of his own humble powers, of Roman money-getting habits, of the carelessness of Latin writers, (his favourite topic,) and many other points. The turns of his style are easy. He never dwells long on one point. He is more of a letter-writer than a critic, and is a satirist rather than a teacher. Towards the end of the letter, he again returns to a style of light and happy banter, and a kindly allusion to his good friend Quintilius, whose loss he had bewailed in one of the most touching of his odes. Thus we part company with Horace in one of the happiest of his happy moods, and leave him using a homely simile. Who would have him other than he is? Whether he succeeded in restraining the eagerness of his young friend, we have no means of knowing; all we know about the elder of Piso's sons is, that he died before his father, being assassinated when prætor of Spain. However, if anything can teach modesty, good-nature, and sense, it is this short book of Horace, call it Epistle, or Art of Poetry, or what you like.

But this is certain, that with little apparent effort, and little trouble, except, no doubt, the careful correction of particular expressions, Horace has given us an immortal treatise. Truly has Keightley called it the Art of Criticism, rather than the Art of Poetry. The same may be said of Boileau's Art of Poetry. Pope has properly named his treatise an "Essay on Criticism." Walckenaer says that Vida's Poetics have received the praises of Scaliger, that they are written in a florid and elegant style, and in verses that imitate the Virgilian rhythm; but that they are weak and diffuse, and violate the Horatian maxim, "In all your precepts remember to be brief." This fault of diffuseness cannot justly be found either with Boileau or Pope. Both these writers are clear, correct, terse, and to the point. They are elegant, but do not sacrifice other qualities to elegance. They both have a large share of the sense and judgment of the Latin writer. They are not without his liveliness; at any rate, the English poet is not. While Horace owes little or nothing to Aristotle's Poetics, the two modern authors owe very much to Horace, and Boileau in particular is a close imitator. As Pope says of him, "He still in right of Horace sways." Indeed, parts of his "Art" are almost translations of Horace, and happy ones too. Boileau, like Horace, does not deny that genius is necessary for a poet, but dwells much on the importance of art. He is the strong advocate of common sense, and of the avoidance of all extremes. He is quite the writer of the Augustan age of France, and has a relation to Louis XIV. not altogether unlike that of Horace to Augustus. He has the same distaste for pompous pretensions in poetry. He warns poets against flatterers as strongly as Horace does. He also speaks of the various kinds of poetry, and their difference. He follows his master closely and happily in his description of the characteristics of the ages of men. For all that, curiously enough, he gives only four lines to the express mention of Horace, to whom he owes so much, lines too without any particular point in them. Voltaire, who styles the Satires of Boileau the failure of his youth, speaks of his Epistles as fine, and of his Art of Poetry as admirable. The praise is deserved, and comes from one who on such a subject as the Epistles of Horace is a good judge, though on many other subjects, as on the Bible, Shakspeare, and Calderon, a very bad one. Still, though Boileau, like Horace, is clear, neat, sensible, correct, though to both writers may be applied the line:

"Si j'écris quatre mots, j'en effacerai trois,"

yet is he wonderfully inferior to the Roman poet, and leaves, at least on an Englishman, the impression of weariness, caused no doubt in part by the want of variety in his style, and by a lack of vigour and spirit.

Most that may be said of Boileau's production is applicable to Pope's "Essay on Criticism," a treatise composed in the same style and manner. Pope is the writer of the Augustan age of England. In order and regularity and the completeness of his plan, Pope is superior to Horace; some of his lines are models of neatness of expression; specially, in his illustration of the manner in which the sound should be an echo to the sense, he has written some of the most perfect lines in any poetry; he feels, and admirably expresses his feeling, that to make a good critic the heart should be right as well as the head; and that pride, prejudice, and envy are almost as great a hindrance to a true judgment in literature, as dulness and ignorance. And yet even Pope's "Essay on Criticism," with all its merits, is wanting in the variety, the life, the playfulness, the graceful negligence, the happy ease, of the inimitable Latin author.

Lord Byron's "Hints from Horace" is an adaptation of the "Art of Poetry" in the manner of Pope; or, as he himself curiously expresses it, "An allusion in English verse to the Epistle Ad Pisones de Arte Poeticâ." The work is a complete failure, though written by a great poet; it is for the most part commonplace and dull; it wants the ease and delicacy of Horace, Pope's epigrammatic felicity of phrase and command of antithesis, and the concise and studied carefulness of workmanship common to both the earlier poets. For the poetical genius of Byron, though more powerful and splendid than that of Horace or Pope, is yet deficient in their peculiar excellencies: and perhaps the consciousness of this deficiency was in a great measure the cause of that extravagant admiration of Pope which Byron felt throughout his life. It is remarkable that Byron himself preferred the "Hints from Horace" to the first two cantos of "Childe Harold," which he had written about the same time; and after an interval of nine years, during which he had written most of those works which have given him his fame, he says, alluding to these "Hints," "I wrote better then than now." This preference for their inferior writings has been not uncommon with poets: so Milton preferred his "Paradise Regained" to "Paradise Lost," and Petrarch his Latin Poems to his Sonnets. Notwithstanding his veneration of Pope, Byron seems to have had little sympathy with Horace, any more than with Virgil. In the latter poet he can only see "that harmonious plagiary and miserable flatterer;" and of the former he speaks as

"Horace, whom I hated so;" and he goes on to speak of "the curse" that it is,

> "To comprehend, but never love thy verse."

Yet in the same passage he well describes the characteristic of Horace's style of satire, (in words somewhat similar to those of Persius,) as

> "Awakening without wounding the touched heart."

Horace was a Greek scholar, an admirer of Greek literature, and yet we cannot account him as one able to enter into the spirit of such writers as Æschylus or Sophocles. His rules about poetry are not applicable to all classical, still less are they prospectively to modern, poetry, except to a certain part of it.

> "The poet's eye, in a fine frenzy rolling,
> Doth glance from heaven to earth, from earth to heaven."

With such a poet as that, Horace's criticisms have no relation. And even the artificial style of poetry owes but little to criticism. Racine would not learn much from the sensible advice of Boileau. Genius inspires the poet, not merely with noble thoughts, but with untaught shapes, the forms in which suitably to clothe these thoughts. The good that criticism can do is negative rather than positive. It is something to deter those who have no genius for writing poetry from trying to be poets, and to warn such that heaven and earth and booksellers alike condemn mediocrity in poetry. And if good poets are rare, so are good critics. Compositions such as those of Boileau and Pope, in which sense, wit, terseness of expression are found, give pleasure. And Horace's "Art of Poetry" is full of information on subjects long past, is not unworthy of the author of the Satires and Epistles, is full of kindly wit and lively wisdom, and has furnished succeeding ages with many a quotation applied to subjects quite different from that on which the line was originally written.

THE ART OF POETRY.

1—23. *Unity and simplicity are necessary in a poem.*

If a painter were to try to unite to a man's head a horse's neck, or to put party-coloured feathers on limbs collected from every kind of animal, so that, for instance, a woman fair to the waist were to end foul in the tail of an ugly fish; if admitted to view, my friends, could you restrain your laughter? Believe me, my dear Pisos, that just like a monstrous picture of that kind would be a poem, whose images are formed as unreal as the dreams of a sick man, in such a manner as that neither foot nor head can be assigned to one uniform shape. You will say perhaps: "Painters and poets have ever had a reasonable liberty to venture as their fancy bids." 'Tis true, I know, and I grant and claim in return this license; yet not to such excess, as that wild creatures may be mated with tame, and serpents coupled with birds, tigers with lambs. It is the fashion now-a-days to stitch to pompous openings of great professions one or two fine patches of brilliant colour to glitter far and wide, with a description of the grove and altar of Diana, or maze of hurrying stream through pleasant fields, or river Rhine, or rainbow; but it turns out this was not the place for such scenes. And perhaps, sir painter, you can paint a cypress well; but what is the good of that, if you are paid to paint a mariner swimming to the shore from his shipwrecked vessel, a ruined man? A wine-jar was to be produced; why from the potter's circling wheel comes forth a pitcher? In short, be your composition what it may, at least let it be simple and uniform.

24—37. *We, who would be poets, must guard against all extremes.*

Most of us poets (I write to a father and sons worthy of their father) mislead ourselves by the appearance of truth. Thus, I strive to be brief, I become obscure; one poet aims at smoothness, and is wanting in vigour and spirit; another lays claim to grandeur, and is bombastic; along the ground crawls he who would guard himself too much, as dreading the gusty storm; he who would diversify with monstrous prodigies a subject that is really one, is as he who would paint a porpoise in the woods, a wild boar amidst the waves: thus an unskilful avoidance of faults leads into error. Near the school of

Æmilius is an ordinary artist, who in bronze can represent nails and imitate flowing locks, but who fails in the entire statue, being unable to execute the whole figure. Now, if I cared to compose any work, I would no more wish to be such an artist as this, than I would choose to live admired for my black eyes and black hair, but disfigured by a crooked nose.

38—44. *We must well consider our powers before we write.*

Ye authors, choose a subject suited to your abilities, and long ponder what your strength is equal to, what it is too weak to support. He who chooses a theme according to his powers, will find neither command of language nor lucid arrangement fail him. And herein lies, unless I deceive myself, the power and beauty of arrangement; if a writer says at once only what ought to be said at once, reserving most points, and omitting them for the present.

45—72. *We may coin new words, when necessary, but this must be done with care: words, like all other things, are subject to change.*

In the arrangement of his words, too, let the author of the long-promised poem shew delicate taste, and care, preferring one word, rejecting another. You will express yourself excellently well, if by a curious combination you make a familiar word seem original. Should it happen to be necessary to indicate by new terms things before unknown, you may invent expressions not so much as heard of by the old fashioned Cethegi, and license will be granted, if not abused; and words, though new and lately invented, will gain credit, if derived from the Greek, and a little altered in form. What! shall the Roman public grant Cæcilius and Plautus a liberty, which they deny to Virgil and Varius? I myself too, if I have been able to contribute a few new words, should not be grudged this liberty, since the writings of Cato and Ennius have enriched their mother tongue, and coined new names for things. 'Tis a license that has been granted, and ever will be, to put forth a new word stamped with the current die. At each year's fall the forests change their leaves, those green in spring then fall; even so the old race of words passes away, while new-born words, like youths, flourish in vigorous life. We must pay the debt of death, we and all our works; whether Neptune be received into the land, and our fleets are defended from the northern gales, a right royal work; or the marsh, long time unfruitful and fit only for boats, now finds food for the neighbouring towns, and feels the weight of the plough; or the river has changed its course destructive to the crops, and has been taught to flow in a better channel; yes, all the works of mortal men shall perish; much less can the fashion and favour of words remain longlived. Many names now in disuse shall again appear, many now in good repute shall be forgotten, if custom wills it so; custom, the lord and arbiter and rightful legislator of language.

73—85. *The various kinds of poetry, epic, elegiac, dramatic, lyric.*

The measure suited to the exploits of princes and captains, and to the sorrows of war, Homer has shown us. Verses joined in unequal pairs contained first complainings, then the thoughts of successful vows: but who was the inventor of these elegiacs with their shorter measure, grammarians still dispute, and undecided is the question. Rage armed Archilochus with his own iambic metre; the comic sock and high majestic buskin chose this foot, as suited for dialogue, and able to overcome the din of the assembled people, and the natural one for the action of the stage. But to the lyre the Muse granted to sing of gods and children of gods, and victorious boxers, and horses that win in the race, and sorrows of enamoured swains, and cups that free the soul.

86—98. *We must suit our style to the different kinds of poetry.*

Settled are the various forms and shades of style in poetry: if I lack the ability and knowledge to maintain these, how can I have the honoured name of poet? Or why through false shame do I prefer ignorance to being taught? A comic subject refuses to be set forth in tragic verse: so too the tale of the Thyestean banquet scorns to be told in lines suited to some ordinary theme, and unworthy of more than the common sock. Let each style keep its appointed place with propriety. And yet at times, too, Comedy will raise her voice, and angry Chremes storms in swelling tones; so the Telephus and Peleus of tragedy often express their sorrows in language akin to prose, and either hero, in poverty and exile, will cast aside bombast and words a cubit long, if he cares at all to touch the heart of the spectator by his piteous tale.

99—118. *The words also must be suitable to the character in whose mouth the poet puts them.*

For poems to have beauty of style is not enough; they must have pathos also, and lead, where'er they will, the hearer's soul. As human countenances answer with laughter to those that laugh, so do they express sympathy with those that weep; if you would have me weep, you must yourself first grieve; thus alone shall I be touched by your misfortunes, Telephus or Peleus; if you deliver words ill suited to your character, I shall either fall asleep, or laugh. Sad words become a face of sorrow; to angry countenances are suited threats; while jests set off a playful look; serious words become a grave brow. For nature shapes our inner feelings to each state of our fortunes; she makes us joyous, or drives us to anger; or to the earth by weight of woe depresses our tortured hearts: then she expresses our passions by the tongue, the soul's interpreter. So, if the words of the speaker are discordant with his fortunes, loud will be the laughter raised by the Roman spectators, knights and rank and file alike. It will make no little difference, whether a god is the speaker, or a hero, a man of mature age, or one still in the flower and fervour of youth, matron of high rank, or bustling nurse, a roaming merchant, or a tiller of a fruitful farm, Colchian or Assyrian, one reared at Thebes or at Argos.

119—152. *A writer should follow the traditions of the Muse; or, if he strikes out something new, must be consistent. No better guide can we follow than Homer.*

Either follow tradition, or, if you invent, let your creation be consistent. If you once more introduce on the stage illustrious Achilles, he must appear as one restless, passionate, inexorable, keen of soul; he must say law was not made for the like of him, appealing to the sword alone. Again, let Medea be haughty, untamed of soul, but Ino bathed in tears, Ixion perjured, Io a wanderer, Orestes melancholy mad. If you trust to the stage an untried subject, and venture on the creation of an original character, it must be kept to the end of the play such as it was when it was brought on at the beginning, and consistent. Hardly will you give to what is general an individuality; you will be more likely to succeed by dividing the subject of the Iliad into the acts of a play, than if in an original poem you bring forward a theme unknown, as yet unsung. A subject open to all will become your own private property, by your not lingering in the trite and obvious circle of events; neither must you care to render word for word, as a literal translator; nor, as a mere copyist, throw yourself into a cramped space, whence either shame or the rules of the piece forbid your moving a step. Begin not, as did the cyclic writer of old: "Of Priam's fate and far-famed war I'll sing." What will this braggart produce worthy of so bombastic a boast? Mountains are in labour; to the birth comes a most absurd mouse. Far more truly acted he, who makes no ill-timed effort: "Sing, Muse, to me the hero, who, after the days of the capture of Troy, visited many towns, saw many customs." Smoke he never means to bring from a bright blaze, but out of smoke gives us light, that after that he may show us picturesque marvels, such as Antiphates and Scylla, Cyclops and Charybdis; nor does he set forth the return of Diomede from the death of Meleager, or the Trojan war from the twin eggs; ever to the end he hastens, and hurries the reader into the middle of events, assuming them as known; what he despairs of so handling as to make it brilliant, that he drops, and so invents, so with fictions weaves the truth, that the middle harmonises with the opening, and the end with the middle.

153—178. *A writer too should observe the characteristics of each age of man.*

Now hear, what I, aye, and the people too, expect. If you want your auditor to applaud you and stay for the curtain, and to be sure to keep his seat till the actor chants the words "Please, sirs, to applaud," carefully must you observe the characteristics of each age, and assign to each the proprieties of shifting dispositions and changing years. First comes the boy, who just knows how to form words, and with steadier foot to walk; he delights to play with his mates, and on slight cause flies into passion, quickly is appeased, and changes every hour. Next the beardless youth, at last free from his guardian, rejoices in horses and hounds, and the grass of the sunny plain of Mars; easily moulded, like wax, to vice, to those who would admonish him rough, slow to provide what is useful, lavish of his money, high-spirited, passionate in his desires, quick to relinquish his fancies. Then comes a change in a man's spirit, for the temper of middle life seeks wealth, and interest, is the slave of ambition, is careful lest it do that in a hurry, which afterwards it must labour to amend. Last of all, many are the discomforts that gather around old age; either because an old man amasses, and then with miserly soul spares and fears to use his stores; or because he performs every act with timorous and chilled spirit, is a procrastinator, a laggard in hope, sluggish, yet greedy of a longer life, crabbed, querulous, ever praising the bygone days of his boyhood, but the corrector and censor of the young. Many blessings does the flowing tide of years bring with it, many does its ebb take from us. Now, lest perchance we attribute an old man's parts to a youth, or a man's to a boy, never must we wander beyond the limits of what suits and is akin to each age.

179—188. *Some things should be represented on the stage, others related to the spectators.*

Events are either acted on the stage, or reported as done off it. Now, less keenly are our spirits stirred by what drops into the ears, than by what is placed before the trustworthy eyes, when the spectator sees for himself. And yet there are things which should be done behind the scenes, bring not these forward; and much should you withdraw from the eyes, presently to be described by an actor's ready speech before the audience; so that, for instance, Medea should not murder her children in front of the spectators, nor impious Atreus cook on the stage human flesh, nor Progne be transformed into a bird, Cadmus into a snake. Scenes put before me in this way move only my incredulity and disgust.

189—201. *Certain rules not to be transgressed. The office of the Chorus.*

Let not a play be either shorter or longer than five acts; or it will hardly be called for and again represented on the stage. Nor let a god intermeddle, unless a difficulty arise worthy of miraculous interposition; nor let a fourth character attempt to speak. Let the Chorus maintain the parts and duties of a single actor; nor let it sing any song between the acts, save what advances and fitly belongs to the plot of the piece. Let the Chorus support the good, and give them friendly counsel, and restrain the angry, and love those that fear to sin; let it praise the fare of a humble board, and admire justice which is a health to a state, and laws and gates that stand open in peace; let it keep secrets, and offer prayers and supplications to the gods, that fortune may revisit the wretched, depart from the proud.

202—219. *Of the music of the stage, and how it changes with the fortunes and manners of the people.*

The flute in the days of old was not, as now, bound with yellow copper ore, nor did it rival the trumpet in power, but was slight and simple with few holes, good to accompany and aid the Chorus, and to fill with its breath benches not yet crowded, whither would flock spectators easily numbered, for they were but few, an industrious, pious, modest people. But when conquests enlarged the territory, and a greater circle of wall embraced the city, and banquets began early, and on holidays each man freely propitiated his genius, then to the rhythms and music was given greater license. For taste could not be looked for from the unlettered rustic, when in the theatre he sat freed from his labours, crowded with the man of the city, the rough and the polite together. Thus to the art of the days of old the flute-player added the dance, and elaborate music, and drew across the stage his robe's long train. Then to the lyre once severe were added new strings, then an impetuous flow of language produced an eloquence as yet unheard, while saws of wisdom keen to discern what was useful, and prophetic of the future, rivalled the utterance of oracular Delphi.

220—250. *The Satyric drama, which accompanied the tragedy, is not the same as comedy, and has its rules and wholesome restraints.*

He who in tragic verse contended for the prize of a common goat, presently introduced on the stage the half-naked forms of the wild Satyrs; he did not lower the dignity of the Muse, and yet he ventured on rough jokes; for he felt that the allurements and pleasures of novelty would alone keep in their seats spectators, who had just assisted at the sacrifice, well drunken, lawless in spirit. And yet it will be right to introduce these mocking and witty Satyrs, and to pass from grave to gay, only in such a way as that any god or hero, just before conspicuous in regal gold and purple, now joining this company, may not be as one shifting from a palace into low taverns, there to use vulgar language; nor yet as one, who, avoiding what is low, affects cloudy bombast. Insult not the tragic Muse by making her babble out silly verses; if she appears amidst the wanton Satyrs, let her be somewhat reserved, as matron bid to dance on holidays. Were I a writer of satyric pieces, I would not choose bald and common terms, nor would I, my friends, so far depart from the tragic style, as though it made no difference, whether Davus was the speaker and impudent Pythias who got a talent by gulling Simon, or Silenus, guardian and attendant of a divine pupil. My play should be composed throughout in familiar terms, so that anybody may hope to do the same, may labour and toil much, attempting the same, and fail; such is the power of sequence and arrangement, so great the beauty that can crown the commonest expressions. When the Fauns are fetched from the woods, my judgment is that they need to be careful, lest they appear like those born where the streets meet, and almost as loungers in the forum, and their verses sound as the words of our effeminate young men, or lest they talk in coarse and disreputable language: for thus are disgusted the knights, the free-born, the rich, who will not endure the play with patience or reward the poet, however much the buyers of roasted chick-peas and walnuts may approve.

251—274. *On the Iambic and Spondee. The Greek taste is to be followed, rather than the license of the Roman poets, in respect of metre.*

When a long syllable follows a short one, the foot is called an Iambic, a rapid foot; whence it would have the name of trimeters appropriated to the iambic measure, though six were the times it beat, from the first to the last being the same throughout. But not so very long ago, that slower and more solemnly the verse might fall on the ear, the Iambic admitted the steady Spondee into a part of its inheritance, with obliging good nature, so as to share the room, and not to yield from the second and fourth place. In the much vaunted trimeters of Accius, this Iambic appears but seldom, and as to those verses of Ennius, which he sent upon the stage like missiles of ponderous weight, the Iambic lays on them the discreditable charge of hasty and careless composition, or of ignorance of the poetic art. It is not every one that can judge and see when verses are unmusical, and our Roman writers have an allowance made for them, unworthy of poets. Shall I then write loosely and carelessly, or shall I suppose that all will see my faults, and so shall I feel secure and be cautious within the limits of pardon? If so, at the best I have but escaped censure, praise I do not deserve. But do you, my friends, study diligently night and day the Greek models. You will answer, perhaps, your forefathers praised both the rhythm and wit of Plautus; their praise, I say, was given too easily, not to say foolishly, to both the one and the other; at least, if you and I can see the difference between rough humour and polished wit, and know how to beat with the thumb, and with the ear to catch the proper rhythm.

275—294. *The origin of tragedy. Its developement. To it succeeded the old comedy, vigorous, but scurrilous. The Latin poets deserve some praise, but their great fault is their careless, slovenly style.*

Unknown was the style of the tragic Muse, till Thespis, as is said, introduced it; he carried his poems in travelling wagons, to be chanted by actors whose faces were smeared with lees of wine. After him came Æschylus, the inventor of the tragic robe and comely mask, who made a stage with planks of moderate size, and taught the actors magnificent diction and stately gait on the buskin. Then succeeded the old comedy, which had no little merit; but its liberty degenerated into licence, and into a violence, which the law must check; the law was submitted to, and then the chorus to its shame became dumb, being deprived of the right of abuse. No style have our poets left untried, nor slight the glory they have earned, when they ventured beyond the Grecian track, and dared to sing of our national exploits, putting on the stage either tragedies or comedies on Roman subjects. Nor would the Latin name be more famed for deeds of valour and for arms, than for literature, were not the toil and trouble of correction a stumblingblock to every one of our bards. But do you, in whose veins is the blood of Numa, censure every poem, which many a day and many an erasure has not chastened, and by repeated improvements has amended to the finishing touch.

295—308. *Genius cannot afford to dispense with the rules of art. The critic has his place in literature.*

That genius is happier than poor wretched art is the creed of Democritus, who excludes from Helicon all poets in their senses; therefore a large proportion of would-be-poets care not to pare their nails or shave their beard, haunt retired spots, eschew public baths. He, think they, will get himself the estimation and name of a poet, who never trusts to the barber Licinus that precious pate incurable by the hellebore of three Anticyras. Ah, what a wrong-headed fellow am I! I get my bile purged from me, as spring draws on; otherwise, there is not a living wight who would write better verses: however, after all it does not matter so much. For now will I discharge the office of a whetstone, which, though it cannot cut, makes iron sharp. No poet I, but yet I will teach the poet's duty and office, whence he draws his treasures, what trains and fashions the bard; what graces him, what not; which are the paths of excellence, and which of error.

309—322. *Knowledge is the foundation of good writing. Poetry without sense is but a harmonious trifling.*

Of good writing the foundation and source is moral wisdom. Now the Socratic dialogues will supply you with matter, and words will follow readily, when matter is provided. The writer who has learnt what our country expects of us, what our friends look for, the love we owe to parents, to a brother, to a guest, the duties of a senator and a judge, the parts of a general sent to command in war, he, I feel sure, knows how at once to give to each character his proper speech. I would advise a well-instructed imitator to have an eye to the model which life and manners give, and hence to draw the language of reality. Sometimes a play embellished with moral sentiments, and rightly representing manners, though lacking grace and force and art, delights the people more, and interests them to the end of the piece, rather than verses void of sense, and prettily-sounding trifles.

323—333. *The Greeks had genius; the Romans are a money-getting race.*

The Greeks had genius, the Greeks could speak with well-rounded mouth: this was the Muse's gift to them; they coveted nought but renown. But the Roman boys are taught to divide the as by long calculations into a hundred parts. Supposing the son of Albinus says: "If from five ounces be subtracted one, what is the remainder?" At once you can answer, "A third of an as." "Good, you will be able to keep your property. If an ounce be added, what does it make?" "The half of an as." Ah! when this rust of copper, this slavish love of saving money has once imbued the soul, can we hope for the composition of verses worthy to be rubbed with the oil of cedar, or to be kept in cases of polished cypress?

334—346. *The object of the poet should be to give instruction and delight.*

Poets aim either to benefit, or to delight, or to unite what will give pleasure with what is serviceable for life. In moral precepts be brief; what is quickly said, the mind readily receives and faithfully retains: all that is superfluous runs over from the mind, as from a full vessel. Fictions meant to please should be as like truth as possible; the play ought not to demand unlimited belief; after the dinner of an ogress, let no live boy be taken from her stomach. The centuries of the senators drive from the stage poems devoid of moral lessons; the aristocratic knights disapprove of dry poems; that poet gets every vote, who unites information with pleasure, delighting at once and instructing the reader. Such a poem brings money to the publishers, and is sent across the sea, and gives immortality to its illustrious author.

347—360. *Perfection in a poem we do not expect, but we do expect care and pains.*

Yet faults there are, that we can gladly pardon; for a chord does not always return the sound which the hand and mind intend, and, when we expect the flat, very often gives us a sharp; and arrows often miss the threatened mark. But the truth is, where most in a poem is brilliant, I would not be offended at a few blots, which inattention has carelessly let drop, or the infirmity of human nature failed to guard against. What then is the truth? If a copyist, often warned, ever makes the same mistake, he is inexcusable; if a harper is always at fault on the same string, he is derided; so, a very heedless writer is to my mind a second Chœrilus, whose rare excellencies surprise me, while still I laugh; whilst I, the same man, am indignant, if good old Homer sometimes nods. However, it is allowable, if in a long work sleep steals over a writer.

361—365. *A short comparison between poetry and painting.*

As painting, so is poetry; some takes your fancy more, the nearer you stand, some, if you go to a little distance; one poem courts obscurity, another is willing to be seen in a strong light, and dreads not the keen judgment of the critic; one poem pleases but once, another, called for many a time, yet still will please.

366—390. *All men, nearly, would be poets; but mediocrity in poetry is insufferable; wherefore be careful before you publish.*

O elder youth, both by your father's teaching are you trained to what is correct, and naturally you have good judgment; yet what I also say, do you make your own, and remember that in certain subjects mediocrity is allowable, and a tolerable success; for instance, a chamber-counsel and a pleader of fair ability falls short of the excellence of eloquent Messala, and yields in knowledge to Cascellius Aulus, and yet he is valued; but mediocrity in poets is condemned by gods and men, aye, and booksellers too. As during pleasant banquets discordant music and perfumed oil coarse in quality and poppy mixed with bitter honey are offensive, for the dinner might have dispensed with these accompaniments: so poetry, the end and nature of which is to delight the soul, if it fall somewhat short of excellence, inclines to what is faulty. One ignorant of a game stands aloof from the contest in the Campus, and, if unskilled in ball or quoit or hoop, remains an inactive spectator, lest the crowded ring raise an unreproved laughter: but he who is no versifier, yet dares to try to make verses. Prithee, why should he not? Is he not free, nay, free-born, above all, is he not rated as possessed of equestrian fortune, and is he not clear from all moral censure? But you, my friend, will say and do nothing against the bent of your genius, such is your judgment, such your sense; however, if at some future time you write something, let it first be read before Mæcius as critic, before your father and me, and let it be kept back for nine years on the parchments in your desk; you can destroy what you have never published; a word once uttered you cannot recall.

391—407. *The origin and office of poetry in early days.*

Once in the woods men lived; then holy Orpheus, heaven's interpreter, turned them from slaughter and their foul manner of life; hence he was said to have soothed tigers and ravening lions; hence too it was said that Amphion, founder of the Theban citadel, moved rocks to the strains of his lyre, and led them by alluring persuasion, whithersoever he listed. In days of yore it was wisdom's office to set the marks between public and private property, between things sacred and profane, to restrain men from vague concubinage, to appoint rights for man and wife, to build cities, to engrave laws on tablets of wood: thus came honour and renown to prophetic bards and their poems. Afterwards, glorious Homer and Tyrtæus roused manly hearts to martial wars by their songs; oracles were delivered in verse, and the path of life pointed out, and the favour of princes sought by the strains of the Muses, and the drama invented, to come at the end of the long toils of the year; so that you, my friend, may see you have no reason to be ashamed of the Muse skilled in the lyre, and Apollo who chants to its melody.

408—418. *Genius is necessary for a poet, and yet, without art and study, genius will fail.*

Whether by genius or by art an excellent poem is produced, has often been the question: but I do not see what can be done by study without a rich vein of intellect, nor by genius when uncultivated: so true is it that either requires the help of either, and that the two combine in friendly union. He who passionately desires to reach in the race the goal, must first endure and do much as a boy, suffer from toil and cold, abstain from love and wine; he who at the Pythian games sings to the flute, has first been to school and feared a master. Nor is it enough to say, "I compose wondrous poems; murrain take the hindmost! I think it a shame to be left behind, and to confess that I am utterly ignorant of that which I never learnt."

419—452. *Let poets avoid flatterers. Quintilius was an honest friend, whose mission it was to tell an author unpleasant truths.*

As an auctioneer collects crowds to buy wares, so a poet, if rich in lands and money put out at interest, bids flatterers flock to the call of gain. But if he be one who can give a handsome dinner, and be bail for a poor man whose credit is gone, or if he can deliver one who is embarrassed by ugly lawsuits, then I shall be surprised, if the fond happy soul is clever enough to distinguish between a false and true friend. You, if you have made or intend to make a present to any one, do not bring the man full of grateful joy to hear your verses: for he will cry, "Beautiful! good! correct!" he will turn pale with wonder over them, he will even drop dewy tears from his loving eyes, he will jump as with delight, he will strike the ground with his foot. As hired mourners at a funeral in words and actions outdo those whose grief is sincere; so does the man who laughs behind your back seem more moved than a real admirer. Patrons are said to press hard with many a cup, and test with wine the man whom they desire thoroughly to try, whether he be worthy of their friendship; so, if you compose poems, be not unaware of the feeling concealed under the exterior, like that of the fox in the fable. If one read a passage to Quintilius, he would say, "Friend, correct this or that." If one said he could not improve it after two or three trials, then he would bid him erase it, and return the ill-formed verses to the anvil of correction. But if one preferred the defence of a fault to the amending of it, he wasted not a single word more, nor threw away his pains to prevent a man from having the fondest love of himself and his own writings, without any rival admirer. A good and sensible man will censure spiritless lines, blame harsh ones, put a smearing mark with the back of his pen to inelegant verses, will prune ambitious ornaments, force you to make plain your obscurities, will blame an equivocal phrase, and note what should be altered; so will he shew himself a second Aristarchus, and never say, "Why offend a friend for trifles?" seeing that these trifles bring serious trouble on the poet, hooted off the stage once for all after an unlucky reception.

453—476. *A poet goes as mad as Empedocles; let all beware of him, and keep out of the way of one who will not be helped.*

Like one troubled with the evil scab, or jaundice, or frantic madness and Diana's wrath, even so the insane poet all men in their senses fly from, and fear even to touch; the boys hoot at him and heedlessly follow. He with his eyes in the sky belches forth verses, and strays about; then, like a bird-catcher intent on blackbirds, falls into a well or pit; he may cry from afar, "Ho, citizens, come to the help!" but not a soul cares to pull him out. If any one does trouble himself to bring aid, and to let down a rope, how can you tell, I say, whether he did not purposely throw himself in, and wishes not to be saved? So I'll tell you the tale of Sicilian Empedocles, how, wishing to be deemed an immortal god, he leapt in cold blood into burning Etna. Let poets have the right and liberty to perish, if they so please. He who saves a man against his will does the same as if he killed him. The poet has so acted more than once, and if now pulled out, will not for the future become a reasonable man, or lay aside the desire for notorious death. Nor is there any good cause to be shown, why he will always be making verses; whether he has defiled his father's grave, or impiously disturbed some ill-omened accursed plot; anyhow, he is raving mad, and like a bear, who has managed to break the opposing bars of a cage, so he puts to flight the lettered and unlettered alike, by his reading that bores to the death; but if he catches any one, him he holds fast, and kills by his recitation, like a leech, that will not leave the skin, till it is gorged with blood.

[*The references are to the lines of the original.*]

NOTES.

ODES.

BOOK I.

I.

1. 'Mæcenas.' C. Cilnius Mæcenas professed to be descended from the Cilnii, who were Lucumos of Etruria. Comp. III. 29, 1. 'Atavus' is literally a great-great-great-grandfather. Comp. also *Sat.* I. 6, 1.

2. 'You that are.' Comp. Virgil, Georg. II. 40.

4. 'to gather,' 'collegisse.' It seems best to explain this perf. inf. as being used in an aoristic sense, to express the habit. 'to gather' appears simply to mean 'to raise a cloud of dust.' 'The goal' is the pillar at the end of the double course, which had to be rounded by the racing chariots.

7. 'citizens,' lit. 'Quirites,' the name applied to the Romans in their civil capacity. It is curious that the probable der. 'Quiris,' should mean 'a spearman:' in early times all the citizens served the state as soldiers.

8. 'threefold honours.' Curule ædile, prætor, consul; this was the regular sequence of the 'curule honours.'

12. 'an Attalus.' The name of several kings of Pergamus, famous for their wealth and patronage of art. Attalus III. bequeathed his possessions to the Roman people. (B.C. 133.)

14. 'Myrtoan main.' That part of the Ægean sea south of Myrtos, an island off the south coast of Eubœa. This epithet, as well as that of 'Cyprian,' seems to be merely ornamental. So too 'Icarian waves,' i.e. the sea between the islands of Samos and Icaria.

15. 'African blasts.' The W. S. W. wind (sirocco). It was thus named, because it blows upon Italy from the coast of Africa. It is still called 'l'Affrico' by the Italians.

19. 'Massic.' This wine was from the slopes of Mons Massicus, between Campania and Latium. It ranked 3rd or 4th among the choicest wines of Italy.

20. 'heart of the day,' lit. 'solid day:' i.e. while the whole or most of it is still to come. Comp. 'integro die,' IV. 38.

25. 'cold sky,' lit. 'Jupiter:' the name of the God of the sky being put, as it often is, for the sky itself. Comp. 'sub divo,' II. 3, 23.

28. 'Marsian boar.' The country of the Marsi (N. E. of Latium) abounded in thickets and forests.

29. 'ivy-leaf;' sacred to Bacchus the inspirer of lyric poetry. 'learned brows.' Comp. Spenser, *Faerie Queene*, Canto I. Stanza 9; 'poets sage.' So Gr. σοφοί. Pind. *Ol.* I. 15.

33. The Scholiast (on Hesiod's *Theogony*, 77) says that Euterpe invented the flute. Polyhymnia was said to have invented the lyre.

34. 'Lesbian lyre;' i.e. the lyric poetry of Lesbos, especially that of Alcæus and Sappho.

II.

6. 'Pyrrha.' The daughter of Epimetheus and Pandora, and the wife of Deucalion.

7. 'Proteus.' The Old Man of the sea. Vid. Virg. *Georg.* IV. 395.

14. 'Tuscan shore;' i.e. from the Etruscan or Tyrrhenian sea at the mouth of the Tiber. Orelli says that the Romans still think the floods of the Tiber are caused by the force of the sea driving back the water from the mouth of the river.

15. 'monuments of the king.' The so-called palace of Numa and temple of Vesta at the foot of the Palatine.

17. 'Ilia' (Rea Silvia) was the mother of Romulus. She was said to have been drowned in the Anio, a tributary of the Tiber; so Horace here represents her as the river's wife. Ovid, (*Amores* III. 6, 45) mentions her as the wife of the Anio. Ilia 'complains' of the assassination of Cæsar, and of the civil wars. Jupiter of the Capitol was the guardian god of Rome.

22. 'Parthians,' lit. 'Persians.' They are often called Persians, or Medes, by Horace, as occupying the ancient kingdom of Persia.

32. 'Diviner,' lit. Augur, i.e. 'Seer.' Comp. German 'auge,' 'eye.'

33. 'Erycina,' Venus, so named from her famous temple on mount Eryx in Sicily.

36. 'our Founder,' Mars. The 'show' in the next line seems to be an allusion to the gladiatorial shows. See I. 28, 17, 'a show for grisly Mars.'

39. 'Marsian.' All the MSS. have 'Mauri;' but the conjecture is so much better, and the change is so slight, that it has been adopted by most commentators. See II. 20, 18.

41. 'a youth.' Augustus was forty at this time; but 'juvenis' is applicable to any man in the vigour of life; and the emperor seems to have liked the name, which suited him better in the earlier days of his power. He is twice called 'juvenis' by Virgil: *Ecl.* I. 42, *Georg.* I. 500. 'kind Maia's winged child.' Mercury.

III.

1. 'So.' The usual sequence would be 'ut reddas,'='on this condition, that you restore,' &c. But by a poetical variation Horace substitutes the pres. subj. alone.

'the goddess,' Venus, who is invoked as a Power of the sea. With 'potens Cypri,' comp. '*Naiadum potens*,' III. 25, 14.

2. 'Helen's brethren,' Castor and Pollux. The phosphorescent light seen on the mast after a storm was supposed to denote their propitious presence. See I. 12, 27. The Italians, by a curious corruption of the name of Helen, have formed the expression 'St. Elmo's fire.'

3. 'the father of the winds,' Æolus.

4. 'Iapyx.' This was a name of the West wind, blowing from Italy towards Greece. 'Iapygia' is one of the names of Apulia, which lies on the eastern coast of Italy.

14. 'Hyades,' 'ὕαδες,' the rainy stars. Virg. *Æn.* III. 576. 'Notus,' the South wind.

20. 'Acroceraunia,' 'the peak of the thunderbolt;' a headland of Epirus, now 'il monte della Chimera.' Virg. *Georg.* I. 332.

27. 'child of Iapetus,' Prometheus.

36. 'the toiling Hercules:' when he brought up Cerberus from Hades.

IV.

8. 'fiery Vulcan.' The Scholiast says that this is an allusion to the thunderbolts forged by the Cyclops for Jove: for thunderstorms return with the warm weather. The idea is that all things renew their vigour with the coming of spring.

11. 'Faunus.' The 13th (Ides) of February was sacred to Faunus. Ovid, *Fast.* II. 193.

'with impartial foot.' This phrase expresses the rudeness and violence of Death's approach. Plautus, *Most.* II. 2, 23.

14. 'Sestius.' L. Sestius was consul together with Augustus, 23 B.C. 'blest,' 'beate.' This word, as it often does, combines the notions of wealth and happiness.

16. 'fantastic Shades.' lit. 'the Shades that are fables;' i. e. ghostly and unsubstantial.

18. 'by the dice's cast.' It was usual to elect by lot one of the company to act as ruler of the feast. II. 7, 25. St John II. 8.

V.

8. 'and stare;' 'emirabitur.' The prefix is intensitive. This is the only place where the word occurs in writers of the Augustan age.

13. 'votive tablet.' Those saved from shipwreck used to hang up on the wall of Neptune's temple a votive tablet and the garments they had worn in the time of their peril. Virg. *Æn.* XII. 766.

VI.

1. 'Varius.' See *Sat.* I. 10, 43.

2. 'a bird of Homer's strain,' lit. 'of Mæonian strain.' Mæonia was an old name of Lydia, and Homer was born at Smyrna in that kingdom, according to one tradition. 'bird,' 'alite,' abl. Perhaps abl. abs. As an abl. of the agent is contrary to usage, some call this an abl. of the instrument; but 'Vario' must be in apposition with 'alite,' and he certainly must be regarded as a personal agent. If Horace did not (as it has of course been conjectured that he did) write 'aliti,' he must have taken this grammatical license to avoid the jingle of the last syllables of 'Mæonii,' 'aliti.'

5. 'Agrippa.' M. Vipsanius Agrippa was the ablest general of Augustus, and married his only child Julia..

8. 'Pelops' murderous house;' the subject of many of the Greek tragedies, the Agamemnon, Eumenides, Electra, &c.

16. 'a match for the gods.' 'δαίμονι ἶσος,' *Iliad*, V. 884.

18. 'with close-pared nails;' so that the combat is only playful. Bentley's conj. 'strictis,' 'drawn,' (like swords,) seems to convey too strongly the idea of ferocity.

VII.

1. 'Let others praise,' lit. 'Others will praise,' i. e. 'will, if they please.'

2. 'with its double sea;' 'bimaris,' Gr. διθάλασσος; as Corinth lies on the isthmus.

3. 'Thebes made glorious by Bacchus,' as being the son of Semele. I. 19, 2.

4. 'Tempe;' the famous valley of the river Peneus, between Olympus and Ossa.

5. 'the city of virgin Pallas,' (Athene,) Athens.

9. 'Argos meet for steeds;' ἱππόβοτον. Pindar calls Argos Ἥρας δῶμα θεοπρεπές, *Nem.* IX. 3. 'rich Mycenæ;' πολύχρυσοι.

10. 'enduring Lacedæmon;' the virtue always especially ascribed to the Spartans.

11. 'fruitful Larissa:' 'Λαρίσσαν ἐριβώλακα,' *Il.* II. 841.

12. 'home of Albunea,' 'the sacred cave of the Nymph.' Now called 'Solfatara.' It is described in Virg. *Æn.* VII. 82.

13. 'Anio,' now 'Teverone.' the 'torrent' refers to the cascades of Tivoli. (Tibur.)

19. 'Plancus.' L. Munatius Plancus constantly changed from one party to another during the civil wars. He was once consul, and received from Augustus the offices of censor and prefect of the City in 22. B.C.

21. 'Teucer.' He was said to have been banished by his father Telamon, because he did not avenge the wrong done to his brother Ajax.

27. 'conductor,' 'auspex.' A consul in command of an army had the right of taking the auspices: hence the word 'auspicia' came to mean 'leadership,' and 'auspex' 'leader.' Comp. Virg. *Æn.* VI. 781.

28. 'Apollo.' The prophecy is more fully given in Eurip. *Helena* 146.

29. 'Salamis.' The new Salamis was in Cyprus.

30. 'ye who oft.' See Virg. *Æn.* I. 198, imitating *Odyss.* XII. 208.

VIII.

3. 'Plain.' The Campus Martius.

6. 'sharp-toothed bits,' &c. lit. 'bits set with wolves' teeth;' from their likeness in shape. Gaul was famous for horses, and at one time supplied the Roman armies. Tacitus, *Ann.* II. 5.

13. 'The son of Ocean Thetis;' Achilles, disguised as a girl, at the court of Lycomedes, king of the island of Scyros.

16. 'the slaughter,' &c. This meaning seems the most appropriate to the might of Achilles. lit. 'forth into slaughter and the Lycian,' &c. The meaning may be 'forth into the slaughter which the Lycian battalions will effect.'

IX.

1. The first part of this ode is imitated from an extant fragment of Alcæus, preserved by Athenæus; X. 430.

2. 'Soracte.' A hill about 13 miles from Rome, in the country of the Falisci, prob. the modern Monte Tresto.

8. 'Thaliarch.' θαλίαρχος, a ruler of the feast.

23. 'forfeit.' Possibly the word (pignus) would be better translated by 'keepsake.'

X.

1. 'Atlas' grandchild;' as being the son of Maia, Atlas' daughter.

2. 'that didst skilfully fashion.' The same praise is given to Mercury by Ovid, *Fast.* V. 665.

9. 'At thee.' The story is told in the so-called Homeric hymn to Mercury, l. 20.

10. 'tried.' Lit. 'while he tries.' The historic present is poetically employed, though followed by past tenses.

13. 'Likewise too.' *Iliad*, XXIV. 445.

15. 'Thessalian watch-fires.' Those of the Myrmidons.

18. 'with golden wand.' Comp. I. 24, 16, and Virg. *Æn.* IV. 242, following Hom. *Il.* XXIV. 343.

XI.

3. Chaldæan tables;' lit. 'Babylonian.' The passion for studying the Oriental science of astrology, which was afterwards carried to such an extent (Juvenal VI. 553, &c.), was introduced at least as far back as the time of Cicero, who speaks of 'Chaldæan calculations.' (*de Divin.* II. 47.)

6. 'since our span is short;' 'spatio brevi;' abl. abs.

XII.

1. The beginning of this ode is an imitation of Pindar, *Olymp.* II. 1.

2. 'Clio.' lit. 'the proclaimer.' She is usually the Muse of history; but sometimes, as here, the Muse of panegyric, as the name implies.

5. 'Helicon,' &c. Mountains sacred to the Muses.

9. 'by his mother's art;' that of Calliope, 'she of the beautiful voice,' the first of the nine Muses.

11. 'strong in the power,' &c. lit. 'persuasive (blandum), so as to lead.' The constr. is like the Gr. ὥστε with inf.

15. 'the firmament;' 'mundus;' lit. = κόσμος, the order of things. Here it is all the visible part of the universe, except the earth and sea.

22. 'Liber,' lit. 'the free god.' He is named as a warrior god on account of his expedition to India and his valour in the war of the giants. (II. 19, 17, &c.) 'Maid,' 'Diana.'

25. 'boys of Leda,' Castor and Pollux. (I. 3, 2, note.)

35. 'Cato's glorious death.' Comp. II. 24. Virg. *Æn.* VIII.

37. 'Paullus.' The consul L. Æmilius Paullus, at the battle of Cannæ.

40. 'Curius.' M. Curius Dentatus.

46. 'Marcellus.' It seems most natural to refer this passage solely to the son of Octavia, the sister of Augustus, who died when about 18. The previous line is in favour of this explanation. Comp. Virg. *Æn.* VI. 861, &c.

47. 'the Julian star.' The use of the adjective makes it probable that the 'star' signifies the glory of all the Julian gens; and not of Julius Cæsar or Augustus only.

54. 'in proper triumph;' 'justo triumpho,' i.e. complete, well-deserved. The word is formal and technical.

56. 'Seres.' They have been generally considered to be the Chinese. Pliny says they excelled in making silk. *Nat. Hist.* VI. 20.

59. 'sacrilegious groves,' i.e. those profaned by crime. The single mention of 'ille,' (he, Cæsar,) in the previous stanza, seems meant to be contrasted with the triple 'thee, thou, thou,' in this, so as to express the deeper homage due to Jove.

XIII.

2. 'waxen arms;' i.e. rounded, and, perhaps, white.

3. 'labouring bile.' It was an established notion that the liver was the seat of passion, whether jealousy, anger, or love. *Sat.* I. 9, 66. *Od.* IV. 1, 12.

11. 'brawls,' &c. Comp. I. 17, 25: Tibullus I. 6, 14.

16. 'the quintessence.' According to the Pythagoreans, the fifth and purest of the elements was ether: whence the modern word 'quintessence.' So the fifth part is here put for the finest part.

XIV.

1. It is doubtful when this ode was written; perhaps about 32 B.C., when the rupture between Octavianus and Antonius was imminent.

5. 'the swooping Africus.' See I. 1, 15, note.

6. 'not bound with cables.' Comp. Acts XXVII. 17.

11. 'a Pontic pine.' Pontus was famous for its pine-forests. Catullus, 4. 9.

15. 'Unless you owe,' &c. The phrase seems to be modelled on the Gr. constr. of

ὀφλισκάνειν with acc. of the thing: e.g. γέλωτα, αἰσχύνην, &c.

17. 'You that were late.' i.e., as it seems, after the campaign of Philippi.

20. 'Shun you the seas,' &c. i.e. 'Avoid running heedlessly upon the rocks and shoals of civil war.'

XV.

1. 'the shepherd;' Paris, who was exposed on Mount Ida, that he might not cause the fall of Troy; and there brought up by the shepherds. So Ἰδαῖον βούταν, Eur. *Hec.* 932.

3. 'rest unwelcome'; i. e. at variance with the restless movement of the winds.

5. 'Nereus;' 'the god of the flowing water.' He is spoken of as a true prophet in Hesiod, *Theog.* 333.

'with an evil omen.' Lit. 'bird;' as omens were taken both from the notes and the flight of birds. Comp. III. 3, 61; *Epod.* 10, 1.

7. 'to destroy.' In the Latin, there is a sort of 'zeugma,' as the sense of 'rumpere' properly agrees only with 'nuptias.'

11. 'ægis.' The der. is prob. αἴσσω, to flash: others connect the word with αἴξ, a goat: so meaning literally the goat-skin lining or pendant of the shield. In Hom. the ægis is the shield of Zeus; afterwards it signified the corslet of Pallas, as in Eurip. *Ion*, 996, Ov. *Met.* VI. 78, and in this passage.

13. 'Venus;' the champion of Paris, who had awarded to her the prize of beauty.

15. 'accompany.' Lit. 'divide your songs with the harp;' i.e. partly play and partly sing them.

17. 'Cretan wand.' The Cretan archery was famous. Virg. *Ecl.* X. 56.

19. 'Ajax.' *Iliad* II. 527; Ὀϊλῆος ταχὺς Αἴας.

24. 'Skilful in the fight.' *Il.* V. 549, μάχης εὖ εἰδότε.

38. 'Tydides,' &c. See *Il.* IV. 405, ἡμεῖς τοι πατέρων μέγ' ἀμείνονες εὐχόμεθ' εἶναι.

34. 'Achilles' angry fleet.' Poetically, for the anger of Achilles himself.

XVI.

3. 'iambics,' i.e. satirical poetry; Horace says that Archilochus adopted the iambic as the proper metre of satire. *Art. Poet.* 79.

4. 'Adrian sea.' See I. 1, 15, note. Comp. l. 9.

5. 'Dindymenè.' A name of Cybele, from mount Dindymus in Phrygia, sacred to the goddess.

8. 'Corybantes,' the frantic priests of Cybele.

13. 'Prometheus.' The legend was, that Prometheus and his brother exhausted all the elements of creation on the other animals, and so were obliged to make up the character of man of qualities borrowed from various creatures. This account of the making of man by Prometheus from mud and water is later than Homer and Hesiod.

14. 'was constrained,' literally, 'is said to have been constrained,' 'coactus' = 'coactus esse.' Comp. Martial 'affatus dicitur undas,' and Juvenal, *Sat.* 10, 'dicitur olim velificatus Athos.' Though the construction is also frequently found in Livy, Prof. Kennedy was the first who pointed out its use in this passage. Formerly, 'coactus' was taken as a participle, and the following 'et' as = 'etiam.'

17. 'Thyestes.' The quarrel between Thyestes and his brother Atreus is referred to.

21. 'the hostile plough.' A usual and very ancient mode of expressing the utter overthrow of a city. Comp. Jeremiah XXXVI. 8.

XVII.

1. 'Lucretilis,' the hill at the foot of which lay Horace's farm. It is now called 'Monte Gennaro.'

2. 'Lycæus,' a mountain of Arcadia, sacred to Pan, with whom Faunus seems here to be identified. Virg. *Georg.* I. 16.

9. 'the wolves of Mars.' The ferocity of wolves caused them to be regarded as sacred to Mars, Virg. *Æn.* IX. 566.

14. 'are dear,' lit. 'are to my heart.' The idiom is frequent in Latin. So in Hebr. Is. XL. 2.

18. 'Teian.' Teus in Ionia was the city of Anacreon.

20. 'Circe crystal-fair.' This translation of 'vitrea' seems more suited to the passage than to explain the word as denoting the colour of the sea; though it is true that epithets of the latter class are applied to Gods of the sea. See III. 28, 10, note.

21. 'harmless Lesbian wine;' i.e. light and soft, and pleasant to drink in the hot weather.

23. 'Thyoneus,' from Thyone, the mother of the so-called 'fourth' Bacchus. Cic *Nat. Deor.* III. 23, 58. With poetical liberty, the god is described by titles derived from two of his reputed mothers. The meaning of the passage of course is that there will be no quarrel, such as might be caused by strong and heady wine.

XVIII.

1. 'Varus.' Probably Quintilius Varus of Cremona, to whom Virgil dedicates his 6th Eclogue, and whose death is lamented in the 24th Ode of this Book. He is mentioned in *Art. Poet.* 438 as a judicious and skilful critic.

'plant;' 'severis.' It seems better to explain this word, as the fut. perf. ind. expressing, like the simple fut., a gentle imperative, than as the perf. sub., which, however, regularly follows 'ne' in prohibitive sentences; e.g. 'do not say it,' 'ne dixeris,' not 'ne dicas;' 'ne dic' is poetical.

2. 'Catilus' walls.' Tibur was said to have been founded by Catillus, the son of Amphiaraus.

8. 'the Lapithæ.' The reference is to the quarrel at the marriage of Pirithous and Hippodamia. Ov. *Met.* XII. 224.

9. 'Thracians,' lit. 'Sithonians,' a Thracian tribe. See I. 27, 1.

'Evius,' a name of Bacchus, derived from the cry of the Bacchanals, εὐοῖ, εὐάν.

11. 'Bassareus.' This title of Bacchus is derived from βασσαρὶς, a fox-skin, such as the Bacchanals wore, βασσάρα being a Thracian word for a fox.

12. 'wrapt in.' The mysteries of Bacchus, preserved in chests encircled with the foliage sacred to the god.

'beneath the open sky,' 'sub divum.' See I. 1, 25, note. The meaning of the whole passage is, 'I will not celebrate the rites of Bacchus against his will, or divulge his mysteries to the uninitiated.'

13. 'Berecynthian.' Mount Berecynthus in Phrygia was sacred to Cybele, the goddess who drove her votaries mad. See Catullus, Ode 63, the 'Atys.' Intoxication is here poetically identified with this frantic inspiration.

15. 'that lifts too high,' lit. 'that lifts more than overmuch.' The phrase occurs again I. 33, 1.

16. 'an honour,' &c. i. e. 'an honour which belies its name.'

XIX.

1. Repeated, IV. 1, 5.

2. 'Theban Semele's boy.' I. 7, 3, note.

8. 'too dazzling-dangerous.' 'nimium lubricus.' From the literal meaning of the word, 'slippery,' the two ideas of 'perilousness' and 'brightness' are derived, and seem to be here intentionally mixed.

10. 'Scythians,' so often mentioned with the Parthians, as the most formidable of the remaining enemies of Rome.

11. 'Parthian;' Virg. *Georg.* III. 31.

14. 'vervain,' 'verbena,' The word was applied to any sacred plant. IV. 11, 7, note.

XX.

2. 'bowls,' 'cantharis.' The word is Greek, and is said to be derived from Cantharus, the inventor of this goblet. It was a vessel with a handle. Virg. *Ecl.* VI. 17. The Sabine wine was put into a cask which had held Greek wine of superior quality, according to a custom still common.

5. 'knight Mæcenas.' Mæcenas never accepted any political rank; the honours of the state were now little more than names, and the knowledge of the great influence he possessed no doubt made the simple name of 'knight' (an untitled man of the middle class) all the more agreeable to him.

'Your ancestral river.' The Tiber, which flows from Etruria. See I. 1, 1, note. 'Mæcenas had evidently been much pleased with his reception by the people on his recovery from one of his many attacks of illness. Comp. II. 17, 25.

9. 'Cæcuban,' which divided with Setine (which Horace never mentions) the highest honours. The district was in Latium, near Fundi. Cales in Campania is the modern *Calvi;* the Falernian district was also in Campania; Formiæ was near Caieta, now *Mola di Gaëta.*

XXI.

1. This hymn to Apollo and Diana, though certainly in no way connected with the Secular Hymn, may have also been composed on the occasion of some public ceremony of religion.

2. Cynthus was a hill of Delos, the native island of Apollo.

6. 'Algidus,' in Latium, about twelve miles from Rome. Comp. *Sec. Hymn* 69; Erymanthus, a well-known mountain in Arcadia; Cragus, a hill in Lycia.

11. It seems best to take 'humerum' as an acc. of limitation governed by 'insignem,' not as agreeing with it.

12. 'his brother's gift,' i. e. which he had received from its inventor, his brother Mercury.

XXII.

1. This ode is addressed to Aristius Fuscus, to whom Horace wrote *Epist.* I. 10. Nothing is known of him, except the little which Horace tells us. Comp. *Sat.* I. 10, 83.

5. 'Syrtes,' dangerous sands off the northern coast of Africa. The word seems to be loosely used here to mean the sands of the sea-shore.

7. 'inhospitable Caucasus.' The epithet, which seems to be taken from the ἀπάνθρωπον πάγον of Æschylus, (*Prom.* 20,) occurs again in *Epod.* 1, 12.

'the river of romance;' i.e. about which many fables are told. Comp. III. 4, 9, 'the ring-doves of romance;' so Wordsworth;

'Lady of the Mere,
Lone-sitting by the shores of old romance.'

10. 'Lalage' (λαλαγέω), 'the talkative,' was a common name of freedwomen.

14. 'Daunias,' part of Apulia; III. 30, 11.

15. 'land of Juba,' Mauritania and Numidia.

17. 'Set me,' &c. i. e. either in the frigid or the torrid zone. See the description in Virg. *Georg.* I. 233, &c.

XXIII.

5. 'with vague alarm.' Comp. *Faerie Queene*, III. 7, 1:

'And every leaf that shaketh with the least
Murmure of winde her terror hath encreast.'

6. 'the approach.' 'Ad ventum' has been suggested instead of 'adventus,' and 'vepris' or 'vitis' for 'veris.' But the usual reading is certainly the most poetical, and does not seem too elaborate for the manner of Horace. Orelli thinks that 'foliis' is the abl. of the instr., not the dat.

'chance to.' The perf. of the original appears to express the casual and ordinary nature of the motion.

10. 'Gætulian lion;' i.e. Libyan. Comp. Virg. *Æn.* V. 351.

XXIV.

3. 'Melpomene,' the Muse of tragedy, is here invoked to inspire the poetry of the dirge.

5. 'Quinctilius;' see I. 18, 1, note.

11. 'entrusted not to them,' i. e. by your vows and prayers.

16. 'with his awful wand.' See I. 10, 18, note.

17. 'the fates.' Contrary to the usual doctrine, the gods are here assumed to be the masters of fate.

18. 'to join his gloomy flock;' 'nigro gregi.' The dat. is used for 'ad' with the acc., as it is in *Sat.* II. 5, 49.

19. 'But patience.' See Plautus, *Capt.* II. 1, 1, ''Tis best to bear the grief you may not cure;' and Virg. *Æn.* v. 710.

XXV.

3. 'that door loves the lintel.' Comp. Virg. *Æn.* v. 163. 'Litus ama;' i. e. 'keep close to the shore.'

10. 'an alley,' 'angiportu.' Lit. 'a narrow passage.' It generally means a blind alley, as in Terence, *Adelphi*, II. 4, 39, and would so be the more solitary.

11. 'the time between the moons.' Theophrastus, 'On Winds,' IV., says that these days are especially tempestuous. The prep. 'sub' here has the signif. of 'about' or 'towards.'

12. The North wind is called the Thracian wind, according to the Greek usage, Thrace being the country lying north of Greece proper.

20. 'Hebrus,' the river of Thrace, is also here used in the Greek manner, (perhaps it occurs in a Greek ode on which this of Horace is modelled,) for any cold wintry stream. The Hebrus is called the mate of Winter, as in III. 18, 6, the wine-bowl is called the mate of Venus.

XXVI.

2. 'Cretan sea.' See I. 1, 14, note.

3. 'by whom,' &c. The word refers to Tiridates and his followers. He, after the expulsion of Phraates, had been elected king of Parthia; and Phraates was at this time (B.C. 15) threatening to attack him with the help of the Scythians. See II. 2, 17.

8. L. Ælius Lamia was afterwards consul, A.D. 2.

9. 'Pimplea.' Pimpla was a hill near Helicon, sacred to the Muses.

10. 'Lesbian quill.' I. 1, 34, note.

XXVII.

2. 'like Thracians.' See I. 18, 9. Thrace was sacred both to Mars and Bacchus.

5. 'scimitar,' 'acinaces;' a Persian word.

10. 'potent Falernian.' Horace calls this wine 'fortis' in *Sat.* II. 4, 24. Athenæus says there were two kinds, the harsh and the sweet; and Catullus, 27. 1, asks for cups of the drier Falernian.

11. 'the brother.' The name, which is clearly only ornamental, seems taken from the Greek.

12. 'with elbow at rest;' for the Romans reclined at table on the left elbow.

19. 'Charybdis;' i.e. a mistress as rapacious as the famous whirlpool. *Epist.* I. 14, 33; 'the grasping Cinara.'

21. 'Thessalian drugs;' the epithet is frequent in poetry. See *Epist.* II. 2, 209. *Epod.* 5, 45.

24. 'Pegasus,' 'Chimæra.' The story is told in Hom. *Il.* VI. 181, &c.

XXVIII.

1. The distribution of the dialogue in this ode is a matter of some difficulty. The division here adopted is that of Orelli, who follows the arrangement of a certain friend, whose name he does not give. It is curious that so careful a writer as Horace should (l. 3) use words which at least imply that the sailor thought that Archytas had already received the rites of the dead, and yet make the philosopher afterwards demand the gift of burial.

5. Archytas of Tarentum was a Pythagorean philosopher, the contemporary of Plato. His death by shipwreck is not elsewhere recorded.

3. Mount Matinus (now Matinata) lies on the coast of Apulia. So the woods of Venusia, the birth-place of Horace, are mentioned in l. 26.

8. 'the sire of Pelops;' Tantalus.

10. The son of Panthus was Euphorbus, who was slain by Menelaus. The legend was that Pythagoras maintained that the soul of Euphorbus had by metempsychosis passed into his own body; and he professed to recognise a shield hung up in a temple, as having once belonged to Euphorbus.

17. 'a show.' See I. 2, 36, note.

20. 'one life,' lit. 'head.' Proserpine was said to cut away a lock from the head of the dying as an emblem that the victim was doomed to Hades. This is mentioned in the story of Dido's death, Virg. *Æn.* IV. 698.

21. Orion sets at the beginning of November. Comp. III. 29, 18.

29. 'Neptune,' for Taras, the founder of Tarentum, was said to have been the son of Neptune.

26. So the ghost of Palinurus to Æneas; 'Cast earth upon me,' *Æn.* VI. 365; and in l. 505 Æneas, addressing Deiphobus: 'I set up in your honour an empty barrow, and with solemn cry thrice called on your spirit.'

XXIX.

1. This ode was written before the unsuccessful expedition of Ælius Gallus to Arabia in 24 B.C.. The Arabs had the reputation of fabulous opulence. Horace playfully remonstrates with Iccius on his lust for wealth, in *Epist.* I. 12.

3. 'Sabæa,' a district of Arabia Felix. Milton, *Par. Lost*, IV.:

'Sabæan odours from the spicy shore
Of Araby the blest.'

4. 'Mede,' the Parthian, as usual.

9. 'Seric,' I. 12, 56, note. Archery is mentioned as an accomplishment especially Oriental.

11. 'river-currents.' Comp. Eurip. *Med.* 410.

14. Panætius of Rhodes was a leader of the Stoics, and the friend of the younger Africanus and Lælius.

15. 'Iberian corslet.' Spain was even then celebrated for its steel.

XXX.

1. Cnidos was a city of Caria, where Phryne is said to have supplied to Praxiteles the model for the statue, of which the Venus de' Medici is thought to be a copy. Coins of Cnidos were

engraved with a figure which bears a general likeness to the Venus de' Medici. Paphos is mentioned by Homer as the haunt of Venus. (*Odyss.* VIII. 362.)

8. Mercury is associated with Venus, as the god of skilful and persuasive eloquence.

XXXI.

1. The reference is to the consecration of Apollo's temple on the Palatine, (which was also the imperial library,) after the battle of Actium.

7. 'Liris,' flowing between Latium and Campania; now the Garigliano. III. 17, 8.

9. 'Cales.' I. 20, 9, note.

13. 'beloved by Heaven,' &c. The passage is of course ironical.

XXXII.

4. 'first tuned.' I. 1, 34, note.

6. 'dauntless in war.' Comp. II. 13, 31, note.

15. The use of 'cunque,' except in composition with other words, is very uncommon, 'cunque vocanti' here = 'quandocunque te vocavero.'

XXXIII.

1. 'Albius.' See *Epist.* I. 4.

'To warn you.' There can be little doubt that it is right to adopt this construction, both because 'ne' is at least but rarely used with the pres. subj. to express a prohibition, and because the analogy of such passages as the following strongly favours this rendering. II. 4, 1. III. 9, 1: &c. See also I. 18, 1, note.

3. 'chant,' 'decantes.' 'De' has here an intensive force, expressing the endlessness and sameness of the elegies. So *Epist.* I. 1, 64.

'because.' 'Cur' is sometimes used for 'quod,' esp. after verbs of accusation, grief, anger, &c. *Epist.* I. 8, 9.

5. 'low brow.' Comp. *Epist.* I. 7, 26.

11. 'brazen yoke.' So III. 9, 17.

13. 'a better mistress.' Orelli, following Peerlkamp, construes 'though love for a better object was beginning to possess me.' There can surely be no doubt that the 'Venus' here means a person, as it does in I. 27, 14, 'quæ te cunque domat Venus;' and in Virg. *Ecl.* III. 3, 68, 'Parta meæ Veneri sunt munera.'

XXXIV.

2. 'Wisdom's foolishness.' This kind of paradox is probably common in all languages, though less frequently found in Latin than in Greek. The 'wisdom' is the Epicurean philosophy. *Epist.* I. 11, 28. So 1 Cor. I. 20.

3. 'versed,' 'consultus,' with gen. The phrase is formed on the analogy of 'juris consultus.'

5. 'Father of the sky,' 'Diespiter. Gr. Διὸς and Lat. 'dies' are words of the same original signif.

9. 'ponderous earth.' The earth is thus styled in contrast to the other elements.

10. 'Tænarus:' now Cape Matapan, where there was said to be an entrance to Hell. Virg. *Georg.* IV. 467.

11. 'confine of Atlas;' as being on the Ocean, at the limit of the world. The phrase seems a translation of the τέρμονες Ἀτλαντικοὶ of Euripides, *Hippol.* 3.

13. 'God,' &c. i.e. 'The power of the Deity is also shewn in many other ways.' Horace is probably thinking of the expulsion of Tiridates from the throne of Parthia by Phraates. Orelli thinks the word 'crest' is particularly applicable to the oriental tiara.

15. 'with flapping.' The same metaphor is used in III. 9, 53.

16. 'sustulit' and 'posuisse' are used aoristically, to denote the habit.

XXXV.

1. 'Antium,' now Azzo rovinato, the capital of the Volsci, where were the temples of two goddesses of fortune, which were consulted as oracles.

2. 'strong,' 'præsens.' The idea of power is derived from the word's literal signification of readiness. So in Psalm XLVI. 1, 'a very present help in trouble.' Comp. III. 5, 2; Virg. *Ecl.* I. 41.

7. 'Bithynian keel,' as that country was famous for its timber. The Carpathian sea was the part of the Ægæan between Rhodes and Crete, and was so called from the island of Carpathus, now Scarpanto.

9. Dacia was to the north of the Eastern part of the Danube.

17. 'fell Necessity;' the κρατερὴ ἀνάγκη of Homer. (*Odyss.* IX. 273).

18. 'large spikes;' lit. 'spikes to fasten beams.' See Æschylus, *Suppl.* 945. The 'spikes' of Necessity had passed into a proverb among the Romans. Cic. *Verr.* 5. 21.

21. 'Thee Hope,' &c. The metaphor is rather confused. The meaning is that Hope and true friends follow a man through all the changes of fortune.

30. 'new-raised swarm;' referring to the expedition of Gallus, mentioned in I. 29.

39. 'forge into another shape;' so that no trace may remain of its former employment.

40. The Massagetæ were a people of Scythia near Mount Imaus.

XXXVI.

1. The return of Numida was probably in 24 B.C. after serving under Augustus in the campaign against the Cantabri.

7. 'Lamia.' See I. 26.

9. 'toga.' The toga virilis was generally assumed after the completion of the 14th year.

10. 'mark of chalk.' Pliny says it was a Thracian custom to mark each day of life by a black or white pebble, and thus to estimate, at death, the happiness of each man's lifetime.

12. 'Saliar mode.' So IV. 1, 28. 'Salium' is prob. an adj., not gen. plur. for 'Saliorum.'

14. 'Thracian draught,' 'amystis,' fr. Gr. ἄμυστις. Lit. a draught without closing the lips, i.e. continuous.

XXXVII.

1. The news of the death of Cleopatra was brought to Rome in 30 B.C. The beginning of this ode is taken from a fragment of Alcæus.

3. 'the couch of the gods.' Referring to the ceremony called 'lectisternium.' See *Dict. Antiq.*

4. 'now 'twere meet.' The use of the imperfect expresses that the date has previously arrived. 'It is full time.'

14. 'distraught,' lymphatam = Gr. *νυμφόπληκτον*. The nymphs were said to inspire men with panic. Ovid, *Her.* 4. 49.

20. Hæmonia was the poetical name of Thrace.

21. 'But she,' 'quæ.' This is an example of a construction, in which the relative agrees with the antecedent in sense though not in grammar; *πρὸς τὸ σημαινόμενον*, as it is called.

24. 'essayed to mend her loss by winning;' 'reparavit.' Orelli seems right in explaining the word, as meaning to win something in exchange for what is given up. He compares the force of the French 'regagner.'

29. Others render 'made more dauntless by her resolve to die;' taking 'morte' as abl. instr.

30. 'Liburnian galleys.' The light Roman ships of war, so called as resembling those formerly used by the Liburnian pirates, a people of Illyria. *Epod.* I. 1.

XXXVIII.

2. Strips of linden bark were used to bind together a variety of flowers and leaves; so such a garland is contrasted with the 'simple myrtle.'

5. 'with busy toilsomeness to add;' 'allabores.' This word is used by Horace alone, and by him only here and in *Epod.* 8. 20.

BOOK II.

I.

1. Metellus was consul in B.C. 60, the year of the first triumvirate, as it is sometimes called. The civil war did not actually break out till ten years later.

3. 'the game of Fortune.' III. 29, 51.
'pernicious leagues;' especially that between Pompey and Cæsar.

9. 'tragedy.' *Sat.* I. 10, 42; Virg. *Ecl.* 3. 86.

12. 'Cecropian,' Athenian, from Cecrops, the first king of Attica.

14. C. Asinius Pollio had been a partisan of J. Cæsar throughout the civil war: he afterwards attached himself to Antony, from whom he received many favours. Though he did not follow his patron in his later actions, he had the generosity to refuse to accompany Octavianus on the expedition which resulted in the battle of Actium. From this time he retired from public life. He was the patron of Virgil, and to him are dedicated the 4th and 8th Eclogues. The 'Dalmatic triumph' was won by his conquest of the Parthini, a tribe adjacent to Dalmatia, B.C. 49.

24. 'Cato.' I. 12, 35, note.

25. 'Juno' is identified with Astarte, the queen of heaven, and tutelary goddess of Carthage.

28. 'an offering.' The citizens who fell at the battle of Thapsus are specially referred to. Jugurtha is mentioned as the most famous of the African kings slain by the Romans.

32. 'Italy;' lit. Hesperia,' 'the land of the West,' which generally means Italy, but sometimes Spain. (I. 36, 4.) The name is taken from Greek poetry.

34. 'Daunian.' I. 22, 14, note.

37. 'dirge.' The *θρῆνοι* of Simonides of Ceus.

39. 'Dionæan.' Dione was the mother of Venus. Sometimes the name is given to Venus herself. Ov. *Fast.* II. 461.

II.

2. 'metal.' Lit. 'plate of metal.' The word is used in a somewhat contemptuous sense.

3. In the orig. the gentile and family names are inverted, 'Crispus Sallustius.' See II. 11, 2; *Sat.* I. 9, 61. The usage is common also in Tacitus; a man was naturally better known by his family name, as being less inclusive than that of his gens.

5. Proculeius is said to have divided his property equally with his brothers, who had lost their own in the civil war.

10. 'Libya,' &c. i.e. the possessions of Carthage in Africa and Spain. 'Gades' is the modern Cadiz.

17. 'Cyrus.' The Parthian monarchs (the Arsacidæ) boasted to be the successors of the Persian kings. 'Phraates.' See I. 26, 3, note.

22. 'lasting,' 'propriam.' The idea of permanence is derived from the lit. signif. 'one's own.' Virg. *Æn.* III. 85.

III.

2. Q. Dellius, like many others, repeatedly changed from one party to another during the civil wars, and finally became the friend of Augustus. Seneca calls him 'the vaulter' of the time.

8. 'cask.' Lit. 'brand.' Each cask was marked with the names of the consuls in the year of the vintage. III. 21, 1. The older the wine, the further it would be from the door; 'interiore,' 'deep-stored.'

9. 'where,' &c. Most of the MSS. read 'quo' not 'qua.' In the next line but one, there is a great variety of readings. That here adopted is 'Ramis, et,' &c., as seeming the simplest and most natural. Orelli, following Regel, reads 'quo' at the beginning of the stanza, and then 'Ramis? quid,' &c. 'Wherefore does the pine, &c.?—Why does the brook, &c.?' understanding, 'if we do not enjoy them,' or some such expression. This is the reading of the oldest MSS., but the sense given is certainly rather forced and abrupt.

14. Some MSS. read 'brevis,' others 'amœnos,' or both.
20. 'Your heir.' II. 14, 25.
21. 'Inachus,' the first king of Argos. III. 19, 1. Here of course the name represents any ancient and noble descent.
23. 'beneath the sky.' I. 1, 25, note.
26. 'the urn,' that of Necessity or Destiny. III. 1, 16.

IV.

1. See I. 33, 1, note.
8. 'a maid.' Cassandra, who was conveyed by Agamemnon to Mycenæ, where she was killed by Clytemnestra, together with the king himself. Æschylus, *Agamemn.*
9. 'barbarians.' The word is used according to the later usage of the Greeks, adopted by the Romans, for all other nations, and perhaps especially for Orientals.
10. 'Thessalian.' Particularly Achilles and his son Neoptolemus.
13. 'you cannot tell.' 'Nescias' is perhaps conditional, and part of the sentence of which 'mæret' is the principal verb. 'If you know not, no doubt she laments,' &c.
22. 'Heart-whole.' Shakespeare, *As you like it*, A. IV. Sc. 1. The word seems to blend with this meaning that of 'Free from all perfidious intent.'
24. 'fortieth year;' lit. 'eighth lustrum.' A lustrum was a space of five years; so named from the general purificatory offering made by the censor at that interval of time.

V.

12. 'many-coloured Autumn.' Other readings are 'varios' and 'vario.' The reading and construction given here are those adopted by Orelli.
13. 'fiercely.' Orelli strangely explains 'ferox' to express 'the wildness of youth.'
15. 'the years,' &c. The years preceding the prime of life are regarded as an addition; those following it, as a diminution. Comp. *Art. Poet.* 175.
23. 'flowing tresses.' 'crinibus' and 'vultu' seem best explained as abl. instr.

VI.

1. Horace wrote for Septimius the letter of introduction which forms the 9th Epist. of Book I.; and he is mentioned in a letter by Augustus, quoted in the life by Suetonius. 'Gades,' now Cadiz.
2. The land of the Cantabrians is the modern Biscay.
3. 'Syrtes.' I. 22, 5, note.
5. 'Tibur.' I. 18, 2, note.
10. 'Galæsus' (*Galaso*) is near Tarentum, (*Otranto*,) which was said to have been founded by Phalanthus, a banished king of Sparta. Virg. *Georg.* IV, 126.
11. 'were ruled,' 'regnata;' which is again used as if it was the participle of a transitive verb, in Virg. *Æn.* VI. 794.
14. The honey of Mount Hymettus in Attica is said to be still noted for its clearness and sweetness.
'yields not,' 'decedunt.' So Virg. *Ecl.* 8. 55; 'decedere nocti.'
15. 'Venafrum,' in the north of Campania.
18. 'Aulon' (Αὐλών), a valley near Tarentum.

VII.

3. 'a Roman;' i.e. with all the rights of citizenship. I. 1, 7, note.
5. The Scholiasts say that the name of the friend of Horace was Pompeius Varus. His return was probably at the time of the amnesty after the battle of Actium.
'chiefest.' It seems more poetical to take 'prime' in this sense, than as = 'earliest.'
8. 'Syrian balm;' 'malobathro.' The der. and the meaning of the word are alike unknown. 'capillos' is the acc. of limitation.
10. 'my target.' Archilochus, Alcæus, and Anacreon are said to have owned to the same act; and Horace may have thought that their example excused him; but the confession of cowardice is disgraceful to the poet as a Roman officer, and unlike the general tone of his writings. For 'sensi,' see IV. 6, 2, note.
12. 'the ignominious ground.' The epithet seems to indicate nothing more than the humiliated condition of a fallen man. *Iliad*, II. 418. The rendering 'prostrated themselves as suppliants' seems artificial and needlessly degrading.
13. 'Mercury,' as the protector of poets. II. 17, 29.
22. 'tankards,' 'ciboria.' Bell-shaped cups in the form of the Egyptian lily.
23. 'shells,' i. e. boxes of this shape.
'pliant,' lit. 'moist.' The Gr. ὑγρὸς is used in this sense.
25. 'Venus.' The highest throw of the four dice; I. 3, 4, 6.
'lord.' I. 4, 18, note.
27. 'Edonians,' a Thracian tribe, the votaries of Bacchus.

VIII.

1. 'faith forsworn,' 'jus pejeratum' seems to be a phrase coined by Horace on the analogy of 'jus jurandum.'
10. 'to cheat;' by swearing by them that she will keep her word.
14. 'the guileless Nymphs.' Comp. Virg. *Ecl.* 3. 9, 'faciles Nymphæ.'
21. 'youthful sons.' In the Lat. 'juvencis.' Comp. II. 5, 6.

IX.

1. 'squalid,' 'hispidos,' lit. shaggy and bristling, like matted hair.
2. The Caspian Sea is famous for sudden storms. Milton, *Par. Lost.* II. 716.
4. 'Armenia.' The range of the Taurus is referred to.
5. 'Valgius.' C. Valgius Rufus was an Epic poet and a rhetorician. He is praised as 'near to Homer,' in a poem ascribed to Tibullus, IV. 1, 179: but the authorship of the verses is doubtful. *Sat.* I. 10, 82.

8. 'Garganus,' a mountain of Apulia.

9. 'dwell upon,' 'urges.' The word is used in the same sense in the last elegy of Propertius, IV. 11, 1.

12. 'term of life,' ævum,' (or ætas) = Gr. γενεά, which some explain as = not the whole lifetime, but the period required for a new generation to grow to manhood; i.e. about 30 years.

14. 'the sire,' Nestor. *Iliad*, I. 250. Antilochus was killed by Memnon.

16. 'Troilus.' A son of Priam, killed by Achilles. Virg. *Æn.* I. 475. His death is said to have been the subject of a play of Sophocles.

17. 'Cease,' &c. The construction is Greek, like λῆξασ' ὀδυρμῶν in Eurip. *Phoen.* 1071. So III. 27, 69.

18. 'newly-won trophies.' The reference is probably to the victories of Augustus in B.C. 20. Comp. Virg. *Georg.* III. 30.

20. 'Niphates,' a mountain of Armenia: but Juvenal, Lucan, and Statius speak of a river of this name; so perhaps does Virgil, *Geor.* III. 30. 'rigent' is applied to frozen land, in IV. 12, 3.

21. 'river of Media,' the Euphrates.

23. 'Gelonians,' a tribe of Scythia, first mentioned by Herodotus, IV. 108.

X.

1. Licinius was a son of the Murena defended by Cicero. He was afterwards, by adoption, A. Terentius Varro Murena. In character he was restless and ambitious, and was put to death in B.C. 23, for a conspiracy against the life of Augustus.

5. 'the golden mean.' *Epist.* I. 18, 9. See Int. to Epistles.

13. 'contrary,' 'infestis' and 'secundis' are abl. of circumstance.

19. 'does not always bend his bow.' Comp. *Sec. Hymn* 33.

21. 'when perils press.' 'Rebus angustis.' The phrase elsewhere denotes poverty, as in III. 22, 1; and 'res angusta domi,' Juvenal, III. 164.

XI.

1. 'Cantabrian,' II. 6, 2, note.

2. 'Quintius.' In the Lat. 'Hirpinus Quintius;' the gentile and family names are inverted, II. 2, 3, note. Perhaps this Quintius is the friend to whom is addressed *Epist.* I. 16.

10. 'the ruddy Moon.' The epithet seems taken from the colour which the moon sometimes shows at her rising. But Propertius, I. 10, 8, uses the epithet of the moon in the middle of her course. If this is not owing to the carelessness of the writer, it is another of the many instances of the vagueness exhibited by the Greeks and Romans in their use of words expressing colour.

15. 'gray locks,' acc. of limitation, as in II. 7, 8.

17. 'Evius.' I. 18, 9, note.

23. 'a comely knot.' Comp. I. 5, 4, and III. 14, 21. 'Spartan' is of course used as equivalent to 'neat and simple.'

XII.

1. 'lingering wars,' from B.C. 41 to B.C. 33.

2. 'accursed Hannibal.' III. 6, 36; IV. 4, 42

3. 'the Sicilian sea.' Alluding to the naval victories of Duilius and Catulus in the first Punic war.

5. 'Lapithæ,' I. 18, 8, note.

7. 'children of earth;' the giants. 'at the peril.' 'contremuit' is followed by an acc., like 'tremisco' in Virg. *Æn.* III. 648.

13. 'Licymnia.' Probably Terentia, the wife of Mæcenas. Her misconduct and fascinating beauty caused a series of divorces and reconciliations between her husband and herself. The looseness of the tie in this case seems enough to remove the objection that it was contrary to the manners of the nation to write in this light style about a Roman matron. This use of the word 'dominæ' is also rather in favour of this explanation, and so is the allusion to the sacred dances of Diana's festival.

14. 'lustrous,' 'lucidum' is used adverbially. Comp. II. 19, 6. III. 27, 67.

15. 'deeply mutual.' This use of 'bene' is not very common. Cic. *Att.* 14, 7, speaks of 'literæ bene longæ.' Comp. the use of the French 'bien.'

21. 'Achæmenes.' The mythical founder of the Persian house of the Achæmenidæ. Mygdonia, a part of Phrygia, was said to have taken its name from an ancient king, Mygdon.

24. 'the Arabians:' I. 29, 1, note.

27. 'which she would rather,' &c. Lit. 'she would be pleased they should be snatched, rather than one asking for them.' 'poscente' is probably governed by 'magis,' the construction being poetically loose for 'eripi magis quam posci,' or (amet) 'eripientem magis poscente.' Other constructions make 'magis poscente' = 'magis quam poscens;' or understand 'a' before 'poscente;' but these do not seem to give an appropriate sense; and it is contrary to usage to explain 'poscente' as an abl. of the agent. I. 6, 2, note.

28. 'is the first.' The construction is modelled on the Greek φθάνοι ἂν ἁρπάζουσα. (Orelli.)

XIII.

1. The accident is alluded to again three times: II. 17, 27; III. 4, 27; III. 8, 8.

4. 'the hamlet.' Mandela, near Horace's farm.

8. 'Colchian poisons.' *Epod.* 17. 35. Virg. *Ecl.* 8. 95.

15. 'Carthaginian mariner,' one of Sidon, or of Tyre, said to be the mother-city of Carthage, seems intended.

18. 'the Parthian.' Virg. *Georg.* III. 31.

19. 'dungeon.' Others explain 'robur' as = 'might;' but the rendering given here agrees best with 'catenas.' The dungeon is the Tullianum. Robur is used in this sense in Liv. XXXVIII. 59, and Tac. *Ann.* IV. 29.

23. 'the pious.' So 'secretosque pios,' in Virg. *Æn.* VIII. 670.

29. 'a holy silence.' Milton, *Par. Lost*, v. 555: 'Worthy of sacred silence to be heard.'

31. 'tyrants banished.' Those of Mytilene; viz. Myrsilus, Megalagyrus, and others. Alcæus himself bore a principal part in their expulsion.

36. 'Furies,' lit. 'Eumenides,' 'the kind goddesses;' a conciliating euphemism.

37. 'the sire of Pelops,' Tantalus.

38. 'beguiled from their labours.' This use of the genitive is Greek, and equivalent to κλέπτεται τῶν πόνων.

40. 'Orion.' III. 4, 71.

XIV.

1. The friend to whom this famous ode is addressed is not otherwise known. Postumus is the name of the friend to whom Propertius inscribes an elegy. (III. 12.)

8. 'Geryon.' The mythic Spanish king, whose oxen were carried off by Hercules. 'Tityos.' Comp. III. 4, 77.

9. 'imprisons.' See Virg. *Georg.* IV. 478.

10. 'all we,' &c. Taken from *Iliad*, VI. 142, οἳ ἀρούρης καρπὸν ἔδουσι.

11. 'must sail across.' The 'e' in 'enaviganda' seems intensitive; 'we must sail quite to the other side.'

16. 'Southern wind,' the sirocco, which is especially pestilential in the marshy country about Rome.

18. 'Cocytus,' Virg. *Georg.* IV. 478. 'Danaus.' See III. 11, 23, &c.

19. 'condemned to.' The genitive is used on the analogy of 'damnatus furti,' &c.

23. 'hateful cypresses,' as being the emblems of death.

25. 'Cæcuban,' I. 20, 9, note.

28. 'pontiff's feasts.' They seem to have almost passed into a proverb. Martial, XII. 18, 12.

XV.

3. 'the Lucrine lake,' in the neighbourhood of Baiæ, near lake Avernus. The 'pools' were fish-ponds. Lucullus and others made it the fashion to form them on an extravagant scale.

4. 'bachelor plane,' i.e. trees of ornament will displace those that are useful.

6. 'fragrance,' 'narium.' The nostrils are curiously put for the odours which they enjoy.

11. 'unshorn Cato,' the censor. Barbers are said to have come to Rome from Sicily in B.C. 300.

12. 'by the precepts.' See I. 7, 27, note.

14. 'the public revenue.' This use of the neuter, (τὸ κοινὸν,) is formed on Greek usage. 'long measuring rods,' lit. 'ten feet long.'

16. 'shaded North,' because buildings with such an aspect would seldom have the sun on their fronts.

17. 'which chance supplied,' i.e. easily found, to build their cottages.

18. 'their towns,' i.e. their walls and public buildings.

XVI.

2. 'surprised.' The more usual form of the word is 'deprensus,' corresponding to the Gr. καταλαμβάνειν. Some read 'pressus,' 'nearly overwhelmed.'

3. 'beam not clear,' so as to guide the mariner's course.

6. 'Medes,' the Parthians, as often.

7. Pompeius Grosphus was a Roman knight, a native of Sicily. He is commended in *Epist.* I. 12, 22.

10. 'clear away,' 'summovet,' the word regularly applied to the lictor's office.

11. 'fretted vault.' 'laqueata' is connected with 'lacunar,' II. 18, 2. These ceilings were inlaid with gold, ivory, mosaic-work, &c.

14. 'salt-cellar gleams,' as being the only plate that he owns. The Romans, like many other nations, regarded the salt with a kind of especial reverence.

15. 'passion.' 'cupido' is always masculine in Horace.

19. 'from his country.' The gen. is used in imitation of the Greek construction, as in Eurip. *Hippol.* 281; ἔκδημος χθονός. So in Ovid, *Metam.* VI. 189.

25. 'that views with joy.' 'in' seems to have the double force of joyful with regard to the present and joyful for the present time.

29. Tithonus, the son of Laomedon, king of Troy, was beloved by Aurora, who obtained for him from Jove the gift of immortality; but she forgot to ask for that of perpetual youth; so that he slowly wasted away.

32. 'the hour' is half personified, as the goddess of circumstance.

36. 'purple.' This brilliant dye obtained from the murex, a species of shell-fish, is now unknown.

38. 'delicate.' Others explain 'tenuis' as meaning 'slight.' In *Art. Poet.* 46, the word certainly has the meaning given here, which seems to suit best with the context.

39. 'who cannot lie;' i.e. 'whose decrees will surely be fulfilled.'

XVII.

3. 'to depart,' 'obire' lit. means 'to undergo,' mortem or fatum being understood. Mæcenas, according to Pliny, did not have one hour's sleep during the last three years of his life.

4. 'chiefest glory.' Comp. I. 1, 2.

11. 'allegiance,' 'sacramentum' is here used in its special sense, of the oath of obedience taken by soldiers.

12. 'to take,' 'carpere,' derives this meaning from the idea that each step 'plucks away' a fraction of the journey.

13. 'Chimæra,' I. 27, 24, note.

14. 'Gyas,' the giant son of Gaia and Uranus, Hesiod, *Theog.* 149.

17. 'looks upon;' i.e. was in the ascendant at my birth.

18. 'terrible Scorpion.' The epithet is simply descriptive, and does not mean 'unpropitious.' All the three stars here mentioned were considered favourable. 'the more prevailing elements;' 'the master in my house of life.'

22. 'Jove's shielding planet.' Jove and Saturn appear to be considered as being both in the horoscope; but the superior influence of

Jove outweighs the malignant power of Saturn. The force of the particle in 'refulgens' is rather remarkable.

25. 'the crowded people,' I. 20, 5, note.

27. 'the tree,' II. 13.

28. 'had carried away.' The pluperf. ind. is used instead of the subj., as being more vivid, since it literally represents the event as having really happened.

'Faunus,' as the protecting god of the country.

29. 'men beloved by Mercury.' Mercury, as being the god of eloquence, is one of the guardians of poets, II. 7, 13, note.

30. 'to offer victims:' to Salus (Health), or to Jove the Preserver.

XVIII.

2. 'roof,' II. 16, 11, note.

3. 'from Hymettus.' Architraves of white marble from the quarries on mount Hymettus near Athens.

4. 'columns,' of Numidian marble (*Epist.* I. 10, 19), called by the Italians *giallo antico.*

6. 'a stranger heir.' Perh. one of the Roman commissioners, who were able to appropriate much of the king's wealth. Others think the reference is to Aristonicus, the illegitimate son of Attalus, who usurped the throne, and was expelled by the Romans under Perpenna, B.C. 129.

7. 'Laconian purple,' from Tænarus in the south of Laconia, II. 16, 36, note.

12. 'a powerful friend.' Perh. the line should be rendered 'my powerful friend,' i.e. Mæcenas.

14. 'my Sabine farm alone,' supply 'prædiis.' A villa in the Sabine country was far less costly and fashionable than one at Tibur, or Tusculum: so Catullus speaks of his own farm, which lay between the two districts, as being called Tiburtine by his friends, and Sabine by his enemies. (44, 1.)

17. 'You.' Any avaricious old man, as appears from the context. The address is rather abruptly introduced.

21. 'to thrust backward.' It was one of the fashionable caprices of the time to encroach upon the sea by means of enormous piles and breakwaters.

23. 'Nay, why,' i. e. 'Quid dicam de hoc, quod,' &c. 'Besides what I have charged you with, there is this also,' &c.

25. 'Your clients' borders.' This was a high crime by the provisions of the Twelve Tables, as being an abuse of a position of trust and influence.

29. 'Yet no palace,' i. e. 'whatever his abode may be here, he will certainly after death be compelled to descend to Hades, like the poorest of men.' Though the sentence is rather curiously formed, there seems no sufficient reason for Orelli's artificial explanation. 'Yet no palace more surely awaits the wealthy heir than the palace bounded by the confine' &c.

34. 'the guard of Orcus,' Charon. Horace seems to be quoting some Greek story not otherwise known.

36. 'he,' i. e. Hell, (Orcus,) not Charon.

40. 'he hears,' &c. Put, for the sake of conciseness, by a kind of poetical paradox, for 'he hears when invoked, and comes though not invoked.' It seems better to govern 'levare' by 'vocatus' ('vocatus ut levet') than by 'audit.'

XIX.

1. 'amid retired rocks.' The frenzy inspired by Bacchus, Cybele, the Nymphs, &c. is always associated with solitude and the wildness of the country. I. 18, III. 25, Catullus, *Ode* 63. No doubt the idea is connected with the effect which a life of solitude often produces on the mind.

5. 'Evoe.' I. 18, 9, note.

8. 'thyrsus,' as the magic wand, whose touch caused madness.

9. 'Thyiades,' fr. Gr. θύω, to rave. *Bacch.* 704.

10. 'The fount that flows with wine.' The bounteous influences of Bacchus are described in Eurip.

12. 'to picture.' It seems more natural to give to 'iterare' this sense of 'reproducing by description,' than that of 'describing again and again.'

14. The punishments of Pentheus, king of Thebes, and Lycurgus, king of the Edoni, for contempt of the worship of Bacchus, are variously related. Eurip. *Bacch.* 633, Theocr. *Id.* 26, &c.

17. 'rivers,' the Hydaspes and Orontes, which he was said to have parted with his thyrsus, and so passed over on dry ground.

'barbarian sea.' The Indian Ocean. The construction presents an instance of ζεῦγμα. Some verb implying 'thou dost calm' must be supplied.

20. 'Thracian Bacchanals,' lit. 'Bistonides,' a feminine adjective in the Greek form. The Bistonides were a tribe in the south of Thrace.

23. 'Rhœtus,' one of the giants. From the part which he took in this war, Bacchus received the name of γιγαντολέτωρ, 'the giant-killer.'

28. 'the soul,' 'medius.' The word does not seem to be elsewhere used in this sense of 'being equally excellent in both qualities.'

29. 'Cerberus.' Bacchus descended to bring up his mother Semele. The story is told in Apollodorus, III. 5, 3.

XX.

1. 'no common wing,' as Horace professed himself to be the earliest of Roman lyric poets. See Int. to Epistles.

2. 'of double shape.' This metamorphosis is also described in a fragment attributed to Euripides (102, *D*).

7. 'perish,' II. 17, 3, note.

8. 'confined.' II. 14, 9, note.

13. 'Icarus,' comp. IV. 2, 2. Virg. *Æn.* VI. 31.

For the hiatus of 'Dædaleo ocior,' see *Epod.* 13. 8, *Æn.* III. 74.

14. 'Bosporus.' III. 4, 30.
15. 'Syrtes.' II. 6, 3.
16. 'Hyperborean plains.' These happy fields behind the North wind, free from storms and frosts, are described by Pindar, *Pyth.* 10. 31.
18. 'Marsian.' I. 2, 39, note.
19. 'Geloni.' II. 9, 23.
20. 'the Iberian scholar,' i. e. 'the Iberian when he shall become a scholar,' though now a barbarian.
22. 'unsightly,' as disfiguring the countenance.

BOOK III.

I.

1. 'uninitiated.' Gr. ἀμύητοι. Comp. Virg. *Æn.* VI. 258.
2. 'a holy silence.' Lit. 'be favourable with your tongues,' i. e. 'utter no ill-omened words.' Perfect silence was of course the safest means to ensure this end, and so the phrase came to have the signification here given. Comp. Gr. εὐφημεῖτε. So in Psalm XXXIX. 2.
4. 'maidens and boys,' i. e. 'I sing hymns which teach pure morality and religion.' The reference is general; but still there is an allusion to the religious chorus formed by youths and virgins, such as that of the Secular Hymn.
5. 'flocks.' Gr. ποιμένες λαῶν.
8. 'with his nod.' *Iliad*, I. 528. *Æn.* IX. 106.
9. 'it may be that.' Gr. ἐστὶν ὅπως.
11. 'the Plain,' the Campus Martius. He speaks as if the old Republic still existed in substance.
14. 'Necessity.' I. 35, 17, note.
16. 'urn.' II. 3, 26.
17. 'above whose,' &c. Alluding to the story of Damocles.
19. 'will not yield,' &c., lit. 'will not laboriously create.' The pains spent in preparing the feast represent the 'recherché' flavour of the dishes produced.
24. 'Tempe.' I. 7, 4, note; and I. 1, 14, note.
27. Arcturus sets Oct. 29; the Kids rise Oct. 6.
30. 'farm.' *Epod.* 16. 45; *Epist.* I. 7, 87. 'tree.' Particularly the olive.
32. 'stars.' The dog-star or Cancer.
33. 'The fish.' II. 15, 3, note, and 18, 21, note.
37. 'Fear,' &c. The verses closely resemble II. 16, 21.
41. 'Phrygian marble.' Ital. *paonazzetto*. Comp. II. 18, 3.
42. 'than a star.' III. 9, 21, and 19, 26.
43. 'wearing' is put for the dress worn. See Virg. *Georg.* II. 466.
44. 'Achæmenes.' See II. 12, 21, note.
45. 'Envy.' Comp. II. 10, 8.
47. 'Sabine.' II. 18, 14, note.

II.

3. 'thoroughly learn.' The compounded prep. is intensitive, as in IV. 11, 34.
5. 'beneath the sky.' II. 3, 23.
10. 'the royal lover.' The prince who has come to be the suitor of the maiden, as Corœbus came to Troy as the lover of Cassandra. *Æn.* II. 341.
13. 'fatherland.' A fragment of Tyrtæus, 7, 1, Bergk, p. 308; and Eurip. *Troad.* 386, somewhat resemble this line, which is, however, more concisely and happily expressed.
14. 'the man who flees.' From Simonides: ὁ δ' αὖ θάνατος κίχε καὶ τὸν φυγόμαχον.
17. The meaning is, that true virtue is indifferent to defeat in competition for office; and that her honour is moral excellence.
20. 'the popular breeze.' *Æn.* VI. 817.
22. 'denied to others;' because too hard for them.
26. 'Ceres.' Probably he speaks of the Eleusinian mysteries; but the Romans also had secret rites sacred to Ceres. Cic. *Verr.* 5. 72.
28. 'to be.' 'ut' is understood after 'vetabo,' as it is after verbs of a contrary signif., as 'volo,' &c.
29. 'pinnace,' lit. the Egyptian bean, the boat being shaped like its pod.
...'Father of the sky.' I. 34, 5, note.
32. 'Punishment.' The idea is frequently found. Tibullus, I. 9, 4.

III.

4. 'lord.' Comp. II. 17, 19: I. 3, 15.
7. 'sphere.' The firmament being regarded as a solid vault.
9. 'by this course;' the consistent practice of virtue.
11. 'roving.' *Æn.* VI. 801.
12. 'rosy lip.' Some render 'brilliant countenance.' The 'roseo ore' of Virg. *Æn.* II. 593 is rather in favour of the first explanation.
13. Bacchus is named as the son of a mortal mother (Semele), and a legendary civiliser of mankind. The tigers which draw him (to heaven) are emblems of the barbarism he subdued.
15. 'Quirinus,' Romulus. Ovid. *Fast.* II. 493.
19. 'judge.' *Æn.* I. 26.
22. 'Laomedon.' Virgil (*Georg.* I. 502) even represents the perfidy of Laomedon as the cause of the calamitous civil wars of the Romans.
24. 'chief,' Paris. Ovid (Œnone to Paris), 'Dux Paris Priamide.' It is awkward to refer the word to Laomedon, long since dead, as Orelli does; and of course it is not applicable to Priam.
25. 'have charms for.' Some take 'adulteræ,' as a gen., with 'hospes.' The position of the word is in favour of explaining it as dat. after 'splendet' like 'mihi ridet,' II. 6, 14.
30. 'Straightway.' The time between the fall of Troy and the flight of Romulus is poetically passed over.
32. 'the Trojan priestess.' Rhea Silvia, the mother of Romulus, was of Trojan blood, as her father, Numitor, was descended from Æneas.

33. 'will resign.' The word is used in the lit. sense with 'nepotem,' and metaphorically with 'iras:' 'I will remit my wrath.'

37. 'Provided that.' Perh. 'dum' should be rendered 'while.' The sense given in either case is almost identical.

43. 'vanquished,' 'triumphatis' is here used as if it was the partic. of a transitive verb, like 'regnata,' II. 6, 11, and in *Æn.* VI. 794.

50. 'while she shows,' &c. lit. 'braver to despise, &c. than to force,' &c. i. e. 'rather showing courage in disdaining to search for gold, than weakness and avarice in applying it to impious purposes.' Comp. Soph. *Antig.* 221; *Æn.* III. 57.

55. 'the fires.' I. 22, 17, note.

60. 'Troy.' It cannot be supposed that Augustus really entertained the idea of removing the seat of government to Troy, though Suetonius mentions it as being believed of J. Cæsar. Orelli thinks that Horace foresaw the evils which would follow such a transference of the capital as was made by Constantine.

61. 'omen;' I. 15, 5, note.

'Troy.' *Æn.* VI. 62.

64. 'consort.' *Iliad*, II. 432; *Æn.* I. 46.

65. 'wall of brass,' i. e. 'of adamantine strength.' III. 16, I.

66. 'Phoebus,' as the founder of the former Troy. Virg. *Georg.* III. 36.

69. The reading of this line is disputed. Perh. 'hoc—conveniet' is that most generally accepted.

IV.

1. 'on the flute.' 'Either on the flute, or with the voice alone, or on the lyre accompanied by the voice.'

2. 'Calliope,' properly the Muse of Epic poetry. Comp. I. 12, 2, note.

9. 'of romance.' I. 22, 7, note.

10. 'Apulia.' The sentence is curiously expressed. The meaning is that though Mount Vultur is partly in Apulia, Horace had wandered to a part of it, which is beyond the boundary. Comp. II. I, 34. The first syllable of 'Apulia,' long in one line and short in the next, is an example of the doubtfulness of the quantity of proper names in Latin, as in Greek. So, *Ītalus* and *Ĭtalia; Prĭamus* and *Prīamides*; &c.

11. 'overcome.' A zeugma. 'Wearied with play and (overcome) with sleep.' *Iliad*, X. 98; καμάτῳ ἀδηκότες ἠδὲ καὶ ὕπνῳ.

14. 'Acherontia' now *Acerenza*, 'Bantia' *Banzi*, 'Forentum' *Forenza*.

17. 'with my body safe.' 'tuto corpore' is abl. abs.

22. 'cool Præneste' (*Palestrina*), because on a hill of Latium; 'Tibur' *Tivoli*. 'Baiæ,' *Baja*, is prob. called limpid, on account of the purity of its atmosphere.

27. 'the tree.' II. 13.

28. 'Palinurus' (*capo di Spartimento*), a cape on the coast of Lucania, named after the pilot of Æneas; *Æn.* VI. 373. Horace does not elsewhere mention this escape from shipwreck.

30. 'Bosporus,' II. 13, 14.

31. 'burning sands.' 'urentes' seems preferable to the other reading, 'arentes,' as being a more distinguishing epithet.

33. 'Britons.' They were said to sacrifice strangers. Tac. *Ann.* XIV. 30.

34. The Concans were a Cantabrian tribe. The Geloni are called 'arrow-bearers' in *Æn.* VIII. 725. The Scythian river is the Tanais, *Don.*

38. Other readings in this line are 'fessas' and 'abdidit.' 'addidit' seems the better word to express the assignment of the veterans as new inhabitants of the towns. Orelli quotes 'additis veteranis' from Tac. *Ann.* XIII. 31.

40. 'Pierian grot.' A compliment to Augustus' literary studies.

41. 'gentle counsel.' Alluding to the clemency which Augustus, following the example of J. Cæsar, displayed after the battle of Actium. The following verses are meant to teach that clemency and goodness, as represented by the gods, are better and stronger than cruelty and violence, as represented by the Titans and giants.

45. It appears best to govern 'terram,' 'mare,' 'urbes,' and 'regna,' as comprising the material universe, by 'temperat;' and by 'regit' the other accusatives, as referring to the persons of gods and men.

50. As 'horrida' stands nearest, 'brachiis' is here rendered as abl. instr. At the same time, 'fidens' seems also, less directly, to govern 'brachiis.'

51. 'the brothers' are the Aloidæ, Otus and Ephialtes. See Virg. *Georg.* I. 280.

54. 'mien,' 'status' expresses a steady and determined attitude.

57. 'ægis.' I. 15, 11, note.

58 'eager;' the Homeric λιλαιόμενος πολέμοιο.

59. 'matron Juno,' as being in an especial sense the matron among the goddesses.

63. 'his native wood,' mount Cynthus, in Delos.

67. 'they likewise hate.' Eurip. *Hel.* 903: μισεῖ γὰρ ὁ θεὸς τὴν βίαν.

77. 'Tityos.' See *Æn.* VI. 595. The bird is the vulture.

79. Pirithous and Theseus attempted to carry away Proserpine. See *Æn.* VI. 397.

V.

1. 'cælo' depends both on 'tonantem' and 'regnare.' III. 4, 50, note.

The perf. in 'credidimus' is aoristic, and denotes the habit, as it often does.

5. 'conjuge' is abl. governed by maritus, as a verb expressing union. So 'fratre marita,' Ov. *Her.* 4. 134; and 'propagine maritat,' *Epod.* 2. 10.

9. 'Marsian;' often mentioned as the most warlike of Italian peoples. Horace frequently introduces the name of the Apulians, his countrymen. These words are studiously placed close to 'sub rege Medo,' to heighten the language of indignation.

10. 'sacred shields.' The 'ancilia' of Mars, the father of Rome. See *Dict. Antiq.* For 'toga,' see *Æn.* I. 282.

12. 'Jupiter.' The Capitol is represented by its tutelary god.

15. 'and proved.' The reading 'trahentis' seems better than 'trahenti,' which is given by one codex only; since the following clause, 'si non periret,' &c. indicates an argument impressed by Regulus upon the senate.

23. 'the gates;' those of Carthage, open as a sign of security. *Art. Poet.* 199.

27. 'loss.' Because the cowardly soldiers are not worth their ransom. There is a taunt in the 'redeemed with gold' of the preceding line, as if being bought in such a way was worthy only of a slave.

'the hues.' Its natural colour.

30. There can be no doubt that 'deterioribus' is a dative, as if it were 'viris deterioribus factis.'

33. 'surrendered,' 'credidit' is strongly contrasted with 'perfidis.' So 'niveum doloso,' III. 27, 25.

37. 'his life,' i.e. a soldier should save his life only by his valour; and he has no right to make peace with the foe.

42. 'as one whose rights were lost.' As a captive, he was 'capite deminutus;' lit. 'lessened by the head;' he had lost his personality as a Roman citizen.

50. 'tormenter.' It has been proved that the story of the tortures inflicted on Regulus rests on no sufficient evidence.

53. 'as if.' Orelli thinks that the allusion is to the practice of submitting to the patron, as arbitrator, the disputes of his clients. It seems more likely that Horace contemplates the patron as having pleaded his client's cause in the public courts. Comp. *Epist.* I. 5, 31.

56. 'Tarentum.' See II. 6, 10, note.

VI.

1. 'of your forefathers:' in the two generations of civil war and anarchy, which had elapsed since the time of Sulla.

5. ''Tis because.' See Int. to Odes, p. 23.

6. 'Principium' is, no doubt, the nom. To take 'hinc' with 'refer' would be very awkward.

9. It has been conjectured that by Monæses is meant the conqueror of Crassus, who is usually known by the name of Surena, which was probably his official title. Pacorus destroyed the army of Decidius, the lieutenant of Antony, in B C. 40.

10. The omens which Crassus met with at setting out for Parthia are often mentioned. Cic. *de Div.* I. 16.

14. 'Dacian,' with whom Antony had formed an alliance. 'The Ethiopian' is put for the Egyptian, with an allusion to Cleopatra.

17. 'Our times.' See Int. to Odes, p. 24.

'Ionian.' The Ionians were notorious for their effeminacy, which they had derived from their connection with the Orientals.

24. 'from her inmost soul,' lit. 'from her soft nail.' The Greek equivalent, ἐξ ἀπαλῶν ὀνύχων, means 'from the *place* where the nails are soft,' i.e. 'from the inner parts,' 'utterly;' and such seems to be the meaning here intended by Horace. The position of the expression, after 'matura virgo,' is also in favour of this interpretation. Cicero, *ad Fam.* I. 6, 2, used the phrase 'a teneris unguiculis cognitus' as meaning 'intimately known.' The rendering formerly adopted was 'from her earliest childhood:' i.e. from the *time* when her nails were soft.

'meditatur' perhaps = 'practises.'

30. 'factor,' 'institor,' is lit. 'one who stands in the place of another' (insisto). These persons are again joined with sailors in *Epod.* 17. 20.

33. 'Carthaginian blood.' See II. 12, 2, note. Antiochus was routed at the battle of Magnesia, B.C. 190, by L. C. Scipio Asiaticus.

38. The Sabine simplicity and austerity were proverbial. Virg. *Georg.* II. 531. Ovid calls the Sabine matrons 'rigidas Sabinas,' in *Am.* II. 4, 15.

41. 'when the sun,' i.e. though they had already worked hard through the day.

45. 'What is there.' For the sentiment, Comp. Virg. *Georg.* I. 199.

VII.

1. 'fair,' 'candidi,' as bringing fine weather.

3. 'Thynian,' i.e. Bithynian. Bithynia is the modern Anatolia. In the next line, 'fide' is the old form of the gen. So 'die,' Virg. *Georg.* I. 208.

5. 'Oricum,' *Erikho*, at the entrance of the Adriatic.

6. 'after,' i.e. after the rising of the She-goat, Sept. 28.

10. 'Chloe' is the hostess. 'Your lover' is Gyges, lit. 'your flames.' So Ovid. *Am.* III. 9, 56, 'while I was your flame.'

13. 'the treacherous woman,' Sthenoboea. See *Iliad*, VI. 155; and for Peleus, Pindar, *Nem.* 4. 54.

20. 'touches upon;' 'movet.' The word is used as in 'mentionem movere,' and seems to suggest the insinuating manner in which the stories are introduced.

22. 'with heart unshaken.' Comp. II. 4, 22, note: and for 'Icarian,' I. 1, 14, note.

23. The name of Enipeus is borrowed from a river of Thessaly: so 'Hebrus,' III. 12. For his accomplishments, comp. I. 8. The 'Tuscan stream' is the Tiber. Virg. *Georg.* I. 499.

29. So Shylock to Jessica, 'Lock up my doors;' &c. *Merchant of Venice*, A. 2. S. 5.

VIII.

1. As to the Feast of the Matrons, see Ovid, *Fasti*, III. 233.

5. 'you that are learned,' in Greek and Latin, (the two polite languages;) and therefore well versed in the literature of religious ceremonies. Orelli compares 'in beiden sprachen,' viz. French and German.

9. 'this day.' Comp. III. 14, 13.

11. 'the smoke.' In order to hasten the ripening of the wine, it was a custom to expose the amphoræ for some years to the hot air and smoke of the bath-furnaces. Horace's wine was probably about forty years old.

13. 'friend.' For this genitive, comp. III. 19, 9, note.
17. 'The City's weal.' Mæcenas was prefect of the City during the absence of Augustus in the East.
18. The Dacians were defeated by M. Crassus in 30 B.C. As to 'the Mede,' see I. 26, 3, note.
22. 'the Cantabrian.' II. 6, 2, note. The Scythians here are identical with the Geloni in II. 9, 23.
26. 'as a man not in place.' Mæcenas never accepted any of the higher offices of state, or raised himself above the rank of a knight. See I. 20, 5, note.

IX.

4. 'The Persians' king.' A proverbial form. So Byron:

'A pleasure worthy Xerxes, the great king.'

8. 'Ilia,' the mother of Romulus.
10. 'skilled to play.' Comp. 'pugnæ sciens,' I. 15, 24.
14. Calais was a son of Boreas. Ornytus is mentioned in *Æn.* XI. 677. The names are of course merely ornamental.
18. 'yoke of brass,' i. e. 'of abiding strength,' I. 33, 11.
21. 'than a star.' III. 1, 42, note: *Iliad*, VI. 401, ἀλίγκιος ἀστέρι καλῷ.
22. 'frantic Adrian.' Orelli well remarks that 'improbus' is applied by the poets to everything which exceeds moderation. Virg. *Georg.* I. 146. *Epist.* I. 7, 63, note.

X.

1. A burlesque specimen of a serenade (παρακλαυσίθυρον) such as is alluded to at the end of III. 8.
5. 'the grove.' The ornamental shrubs in the peristylium. Smith, *Dict. Antiq.* 'Domus.'
7. 'and how.' The zeugma must be supplied by 'sentis,' or some such word.
8. 'clear influence;' referring to the frosty air. 'Jupiter,' as god of the sky.
10. 'as the wheel.' The metaphor is taken from a well-rope, or some similar contrivance.
12. The Etruscans were notorious for luxury.
14. 'violet hue.' The white violet. Petrarch, *Son.* 187:

'Un pallor di viola e d' amor tinto.'

15. 'Macedonian,' lit. 'Pierian.' Pierus was a mountain between Macedon and Thessaly.
18. 'Moorish.' Comp. I. 22, 2,
20. 'water of the sky.' So *Epist.* II. 1, 135.

XI.

1. 'Amphion,' as in *Art. Poet.* 394.
4. 'seven.' Invented by Mercury, according to the so-called Homeric Hymn; Terpander claims to be the inventor (or rather the bringer of the invention into Greece), in a fragment of his poetry which has been preserved.
6. 'now a friend.' *Odyss.* XVI. 270.
10. 'boundingly, exsultim.' The word is not found elsewhere.
13. 'tigers.' The line seems modelled on Virg. *Georg.* IV. 510.
15. Orelli takes 'immanis' as gen. agreeing with 'aulæ.' But the terrible appearance of Cerberus, not the vastness of Pluto's palace, is surely the principal point in the line.
17. Many commentators reject the whole of this stanza, as spurious; while others have suggested a variety of emendations, to get rid of the prosaic 'ejus.' But the word occurs again in the Odes, IV. 8, 18.
25. 'daughters of Danaus.' For the story, comp. Ovid, *Her.* 14.
26. 'void of water;' the genitive is on the analogy of 'plenum aquæ.' Cic., *de Orat.* I. 9, 37, uses the phrase 'inania verborum.' 'Fundo' is better taken as abl. of place, than of the instr.
35. 'nobly false.' So Cic. *pro Mil.* 27; 'mentiri gloriose.'
47. 'Numidia;' as a land of barbarous savages.
51. The 'tomb' is apparently to be a cenotaph recording the love of Hypermnestra.

XII.

1. This ode seems to be an imitation of a poem of Alcæus, the first line of which has been preserved by Hephæstion. The Ode of Alcæus is in the form of a monologue; perhaps this is so too; but l. 4 is rather against the notion, nor is it necessary to assume that Horace would probably follow Alcæus in such a detail.
3. 'uncle's,' a proverbial phrase. *Sat.* II. 3, 38; 'ne sis patruus mihi.'
5. 'craft,' 'Minerva,' as the especial patron of spinning. *Æn.* VIII. 409.
6. 'Hebrus.' III. 7, 23, note.
8. 'Bellerophon,' as the rider of Pegasus.
11. 'quick to intercept.' The constr. is Greek, as in I. 15, 18; 'celerem sequi.' 'excipere' = δέχεσθαι, with the idea of stopping the boar at the moment he comes from cover.

XIII.

1. This fountain was probably not near Venusia, as some have thought, but on Horace's Sabine farm. It has of course been identified by travellers with various springs in the neighbourhood.
2. 'flowers.' Varro says that on the Feast of Fountains wreaths were thrown into the springs, and the wells decked with flowers.
13. 'one of the.' This partitive gen. is used in the Greek manner: so Strabo, Ἑρμιόνη ἐστὶ τῶν οὐκ ἀσήμων πόλεων.

XIV.

1. 'O people.' 'Plebs' has now lost its old meaning, and is used as = 'populus.' Virg. *Georg.* II. 509.
5. 'peerless lord,' Augustus. Some translate 'in her one husband,' when the phrase (less suitably to the context) would apply not to Livia only, but to all matrons.

6. 'to sacrifice,' 'operata' has the force of a pres. particip. as in Virg. *Georg.* I. 339; or rather, of the inceptive force of the present, which is almost equal to a future: 'prodeat et operetur.' operor and facio (like Gr. ῥέζω) have the signif. of 'to sacrifice,' i.e. 'to do' in a special religious sense.

8. 'wreath.' This was worn by all matrons, to distinguish them from freedwomen: but here it has a special application to the sacrifice in which they are engaged.

11. 'ill-omened,' III. 1, 2, note.

14. 'tumultus' is used with the special signif. of an outbreak in Italy. *Æn.* VI. 857.

18. 'the Marsian' (social) 'war.' This wine would now be about 65 years old. Spartacus was leader of the Servile war, which followed the Social war, and was quelled in B.C. 71.

21. 'melodious,' 'argutus' is again used in this sense in *Epist.* II. 2, 90; and in Virg. *Ecl.* 9. 36.

22. 'sweet with myrrh.' This seems the sense of 'myrrheum,' rather than 'having naturally a fragrance like myrrh,' as some explain the word. Others take the word as one of colour, 'dark-brown.'

28. L. Munatius Plancus was consul in B.C. 42, when Horace was 22.

XV.

1. The names in this ode are all Greek, and probably fictitious.

3. 'tasks.' Her elaborate attempts to preserve the appearance of youthful beauty.

4. 'seasonable.' The rendering seems more pointed than 'swiftly approaching.'

10. 'Thyiad,' II. 19, 9, note.

14. Luceria was a town of Apulia, noted for its wool. The sentence means, 'spinning suits you better than feasting.'

16. 'casks,' comp. I. 35, 26.

XVI.

2. 'doors.' According to some 'doors of oak;' which seems rather prosaic after the 'tower of brass.'

3. 'had fenced in.' The pluperf. ind. is for the subj., as in II. 17, 28, where see note.

7. Some such word as 'sciebant' is readily understood before 'fore:' 'deo' is the dative.

12. 'the Argive augur' was Amphiaraus. Smith, *Dict. Biogr.* The 'house'='the family.'

14. 'the man of Macedon.' Philip, the father of Alexander.

16. 'captains.' Referring probably to Menas, the admiral of Sextus Pompeius, who repeatedly changed from one party to the other. *Epod.* 4.

17. 'money as it grows.' So Juvenal, XIV. 139.

20. 'glory of the knights.' I. 20, 5, note.

21. 'The more that each man.' Int. to Odes, p. 24.

23. 'as a deserter.' Horace was never rich; but the word is here used loosely, to express utter aversion.

26. 'Apulian.' III. 5, 9, note.

28. 'unenriched.' *Epist.* I. 2, 56, 'A miser is ever in want.'

31. 'in the sway.' Alluding apparently to the possessor of large estates in Africa.

32. 'though he knows it not.' Lit. 'being happier in lot, it escapes the notice of him,' &c. A curious adaptation of a Greek idiom: τὸν πλούσιον λανθάνει ὀλβιώτερον ὄν.

33. 'Calabrian.' II. 6, 14. 'Læstrygonian = Formian, as Lamus, king of the Læstrygonians, was said to have founded Formiæ.

41. Alyattes was the father of Crœsus. 'Mydonian.' II. 12, 22, note.

XVII.

1. 'Ælius.' Comp. I. 26. For Lamus, see preceding ode, l. 33, note.

2. elder 'Lamias.' Apparently, those who lived antecedently to existing records. 'ferunt' is opposed to 'memores fastos.'

5. Heinsius conjectured 'ducit' for 'ducis,' making 'genus omne' its subject. But there seems no sufficient reason for the alteration. 'Tu' is omitted in a somewhat similar case, II. 17, 30.

7. Marica, the goddess of the coast of Minturnæ. For 'Liris' see I. 31, 7, note.

9. 'a monarch.' Translated from the Homeric εὐρυκρείων.

10. 'seaweed.' So in Virg. *Ecl.* 7. 42.

13. 'crow.' III. 27, 10.

14. 'to-morrow,' which was perhaps the monthly festival of the Genius and the Lares. If it was the birthday of Ælius, this would probably have been more clearly expressed. As to the Genius, each man's guardian god, who came into the world and left it with him, comp. *Epist.* II. 1, 144; 2, 187; *A. P.* 210.

XVIII.

5. 'in the fulness of the year,' i.e. 'at its close.'

6. 'Venus.' So Ovid, 'Venus in vinis.'

12. 'hamlet.' Mandela. II. 13, 4.

XIX.

1. The mythical period between Inachus, the first king of Argos, and Codrus, the last king of Athens, has been calculated to be 800 years.

3. 'the race of Æacus.' Achilles, Ajax, &c.

7. 'at what hour;' after 'quota,' 'hora' is to be supplied.

8. 'Pelignian,' i.e. equal to that among the Peligni, at Corfinium or Sulmo.

9. 'in honour of.' Supply 'poculum in honorem,' or some similar form. For 'midnight,' comp. III 28, 16.

11. The Murena, whose election into the College of Augurs is to be celebrated, was perhaps the friend to whom is addressed II. 10.

12. 'fair cups.' The most plausible explanation seems to be this. 'Since the sextarius contains 12 cyathi, let the mixture be 3 of wine and 9 of water, or vice versa;' 'fair' will then='complete.'

14. 'ecstatic.' Gr. ἐμβρόντητος. As to poets' love of wine, see *Epist.* I. 19, 2.
16. 'the Grace,' as the emblem of courtesy and temperance.
17. 'that clasps;' no doubt alluding to the arrangement of the figures in the famous group of statuary.
18. 'Berecynthian.' I. 18, 13, note.
26. 'Hesper.' III. 1, 42, note.

XX.

3. 'spiritless.' 'Inaudax,' 'ἅπαξ λεγόμενον.' The word does not occur again in Horace or any other writer.
7. 'a mighty conflict.' This is in apposition with the sentence.
8. 'whether the greater booty.' Though there is only a single object of the contest, the phrase seems to convey clearly enough the general idea of superiority; nor is there any adequate reason for the awkward emendation 'cedat, Major an illa,' (futura sit).
11. 'to have placed.' The perf. infin. is here used, because the act is regarded as preceding that expressed by the pres. in l. 13.
15. 'Nireus.' The handsomest of the Greeks, next to Achilles. *Iliad*, II. 673.
16. 'he who was.' Ganymede. *Æn.* I. 28. 'the hill of waters.' Homer's πιδήεσσα. Ovid: 'celeberrima fontibus Ida.'

XXI.

1. Manlius, B.C. 65.
4. 'gracious,' 'pia.' Not only because it may bestow slumber, but generally, as the creator of pleasure and mirth.
5. 'in whatever quality,' i.e. 'whatever effects you are destined to produce. 'exquisite' 'lectum' seems on the whole to='chosen' in the general sense; i.e. 'choice.' Orelli thinks that the word means 'treasured up.'
7. 'Come down,' from the store-room (apotheca) in the upper part of the house. Comp. III. 8, 11, note.
9. 'Socratic dialogues,' i.e. in Plato. The phrase seems simply='deep philosophy.'
11. 'Cato,' the Censor. Seneca says that Cato was fond of wine.
16. 'with the blithe juice,' &c., lit. 'with blithe Lyæus (λύαιος), 'the god of frankness.' Orelli takes 'Lyæo' as dat.
18. 'and strength.' Some join 'vires' with 'cornua.' As to the latter word, comp. Ovid, *Ars Am.* I. 239; and Psalm XCII. 10.
20. 'crests.' I. 34, 14, note.
22. 'Graces.' III. 19, 16, note.
23. 'shall prolong' the feast which you adorn.

XXII.

3. 'thrice,' a religious number, I. 28, 36, &c.
4. 'of triple shape;' in heaven Luna, on earth Diana, in hell Hecate.
8. 'to present with;' pres. subj. expressing the object.

XXIII.

1. 'upturned.' The usual action of prayer. *Iliad*, VII. 177; *Æn.* IV. 205.
2. 'Phidyle.' From Gr. φείδεσθαι.
5. 'Sirocco.' I. 1, 15, note.
8. 'deadly season,' II. 14, 15, note. For 'pomifero anno,' comp. *Epod.* 2. 29; *Æn.* VI. 311.
9. 'Algidus,' I. 21, 6, note. Alba too was in Latium, and not far from Rome.
14. 'ewe,' 'bidens,' 'with two teeth.' When a sheep is in its second year, only two of the permanent teeth being developed, it appears to have only two teeth. Gellius says the word is derived from annus, like biennis.
17. 'clear from guilt,' (immunis,) lit. 'free from obligation.'
'tetigit' is aoristic: so is 'mollivit.' The grammatical construction of this difficult sentence seems to be *manus non mollivit* (is not wont to appease) *blandior* (*blandius*) *Penates sumptuosa hostia.*

XXIV.

2. 'Arabs.' I. 29, 1, note. Their treasures are called 'untouched,' because not yet seized by Rome.
3. 'although.' III. 1, 33, note.
4. The Apulian sea on the East of Italy, and the Etruscan on the West.
6. 'Necessity' is here almost identical with Death. 'The loftiest tops'=the proudest heights: the metaphor is probably from a lofty building. Comp. I. 35, 18, note.
8. 'the snares of death.' See Psalm XVIII. 5; but there the phrase means 'the deadly snares laid by foes.'
9. 'Scythians.' I. 35, 9: Æschyl. *Prom.* 709. The Getæ were a Thracian tribe adjacent to the Dacians.
12. 'unallotted.' 'Immetata' is ἅπαξ λεγόμενον. 'Fruges et Cererem,' is a 'hendiadys' for 'fruges Cereris.'
16. 'Æquali sorte vicarius'='Æqualem sortem vicissim suscipiens.' For 'Defunctum laboribus' comp. II. 19, 38.
18. 'refrains from harming.' This a μείωσις for 'does not plan their destruction.'
21. 'parents.' Those of the wife. Orelli seems to take 'parentium' as referring to the wife herself.
25. 'impious.' A usual epithet of civil war. II. 1, 30.
35. 'without morals.' Lit. 'without customs,' as forming the standard of national morality. Comp. IV. 5, 22, which is a panegyric of the reforms effected by Augustus. The present ode seems indirectly to eulogise his intentions.
37. 'that quarter,' &c. The frigid and torrid zones. I. 22, 17, note.
41. 'into the Capitol;' to be laid up as sacred to Jupiter.
42. 'that deep disgrace.' *Sat.* II. 3, 92; Eurip. *El.* 375; Ovid, *Amor.* 8.
46. 'invites us.' The pres. is used, as more vivid than the fut. 'is sure to invite us.'

47. 'pearls.' 'lapis' often has this signif. when coupled with 'gemma.' Ovid, *de medic. faciei*, 8.
48. 'vile,' 'inutile:' a 'litotes' for 'pernicious.'
58. 'gaming:' which was always looked upon by the Romans as a practice extremely disgraceful. See Cicero, *Catil.* II. 10, 23.
59. 'broken faith;' lit. 'treacherous faith.' Comp. I. 18, 16, note.
60. 'consortem socium' = 'sortis socium:' 'the partner of his capital.'
62. 'monstrous bulk.' See III. 9, 22, note.

XXV.

1. Compare with this ode, II. 19.
2. 'groves.' II. 12, 1, note.
4. 'audiar' is pres. subj. deliberative.
6. 'to plant among the stars;' to immortalise.
8. 'unuttered.' *Epist.* I. 19, 32.
11. 'Thrace.' I. 18, 9, &c. 'non secus—ut' = 'non secus—ac;' so 'æque—ut,' I. 16, 7.
16. 'to o'erthrow;' in the strength of their frenzy. Eurip. *Bacch.* 1109.
20. 'vineleaves.' IV. 8. 33.

XXVI.

1. 'effective soldier,' i. e. so long as my youth lasted.
2. 'my warfare.' Ovid, *Am.* I. 9, 1, 'Militat omnis amans.'
3. 'now;' so in *Epist.* I. 1, 5.
5. 'the left.' As the statues looked towards the South, this would be the East, a favourable side.
7. 'bows,' to frighten the porter.
10. 'Memphis,' according to Strabo, the largest city of Egypt, next to Alexandria. 'Sithonian' = Thracian: I. 18, 9, note.

XXVII.

1. The screech-owl is still called *parruzza* in the dialect of Venice.
2. 'start;' meet them at the beginning of their journey.
3. 'Lanuvium.' That is, running down into the Appian way from the woods about this town of Latium.
7. 'chance to affright;' the perf. is aoristic. Some think that 'mannus' (a Gallic word) means a mule.
10. 'the bird,' the crow. Virg. *Georg.* I. 388.
11. 'of prophetic note,' 'oscines' (os cano) were birds which gave omens by their note; 'præpetes' by their flight.
13. ''tis my wish,' grammatically 'per me' is to be understood after 'licet.'
15. 'magpie.' This is a good omen in Plautus, *Asin.* II. 1, 12.
18. 'Orion.' I. 28, 21, note.
20. 'what misdeeds,' &c. By causing unexpected shipwreck. For Iapyx, see I. 3, 4, note.
21. 'our foes.' So Virg. *Georg.* III. 513.
27. 'all around her,' 'medias' is rather curiously used but appears to mean 'which she was in the midst of.' expalluit governs an acc. in *Epist.* I. 3, 10.
33. 'hundred towns,' ἑκατόμπολις, *Iliad*, II. 649. *Epod.* 9. 29.
35. 'Filiæ' is dative of the agent.
37. 'whence, whither:' the abruptness of the double interrogative is suited to the situation of the speaker. So Turnus, *Æn.* X. 670; and Dido, *Æn.* IV. 371.
41. 'the ivory gate,' the passage of false dreams. *Æn.* VII. 894.
50. 'shrink from.' This use of 'moror' is uncommon, unless it should be explained as meaning, 'to keep Orcus (Pluto) waiting for me.' Comp. 'demoror umbras,' Stat. *Theb.* 7. 364.
61. 'with points of death.' Others take 'leto' as a dat. = for the purpose of inflicting death.
64. 'spinning,' the usual employment of slaves. Pensum (pendo) is literally a task allotted by weight.
67. As to 'perfidum ridens,' see II. 12, 14, note.
70. The use of the genitive after 'abstineto' is Greek, = ἀπέχου τῆς ὀργῆς. IV. 9, 37.
73. 'Uxor esse nescis' = γυνὴ ἀγνοεῖς εἶναι.
75. 'half the divided world,' Europe and Asia only being considered. Soph. *Trachin.* 100.
76. 'Nomina' is plur. for sing. The idiom is common in Latin poetry, and generally contains the idea of greatness.

XXVIII.

2. 'treasured.' II. 3, 8, note.
7. 'to pluck down.' III. 21. 7, note.
8. Bibulus was consul in B.C. 59; so that this wine would be about 35 years old.
10. 'green tresses.' The colours of the sea are often applied to its divinities. So Virg. *Georg.* IV. 388, 'Cæruleus Proteus.'
14. 'sparkling,' 'fulgentes.' They are called 'nitentes' in I. 14, 19.
15. 'team of swans.' IV. 1, 13.
16. Night is also spoken of as a deity in III. 19, 10.

XXIX.

1. 'scion.' I. 1. 1, note.
2. 'broached,' lit. 'turned;' to pour the wine from the amphora into the bowl.
6. Æsula was a Roman colony in Latium, on the slope between Præneste and Tibur.
8. 'Telegonus;' the son of Ulysses and Circe, who was said to have killed his father by mistake. He was the legendary founder of Tusculum.
10. 'pile,' the house of Mæcenas on the Esquiline.
12. 'the smoke.' 'Mirari,' by a kind of zeugma, seems to refer properly to 'opes' alone; yet the smoke and din would both be signs of wealth.
15. 'canopy.' See *Sat.* II. 18, 54. 'explicuere' is aoristic.
17. Cepheus (Andromeda's sire) rises 9th July, Procyon on the 15th. The sun enters Leo, 20th July.

26. 'the City,' of which Mæcenas was Prefect. For 'Seres,' see I. 12, 56, note: 'regnata,' II. 6, 11, note.

28. 'Bactria,' now Balkh, a province of Bokhara. 'Tanais' (the Don) is put for the Scythians, who, it seems, were then in a state of dissension, like the Parthians, III. 8, 19.

33. 'regulate,' i. e. 'make the best use of.'

35. 'the stream;' 'the Tiber.' III. 7, 28, note.

34. 'channel.' One codex reads 'æquore' for 'alveo:' but the fact that the former was more likely to be altered into the latter, than vice versa, is hardly a sufficient reason for making the change.

41. 'master of himself;' = Gr. αὐτάρκης, or ἐγκρατὴς ἑαυτοῦ.

43. 'I have lived.' The expression is used in the same sense by Dido in *Æn.* IV. 653.

46. 'overspread.' Perhaps this should be considered a zeugma, as 'occupato' does not very well suit 'sole puro;' in this case some such word as 'illustrato' must be supplied.

47. 'shape anew,' 'diffingas.' Comp. I. 35, 39, note.

50. 'game.' II. 1, 3. Dryden's paraphrase of this latter part of the ode is certainly finer than the original.

54. 'resign,' lit. 'unseal:' the metaphorical signif. is borrowed from the cancelling of a covenant.

57. 'Africus.' Comp. I. 14, 5, note.

59. 'to resort to,' so 'descendere in preces,' *Æn.* V. 782.

64. 'Pollux.' So 'geminus Castor' is used by Ovid, *Ars Am.* I. 746.

XXX.

1. Comp. Ovid, *Met.* XV. 871. Shakespeare, *Sonnet* 55,

'Not marble, nor the gilded monuments
Of princes, shall outlive this powerful rhyme.'

3. 'which.' 'Quod' with the subj. here expresses the result; 'ut nequeat.'

'raving,' 'sui' is understood: 'void of self-control.' *Epod.* 16. 61.

7. 'the queen of death:' the root of the word is probably the same as that of 'libitum:' so that it would mean literally 'the pleasing goddess,' by a euphemism like that of 'Eumenides,' 'the gentle goddesses.' Libitina is identified sometimes with Proserpine, sometimes with Venus; the latter association is explained by the derivation of the word.

8. 'the Capitol,' *Æn.* IX. 448. The pontifex maximus is called 'Vesta's priest' by Ovid, *Fast.* III. 699.

10. To connect 'qua' with 'dicar' would greatly narrow the poet's fame. As to the Aufidus, see IX. 14, 25; Gen. Int. p. 1.

11. 'Daunus.' The mythical king represents Apulia itself. Comp. 'siticulosæ Apuliæ,' *Epod.* 3. 16.

12. 'Regnavit' with gen. is Greek constr. = ἦρξε λαῶν.

13. 'the first.' See Int. to Epistles.

15. 'Delphic' = 'Apollinari,' IV. 2. 9.

16. Melpomene, usually the Muse of tragedy, here is the mistress of serious lyric poetry.

BOOK IV.

I.

2. 'warfare.' III. 26, 2.

4. 'Cinara.' See Int. to Odes, p. 22.

5. Repeated from I. 19, 1.

6. 'lustres.' II. 4, 24, note.

9. By 'in' with acc. is expressed the passage of the goddess.

10. Paullus Fabius Maximus, the friend of Augustus, and consul B.C. 11, would be now about 40; so that it has been thought that this Paullus is his son. But see I. 1, 41, note.

'shining swans.' So in *Æn.* I. 590, 'lumen purpureum.' The almost opposite meanings of this word afford a remarkable instance of the vague use of words of colour by the ancients.

'ales.' The epithet is poetically given to Venus, though referring, of course, to her swans.

12. 'heart,' lit. 'liver.' So Gr. ἧπαρ. I. 13, 3, note.

19. 'Alba's meres,' near which, it seems, was the villa of Maximus.

22. 'Berecynthian.' I. 18, 13, note.

28. 'Salian.' I. 36, 12, note.

31. 'wine.' So *Epist.* I. 19, 11.

36. 'fails my tongue.' *Æn.* IV. 76.

II.

2. 'Dædalus.' II. 20, 13, note.

3. 'Nitens' is used in a similar sense in *Æn.* IV. 252.

4. 'name.' III. 27, 76, note.

10. 'dithyrambs.' See III. 25.

16. 'Chimæra.' I. 27, 24, note.

18. 'exalted.' I. 1, 6.

24. 'Orcus.' Lit. 'grudges to yield him to Orcus;' i.e. preserves him from oblivion.

25. 'swan of Dirce.' Pindar; Dirce was a fountain near Thebes. Gray calls Pindar 'the Theban eagle,' at the end of his *Progress of Poesy*.

27. 'Matine.' I. 28, 3, note.

28. 'more' refers to natural disposition; 'modo' to habit.

35. 'the sacred slope' was probably that part of the Sacred Way which is between the Forum and the Arch of Titus.

36. The Sygambri were a German tribe between the Rhine and the Lippe.

38. 'Fate.' See Int. to Odes, p. 23.

40. 'the ages.' Referring to the Great Year. See Int. to the Secular Hymn.

41 'joyous days,' such as the Augustalia, instituted B.C. 19.

49. Triumph is personified, as in Epod. 9. 21. Some MSS. read 'Tuque,' and all but one 'procedis:' but there can be little doubt that the reading here given (which was adopted by D. Heinsius and Bentley) is right, as the address to Augustus would be awkwardly abrupt.

56. He contrasts his own humble means with his friend's wealth, as in II. 17, 32. 'in' expresses the purpose.

59. 'received,' 'duxit.' The white crescent is here of course a natural mark; but the word would generally denote a process after birth; ='contracted.'

III.

1. 'Melpomene.' III. 30, 16, note.

5. 'Achæan'='Olympian,' apparently; but Orelli thinks otherwise.

6. 'of Delos'='of Apollo:' see III. 30, 15.

9. 'to the Capitol;' i.e. as he approaches it in triumph.

12. 'Æolian,' that is 'lyric;' this being the dialect in which were composed the writings of Alcæus, Sappho, &c. III. 30, 13.

17. 'golden shell;' the χρυσέα φόρμιξ of Pindar, *Pyth.* I. I.

18. 'Pieri' is Gr. vocative. This word is seldom used in the singular. Ovid, *Fast.* IV. 222.

21. 'muneris' is a partitive gen., lit. 'This is a portion of thy bounty.'

24. 'a poet's breath.' Some take 'spiro' more literally, as='I live:' but this rendering gives no satisfactory meaning, and is much less poetical. Comp. II. 16, 38; IV. 6, 29.

IV.

1. The apodosis does not begin till l. 17: '(talem) videre,' &c. This long and elaborate sentence is no doubt intended to give the subject an imposing dignity and grandeur. For the same reason the poet dwells upon the description of the Vindelici, the people conquered by Drusus.

5. 'Erewhile.' Some take 'olim' as signifying an indefinite point of time; but 'now,' in l. 11, seems against such a rendering.

11. 'serpents.' A struggle between an eagle and a serpent is described in *Iliad*, XII. 200.

15. 'weaned.' The double ablative is admitted, because 'lacte depulsum' conveys only a single notion, such as in late Latin would be expressed by one word, 'ablactatus.'

21. 'I stay not.' The perf. perhaps denotes an idea formed in past time; 'I have resolved not to inquire.' Comp. a similar use of the aorist in Greek.

24. 'in their turn.' The preceding 'victrices' seems strongly in favour of this translation: but the word is also explained as='utterly conquered.' It appears to have the latter signif. in Cicero *pro Sulla* 1, and perhaps in Lucretius, v. 409.

29. 'brave and good.' A regular formula. *Epist.* I. 9, 13. Comp. Greek καλὸς καὶ ἀγαθός.

36. 'minds,' &c. The neuter resembles the Greek usage: τὰ εὐφυῆ.

38. 'Metaurus.' This battle, which decided the fate of Hannibal's expedition, was fought in B.C. 207.

41. 'success.' Lit. 'spelt;' for in primitive times the successful warrior was rewarded with a present of corn. The word is used literally by Plautus, *Amph.* I. 1, 43.

42. 'fiend,' 'dirus,' which properly='that which is accursed,' or 'that which brings a curse,' is a constant epithet of Hannibal. II. 12, 2, &c.

45. 'usque' is used in its proper sense of 'continuously.' The word is not very often used (except by Horace) without a preposition. See I. 17, 4; II. 9, 3.

49. 'treacherous,' as nations usually call their enemies. It is regularly applied to Carthage, and especially to Hannibal. Livy, XXI. 4.

51. 'perversely,' ultro.' We go so far in the wrong direction (ultro) that we not only flee from, but even pursue, &c.

'splendid.' The phrase is formed on the analogy of 'spolia opima.'

53. 'The race.' Comp. *Æn.* I. 67.

57. 'an ilex-tree.' See Gen. Int. p. 8.

63. 'the Colchians.' Alluding to the dragon's teeth sown by Jason. Echion was one of the earth-born men, and the son-in-law of Cadmus the founder of Thebes.

69. 'messengers.' Like those who poured out before the Carthaginian senate three bushels of golden rings taken from the Roman knights slain at Cannæ.

73. Some have ascribed these lines to the poet; but the compliment is greater from the lips of the enemy.

76. 'points of war.' 'Acuta belli' is like 'aspera belli,' Livy, XXXIII. 11, &c.

V.

10. 'Carpathian.' I. 35, 8, note.

13. 'with omens;' by endeavouring to discover such as are favourable for his return.

18. 'Prosperity,' 'Faustitas,' ἅπαξ λεγόμενον. The word seems to be put for Fausta Felicitas, a divinity of the Roman religion.

22. 'morality.' III. 24, 35, note.

25. 'paveat' is deliberative subj.: the phrase is equivalent to 'Quis est qui paveat?'

28. 'Iberia.' The Cantabri in particular are referred to. III. 8, 22, note.

29. 'passes through the day.' Lit. 'brings the day to an end.' Comp. Virg. *Ecl.* 9. 51.

30.' 'weds.' *Epod.* 2. 9.

31.' 'to the second course,' which was the principal course. So Virg. *Georg.* II. 101 speaks of the wine of Rhodes as 'welcome to the gods and to the second course.'

32. 'invites.' Virg. uses 'adhibeo' in this sense, in *Æn.* V. 62.

35. 'worships,' 'prosequor,' lit.='to escort, attend upon:' whence Horace derives this secondary meaning.'

37. 'holidays.' 'ferias' here='days of peace and prosperity.'

38. 'when the day is all before us,' lit. 'when the day is entire,' 'integer.' Comp. the use of 'solidus' in a slightly different sense in I. 1, 20, note.

39. uvidi=Gr. βεβρεγμένοι.

VI.

1. 'Niobe.' The story is told in Ovid, *Met.* VI. 155. As to Tityos, comp. III. 4, 77.

2. 'felt.' The word is used in a similar sense, to express grief and pain, in II. 7, 10.

4. 'Phthian;' as his soldiers, the Myrmidons, came from Phthiotis in Thessaly.

10. 'pine.' The simile is from the *Iliad*, v. 560.

14. 'ill-timed revelling.' *Æn.* II. 249; in which book the story is told in full.

17. 'the captured.' Other readings are 'victor' and 'raptor.' Perhaps the word actually used by Horace has been lost; 'gravis' = Gr. βαρύς.

21. 'Venus.' See *Æn.* I. 257.

23. 'ducere,' like ἐλαύνω, denotes the gradual extension of the line of the wall.

24. 'omen.' See I. 15, 5, note.

26. The Xanthus is probably a river in Lycia, sacred to Apollo; not the famous stream of Troy.

27. 'Daunian,' i.e. Apulian, which here = Latin. III. 5, 9, note.

28. 'Agyieus,' ἀγυιεύς. This Greek epithet is here used, as it seems, purely as an ornamental epithet.

29. 'inspiration,' IV. 3, 24, note.

30. 'flower.' See Int. to Sec. Hymn.

35. 'Lesbian.' I. 1, 34, note.

39. 'finger,' i.e. the rhythm of the verse, as if marked by the motion of the thumb.

38. 'Noctiluca' = νυκτιλαμπής.

42. 'days.' For the feast lasted three days and nights.

43. 'rendered.' The word here signifies the expression of the verses by voice, gesture, and dance. Comp. IV. 11, 34.

VII.

1. Compare with this ode, I. 4.

3. 'mutat vices' is a phrase like Gr. ὄψιν ἰδ.ιν, &c. Lit. 'changes her variations:' i.e. passes through them.

9. 'treads on the steps.' 'proterit' well expresses the rapid transition from spring to summer in the south of Italy.

13. 'their losses.' Comp. Catullus 5. 4: 'Soles occidere et redire possunt,' &c.

15. 'father Æneas' seems preferable to 'pious,' as the latter is too strongly contrasted with 'rich' in the same line. 'Wealthy' is a regular poetical epithet of kings. The passage implies that death will make us equal with those who lived so long ago, that they have become little more than mythical names.

16. 'dust and shadow.' Soph. *Electr.* 1158: σποδόν τε καὶ σκιάν.

20. 'own dear heart.' Comp. Gr. φίλη ψυχή.

21. 'august.' Some take the word as = 'honourable to yourself;' a meaning which seems very inappropriate here.

26. 'Hippolytus:' whose story is the subject of the play of this name by Euripides, and of the *Phèdre* of Racine.

VIII.

1. 'munificently.' For this use of 'commodus,' comp. III. 19, 12; *Epist.* II. 1, 226.

3. 'tripods,' as in *Odyssey*, V. 13.

5. 'works of art.' The word seems to be used in this sense in the plural only. *Epist.* I. 6, 17; *Æn.* V. 359.

6. Parrhasius of Ephesus flourished 400 B.C.; Scopas of Paros about 430 B.C.

17. The absence of a cæsura in this line is generally explained by the difficulty of introducing otherwise the word 'Carthaginis.' Yet it might have occurred in the first half of a line, if preceded and followed by a monosyllable; or 'Carthago' might have easily been used.

18. 'of him who.' Many ingenious explanations have been given, to overcome the difficulty presented by the fact that it was Africanus the younger who actually took Carthage. It seems best on the whole to assume that Horace deliberately confused the exploits of the two Africani, so as to represent the capture of Carthage, the great prize of the war, as actually achieved by the patron of Ennius.

20. 'Calabrian.' Those of Ennius, a native of Calabria.

24. 'jealous.' Comp. IV. 2, 24.

27. 'poets.' Especially Pindar, who often extols the merit of Æacus. *Isthm.* 7. 23.

'isles of wealth.' *Epod.* 16. 42. They were the μακάρων νῆσοι of the Greeks, and were supposed to be islands lying in the far West; perhaps the Canaries or Madeira.

29. 'heaven' = immortality. 'Hercules.' See III. 3, 9.

31. 'the sons of Tyndarus;' Castor and Pollux. I. 3, 2, note.

34. 'Liber.' Bacchus himself, according to one legend, was a deified mortal. III. 3. 13. Comp. III. 25. 20.

IX.

1. 'Lest.' See I. 33, 1, note.

2. 'Aufidus.' Gen. Int. 1.

3. 'by arts.' III. 30, 13, note.

5. 'Mæonian.' I. 6, 2, note.

7. 'Cean.' II. 1, 38, note. 'Alcæus.' II. 13, 31, note. Statius applies to Stesichorus the epithet 'ferox.'

12. 'the Æolian girl,' Sappho. II. 13, 24.

15. 'mirata' has not a participial force, but is the perf. = 'mirata est.'

17. 'Cydonian' = Cretan, as in Virg. *Ecl.* 10. 39. Cydon was a city of Crete.

18. 'not once.' It seems more poetical to take the phrase not literally, but as meaning, 'not once only has there been a siege like that of Troy.'

26. 'unwept,' 'illacrimabilis' is also used in the active sense. II. 14, 6.

29. 'Worth hidden.' Mr Theodore Martin compares *Measure for Measure*, A. I. S. 2.

'For if our virtues
Did not go forth of us, 'twere all alike
As though we had them not.'

38. 'money.' Comp. 24. 43; *Epist.* I. 1, 53.

39. 'consul' is in apposition with 'animus;' you have a mind that is consul, &c. As four lines intervene, the metaphor is less startling; 'Though literally consul for one year only,

your mind continues to hold the genuine consulship, in its perfect honesty and integrity.' Comp. *Epist.* I. 1, 59.

41. 'judge,' in the literal sense: Lollius was one of the 'judices selecti.' *Sat.* I. 4, 123, note. Smith, *Dict. Antiq.*

43. 'battalions.' The enemies and corrupters of judicial impartiality and virtue.

50. 'worse,' 'pejus' is here an adverb, not an adjective. So in *Epist.* I. 17, 30. Lollius is described as 'the perfect man' of the Stoics. *Int. to Odes*, p. 24.

X.

1. 'gifts of Venus.' δῶρ' Ἀφροδίτης is used in a similar sense, *Iliad* III. 54.

5. 'shaggy.' Comp. the signif. of 'hispidos' in II. 9, 1.

7. 'the mind.' The sentiment and language closely resemble Terence, *Hecyra*, I. 1, 17.

XI.

4. 'abundance.' So in Cic. *Tusc. Disp.* V. 32, 91: 'vis auri.'

7. 'vervain,' 'verbena' is used to signify any sacred plant. *Æn.* XII. 120.

8. This instance (spargier) is the only one of the use of the archaic form of the infinitive in the lyric poetry of Horace.

12. 'through the roof.' In this case 'vertice' is a local abl. Orelli takes it as abl. instr. 'in an eddying stream.'

16. April (aperio) is the month of Venus, as being the season when Nature opens fresh life. But see Paley on Ovid *F.* 4, 62.

19. 'tide of years.' See II. 5, 15, note.

28. 'Bellerophon.' Comp. III. 12, 8. See Pindar, *Isth.* 7, 60.

34. 'truly learn.' See III. 2, 3, note.

35. 'render.' See IV. 16, 43, note.

XII.

2. 'Thracian.' I. 25, 12, note.

6. 'bird,' the swallow, into which Procne was transformed, and her sister Philomela into a nightingale; Ovid *Met.* 6, 424; but according to the Greek version, which Virgil, *Ecl.* VI. 81, seems to follow, the transformation is vice versa.

8. 'kings.' Though Tereus only is particularly meant, the plur. is used as characterising barbarian kings in general.

11. 'The god' is Pan. Virg. *Georg.* I. 16. The hills are dusky with pine forests.

14. 'Cales.' I. 20, 9, note.

15. 'client.' This line, and 'thoughts of gain,' *l.* 25, an expression which Horace would hardly use of his friend, even in jest, are against the idea that the ode is addressed to Virgil the poet. Horace would speak of Virgil as the friend, not as the client of Mæcenas and Pollio, nor could they be described as 'youthful nobles.' Besides, Virgil, who died B.C. 19, would hardly be living at the date of this ode.

18. At the warehouse called the stores of Sulpicius Galba, wines, &c., of a choice character were sold.

19. 'largus donare' is a Greek constr. So is 'amara curarum,' = τὰ πικρὰ τῶν μεριμνῶν. For 'to wash away,' comp. III. 12, 2.

26. 'the dark fires' of the funeral pile. 'Dark' = 'mournful.'

28. ''tis sweet.' Comp. *Epist.* I. 5, 15.

XIII.

1. This ode is written in the same manner as III. 15, and I. 25.

8. 'Keeps his watch.' The phrase seems taken from Sophocles, *Antig.* 782:

Ἔρως,——
ὃς ἐν μαλακαῖς παρειαῖς νεάνιδος ἐννυχεύεις.

13. 'Coan.' These dresses are generally believed to have been of silk; but the fact that they were always nearly transparent seems against this notion. Comp. *Sat.* I. 2, 101.

14. 'pearls.' So in 3, 48: see note.

15. 'public,' and therefore well known to all.

20. 'surpuerat' is for 'surripuerat,' as 'surpite' for 'surripite,' in *Sat.* II. 3, 283.

22. 'a form.' 'facies' is in apposition with the subject of 'habes,' by a kind of poetical confusion of Lyce herself with her personal beauty, 'artium' is the gen. of quality. For Cinara, see Int. to Odes, p. 22.

XIV.

2. By some 'plenis' is taken as governing 'honorum;' but 'plenis' (amplest) appears to mean, 'such as fully reward your merits.'

8. 'Vindelici.' IV. 4, 18.

10. 'Genauni.' Probably the inhabitants of the Valle di Non, and the Breuni of Brunecken, or, perhaps, the Val di Bregna.

13. 'a single requital.' He inflicted double the loss he had sustained. The form is opposed to 'pari' and 'mutuâ vice.'

20. 'much as.' 'Prope' has been thought rather to disparage the exploit of Tiberius: but Comp. *Sat.* II. 3, 268; and the use of Gr. σχεδόν.

22. 'piercing through the clouds;' i. e. 'bringing the autumnal rains.' The Pleiades rise on the 10th Oct. 'impiger' with infin. is Gr. constr., as usual.

25. 'Aufidus.' See Gen. Int. p. 1. Rivers were called horned, probably on account of their windings and branching tributaries; some explain the epithet as referring to their violence; others to the roaring of their torrents. Virg. *Georg.* IV. 371; Eurip. *Ion.* 1261; *Iliad*, XXI. 237.

26. 'Daunian.' III. 30, 11, note.

33. 'you.' This ode (unlike the 4th of this book) is so framed as to be a eulogy of Augustus rather than Tiberius; perhaps because Horace knew that the exploits of Drusus were really far superior to those of his brother.

34. 'For.' The meaning is that Tiberius conquered the Vindelici 15 years after Augustus took Alexandria, (30 B.C.). 'quo die' would literally = 'on the anniversary of that day;' but the words are not used in their exact sense. For 'lustre,' see II. 4, 24, note.

41. 'Cantabrian.' II. 6. 2, note.

44. 'Rome.' Comp. IV. 3, 13.
45. Lucan says the same of the Nile, x. 294.
48. 'beluosus,' is the Homeric μεγακήτης. Horace had perhaps heard of whales abounding in the Northern sea.
49. 'Gallia;' as Lucan also says, I. 454.
50. 'hardy.' The reference is to the Cantabrians especially.
50. 'Sygambri.' IV. 2, 36, note.

XV.

1. 'Phœbus.' Virgil says the same of himself; *Ecl.* VI. 3.
2. 'Tuscan main.' III. 24, 4, note; I. 1, 14, note.
4. 'Cæsar.' With the whole of this passage, comp. *Sec. Hymn*, 53, &c: IV. 5, 17, &c.
7. 'Parthians.' III. 5, 5. 'Derepta' properly means 'taken by force:' and Horace means to suggest that the standards were recovered by the might of Augustus, though indirectly.
9. 'Quirine Janus,' lit. Janus of the spear; I. 1, 7, note: Janus being regarded as the god of battles, whose arcade Augustus thrice closed.
12. These 'ancient virtues' are enumerated in *Sec. Hymn*, 57.
15. 'Porrecta'='Porrecta est.' So 'Mirata,' IV. 9, 15, &c.
17. 'guardian.' Comp. III. 14, 14, note.
20. 'Embroils.' 'inimico' is a form which seems to have been first used by Horace.
22. 'decrees.' *Sec. Hymn* 55, note.
29. 'who fulfilled.' 'Virtute fungi' is formed on the analogy of 'vitâ fungi,' &c.
30. 'Lydian.' This epithet is here purely ornamental, and must not be pressed; for Plato contrasts the Ionian and Lydian melodies with the Dorian and Phrygian, as being unwarlike and convivial. So Dryden:

"Softly sweet, in Lydian measures,
Soon he soothed his soul to pleasures."

—'remixto,' lit. mixed again;' i. e. 'perfectly blended.'
32. 'Venus.' *Sec. Hymn* 50, note.

SECULAR HYMN.

1. 'mistress of the woods.' Comp. 'potens Cypri,' I. 3, 1.
2. 'shining beauty of the sky.' Virg. *Georg.* I. 5. 'clarissima mundi lumina.'
5. 'the verses of the Sibyl.' See Introduction.
14. 'Lenis aperire' is a Greek constr. like 'largus donare,' II. 12, 19. &c. Εἰλειθυῖα (Ilithyia) is a quasi participial form=ἐληλυθυῖα, the goddess who *comes* to succour. The name Lucina (the bringer of light, i. e. safety) was also applied to Juno. For the option of the names, comp. *Sat.* II. 6, 20.
19. 'feraci' agrees with 'lege,' as it is the law which is to cause this fruitfulness, though indirectly. 'lege maritâ' is a very concise form, and one not elsewhere found. The law is the lex Julia de maritandis ordinibus. See Smith, *Dict. Antiq.* The native population of Italy had already begun to decrease, as it afterwards continued to do to a most ruinous extent.
21. 'years eleven times ten.' See Introduction.
25. 'truly to predict.' A Greek constr. as in l. 14.
26. 'uttered,' i. e. 'by you.'
32. 'of Jove,' as the monarch of the sky.
33. 'with thy shaft laid by.' That is, not inflicting any plague on the Roman people. Apollo seems to be here regarded as the god of sudden death, according to the Greek notion, as in the first book of the *Iliad.*
38. 'Etruscan shore.' See I. 2, 14, note
41. 'unharmed.' 'sine fraude' is used in the same sense in II. 19, 19.
43. 'opened.' The same word (munio) was used by the Romans for making a wall and making a road; and indeed the two operations were not unlike. See Smith, *Dict. Antiq.* 'via.'
45. 'Ye gods.' Apollo and Diana.
49. 'white oxen,' as prescribed in the Sibylline verses.
50. 'Venus.' For Augustus professed to be her descendant, as the representative of the Julian gens, descended from Iulus, the son of Æneas. *Æn.* I. 288.
54. 'the Mede' is the Parthian, as usual. 'Alban'=Roman, as the Romans were said to have come from Alba Longa. In the next line, the 'replies' are the same as the 'Edicta Julia' in IV. 15, 21; the conditions of peace imposed by Rome. Horace carefully avoids throughout the ode all mention of the ill-omened civil wars.
58. 'antique Modesty.' Virgil applies the epithet to 'Fides' in the well-known passage at the end of *Æn.* VI.
61. 'Augur.' I. 2, 32, note. Apollo is here described with three of his attributes; augury, music, and medicine.
67. 'lustre.' See II. 4, 24, note. Orelli makes 'felix agree with 'lustrum;' but it seems more forcible when taken with Latium, and the collocation 'felix alterum in lustrum' is awkward.
69. 'Algidus.' Comp. I. 21. 6. As to 'the fifteen men,' see Introduction.
75. 'trained.' Comp. the conclusion of IV. 6.

—'a chorister,' Lit. 'a chorus.' Though 'I, a chorus,' would be inadmissible in English, the omission of the pronoun in the Latin form sufficiently softens the literal incongruity of the expression.

EPODES.

I.

1. 'You will go.' For subject of Epode, see Introduction to Epodes, p. 89.

2. 'Liburnian galleys,' i.e. swift light vessels used by the Liburnians, a tribe of pirates on the Illyrian coast, here contrasted with the tall ships having ten banks of oars, and carrying towers on them, from which Antony's troops fought. *Od.* I. 37, 30, note.

4. 'all your own.' 'Tuo' is ablative case. Literally: 'to sustain every danger of Cæsar by means of your own danger.'

27. 'change Calabrian for Lucanian pastures.' In Calabria were plains, in Lucania hills, where it was cooler in summer.

30. 'Circæan:' for Telegonus, son of Circe, was the mythical founder of Tusculum, now Frascati, built on a hill. *Od.* III. 29, 8, note.

33. 'Chremes,' a miser in a play. See I. *Sat.* X. 40.

II.

10. The elm or poplar were the favourite trees to which to wed the vine. The plane-tree was a bachelor. *Od.* II. 15, 4, note.

21. 'Priapus' the guardian of gardens. See I. *Sat.* VIII.

22. 'Silvanus' is here confounded with 'Terminus.' A wood may have been the girdle of the farm.

29. 'season,' 'annus.' See Virg. *Ecl.* III. 57. *Æn.* VI. 311. *Tib.* I. 1, 19. *Odes* III. XXIII. 8, note. 'thundering.' Thunder often accompanies rain in southern climates, as in Palestine.

41. 'Sabine matron.' The Sabine matron was supposed to be the type of simple honesty and old religious feeling. *Od.* III. 6, 38, note.

49. 'Lucrine fish,' i. e. the oysters for which the Lucrine lake near Baiæ was famous.

53. 'The African bird:' perhaps the guinea-fowl.

59. 'feast of the god of bounds.' It was celebrated at the close of the old year, at the end of February, one of the old feasts of Rome, when the people, dressed in white, kept religious silence round the rustic altar of the god Terminus, to whom was sacrificed a lamb or pig. Ov. *Fast.* II. 639.

69. 'on the Ides.' Interest was calculated by the month, and on the Ides, in the middle of the month, payment was made.

III.

8. For Canidia, see Introduction, p. 91.

IV.

1. See Introduction, p. 90, for subject of the Epode.

3. 'Iberian cords,' i.e. made of Spanish broom.

6. 'The Sacred Way' led from the North side of the Capitoline Hill to the Flaminian gate. The Arch of Titus was afterwards built over it. It went along the upper end of the Forum. Along it walked Horace, as well as the conceited military tribune.

9. 'turn their faces.' Others take it of the change of colour in the faces; so in *Sat.* II. 8, 35: but the word 'pallor' gives it this meaning.

11. 'triumvirs' rods.' These triumvirs were police magistrates.

16. 'braving Otho's law.' Perhaps all that is meant is, that he broke the spirit of Otho's law, who intended the fourteen front rows on the floor of the theatre for persons of birth.

19. 'pirates.' Alluding to the fleet of Sextus Pompeius.

V.

1. 'But.' The opening is intended to express abruptness.

7. 'my purple stripe;' worn by children of free parents.

21. 'Iolcos and Iberia.' Iolcos, a town of Thessaly, and Iberia, part of modern Georgia, were famous for poisonous drugs.

26. 'lake Avernus.' So Virg. *Æn.* IV. 512.

35. 'bodies poised upon the chin.' That is, swimmers.

43. 'of Ariminum,' an Umbrian town, now Rimini, at the mouth of the Marocchia.

58. 'dogs of Subura.' That part of Rome between the Esquiline and Viminal hills, populous, and of low repute.

76. 'Marsian enchantments,' the Marsian witches were famous.

86. 'Thyestean curse,' such as Thyestes might have poured forth, after the Thyestean banquet, against Atreus.

87. 'Magic drugs, &c.' Many renderings have been given of this passage; which of them is right, must be uncertain. Some have taken 'magnum' as an interjection, and others 'humanam vicem' as 'after human fashion.'

100. 'birds of the Esquiline.' On this spot criminals were executed, and their bodies torn by vultures. Compare the description in *Sat.* I. VIII.

VI.

1. An Epode after the spirit of Archilochus.

5. 'Molossian hounds or dogs of Sparta's breed.' So Virg. *Georg.* III. 405, unites the two kinds together.

13. 'like him rejected;' the famous Archilochus of Paros, whence satires are called Parian Iambics. See *Ep.* I. 19. 25, and *Ars Poet.* 79, and Introd. to Epodes, p. 89.

14. 'fierce foe,' Hipponax of Ephesus, about B.C. 540. Bupalus was a sculptor, who represented Hipponax's ugly face.

VII.

1. See Introd. to Epodes, p. 89.

8. 'Sacred Slope,' i.e. that part of the Sacred Way or Street which sloped down from the Capitol.

12. 'not against their own kind.' Compare Ariosto, *Orl. Fur.* Canto v. Stanz. 1.

19. 'innocent Remus:' on the other hand, in Virg. *Æn.* 1. 292, the union of Quirinus with his brother Remus is a sign of peace and prosperity to the empire.

IX.

4. 'O blest Mæcenas.' Probably, simply= 'blest by Heaven;' rather than 'glad at the news,' or 'wealthy,' or 'happy in wealth.'

6. 'Phrygian.' In the original 'barbarian.' *Od.* II. 4, 9, note.

7. 'Neptune's son,' in satiric allusion to his boast of being Neptune's son. 'of late,' about 5 or 6 years ago.

'straits' of Sicily.

12. 'sold into slavery.' In the Latin 'emancipated;' but the English word is used in the opposite sense; for here it means, 'passed by sale from one master to another.'

'a woman,' Cleopatra. Compare Ode I. 37, 32.

17. 'Then to our side.' Here the MSS. vary. Some take it 'But chafing at this, the Gauls,' &c.

23. 'so great a captain,' i.e. Marius.

25. 'Africanus,' the younger.

35. 'qualmish sickness.' So Athenæus says that the Cæcuban wine was a good tonic.

X.

2. 'Mævius' is thought to be the bad poet whom Virgil disliked. *Eclog.* 3. 90. Horace wishes a good voyage to good poets, *Od.* I. 3; a bad voyage to bad poets.

14. 'impious Ajax,' because he profaned the temple of Pallas.

24. 'to the Tempests.' Cicero says that Roman admirals, before sailing, offered a victim to the waves.

XI.

An epode probably taken from the Greek, and not unlike some of Petrarch's sonnets.

XIII.

6. 'in my natal year.' See *Od.* III. 21, 1. A.U.C. 689, B.C. 65, on the 8th of December.

7. 'the god.' Sometimes the ancients spoke of no particular god, but of God in a higher and truer strain.

8. 'Achæmenian,' i.e. Persian. *Od.* II. 12, 21, note.

11. 'tall pupil.' But it may mean 'great,' that is, destined to be great when a man.

13. 'land of Assaracus,' Troy, of which Assaracus was a king. Virg. *Æn.* I. 284.

16. 'azure mother,' Thetis, the goddess of the azure sea.

XIV.

7. 'the iambics I began.' Some think the book of Epodes is meant; but Doering is probably right in thinking the words refer to a particular ode or epode.

13. 'You yourself are burning.' Terentia probably is meant, the wife of Mæcenas, who tormented him with other flames besides those of love, divorced by him and again taken back, so that it was said he was married often, but had only one wife. *Od.* II. 12, 13, note.

XV.

15. 'in Flaccus.' Only twice has Horace so called himself; here, and in 2nd *Sat.* I. 18. Dacier and Walckenaer think that here there is a play on the word 'Flaccus,' which means 'weak.'

20. 'Pactolus may flow with gold.' The golden rivers were Pactolus, Hebrus, Ganges, Tagus.

21. 'mysteries of Pythagoras,' touching the transmigration of souls.

22. 'Nireus.' The beautiful poltroon of the Iliad.

XVI.

1. 'a second age' or generation, the first one being that of Sulla.

3. 'Marsians.' This refers to the social or Marsian war, B.C. 90—88.

5. 'Capua,' which aimed to be the capital of Italy after the battle of Cannæ. See Livy, XXIII. 6.

'Spartacus,' captain of slaves and gladiators. B.C. 73.

6. 'Allobroges' refers to the conspiracy of Catiline, B.C. 62.

7. 'Germany,' refers to the Cimbric war, B.C. 101.

13. 'bones of Quirinus.' Quirinus was a god in heaven; but the legends of Rome and Greece are always inconsistent.

17. 'Phocæa's people.' The oath of the people of this Ionian city is given by Herodotus, I. c. 165. They founded Marseilles, Mæonaca in Spain, Aleria in Corsica.

28. 'Matinum's peaks.' Mountain in Calabria, near the end of Italy, now called 'Maro.'

41. 'that wanders round the world.' Probably the idea is taken from the old notion of the Ocean flowing round the earth.

46. 'its proper tree.' There is no need of the trouble of grafting in these happy isles.

52. 'deep soil,' i.e. a rich soil. Others take it as 'mountainous;' or it may be the soil 'with tall grass.' Others again join the epithet closely to the verb, as if the ground rose with the snakes rising from the ground.

66. Sertorius, as Plutarch says, had such a desire to flee away and be at rest in these happy isles.

XVII.

7. 'your rapid wheel.' The sorceresses' wheel was called rhombos. Yonge inclines to take the word 'citus' as a participle, and join it with 'retro,' 'whirled back;' and compares *Epod.* 9. 20.

8. 'grandson of Nereus.' Achilles, son of Thetis, daughter of Nereus. Achilles first

wounded, and then cured Telephus, king of Mysia.

29. 'Sabine,' 'Marsian.' The women of these countries were famous as witches.

32. 'blood of Nessus.' The subject of the *Trachiniæ* of Sophocles.

35. 'Colchian.' The enchantress Medea was a Colchian.

41. 'shall you move among the stars.' Like Ariadne.

44. 'the bard,' Stesichorus, whose recantation was famous.

48. 'on the ninth day,' the day on which the ashes of the dead were buried. Nine was a holy number in connection with the spirits of the departed.

56. 'the mysteries of Cotytto,' of Thracian origin, celebrated by priests called Baptæ, at night, introduced into Athens. Juv. II. 91.

58. 'Esquiline Hill.' See above, *Ep.* v. 100, and I *Sat.* VIII.

60. 'Pelignian hags,' to be ranked with Sabine and Marsian.

71. 'Noric sword.' An epithet from a country or place so common in the later writings of Horace. Noricum, now Carinthia, Styria, and part of Bavaria, was famous for its steel. So *Ode* I. 16, 9.

74. 'mounted on your hated shoulders;' like the old man in the story of Sinbad the sailor.

76. 'images of wax.' The same belief is mentioned in Theocritus, Virgil, Ovid. See also I. *Sat.* VIII. 30.

SATIRES.

BOOK I.

I.

10. The great men of Rome must have had their slumbers broken very early by the visits of their clients. It was almost as bad, says Cicero jesting, as the trumpet in the camp in morning.

14. 'Fabius,' a native of Gaul, who wrote several books on the Stoic philosophy, probably long-winded. Horace was very intolerant of bores.

58. 'Aufidus,' 'Ofanto,' called by Horace the 'roaring,' 'violent,' 'impetuous,' 'bull-shaped.' It was near a southern tributary of it that Horace was born.

77. 'your slaves.' This was one of the troubles of the men of old days.

95. 'it is a short story.' Horace's stories are usually short: he is afraid of being a bore.

102. 'Nomentanus.' Sallust the historian hired his cook for 100,000 sesterces.

106. 'a mean.' Aristotle's golden mean, which recommended itself to Horace's common sense.

108. 'how that no miser.' Probably the 'ne' is to be omitted, though the hiatus is not common.

120. 'blear-eyed Crispinus.' Blear-eyed was Horace; but not a bore, nor a Stoic prig, like Crispinus.

II

1. 'guilds of singing girls,' literally, 'colleges.' Any body of men legally united were a college among the ancients. From this, the early fathers of the Church spoke of the college of the Apostles. The singing girls were Syrian girls who came to Rome.

2. 'buffoons,' who stuck like mud to the rich.

3. 'Tigellius.' Cicero and Calvus the poet disliked him; the two Cæsars and Cleopatra liked him.

14. 'Sixty per cent.' Five per cent. by the month, five times as much as was usual, which interest was deducted from the principal, as discount, when the money was lent.

16. 'bonds of minors.' The 'toga virilis' was put on at the age of seventeen. The money-lender ran a risk, and so required exorbitant interest; for the Roman law wisely made such contracts absolutely invalid.

20. 'the father in the play.' Menedemus in the play of the self-tormentor, by Terence.

III.

3. 'child of Sardinia.' Sardinians, like Cretans, Cilicians, Cappadocians, Mysians, Phrygians, Nazarenes, had a bad name; one was worse than another: the slaves were worthless; poisonous and bitter were its herbs; a Sardonic smile was a grin or sneer.

4. 'Cæsar,' Augustus. 'His father,' Julius.

7. 'Io Bacche.' A convivial song.

8. In Virg. *Æn.* VI. 646, we have the heptachord; but here the tetrachord.

25. 'your own failings.' But others read 'male lippus,' 'wretchedly blear-eyed.'

27. 'Epidaurian serpent.' There were serpents at Epidaurus, sacred to Æsculapius, afterwards worshipped at Rome.

47. 'Sisyphus.' Antony's dwarf, two feet high, as cunning as Sisyphus the man of craft. 'Varus,' 'Scaurus.' Cognomens of families at Rome, originally given, as such names often were, for bodily peculiarities.

57. 'a poor creature.' But it is not unlikely that the word 'demissus' is in a good sense, as in Cicero: then translate: 'there lives among us an honest, modest man; we call him slow and dull.'

64. 'have thrust myself on you.' Again he fears he may be a bore.

73. 'lumps' and 'warts' answer to the 'beam' and 'mote.'

77. 'who are no philosophers.' A cut at the Stoics.

78. 'right reason,' the rule of the Stoic.

82. 'Labeo.' It is not known who this Labeo was.

83. 'how much more outrageous.' Keightley well says: 'What an idea this comparison gives of Roman barbarity to slaves.'

87. 'black Calends,' day of the exacting of payment.

89. 'wearying histories.' So the poor Italian in the story preferred the galleys to having to read the history of Guicciardini.

91. 'old Evander,' mythical king of Italy, Æneas' host in the VIII. *Æneid:* but the scholiast, followed by Doering, understands the passage as speaking of a dish made by Evander, a famous carver, brought by Antony to Rome from Alexandria.

96. 'Those who hold all sins equal,' i.e. the Stoics, the pedants of antiquity, the foes of common sense, and of kindly feeling.

98. 'expediency itself.' This is the Epicurean doctrine; but Horace with his usual good sense qualifies the assertion by the word 'nearly.'

99. The Epicurean account of the origin of the world.

111. 'That laws were introduced, &c.' The opposite view was that of the Stoics, namely, that law was anterior to wrong. Compare St Paul, Epistle to the Romans, VII. 8.

123. 'With royal power.' The allusion is to the assertion of the Stoics, that the philosopher is the genuine king.

127. 'father Chrysippus,' the glory of the school of Stoics, whose fame eclipsed that of the founder, Cleanthes. He was born B.C. 280.

IV.

1. Eupolis, Cratinus, Aristophanes, of the old comedy, answer to Æschylus, Sophocles, Euripides in tragedy.

7. 'He has changed only the feet.' Lucilius wrote chiefly in hexameter verse.

21. 'Fannius' Quadratus. It seems as if he had taken his works and bust to the public library. He was a lengthy and silly poet.

28. 'Albius.' Not the poet Tibullus.

60. 'after that Discord grim.' Lines taken from Ennius.

63. 'on some other occasion I will enquire.' Either Horace never kept his promise, or his enquiry has not come down to us.

70. 'Caprius and Sulcius;' two lawyers and informers.

71. 'columns.' The booksellers put their books in stalls in the porticos.

72. 'For Hermogenes Tigellius,' see *Sat.* II. 3. *Sat.* III. 4.

86. 'four on each couch.' In the party described in *Sat.* Book II. VIII., there were only three on each couch. Cicero says the Greeks crowded their parties.

94. 'Capitolinus.' This cognomen of a family of the Petilian gens was in this case very appropriate; as this man was said to have stolen the crown from the image of Jupiter in the Capitol.

105. 'my good father.' This is the first mention of him.

123. 'select judges,' a certain number, 360 men, chosen yearly by the Prætor of the city to be jurymen to try criminal cases. Here they are regarded as models of respectability.

132. 'advancing years.' Horace was probably about 35 years old at this time.

134. 'arcade,' or portico, where he took his walk.

143. 'like the Jews.' See St. Matt. XXIII. 15. Compare treatise of Danz (Jena, 1688) on the zeal of the Jews in making proselytes.

V.

This satire is said to be imitated from a similar poem of Lucilius. The journey seems to be that of Mæcenas in the year B.C. 37, when Antony went to Brundusium, and then, not being allowed to land, went on to Tarentum.

1. 'Aricia,' now La Riccia, sixteen miles from Rome.

3. 'Forum Appii.' Here came St. Paul, a traveller of a very different kind. Acts XXVIII. 15.

9. 'and now night &c.' A mock heroic passage, very likely from some old writer.

11. 'boatmen.' The canal is mentioned by Strabo as running parallel to the Appian road, and often used by passengers by night.

16. 'a passenger,' or a traveller along the tow-path.

23. 'fourth hour,' i.e. about nine o'clock in the morning.

24. 'Feronia.' She was the goddess of enfranchised slaves.

26. 'Anxur,' now Terracina. It was formerly a bathing-place, resorted to in summer.

34. 'Fundi,' now 'Fondi.' Here the ancient appearance of the Appian road, composed of large flag-stones, was seen by Eustace. See Eustace's *Classical Tour*, Vol. II. p. 138.

'prætorship.' Mock Roman style.

36. 'prætexta,' i.e. toga, with purple border. 'Laticlave,' 'broad purple stripe.' 'Pan of live coals,' probably used for sacrifice.

37. 'In the city of the Mamurra family,' i.e. Formiæ, now Mola-di-Gaëta. The place is famous for the supposed remains of the villa and tomb of Cicero.

40. 'Plotius, Virgil, and Varius.' These two, here and in 1 *Sat.* X. 81, joined with Virgil, revised his *Æneid* after his death.

45. 'Campanian bridge,' over the river Savo.

46. 'purveyors,' appointed by the government to furnish those travelling on public business at a certain rate.

54. 'stock of the Osci,' i.e. one of the common people of the country.

55. 'his mistress still lives,' i.e. he was a runaway slave.

71. 'Beneventum' claimed Diomede for its founder; it has been under Roman, Gothic, Greek, Lombard, Norman, Papal, and Italian rule.

78. 'Altino,' Atabalus, which blew from the east.

87. 'a little town with a name, &c.' Supposed to be Equotutium, or Equotuticum.

91. 'Canusium,' now Canosa, on the Aufidus, where Greek and Oscan were spoken. It stood south-west of Cannæ.

97. 'Barium,' now Bari, on a rocky peninsula. 'Egnatia, built when the Nymphs were angry;' because the water there was so bad.

100. 'Apella,' a common name for freedmen, to which class so many Jews belonged. Acts of Ap. VI. 9. Tacitus, *Ann.* II. ch. 85, says it was proposed in the senate that 4000 freedmen of the Jewish religion should be banished. Philo mentions that they dwelt on the other side of the Tiber, and most of them were freedmen.

104. 'Brundusium,' 'Brindisi;' here Virgil died. The town seems now likely to recover its former importance.

VI.

1. 'Lydian Etruria,' from the supposed Lydian settlement in Etruria, mentioned by Herodotus, and alluded to by Virgil.

9. 'Servius' Tullius, according to the legend, the son of a slave.

20. 'Decius,' who devoted himself at the battle of Vesuvius. Juvenal, too, speaks of the plebeian origin of this noble soul.

21. 'the censor Appius,' the model censor of B. C. 312.

27. 'four black straps,' which went up the high shoe of the senators.

39. 'Cadmus,' said to have been the public executioner.

41. 'Paullus or Messala' as we might say, a Howard, or Percy.

59. 'Saturium,' near Tarentum in Calabria.

75. 'The Ides of eight months in the year.' So Yonge, Hermann, and Keightley. There would be four months holidays in the heat of summer.

79. 'so far as would be observed.' But others take it, 'as was proper in a populous city.'

86. 'as auctioneer or collector like himself.' This passage is referred to at the beginning of the life of Horace by Suetonius.

104. 'dumpy mule.' Others translate 'crop-tailed.'

120. 'Marsyas,' whose statue was in the Forum.

121. 'Novius,' a fraudulent usurer.

VII.

1. Supposed to be the earliest of the extant poems of Horace. If so, Horace improved greatly.

'on the proscription list' of the triumvirs.

2. 'Hybrid,' as having an Asiatic father, and Roman mother.

5. 'Clazomenæ,' one of the twelve Ionian cities, famous as the place where Anaxagoras was born.

16. 'Diomede and Lycian Glaucus,' taken from *Iliad*, VI.

18. 'Brutus was prætor.' He was not so formally, as he was acting in defiance of the senate.

19. 'Province of Asia,' of which Ephesus was capital, said by Cicero, too, to be the richest of the provinces.

20. 'Bacchius—with Bithus,' two gladiators.

28. 'The man of Præneste.' Rupilius Rex.

31. 'cuckoo.' The joke is said to be taken from the 'cuckoo' having come, and the vine-dresser not having yet pruned his vines, and so behind-hand.

32. 'a Greek.' Thus he was sharp as a Greek, with Italian vinegar as well.

VIII.

1. 'stem of a fig-tree.' The wood of the fig-tree was considered very poor.

8. 'narrow cells.' The little rooms of the slaves, like cells in convents.

14. 'Esquiline hill,' separated from the Viminal by the Subura. On it were the baths of Titus, and the temple of Minerva Medica. Near the house of Mæcenas, from which Nero beheld the burning of Rome, Virgil is said to have had a house.

15. 'terrace,' raised, as a bulwark, by Servius Tullius.

25. 'the elder Sagana:' probably she had a younger sister.

29. 'the ghosts,' deified by the Roman belief, as Manes (mansuetus), or good spirits, like our 'good folk,' in hopes of propitiating them.

50. 'enchanted bonds,' called by the Romans 'licia;' i. e. threads of different colours, having a loop.

IX.

1. 'The Sacred Street.' This famous street extended from the valley beneath the Esquiline hill, by one side of the Forum to the ascent up to the Capitol. The arch of Titus was afterwards built across it.

18. 'Cæsar's gardens,' bequeathed to the Roman people by Julius Cæsar.

25. 'Hermogenes.' See I. *Sat.* III. 129.

35. 'Vesta's temple,' to the west of the Palatine hill, not far from the Tiber.

60. 'Fuscus Aristius,' to whom is addressed the 22nd *Ode* of 1st book, one of Horace's literary friends, an excellent man, fond of a town life, perhaps too fond of money also.

69. 'the thirtieth sabbath;' a well-known difficulty. Perhaps Aristius Fuscus has caused us this difficulty, by wittily inventing this thirtieth sabbath for the occasion.

76. 'I give my ear to be touched;' by which Horace promised to be a witness, when called upon, and so escaped for the present.

78. 'Apollo,' an allusion to Homer; but, besides that, Horace was a poet, and so Apollo was his patron.

X.

The first eight lines, not noticed by the scholiasts, but found in some MSS., though not written by Horace himself, are probably ancient.

1. 'Yes, I did say;' i. e. in the fourth Satire, which evidently had been censured.

6. 'Laberius' farces.' He was a Roman knight, who wrote mimes or farces. A prologue by him is still extant.

18. 'that monkey;' supposed to be the Demetrius of vv. 79 and 90.

19. 'Calvus,' a contemporary of Cicero: he was an orator as well as poet. 'Catullus.' This is the only passage in Horace where Catullus is mentioned. See Int. to Epistles, p. 161.

26. 'Petillus.' See *Sat.* I. 4, 94.

28. 'Pedius' was adopted by the nephew of Julius Cæsar.

29. 'Corvinus' Messala, praised by Horace, Tibullus (whose patron he was), Valleius Paterculus, Quintilian, Pliny, Seneca, Tacitus. His writings, famous for their latinity, are lost. He was Horace's friend in Brutus' army. He was a warrior as well as orator, and retained his republican frankness.

30. 'mongrel talk,' Oscan and Greek.

36. 'Alpinus.' Furius is so called, because, besides murdering Memnon, and muddying the Rhine, he made Jupiter spew over the Alps. See II. *Sat.* V. 40.

38. 'Tarpa,' who licensed plays.

43. On 'Pollio,' general, historian, tragedian, orator, senator, see II. *Odes*, I, 14, note.

44. 'Varius.' Horace's friend, mentioned with Virgil, author of a tragedy called Medea, and of a poem on Death.

45. 'Virgil's gift.' It would clearly seem that the *Æneid* was not then published; and, perhaps, not the *Georgics*.

46. 'Varro Atacinus' was a poet not much older than Horace, called Atacinus, from the river Atax in Gaul, now the Aude.

48, 'inventor,' i.e. Lucilius.

53. 'Accius,' a tragic poet born B.C 170, whose poems, taken from the Greek, are often quoted by Cicero.

66. 'kind of poetry untouched by the Greeks;' i.e. satire.

67. 'earlier poets;' Livius, Nævius, Ennius, Accius, Pacuvius.

75. 'in common schools,' like the poems of Livius, which got Horace many a whipping. Horace, in spite of his wish, has been used in many a school, common, and good too.

82. 'Octavius;' not, of course, Augustus. The present passage is remarkable, as mentioning so many friends of the poet, who associated with the leading men of his age.

BOOK II.

I.

This satire is imitated by Pope.

4. 'Trebatius' Testa, the friend of Cicero, to whom Cicero wrote letters, and addressed his *Topics*. He was younger than Cicero, older than Horace, a man of a quiet spirit.

17. 'Scipio' the younger. Lucilius served under him in the Numantian war.

35. 'Venusia,' now Venosa. It was made a colony in B.C. 291.

36. 'Samnites,' in the original Sabines, but the Samnites were of Sabine origin.

47. 'Cervius;' no doubt an informer.

63. 'Lælius,' the friend of Scipio, so well known as a speaker in Cicero.

66. 'a title fairly won.' That of Africanus.

67. 'Metellus' Macedonicus, a political opponent of Scipio.

75. 'station.' The original word includes also 'wealth.'

81. 'sacred laws.' The XII tables.

86. 'The prosecution,' &c. Lit. "The tablets (on which the 'judices' recorded their votes) will be broken up by laughter." The word 'solventur' refers rather to the opinion of the 'judices,' than to the actual tabulæ. This seems the best explanation of a difficult passage. 'Risu' is abl. instr.

II.

11. Grecian fashions;' as the ball, or the quoit.

22. 'lagois,' whether bird or fish, seems to be so called from having a taste like a hare.

32. 'among the bridges;' between the Fabrician bridge and the Sublician.

38. 'a hungry stomach seldom,' &c. Some take it 'a stomach not often hungry.'

44. 'elecampane,' a plant whose root had a pungent taste, and was of much repute as a stomachic.

47. 'Gallonius,' the auctioneer mentioned in Lucilius, who spent all his money on this sturgeon, and other fish, and yet never dined well in his life.

50. 'a would-be prætor;' Asinius, or Sempronius Rufus, who was rejected when he stood for the prætorship. So, a wag said, the people had avenged the death of the storks on which he had dined.

68. 'easy-natured;' or it may be so 'simple,' as to forget the decencies of life.

92. 'Oh that the early world,' &c. Again, as so often, in the mock-heroic style.

97. 'angry is your uncle,' whom the ancients regarded as severe and harsh.

114. 'allotted farm,' i.e. measured out by the surveyor for the veteran to whom it had been granted.

122. 'dried figs,' i.e. split, and laid on each other. Gargallo translates the words 'fichi appassiti a coppia.'

133. 'Umbrenus.' Compare Virg. *Eclogues* I. and 9. The confiscation probably took place after the battle of Philippi, B.C. 42.

III.

This is far the longest and most systematic of the Satires of Horace. From it we learn much about Horace himself.

5. 'refuge here;' at your quiet farm, a proper place for study.
8. 'innocent wall.' The thumped wall is personified.
11. 'Plato.' Some think the philosopher, others the comic poet classed with Menander, Eupolis, Archilochus, whose writings might help Horace in his Satires.
13. 'envy;' the jealousy entertained for the successful poet.
17. 'with a barber;' for he had grown a philosophic beard.
18. 'middle Janus;' the central of the three arcades on the north side of the Forum; or, perhaps, the space between them.
21. 'Sisyphus,' founder of Corinth, 'the most crafty of men.' Vessels of Corinthian bronze were famous.
25. 'god of gain,' Mercury. Mercurial in English has a different sense from that here. So 'Jovial' in Shakespeare, *Cymbeline*, A. IV. Sc. 2, where 'Mercurial' also is used literally.
33. 'Stertinius.' A stoic professor of that day.
36. The 'Fabrician bridge' crossed the Tiber at the island to the west of the Capitol.
53. 'with his own tail hanging;' like wearing a fool's cap, as Keightley says.
60. 'Fufius' was an actor, who played the part of Ilione in the tragedy of Pacuvius. Being drunk, he fell asleep, and Catienus, the other actor, could not waken him, though he shouted as if he were 200,000 men. Some, as Keightley, the Delphin editor, and Doering, take it as 1200. Perhaps the shouts were from the people.
69. 'Nerius,' an usurer. 'Cicuta,' another usurer.
72. 'he will laugh immoderately.' So Shilleto takes it. Literally 'with other peoples' jaws.' In Homer, (*Od.* XX. 347,) the same expression means 'unnatural laughter.' Thus Virgil translates Homer's 'crowning cups with wine' into 'crowning them with chaplets.'
77. 'arrange your toga,' i.e. listen composedly to my lecture.
83. 'Anticyra,' island in the Maliac gulf, where hellebore, given by the ancients for melancholy, grew abundantly.
86. 'Arrius,' a vulgar man, who gave a grand entertainment. Arrius in Catullus put in the letter 'h' out of place.
100. 'Aristippus,' the founder of the Cyrenaic sect. As the Cynics were an exaggerated form of Stoicism, so was the Cyrenaic sect of the Epicurean school.
141. 'calling one a Fury.' See Eurip. *Orestes*, 264. 'his magnificent anger;' but some say the word is used medically 'to express the bright colour of the bile when disordered.' But compare 'splendidè mendax,' *Ode* III. 11, 35.
143. 'wine of Veii,' a very poor sort of wine.
161. 'Craterus,' an eminent physician, who once attended Atticus' daughter.
169. 'ancestral fortune;' but Macleane and others explain the words as 'according to the standard of ancient times.'
181. 'outlawed and accursed.' Like 'Anathema.' Literally, 'one who could not make a will, and one devoted to the infernal gods.'
182. 'vetches, beans and lupines;' pulse distributed to the people by the Aediles.
185. 'Agrippa,' who in his ædileship was very munificent.
217. 'would not the prætor interfere;' i.e. by an interdict, according to the law of the XII Tables. The prætor named the person who was to be committee (curator) to the insane man. *Epist.* I. 1, 102, note.
223. 'Bellona.' On the 'day of blood,' the 24th of March, the priests of Bellona in their frenzy cut themselves with knives, till the blood gushed out. The day is omitted in Ovid's *Fasti.*
228. 'Tuscan street;' street to the south of the Forum.
229. 'Velabrum,' full of shops, near the river, once a swamp, lay to the north-west of Circus Maximus, and to the south-west of the Forum, between the Aventine and the Capitol.
239. 'the son of Æsop;' i.e. Clodius, the son of the famous actor.
254. 'Polemo,' who was converted by Xenocrates, the head of the Academic school after Speusippus.
260. 'And he deliberates.' This passage is taken from the first scene of the *Eunuchus* of Terence.
265. 'the slave,' Parmeno.
272. 'Picenian fruit.' See below, *Sat.* II. 4, 70.
275. 'add blood to folly,' &c. i.e. 'add bloodshed to your mad passion; and make bad worse;' taken from a saying of Pythagoras, 'to stir the fire with the sword.'
277. 'Marius and Hellas;' persons now unknown.
280. 'cognate terms;' words differing in form, the same in meaning.
281. 'where streets meet;' where the statues of the Lares stood.
304. 'unhappy son,' Pentheus. See Eurip. *Bacch.*, Ovid. *Met.* III. 700.
309. 'about two feet.' See *Epist.* I. 20, 24.
322. 'your dreadful temper.' See *Ep.* I. 20, 25.

IV.

2. 'by my method;' memoria technica.
3. 'him whom Anytus prosecuted.' Socrates.
19. 'Mead.' Others read 'mixto;' i.e. 'mixed with water.'
55. 'wine of Surrentum,' a light wine mixed with the lees of the strong Falernian.
63. 'of compound sauce.' But some take it as 'the two kinds of sauce.' But 'duplicis' would seem to be opposed to 'simplex.'
66. 'Byzantine jar,' because the tunny-fish was caught near Byzantium.
68. 'Cilician;' literally 'Corycian.' Corycus was a mountain in Cilicia, famous for saffron.
94. 'hidden sources—blessed life.' This seems, as Macleane says, to be a parody of Lucretius.

V.

1. 'Teiresias.' This is an amusing parody on the interview between Teiresias the prophet and Ulysses in the eleventh book of the *Odyssey*.

14. 'even before the household god,' i.e. the Lar, to whom the first-fruits were offered. He was the family god, the good genius of the house, connected with the departed ancestors of the family.

18. 'Dama,' a common name for a slave.

20. 'I'll bid my stalwart—I've borne.' A parody on Homer.

32. 'the prænomen.' Either because the use of it, like a Christian name amongst us, implies familiarity; or the man addressed, once a slave, likes to hear the name used that reminds him of his manumission.

39. 'whether the flaming—wintry Alps.' This is a parody of the bombastic Furius. See *Sat.* I. 10, 36.

44. 'more tunnies;' i.e. more rich fools: so Swift uses 'gudgeons' for people easily ensnared.

56. 'quinquevir,' a member of some board of commissioners, 'a notary,' a public officer. Horace was himself one. See *Sat.* II. 6, 36.

59. 'will happen or will not.' This seems to be a joke, as a pompous truism.

63. 'of the race of Æneas,' as Virgil represents Augustus in the *Æneid.*

84. 'There was at Thebes.' Thebes is the place mentioned, as Teiresias was a Theban.

101. 'And is my old comrade.' In the original 'ergo,' the word used also in *Ode* I. 24, 5, after death.

109. 'for a nominal consideration;' just for a single sesterce; as in the English form, 'in consideration of the sum of ten shillings.'

VI.

The most delightful of Satires, which is no Satire; it is imitated by Swift, and the latter part added afterwards by Pope. See Walckenaer, Vol. I. p. 373.

1. 'a piece of land.' Here is a short description of his Sabine villa with the brook Digentia.

3. 'besides.' Compare *Epod.* I, 31, a passage of similar contentment. Some render 'over these;' and so, just over Horace's villa was mount Lucretilis, now Gennaro.

5. 'son of Maia,' Mercury, invoked as the god of gain, and the patron of Horace the poet.

13. 'Hercules,' like Mercury, also the god of fortunate findings, as of treasure trove.

20. 'Thou father of dawn;' the same god as Janus, i.e. Dianus, originally the god of the day.

23. 'I am hurried away by thee,' i.e. by Janus, as setting Horace onwards for the business of the day.

32. 'Now that this is my delight,' i.e. to get back to Mæcenas.

33. 'Esquiline Hill;' once a common burying place, now the abode of Mæcenas.

35. 'Puteal,' built by Scribonius Libeo in the Forum, where the money-lenders met.

36. 'the notaries,' who wanted to obtain the interest of Horace, once himself a member of their body.

40. 'Seven years and more.' If Horace was introduced to Mæcenas about B.C. 38, this Satire was written B.C. 30, when Horace was 35.

44. 'the Thracian Gallina,' a gladiator of the so-called 'Thracian' sort of gladiators. Perhaps 'Syrus' was a Mirmillo.

55. 'to the veterans;' who were discontented after the battle of Actium, B.C. 31.

63. 'the relations of Pythagoras,' for Pythagoras forbad his disciples eating beans, in which, said he, were the souls of the dead. See Ovid, *Metamorph.*, last book.

69. 'unreasonable laws,' imposed elsewhere by the governor of the feast.

114. 'mastiffs;' in the original 'Molossian dogs;' so called from Molossia, a region of Epirus.

VII.

4. 'freedom of December,' i.e. the Saturnalia.

10. 'changing the stripe of his tunic.' He was a senator; and might, if he chose, wear the laticlave; but sometimes he would wear only the narrow stripe, like a knight.

14. 'all the Vertumni.' Vertumnus was the god of change, who, as Tibullus said, 'wore a thousand ornaments, and all gracefully.'

33. 'when the lamps are just lighted.' To dine late was by the Romans accounted simple, and this simplicity Mæcenas affected.

43 'five hundred drachmæ' amounts to, say, £17, or £18, the price for a poor sort of slave.

45. 'the porter of Crispinus.' The porter retailed the lectures of his blear-eyed philosophic master; *Sat.* I. 1, 120.

76. 'prætor's rod.' The prætor laid a rod on the shoulder of the slave, as he gave him freedom.

79. 'a substitute.' Literally, 'a vicar,' a slave to wait on a slave, which slave was as a master to him.

86. 'like a sphere;' for the ancients thought a globe was the most perfect shape.

95. 'by Pausias;' a painter of Sicyon, about 350 B.C.

96. 'Fulvius, Rutuba, Placideianus;' gladiators.

118. 'you shall join the eight labourers,' where he would have to grind in a mill, get well beaten, work in chains.

VIII.

3. 'to dine early;' which by the Romans was accounted luxurious. See above, *Sat.* II. 7, 33.

6. 'Lucanian boar;' for these and the Umbrian boars were esteemed as good, being fed on the acorns of the Apennines.

7. 'the father of the feast:' the host, who acted as governor of the feast.

9. 'skirret;' called also skirwort: its root has the taste of a parsnip.

14. 'Hydaspes,' an Indian, named from the river Hydaspes.
15. 'home-made Chian.' See Persius, VI. 39, who appears thus to have understood Horace: but some say 'without salt-water in it:' while Yonge thinks Persius and Horace mean 'without power,' wanting in body.
20. 'on the highest couch,' the couch on the right, facing the lowest couch. The place of honour was the corner of the middle couch, where was Mæcenas, next to the host's parasite on the lowest couch. See St. Luke XX. 46; xiv. 8.
22. 'friends he had introduced;' uninvited; literally 'shadows;' in Italian 'ombre' in Gargallo's translation.
26. 'as to the rest of us,' all except Mæcenas; or, perhaps, all except the host.
34. 'shall die unavenged;' in Epic style, as are many bits of the Satires of Horace.
39. 'large cups;' literally, of Allifæ, a town of Samnium on the Vulturnus.
42. 'sea-eel;' muræna, or lamprey, which the ancients esteemed. Hortensius, the orator, cried at the death of one which he had kept in a fish-pond.
50. 'Lesbian;' in the original 'Methymnæan.' Methymna was the second town of Lesbos, the birth-place of Arion and Hellanicus.
52. 'sea-urchins;' animals with firm shells covered with spires.
54. 'the tapestry,' which hung from the ceiling of the room.
58. 'Rufus,' i.e. Nasidienus.
77. 'calls for his slippers;' for the ancients at their meals took off their sandals or slippers.
79. 'I should have preferred this to any play.' This is suitable, as addressed to Fundanius, who wrote comedies. *Sat.* I. 10, 42.
89. 'hares' wings,' which the ancients thought the best part. See *Sat.* II. 2, 44.
95. 'Canidia.' This is the last time she is mentioned.

EPISTLES.

BOOK I.

I.

1. Pope's imitation of this Epistle may be usefully compared with the original. He has also imitated Epistle 6, and part of 7, in this book; and the two Epistles of the 2nd book.
'lay.' The sense of the passage shows that the word is here applied to his writings generally, not to the Odes alone. Also, he uses the word 'Muse' of his Epistles, as in I. 8, 2.
4. Veianius was a well-known gladiator. As to the dedication of his arms, comp. *Od.* III. 26.
6. By 'the edge of the arena' is meant the 'podium,' where sat the spectators of highest rank.
7. 'unobstructed,' i.e. by error or prejudice.
9. 'in the end.' It seems best not to press the phrase so as to make it refer to the end of the course. For 'strain his flanks,' comp. Virg. *Georg.* III. 506.
14. 'bound.' The word is specially used of a debtor assigned to his creditor. 'in' expresses the act of repeating from dictation. So in *Epod.* 15, 4.
16. 'I turn practical.' He is speaking of the Stoic philosophy.
18. Aristippus was the founder of the Cyrenaic school, which generally resembled the Epicurean. For the doctrine of the next line, see *Epist.* 6, throughout.
21. 'who work for debt.' Lit. 'who owe work;' who are working off arrears of labour.
22. 'supervision.' For the widow would have the control (custodia) of the children, though she could not act as their guardian (tutor).
28. 'you may not.' Supply 'quum' or 'quamvis' before 'non.'
29. 'when your eyes are sore.' Comp. *Sat.* I. 5, 30.
30. Glycon, like Veianius, was a well-known character of the time.
34. 'spells.' The maxims of philosophy; so, the 'purificatory rites' of l. 37.
41. 'the beginning of virtue;' 'prima' must be taken as agreeing with 'virtus,' as well as with 'sapientia.'
45. 'with speed.' Comp. *Od.* III. 24, 36.
50. 'the great Olympian games.' The phrase is a translation of στεφανοῦσθαι Ὀλύμπια. The acc. is one of limitation. 'to be crowned as regards the Olympian festival,' ἱερά. So 'without the dust'=Gr. ἀκονιτί.
52. 'gold is meaner than virtues,' as village games are inferior to the Olympian.
54. 'Janus.' The space between the arcades of Janus formed the exchange of Rome. *Sat.* II. 3, 18, note.
56. 'Satchels.' The merchants' purses are compared to school-boys' satchels. This line, repeated from *Sat.* I. 6, 74, has been supposed to be spurious here; but, as it seems, without sufficient reason.
58. The four hundred thousand sesterces were the property qualification of a knight.
59. 'you shall be king.' There is a play, in the Lat., on 'rex' and 'recte.' The meaning is: as he who plays best, wins, so the perfect life, not the greatest wealth, should be most valued.
61. 'to feel no guilt within,' lit. 'to be

conscious of nothing with one's self;' to have nothing on the conscience.

62. The Roscian law reserved the first 14 rows of the orchestra stalls in the theatre for those who had at least the property qualification of a knight. *Epod.* 4, 16; Juvenal, III. 159.

67. 'have a closer view.' See last note. 'lamentable' is, of course, used in a satirical sense. Nothing is known of Pupius.

76. 'a many-headed monster.' Alluding to the hydra. So Shakespeare, *Coriolanus*, A. IV. Sc. 1: 'the beast with many heads.' And Scott, *Lady of the Lake:*

'Thou many-headed monster thing.'

79. 'their preserves,' i.e. inveigle them so far as to make sure of coming in for their property.

80. 'secret usury' seems to mean, above the legal rate of 12 per cent. per annum; or, on money lent to those who are legally infants. A very similar phrase is used in a good sense in *Od.* I. 12, 45.

84. 'the lake,' the Lucrine lake. *Od.* II. 15, 3, note.

85. 'unreasoning,' 'vitiosa' here='full of defects.' In *Od.* II. 16, 21, it means 'that which causes defects.'

86. 'auspices.' See *Od.* I. 7, 27, note. Teanum is about 30 Roman miles from Baiæ (Baja).

87. 'is in his hall.' This was the sign that the house was occupied by married people.

90. 'Proteus.' See Virg. *Georg.* IV. 387, &c.

93. 'sea-sick,' and accordingly discontented, of course.

94. 'capillos' is rather a curious instance of the acc. of limitation. Comp. Virg. *Georg.* IV. 337. 'occurri' in the next line is an instance of the aoristic use of the perfect, so common in Virgil and Horace.

'inæquali tonsore' must be explained as an abl. abs. The adj. agreeing grammatically with 'tonsore' is meant to describe the quality of his workmanship. *Od.* I. 6, 1, note.

100. 'exchanges' &c., i.e. does so without reason.

101. 'like other folks.' This adverbial use of the adj. seems best explained as an acc. of limitation. 'Mad to the extent of what is usual.'

102. 'appointed by the prætor,' in default of a relation legally qualified.

105. 'safeguard,' &c. Pope's 'guide, philosopher, and friend.'

108. 'sound.' 'Sanus,'=Gr. ὑγιής. 'Perfect in mind and body.'

II.

2. 'Præneste.' This was one of Horace's favourite country retreats. See *Od.* III. 40, 22.

3. 'what is fair,' &c., *τὸ καλὸν, τὸ αἰσχρὸν, τὸ συμφέρον.*

4. Chrysippus, *Sat.* I. 3, 126. Crantor, a disciple of Plato. Comp. Milton: 'our sage and serious poet Spenser, whom I dare be known to think a better teacher than Scotus or Aquinas.'

7. 'barbarians.' *Od.* II. 49, note.

9. 'to cut away the cause,' by giving up Helen.

13. 'the one,' Agamemnon, in his love for Chryseis, *Il.* I. 113.

19. 'that wary man.' A paraphrase of the opening of the Odyssey. Comp. *Art. Poet.* 141.

23. 'the Sirens' lays,' &c., as representing the allurements of pleasure. So in *Sat.* II. 3, 14.

29. 'in attending to,' &c. Lit. 'in taking care of their skin;' a common phrase in Latin. *Sat.* II. 5, 38; *Epist.* I. 4, 15. Of course this passage is merely in jest.

39. 'from year to year.' The phrase seems to = 'ex anno in annum.' *Epist.* I. 11, 23, note.

40. 'half the act.' Ἀρχὴ δέ τοι ἥμισυ παντός. 'Now the beginning is half the whole.' The author of the saying is unknown: it has been ascribed to Pythagoras.

42. 'like the clown.' The allusion seems to be to a fable now lost.

44. 'money.' Comp. French 'argent.' The word 'argentum' is mostly used to mean 'plate.' But the word is employed in the present sense in *Sat.* I. 1, 86, and in *Sat.* II. 6, 10.

48. 'is wont to remove.' The perf. (deduxit) is aoristic.

52. 'warm applications to the gout.' As they would only increase the pain. The Romans were extravagantly fond of warm baths. The so-called 'Turkish bath' should rather be the 'Roman bath.'

55. 'Scorn pleasures.' This series of sententious sayings (γνῶμαι) points altogether to the excellence of moderation and self-control.

58. 'Sicilian tyrants;' Dionysius, &c. Comp. *Od.* III. 1, 18.

61. 'to gratify.' 'odio' is dat. 'of advantage' after 'festinat.'

64. 'with neck still pliable,' 'cervice' is abl. of quality; and 'viam' in the next line is probably acc. cognate. Some govern it by 'monstret.'

67. 'begins its service.' 'militat' is a good example of the inceptive force of the present.

68. 'heart still clear.' Comp. *Epist.* I. 1, 7, note.

70. 'if you lag behind,' &c. See analysis.

III.

1. Nothing definite is known of Florus, to whom is also addressed the 2nd Epistle of the 2nd Book. Porphyrio says that he edited satires of Ennius, Lucilius, and Varro. Probably he modernised their phraseology.

3. 'Hebrus.' *Od.* I. 25, 20, note.

4. 'towers;' those commemorative of Hero and Leander. 'Asia' is the Roman colony so named.

6. 'description of works.' It seems better to take 'operum' as partitive gen. after 'Quid,' than as governed by 'studiosa.' Comp. the absolute use of 'peritus' in *Od.* II. 20, 19.

9. Nothing is known of this Titius. 'The Pindaric spring'=lyrics in the style of Pindar.

See *Od.* IV. 2, 1. For 'expalluit' with acc., comp. *Od.* III. 27, 28.

13. 'Theban'='Pindaric.' 'At the prompting.' See *Od.* I. 7, 27, note.

14. 'mouth,' 'ampullari'=Gr. ληκυθίζειν. And comp. *Art. Poet.* 97.

15. 'mihi' (dat. ethic.) nearly ='meus:' but also contains the meaning of 'tell me.'

'Celsus' is perhaps the friend to whom the 8th *Epistle* of this Book is written.

17. The temple of Apollo on the Palatine was the Imperial Library, founded by Augustus. The reference is, of course, to plagiarisms from well-known authors.

19. 'the wretched crow' in Æsop's fable. The passage is not to be taken too seriously.

21. 'flitting.' So he speaks of himself as a bee, in *Od.* IV. 2, 27.

23. 'jura' (for sing. 'jus civile,') is a sort of acc. of limitation: 'to give opinions, so far as concerns the common law.'

25. 'ivy.' See *Od.* I. 1, 29, note.

26. Literally 'applications of cares.' Celsus says that there are cold, dry, and wet, as well as hot 'fomenta.' 'Cold' is the word used here, as opposed to the warmth of genius. The allusion is to avarice and ambition.

30. 'whether,' &c. The readings waver between 'si' and 'sit.' In the former case, supply 'sit;' in the latter, 'utrum.'

31. 'badly sewn.' The metaphor is from a wound imperfectly dressed.

35. 'that are not such.' 'indigni' followed by inf. is an application of a Greek construction not uncommon in Virgil and Horace.

IV.

1. 'Albius.' See *Od.* I. 33. His family estate was at Pedum (prob. Zagarola), not far from Tibur.

3. Cassius of Parma is said to have been a military tribune together with Horace in the army of Brutus, and to have been afterwards put to death by the victorious party. His 'pieces' were probably elegies, like those of Tibullus.

6. 'You never were.' Such is the force of the imperf. 'eras.' 'You never were, and are not now.'

9. 'who, like you,' &c. The readings differ greatly: 'quam' or 'quam ut' for 'qui' being the principal variations. The reading and construction adopted here are those of Lambinus. The passage seems thus to give the best and most natural sense. There can be no reasonable doubt that 'alumno' is a dative.

12. ''Twixt hope and care,' &c. A commonplace in Horace's usual tone. Comp. *Od.* IV. 7.

15. 'plump and sleek.' See *Life* by Suetonius, p. 19.

'in high condition.' *Epist.* I. 2, 29, note.

16. 'a hog.' A common taunt used by the Stoics. Cicero *in Pison.* 16, 37: 'Epicurus, our friend, you who issued from a sty, not from a school of philosophy.'

V.

1. 'Archias,' a well-known cabinet-maker at Rome, as it appears.

2. 'miscellaneous salad.' 'olus' is a sort of cognate acc. after 'cœnare.' The use of 'omne' is curious. Orelli compares the Gr. τὸ ἐπιτυχὸν, but the words are not identical.

4. 'consule,' abl. abs. according to the usual construction, is understood with 'Tauro.' He was consul with Augustus, B. C. 26.

'drawn off into jars,' 'bottled,' as we should say.

5. Sinuessan only ranked as a third-class wine.

6. 'obey my orders,' as master of the feast. 'meum' is, rather abruptly, to be supplied with 'imperium.'

9. Moschus was a rhetorician of Pergamus. He was accused of poisoning, and defended by Torquatus, whose leader was Asinius Pollio.

'Cæsar' is probably Augustus; though the word by itself refers to Julius, in *Od.* I. 2, 44. The birthday of Augustus was Sept. 23; that of J. Cæsar, July 12; but the former, at least in Italy, might properly be said to be in the summer.

12. 'quo' seems best explained as the old form of the dative; 'optem,' or some similar word, being understood after 'fortunam.' The phrase occurs in Ovid, *Am.* II. 19, 7. The reading of this line is much disputed.

13. 'through regard for his heir.' Comp. *Od.* IV. 7, 19.

14. 'scatter flowers.' The phrase seems to be used indefinitely, to express a certain recklessness of festivity.

16. 'effect,' in the imagination of the drinker. 'designo,' lit. ='to mark out.' The sense it bears in this line is not common. Comp. Terence, *Ad.* I. 2, 6. On the whole passage, comp. *Od.* III. 21, 13, &c.

21. 'efficiently.' The sense seems to be: 'as one who is efficient and also willing.'

25. 'elimino' is not elsewhere used, except in the literal sense of 'to turn out of doors.'

26. The friends here mentioned are otherwise unknown to us, though it has been attempted to identify them with persons elsewhere spoken of.

28. 'introductions.' See *Sat.* II. 8, 22, note. Horace, Torquatus, and the three other friends, would make five guests, leaving four more to be invited, so as to make the usual number, nine.

30. 'to bring,' lit. 'to be.' 'quotus' agrees with the person, according to the usual idiom. Orelli compares Martial, XIV. 217.

31. 'by the back-door.' Horace ends with a joke, as he often does, and as is suited to the character of this Epistle.

VI.

1. 'To wonder at nothing.' The same doctrine is dwelt upon in *Od.* II. 6. This idea, that composure and rest and the absence of excitement form the highest happiness, seems to be an element in the Buddhist doctrine of the Nirvânâ: it has also found a place, under various forms, in the religious beliefs of other nations. Among the Romans it was represented in a more practical shape (agreeably to

the temperament of the nation), by such characters as Cato, &c. Plato, on the other hand, says that wonder (τὸ θαυμάζειν) is particularly the feeling of a philosopher. The phrase seems to refer to the energy of inquiry: for Plato's master, Socrates, was certainly a model of composure and self-control.

6. 'gifts of the sea,' i.e. pearls, and the famous purple dye, now lost, which was extracted from the juice of a shell-fish.

'Arabs.' See *Od.* I. 29, 1, note.

7. 'favours.' Political honours are, of course, referred to.

13. 'chance to see,' 'vidit' is used in the aoristic sense of the perfect.

17. 'Go now,' 'I nunc' is sarcastic, as it usually is. Virg. *Æn.* VII. 425. *Epist.* II. 2, 76.

'works of art,' 'artes' is used in this sense in *Od.* IV. 8, 5.

21. The sting is in the fact that Mutus got the land without any work of his own. Mutus is not otherwise known to us.

24. 'Whatever is beneath the earth.' The sense is, that all material possessions are short-lived, and will soon be swept away by death. This is a favourite truism of Horace.

26. 'Agrippa's colonnade,' i.e. that constructed and adorned by M. Vipsanius Agrippa. *Od.* I. 6. The Appian Way was the great south road from Rome. See *Sat.* I. 5, 6, &c.

27. 'Numa.' See *Od.* IV. 7, 15, note.

28. 'If your chest,' &c. This is an instance of Horace's frequent comparison between the defects of the mind and of the body. The same line occurs in *Sat.* II. 3, 163.

31. 'you think virtue to be words.' The last utterance of Brutus, according to Dio, consisted of two Greek iambic verses, of which this is a translation:

"Poor Virtue, you were but a word; yet I
Practised as real what was Fortune's fool."

32. 'a forest fagots,' i.e. 'you think a sacred grove to be simply so much timber: you are purely matter-of-fact; you have no imagination.'

'get into harbour before you,' 'occupet' = Gr. φθάνειν with the participle. *Od.* II. 12, 28, note.

33. Cibyra was a town of Phrygia, celebrated for its iron manufactures. To 'miss the market' seems to refer to the market of purchase, not that of sale; i.e. 'lest another, arriving before you, buy the goods at a lower price.'

34. 'a thousand talents' = about £200,000.

37. 'high birth and beauty.' That is, of course, 'money will make people call you noble and handsome, even if the contrary be the truth.'

39. 'the king.' Cicero speaks of his poverty in his letters to Atticus, VI. 1, 4. The sense of the passage is rather loosely connected. It is; 'be anything rather than poor; aim at the superfluous wealth of Lucullus, and shun the poverty of the Cappadocian king.'

42. 'How.' Quî (quo) = Quomodo.

44. 'purple cloaks.' Though the word (chlamys) does not literally convey so much as this, yet here it is used in a particular and emphatic sense. 'ut' is readily understood before 'tolleret;' and 'prætor,' as a subject. Plutarch says that he was the official who was bringing out the show.

45. 'Meagre.' The passage is sarcastic.

46. 'knaves.' This word, = 'thievish slaves,' is also so used by Virg. *Ecl.* III. 16.

51. 'across the tradesman's scales.' This seems the best explanation of a difficult passage. Orelli says that it is confirmed by a drawing which represents a shop in Pompeii, preserved in the Museo Borbonico at Naples. The other best known explanation is rather grotesque: 'to stretch out your hand beyond the centre of gravity;' so that you run the risk of tumbling down.

54. 'the ivory curule chair,' alluding particularly to the consulship. Horace writes as if the republic still existed practically.

58. We know nothing of this Gargilius.

60. 'before the eyes of the people,' so that they might imagine that he was a great hunter. The general sense is 'let us devote ourselves to good living; and, if we hunt at all for our game, let it be only make-believe.'

61. 'let us bathe.' It was thought that this would renew the appetite. There is a very similar passage in Juvenal, I. 142. See *Epist.* I. 2, 52, note.

62. 'to be classed among the Cærites,' i.e. to lose our civil rights. Gellius says that they were the inhabitants of Cære in Etruria; and that they were the first people who were admitted to the privileges of Romans, without the franchise: and so the censor enrolled among them any person deprived of his full rights as a citizen.

63. 'forbidden pleasure.' When they killed the oxen of the Sun. *Odyss.* XII. 297.

65. Mimnermus was an elegiac poet of Colophon. According to Porphyrio, he placed the chief good in indifference. The cynical and splenetic Swift is, rather oddly, the Mimnermus of Pope.

"If Swift cry wisely, 'Vive la bagatelle!'
The man that loves and laughs must sure do well."

VII.

2. 'August.' In the Lat. 'Sextilem.' The name of this month was not changed to that of 'Augustus,' till about the time of Horace's death, B.C. 8.

6. 'undertaker.' The word literally means 'one who arranges.' 'lictor,' the appointed servant of an officer of state, is here applied with a sort of grim humour. The word is used in the general sense of 'an attendant,' also in Plautus, *Pœn. Prol.* 18. The unhealthiness of Rome in the autumn was (and is now still more) notorious. *Od.* II. 14, 16; *Sat.* II. 6, 19.

7. 'fond mother.' Such is the force of the diminutive 'matercula.' See l. 65, note.

8. 'courtesies.' Especially those rendered to a patron, the calling on friends, &c.

10. 'But when,' 'si' is used in this sense in *Sat.* II. 3, 10.

rner,' i.e. wrapped up
f.
c and rude. The Cala-
comparatively uncivil-
od.
nd;' a polite refusal.
nodern Italian 'tante

here employed in its
mmonly = 'sown corn

lf ready.' The con-
ratus' is Gr. See *Od.*

upine-seeds,' used as
, &c.
merentis' = 'bene me-
. VI. 664.
.' 'latus' is often used
strength, as in Cicero,
brow,' i.e. seeming so,
lustered at the sides.

rds.' 'loqui' and the
are here used substan-
article: τὸ γελᾶν, &c.
t. to Odes, p. 22.
MSS. Bentley ingeni-
dula,' 'a dormouse,'
by most modern com-
reasons for the change
too large an animal to
o a corn-bin, and does
Æsop's fables are full
ch as that of various
ther, of the lion eating

npellor' is used in the
297. It nearly = 're-

Od. I. 29, 1, note.
ften used by clients, in
Epist. I. 17, 20. For
6, 54.
ne,' lit. 'have heard;'
is attempted to trans-
lish. *Par. Lost*, III. 7:
pure ethereal stream?"

.' The pres. indic. of
express his confidence
power.
The passage is taken
nduring' = πολύτλας.
he whole phrase seems
here is no sufficient
patiis' (as Orelli does)
se of 'race-courses.'
Comp. 'dominæ Romæ,'

vds.' Comp. 'vacuæ
31: and with 'peaceful
ntum,' *Sat.* II. 4, 34.
was consul in B.C. 91.
de Orat. 3, 1, 4,) as
and particularly deter-

,' about 2 p.m.

48. 'Carinæ,' a fashionable quarter of Rome, where were the mansions of Pompey, Q. Cicero, &c.

50. 'just shaved.' The word ('adrasum') has the same force in Petronius, c. 32.

'then empty.' Most people would have been shaved earlier; but Mena on this day was taking his ease.

51. 'his own nails,' i.e. not having them dressed by the barber. But the word, which seems = Gr. φίλους, gives additional expression to the lazy carelessness of the attitude.

52. 'Demetrius,' a Greek page. Greek servants, as is often mentioned by Juvenal, were fashionable at Rome.

53. 'what place,' i.e. 'what country?' Lit. 'from whence from home?' So in *Æn.* VIII. 114.

54. 'his patron.' This appears to mean, 'or, in case he is a freedman, who is his patron?'

56. 'known,' &c. There is much doubt whether it is right to take the passage thus, or to take 'notum' absolutely, or to connect it with the next line. The force of 'notum,' taken by itself, does not seem very pointed. If 'notum' be taken with the next line, 'gaudentem' governs 'sodalibus,' &c. According to the arrangement adopted here, these ablatives are those 'of quality.'

61. 'ut' is understood before 'veniat,' according to the usual idiom.

'not quite.' Orelli says that 'non sane' = οὐ πάνυ. And this is certainly sometimes the meaning of the Greek phrase; though it has been violently contended that it always = 'by no means.'

62. 'very kind.' See note on l. 16.

63. 'Can it be,' &c. This is the 'deliberative' subj.

'the rascal.' 'improbus' seems always to contain the notion of excess; here, of excess in perversity. Comp. 'improbus anser,' Virg. *Georg.* I. 119, which Conington proposes oddly to translate 'the unconscionable goose.'

65. 'second-hand goods.' 'scruta' = Gr. γρύτη. The old commentator says that the popular form of the word was 'grutæ.'

'the poor.' 'popello.' The diminutive is slightly contemptuous. Sometimes it expresses a sort of endearment; as in l. 7, and in *Epist.* I. 4, 8. Comp. the French 'petit papa,' the Italian 'signorino,' &c.

66. 'accosts.' Orelli well compares Gr. φθάνει προσαγορεύων.

70. 'As you please.' The shade of meaning is slightly different in l. 19.

71. 'the ninth hour.' About 3 p.m.

72. 'meet and unmeet.' Gr. ῥητὰ ἄῤῥητα. In this and the next line it is gently, but clearly hinted, that Mena showed himself not well versed in the usages of good society, and that he drank more wine than was good for him.

76. 'the Latin Holidays.' These did not occur at any fixed period, but were proclaimed by the Consul, according to the convenience of public business.

77. 'carriage.' Some explain the phrase as meaning 'when mounted on nags.' But the

use of the plural, and the age of Philippus, are against this construction. 'Mannis' is also held to mean 'mules.' *Od.* III. 27, 7.

'Sabine country,' which was not very beautiful, and where the climate was rather cold.

80. 'seven thousand sesterces'=about £56. Money (in the time of Horace, at least,) was cheap; but so was land in the country, though not at Rome.

84. 'prates.' Comp. *Od.* I. 18, 5.

'makes ready.' 'vitibus' is easily understood after 'præparat.'

85. 'half kills himself,' lit. 'dies over his pursuits.' 'studiis' is dat. 'passion for gain.' This phrase seems taken from Virg. *Georg.* IV. 177, where it is applied to bees.

87. 'disappointed.' Comp. *Od.* III. 1, 30.

91. 'you seem to me.' The composed manner of the old lawyer is amusingly contrasted with the angry despair of Mena.

92. 'Pol'='per Pollucem.' The phrase is very common in Plautus and Terence.

94. The 'Genius' of each man came into the world at his birth, and left it at his death, and was a sort of guardian angel. *Epist.* II. 2, 187, note.

98. 'should measure himself;' i.e. 'should find out what suits him, and what does not.' Comp. the subject of *Sat.* I. 1.

VIII.

1. Celsus is probably the friend who is mentioned in I. 3, 15. It seems right to explain the infinitives in this line as substantival=Gr. τὸ χαίρειν καὶ τὸ εὖ πράττειν.

3. 'threaten.' Comp. *Sat.* II. 3, 9.

4. 'perfect nor pleasant.' This is the only one of Horace's compositions which can be said to be written in at all a morbid tone. See Gen. Int.

6. 'distant pastures.' Orelli mentions the large pasture-lands of Calabria and Cisalpine Gaul. The word 'longinquis' seems also to express the idea of large extent.

7. 'all my body.' That is, 'the least healthy part of my body is sounder than the healthiest part of my mind.'

10. 'shield me from.' The usual construction after 'arceo' is acc. of the thing repelled: but this is an inverted construction, in the style of Virgil: so in *Art. Poet.* 64. 'Cur'='propterea quod,' is used in the same way in *Od.* I. 33, 3.

12. 'fickle as the wind.' Horace makes the same charge against his slave, in *Sat.* II. 7, 28.

14. 'his youthful patron.' Tiberius was at this time about 22. 'the staff.' Comp. *Sat.* I. 7, 23, &c.

15. 'wish him joy.' 'Gaudere'seems='illum gaudere jubere.'

16. 'delicate ears.' This is again a different shade of meaning conveyed by the diminutive. Comp. *Epist.* I. 7, 65, note.

IX.

1. This *Epistle* is praised, as a model of a letter of introduction, in the *Spectator*, No. 493, as Mr Theodore Martin observes.

3. 'actually,' 'scilicet.' This force of the word is uncommon; though it is often used in an ironical, as well as in its properly demonstrative sense. *Æn.* IV. 379.

4. 'what is honourable.' The indefinite use of the neuter seems=Gr. τὰ καλά.

9. 'a dissembler.' Such as Aristotle describes in the *Ethics*, IV. 3, as 'one who seems to deny or disparage what he really possesses.'

11. 'stooped.' This seems the force of the word, meaning, as in Cicero, *in Cæcil.* I. 1, something which to a certain extent lowers self-respect.

'the prize.' This word, used ironically, ='disgrace.'

13. 'among your flock,' i.e. 'among your staff.' 'gregis' is the partitive genitive.

X.

1. 'Aristius.' See *Od.* I. 22. 1, note. In the present epistle the ideas are mostly Stoical: and Horace seems to have had a real admiration for this school of philosophy, though he often makes jokes on certain forms which it assumed.

2. 'actually.' Comp. *Epist.* I. 9. 3, note.

3. 'twins,' lit. 'being almost twins,' &c. 'animis' is abl. of quality. After the second 'alter,' 'negat' must be understood. l. 4. is a sort of parenthesis.

8. 'am a king.' This is the language of a Stoic. Comp. *Epist.* I. 1, 107.

9. 'loud applause.' Comp. the meaning of the same phrase in *Æn.* VIII. 90. There, on the whole, it seems to refer to the voices of the crew.

10. The priest's 'sweet wafers,' a surfeit of which made his slave run away, here denote the artificial, as opposed to the natural life, which is signified by bread.

13. 'to live,' &c. A well-known doctrine of the Stoics. Δεῖ ὁμολογουμένως τῇ φύσει ζῆν. Cicero uses the same phrase as Horace, in *de Off.* III. 3, 13.

15. 'winters are milder.' If the phrase has any point at all, it must mean that in the country you have more freedom of choice in selecting a place of abode, than you have in the town. Comp. *Od.* II. 7, 17.

16. The 'dog-star' rises on the 20th of July, and the Sun enters Leo on the 23rd. The word 'momenta' seems rather to mean 'influence,' (as it often does,) than 'season,' as some explain it.

17. 'full of fury;' as if made so by the 'stinging Sun.'

18. 'distracts.' Another reading is 'depellat'; but 'divellat' certainly seems the most expressive, as it is also the less common of the two.

20. 'the leaden pipes' which received the water from the enormous aqueducts which supplied Rome.

21. 'which dances noisily.' Comp. *Od.* II. 3, 11.

22. 'Why,' &c. i.e. 'We even try to reproduce nature in the midst of the town.'

24. 'ut' or 'licet' is, of course, understood before 'expellas;' the other reading, 'expelles,' seems clearly wrong.

26. 'to compare,' &c. That is, to distinguish the real Tyrian (Sidonian) purple from that manufactured in Italy. 'ostro' is the dative.

28. 'his heart,' lit. 'marrow.' So in *Æn.* IV. 66; Psalm XXXI. 10. The passage means, that artificial knowledge on minute and technical points is worthless, when compared with discernment on the great truths of natural philosophy.

30. 'the man,' &c. Comp. *Epist.* VI. beginning. 'overmuch.' See *Od.* I. 18, 13, note.

34. 'a stag,' Aristotle (*Rhet.* II. 20, 5) says that Stesichorus employed this fable to prevent the people of Himera from accepting the sovereignty of Phalaris.

40. 'in his covetousness.' See *Epist.* I. 7, 63, note.

41. 'for ever,' 'æternum' is an adverb, like 'lucidum' in *Od.* II. 12, 14.

42. 'in the story,' 'olim' is often used in somewhat the same sense, as in *Sat.* I. 1, 25.

45. 'and not let me go,' &c. Horace courteously throws upon himself the contemplated possibility of becoming covetous.

48. 'twisted rope,' i.e. simply 'twined rope.' The metaphor is very clear; and it seems useless to attempt to identify it with the notion of a pulley, a cart-rope, a game, &c.

49. 'am dictating for you,' i.e. 'am dictating to my amanuensis, to be sent to you.' In the Latin 'was dictating:' for the Romans used tenses applicable to the time at which the letter would be read.

Vacuna was an ancient Sabine goddess, said to correspond to the Roman 'Victoria.'

50. 'Excepto' is abl. abs. 'cetera' is acc. of limitation.

XI.

1. Bullatius is otherwise unknown.

2. 'pretty Samos;' probably referring to its buildings, especially its temple of Herè.

5. 'cities of Attalus:' Pergamus, Tralles, Thyatira, Myndus. *Od.* I. 1, 12, note.

6. Lebedus was one of the twelve cities of Ionia. It seems from the next line, that Bullatius had been the comrade of Horace in the army of Brutus.

7. Gabii and Fidenæ were two deserted towns of the Prisci Latini. They are coupled by Virgil, *Æn.* VI. 773; and by Juvenal, X. 100.

10. 'the deep.' Comp. Lucretius, II. 1. Here the sentiment is Stoic; 'the perfect man can be happy in the most desolate and wild of places.'

14. 'caught cold,' lit. 'gathered cold.' So 'sitim collegerat,' Ovid, *Met.* V. 446.

17. 'in perfect soundness.' 'Incolumi' is here a word of the Stoic philosophy, like 'sanus' in I. 1, 108.

18. 'at midsummer,' 'æstivo' is readily understood after 'solstitio.'

'athlete's dress.' 'Campestre' (subligaculum) is lit. 'a dress for the Campus Martius.'

19. 'August.' I. 7, 2, note.

22. 'bless you with,' 'fortuno' was a word used in religious formulas.

23. 'from year to year,' lit. 'for a year;' but it seems better to explain the phrase as having the former sense, than as denoting an indefinite time. So in I. 2, 38.

27. 'they change.' Comp. *Od.* II. 16, 19.

28. 'a vigorous idleness,' in always beginning but never achieving.

30. 'at Ulubræ,' i.e. 'anywhere, even at Ulubræ.' This was a little town near the Pomptine marshes. It is called 'vacuæ' by Juvenal, X. 102.

XII.

1. 'Iccius.' Comparing this Epistle with *Od.* I. 29, we see that Iccius, though a dabbler in philosophy, had an eye to the main chance, like many other philosophers.

'Agrippa.' Probably he got these estates in Sicily after his defeat of Sextus Pompeius off the coast of Sicily.

5. 'your digestion is good.' Horace speaks as one who knew what that dreadful monster, indigestion, was.

7. 'nettle broth,' said to be still used in Scotland.

12. 'Democritus' of Abdera, founder of the atomic system.

16. 'inquiring,' &c. Comp. Virg. *Æn.* I. 742.

20. 'Empedocles,' a very early philosopher, B.C. 520, contrasted with 'Stertinius,' a modern and voluminous oracle of the Stoics.

21. 'fish,' 'leeks and onions.' 'fish,' a luxury: 'leeks and onions,' common food; and, besides, the mention of fish alludes to Empedocles, the 'leeks and onions' to Pythagoras, to whose philosophy Iccius may have been attached.

26. 'Cantabrians,' reduced B.C. 26.

27. 'Armenians to Claudius Nero,' i.e. Tiberius. Here is one of the usual exaggerations of Horace and Virgil; and generally the Romans were 'awful liars' about their enemies.

'Phraates on bended knee.' This 'bended knee' is really too bad as an exaggeration.

29. 'Plenty' with her cornucopia, the horn of Amalthea. Comp. *Od.* I. 17, 15. Velleius Paterculus says that when the civil wars of Rome were over, cultivation was restored to the fields, thanks to Augustus. *Od.* IV. 15, 4.

XIII.

8. 'Asina,' a poor joke. Walckenaer compares the name, Asina, Asinus, or Asinius, with the names Porcius, Suillius, Oilius, the Porkers, Swineheads, Sheepshanks of antiquity.

14. 'Pyrrhia,' a slave of a 'ruddy' complexion, in a play of Titinius or Titinnius, a writer of comedies, whose date seems uncertain. Very few fragments of his plays are left.

19. 'break what is entrusted to your charge,' i.e. 'disregard,' with a parting allusion to a stumbling donkey, though donkeys usually are sure-footed.

XIV.

3. 'Varia,' now 'Vico Varo,' on the Via Valeria, situated near the Anio, 'Teverone,' N.E. of Tibur, S.W. of Mandela, now 'Bardela,' and E. of Horace's villa.

6. 'Lamia,' Lucius Ælius, Horace's own dear friend, a dear friend to Numida, who kissed him often on his return from Biscay. He boasted to be descended from Lamus, founder of Formiæ, king of the Læstrygonians.

9. 'barrier.' The figure is from the races of the Circus.

16. 'my consistency.' Inconsistent Horace is now at last consistent in his love of the country.

23 'the nook of the world.' Horace's farm embosomed in the hills was quite a nook.

29. 'the stream.' The Digentia, 'Licenza,' which flows into the Anio near Mandela.

33. 'grasping Cinara.' Yet he speaks, *Od.* IV. 1, 3, of 'the reign of the good Cinara.' Few were her days. Perhaps she is called 'good,' as 'of the dead we should say only good.' By an early death, the girl escaped the lot of long-lived Lyce.

36. Or it may mean, as Macleane thinks, 'I am not ashamed to amuse myself, but should be, if my amusement never stopped.'

43. 'lazy ox.' But others take 'lazy' with the 'horse.'

XV.

1. 'Velia' or Elea, famous for the Eleatic, or logical school of philosophy, a town in Lucania.

'Salernum' at the head of the gulf of Salerno, an important town in the middle ages.

2. 'Baiæ.' The most fashionable of watering-places, full of villas. The sea has gained on the shore there, and an earthquake has changed the look of the country.

3. 'Antonius Musa,' who cured Augustus. Antonius was another of Augustus' doctors. Craterus too was an eminent physician of those times.

4. 'bathe in cold water.' The water-cure was in part known before the days of Preissnitz.

9. 'Clusium.' Now 'Chiusi' on the Clanis. Near it was the 'lacus Clusinus.'

'Gabii,' to the east of Rome, on the lacus Gabinus.

11. 'Cumæ,' the most ancient of Greek colonies, to the north of Baiæ. Narses destroyed it in the Gothic war.

17. 'I can put up with any wine.' So he tells Mæcenas, *Odes*, I. 20, 1, he shall only give him cheap Sabine.

24. 'any Phæacian.' The Phæacians, the Epicureans of the heroic age, subjects of king Alcinous, loved feasts, music, dancing, good clothes, warm baths, comfortable beds. *Odyss.* VIII. 248.

26. Mænius.' See *Sat.* I. 1, 101.

XVI.

4. 'its form and situation.' The valley in which was Horace's farm, visited by his admirer, the Abbé de Chaupy, ran N.W. and S.E. between Mount Ustica and Rocca Giovine, on which was the temple of Vacuna. Through it ran the Digentia (Licenza). Horace's villa was at the upper end of the valley near the fountain Bandusia, just under Lucretilis hill, now Gennaro, on which he imagined the god Faunus often dwelling. Meadows were at the lower part of the little valley, where the Digentia joins the Anio.

5. 'a line of hills,' i.e. as Macleane explains it, the range of mountains from Tibur nearly to Carseoli.

13. 'Hebrus.' It seems odd of Horace, comparing his little stream with the great river of Thrace.

16. 'September's days,' when blew the leaden Sirocco, the month so gainful to the goddess Libitina, and her undertakers.

27. 'May Jove,' &c. said to be taken from Varius' panegyric on Augustus.

49. 'my Sabine bailiff.' But some take it for 'a plain honest man;' for Sabine honesty was a proverb. Walckenaer explains it of Horace, 'le petit Sabin.'

51. 'the gurnard' or gurnet,' so Yonge, Doering, and Charpentier; but some take it for the 'kite,' as do Keightley and Gargallo.

57. 'every forum.' Macleane, in his note, says there were three principal fora in Rome, and in each at least one basilica; and at the end of it a 'tribunal.'

60. 'lovely Laverna;' who, with Mercury, patronized thieves, perhaps from the same root as λαθεῖν or λαβεῖν. Thieves were called 'laverniones;' and there was a gate 'Lavernalis' with an altar of this respectable goddess near it.

69. 'Now when you can sell.' It is hard to see the connection, and Keightley says there is none; but Yonge, Macleane, Walckenaer, seem to think that Horace means, 'the man is no man, only good as a slave.'

73. 'Pentheus,' from *Bacchæ* of Euripides. Walckenaer says 'Voilà bien la philosophie stoïcienne dans toute son apreté, cette philosophie, qui faisait du suicide un devoir.'

78. 'by which I suppose.' Horace may be jesting, bantering the Stoics. But it is more likely that the passage is serious, as Horace praises the suicide of Cato.

XVII.

8. 'Ferentinum,' on the Via Latina, 46 miles to the S.E. of Rome, now 'Ferentino;' but Walckenaer thinks it is the town N. of Rome in Etruria, now 'Ferento.'

13. 'Diogenes.' The story is in Diogenes Laertius.

14. 'princes.' Aristippus had been on a visit to Dionysius of Syracuse.

18. 'the snarling Cynic.' There is something remarkable in the staff, cloak, wallet, lamp, tub of Diogenes: but the difference is essential between Diogenes and St. Francis of Assisi, the ascetic of heathenism, and the ascetic of Christianity.

30. 'of Milesian texture;' the wool of Miletus and its dye were celebrated.

33. 'to shew before our citizens captive

foes,' alludes to the Roman triumphs, to an old Roman the height of glory.

36. 'get to Corinth.' A proverb for a difficulty. It puzzled even the ancients.

60. 'holy Osiris,' the Egyptian god of the spiritual world, of whom the bull Apis was the incarnation. Isis, the wife of Osiris, was a popular object of worship at Rome.

XVIII.

1. Lollius. See *Odes*, IV. 9, 33.

9. 'but virtue is a mean.' The mean or mediocrity, dear to Horace in everything but poetry.

10. 'lowest couch.' See *Sat.* II. 8.

19. 'Castor or Dolichos,' two gladiators. Comp. *Sat.* II. 6, 44.

20. 'the Minucian.' Oddly enough, next to nothing is known of this road.

31. 'one Eutrapelus,' said to be P. Volumnius, a friend of Cicero and M. Antony, those great enemies to one another. 'Eutrapelus' means 'a gentlemanlike wit,' and reminds one of the made names in the *Spectator*, in the *Rambler*, and Law's *Serious Call*, and the *Pilgrim's Progress*.

36. 'a gladiator.' In the original 'Thrax.' See *Sat.* II. 6, 44.

41. 'Zethus and Amphion.' The hunter, and the musician, the rough and gentle. Compare the brothers Halbert and Edward in the novel of the *Monastery*; and the characters of Esau and Jacob.

46. 'Ætolian nets,' with an allusion to Meleager, the Ætolian hunter of Calydon. The epithet reminds one of the epithets of the *Odes*.

56. 'that general,' Augustus.

59. 'out of tune and harmony,' contrary to good taste and your station in life. The musical words are applied to ethics, in the manner of Plato.

82. 'Theon's tooth.' The Scholiast says he was an abusive freedman, whom his patron turned out of his house, and in his will left him a farthing to buy a rope to hang himself.

100. 'whether virtue is a lesson,' &c. See the opening of Plato's dialogue, the *Meno*: 'Is virtue a lesson, or a habit, or neither the one nor the other, but a gift of nature?'

105. 'Mandela,' now 'Bardela,' just where Horace's little valley opened into the more exposed valley of the Anio.

112. Horace wants life and worldly means, but does not want grace to make him good: also he prays he may live for himself, not for others: but he was better than his creed, as we are worse than ours.

XIX.

1. 'old Cratinus,' the oldest of the three writers of the old Comedy.

6. 'Homer, from his praise of wine.' Homer calls wine 'sweet as honey to the soul,' 'suited to the taste,' 'good for a man.'

7. 'father Ennius.' Priscian quotes Ennius as saying, 'Never a poet, except when gouty:' the gout cannot have been so bad in the days when there was no port.

8. 'Libo's hallowed plot.' See *Sat.* II. 6, 35. An inclosure in the forum, dedicated by Scribonius Libo, according to an order of the Senate, when the spot had been struck by lightning. See Facciolati on the word 'puteal.'

13. 'were to ape Cato.' Compare the proverb 'l'abito non fa il monaco.'

15. 'Iarbita,' said to be Cordus, a Moor, so called after the Moorish king Iarbas, who appears in the 4th *Æneid*. Timagenes was a declaimer.

23. 'Parian Iambics.' Horace seems to mean his *Epodes*, written by him twenty years before. But there are Iambics in Catullus.

25. 'Lycambes.' See *Epod.* 6. 13.

30. 'father-in-law,' Lycambes of Thasos.

31. 'bride,' Neobule.

32. 'Alcæus.' Horace does seem to have been the first Latin who wrote Alcaics.

37. 'I hunt not for the applause,' &c. Comp. Pers. I. 53, who describes similar gifts.

40. 'to curry favour.' Horace speaks as an electioneerer.

43. 'Our Jove,' on earth, Augustus, 'who held divided empire with Jove.'

XX.

1. 'Vertumnus and Janus.' Horace's publishers, the brothers Sosii, must have had their shop near the temples of these two gods in the Vicus Thurarius and the Argiletum, near the Forum. From Mart. *Ep.* I. 3, 1, and *Ep.* I. 117, 9, it appears the booksellers lived there in Martial's days, a hundred years afterwards.

3. 'You hate the locks and seals.' So Martial addresses his book: 'You prefer, sir, to dwell in the booksellers' shops, though there is plenty of room in my writing-case.'

5. 'Well then, off with you.' So Martial: 'Off with you, self-willed one, fly through the ethereal breezes.'

7. 'when severely criticised.' So Martial again to his book: 'You know not, alas! you know not, the disdain of Lady Rome; be sure that the city of Mars knows too much for such as you.'

13. 'Ilerda,' now 'Lerida.' Here the Pompeians were beaten by Cæsar. (See *Civ. War*, I. 37.) It was a municipium. In after days it was the Salamanca of Arragon. In the Peninsular war it was the scene of horrid cruelty by the French.

27. 'my forty-fourth December.' He was born on the 8th of December, B.C. 65.

28. 'Lollius received Lepidus.' In this year (B.C. 21) Lollius was chosen consul with Augustus. Augustus declined: then Lepidus was appointed.

BOOK II.

I.

An Epistle, as Macleane remarks, with 'much polish in its versification;' as, of course, has its imitation by Pope.

3. 'gracing it by morals.' This alludes to the laws of Augustus about marriage, and his sumptuary laws.

5. 'Liber,' confounded with Dionysus, or Bacchus, who was one of the civilisers of Greece. Paley, on *Fasti* IV. 785, connects the name 'Liber' with libation. Cicero says he was so called, as a 'child' of Ceres.

10. 'He who crushed.' Hercules.

23. 'the Twelve Tables,' the foundation of Roman law, B.C. 452.

24. 'the treaties,' such as those made with the town of Gabii by Tarquinius Superbus.

26. 'books of the priests,' as annales maximi; these are among the sources of early Roman history.

28. 'the oldest writings of the Greeks.' This must mean Homer, and hardly any other author.

31. 'The olive has no stone,' &c.; a kind of 'reductio ad absurdum.'

45. 'the hairs of a horse-tail.' The commentators think that Horace refers to the story of the horse's tail in the life of Sertorius.

47. 'like a sinking heap.' There must here be an allusion to the argument called 'sorites.'

51. 'seems to trouble himself but little;' so careless is he as a writer. Others explain; 'he need not care.'

52. 'his dream.' Persius, *Sat.* VI. 10, also laughs at Ennius' dream, told in the opening of his *Annals*. He was the Roman Homer who had passed through the body of a peacock, after Pythagoras' fashion.

53. 'Nævius,' B.C. 235, wrote of the Punic war in Saturnian rhythm, libelled the Metelli, had served in the 1st Punic war, wrote also tragedies and comedies.

56. 'Pacuvius,' B.C. 190; sister's son of Ennius; scorned Euripides, then the popular poet, and would only translate Æschylus and Sophocles.

'Accius,' B.C. 170; rather 'Attius,' was fondest of Æschylus; he also wrote 'prætextatæ,' i.e. historical plays like those of Shakspeare.

57. 'Afranius,' B.C. 100. He was thought to be the Roman Menander.

58. 'Plautus,' B.C. 220. His plays, though not so elegant as those of Terence, are more lively and bustling.

'Epicharmus,' of Cos, B.C. 490, was at Gelon's and Hiero's court with Pindar: wrote comedies, and is called the inventor of Comedy.

59. 'Cæcilius,' B.C. 200, was a slave, like Terence. The verses of Vulcatius found in Aulus Gellius give him the palm of comic Latin writers.

'Terence' of Carthage; B.C. 165.

62. 'Livius' Andronicus, B.C. 240, made an abridgment of the *Odyssey*, and wrote tragedies represented on a stage in the circus.

68. 'Jove sanctions my judgment.' Or, 'Jove keeps me from a mistake.'

71. 'Orbilius,' of Beneventum; once a soldier; began to teach when he was 50, when many stop; wrote a book to complain of parents; got more fame than money: Domitius Marsus also mentions his cane and birch.

79. 'Atta's play.' Atta, B.C. 90, wrote comedies.

'saffron,' with which the stage was sprinkled.

82. 'dignified Æsopus,' would then be like our stately Kemble. Cicero calls him a master in his art.

'Roscius;' so good, that whoever was good at anything, was called a Roscius in it. They were both contemporaries and friends of Cicero.

86. 'song of the Salii,' priests of Mars on the Quirinal, famous for their banquets, dances, hymns. Quintilian says that even the Salii themselves hardly understood it, it was so old.

93. 'wars.' Horace must mean the Persian wars. Unluckily, Greece never put wars aside, till liberty was lost. Also by 'Greeks' Horace must mean Athenians.

110. 'dictate verses.' We should say 'write verses;' but the ancients hardly ever took the trouble to write, but dictated to their slave, the amanuensis. Comp. Rom. XVI. 22, 'I, Tertius, who wrote this epistle.'

112. 'more lies than the Parthians.' The Parthians had taken the place of 'Punic faith' in Roman language. No doubt if Hannibal had succeeded, we should have had 'Roman faith' instead.

114. 'southernwood,' a fragrant plant.

132. 'hymns of prayer,' such as the *Secular Hymn*.

134. 'the chorus,' of youths and girls, thrice nine of each.

135. 'implores rain from above.' Sacred rites were in use at Rome to pray for rain in time of drought. Outside the gate Capena was a stone called 'manalis,' which they used to bring inside the gate to fetch rain from the skies. See note in Delphin edition.

138. 'gods below,' especially at the Lemuria, on the 9th of May. See Ov. *Fast.* V. 421.

139. 'our rural ancestors.' Comp. Virg. *Georg.* II. 385; Tibull. *Eleg.* II. 1, 55. On which passage Gerlach remarks that 'in those old days the sparks of genius were kindled by the worship of the gods; and among the Latins the use of masks and alternate verses encouraged especially dramatic poetry;' in which however the Latins were not destined to attain to any great excellence: the best dramatic poetry of the Romans is to be found really in Horace's *Satires*.

145. 'Fescennine licence.' See Liv. VII. 2. These are the 'unpolished verses,' spoken of by Virgil, and the 'rustic words' mentioned by Tibullus. They were used especially at weddings. Fescennia was a town in Etruria. Augustus himself, who was a joking man, though his jokes are bad, so far as we know, is said to have written some verses of this kind. The third eclogue of Virgil is perhaps something like them. See, too, *Sat.* I. 5, 32, and 7, 28, where the man of Præneste indulges in Fescennine licence, but meets his match in the Greek.

149. 'honourable families,' i.e. honoured with the names of those who had held curule offices.

154. 'death by cudgelling,' a severe punish-

ment for such an offence; but barbarous are the punishments of a barbarous age.

158. 'Saturnian measure.' Macaulay has compared it to our nursery rhymes. It was an iambic verse with a syllable at the end, or it may be called a trochaic verse with a syllable before, or it may be regarded as two verses, the first iambic, the second trochaic. The oldest known specimen is the carmen Saliare, called Axamenta, as written on 'axibus,' that is, on boards.

165. 'were satisfied;' judging from the remains that have come down to us, we should say they were easily satisfied with themselves.

173. 'Dossennus.' The Scholiast says a writer of Atellanæ, i. e. farces performed in Oscan; but it is thought by K. O. Muller, Keightley, and Yonge, that his name may be that of a character in a play of that stamp. In that case 'in' would mean 'among.'

194. 'Democritus,' the laughing philosopher.

202. 'Garganus,' in Apulia.

207. 'Tarentine dye.' Tarentum, on the east coast, and Baiæ on the west, were both famous for the dye made of the juice of a certain shell-fish. The colour is lost.

216. 'gifts worthy of Apollo;' the library which Augustus had added to the temple built by him to Apollo on the Palatine.

230. 'the guardians of a virtue.' The poets who were to be entrusted with the glories of Augustus are here compared to the public guardians of the temples.

232. 'Alexander the Great,' who had not such good taste in literature as Augustus.

233. 'Chœrilus,' who, Plutarch and Q. Curtius say, accompanied Alexander in his expeditions to record his exploits, receiving philips for his good verses, stripes for his bad ones, and getting more stripes.

239. 'Apelles,' of Cos, flourished B.C. 330; mentioned by Cicero with Zeuxis and Aglaophon. His picture of Venus Anadyomene, considered the model of his graceful style, was purchased by Augustus.

240. 'Lysippus,' of Sicyon, a statuary of such diligence, as to leave behind him 1500 pieces. The chariot of the Sun at Rhodes was one of his greatest works. He is mentioned by Cicero with Myron and Polycletus.

244. 'Bœotia's dull atmosphere,' contrasted with that of Attica. Dr Parr was pleased to call Warwickshire the Bœotia of England, 'which produced Shakspeare, and was effete.'

269. 'carried down.' Because the Tuscan street, where the poor lived in Rome, was near the river. There stood the temple of Ops.

II.

1. 'good and great Nero.' Tiberius, afterwards Emperor. He is highly praised by Velleius Paterculus for his beauty, noble form, his abilities and character, II. 94.

15. 'under the stairs;' or it may be 'the whip hanging up under the stairs.'

26. 'In Lucullus' army.' Keightley says that Beaumont and Fletcher founded their play of the *Humorous Lieutenant* in part on this story.

44. 'to distinguish right from wrong.' Literally 'crooked from straight,' morally; though some think that geometry is here meant, to which Plato attached much importance.

45. 'Academus' grove;' whence Plato's followers were called the Academic sect.

55. 'the years.' Horace was now about 54. He had three years more to live.

60. 'like Bion's;' who flourished B.C. 270, a different man from the bucolic poet.

68. 'Quirinal,' 'Aventine.' The Quirinal was in the northern part of Rome, the Aventine in the southern, with the Circus Maximus, the Forum, the Palatine, between them.

81. 'a genius,' &c. Walckenaer thinks Horace here describes himself with the shy habits of a student. But Horace was not anything like seven years at Athens.

89. 'a Gracchus,' an orator like Tiberius or Caius. 'a Mucius' Scaevola; learned in the law.

105. 'without requital.' Compare the opening lines of Juvenal.

110. 'an upright censor.' Keightley thinks that Horace here has a reference "to the purgations of the senate made by Augustus." The terms are chosen with great skill so as to apply at once to the senators and to words.

114. 'shrine of Vesta.' The soul of the poet, compared to the shrine, into which none but the Vestals entered.

117. 'Cato and Cethegus.' Cato the censor: and M. Cornelius Cethegus, according to Cicero, (*Brutus*, XV. 57,) the first known to have been an orator in Rome, of whom Ennius, quoted by Cicero, says, in his 9th book of *Annals*, that he was 'as a culled flower of excellence, and the very heart of the goddess of persuasion.'

128. 'There lived one,' &c. A like story is told by Ollian, in Athenæus, by Pseud.-Aristotle; and, Orelli says, by Huarte, a Spanish author. The passage is imitated by Boileau, *Sat.* IV. 103, and by Pope. Boileau ends with the line, 'En me tirant d'erreur m'ôte du paradis.'

144. 'to master the harmonies;' i. e. to study philosophy, which should be to the old what poetry is to the young.

146. 'If no draughts of water,' &c.; now he is addressing himself, not his friend Florus.

158. 'legal purchase,' literally 'scales and brass;' for the buyer touched the 'scales' with a piece of money.

170. 'the poplar planted;' which would be sacred to the god Terminus.

177. 'rows of houses.' The meaning of the word 'vicus,' which is applicable to the country and town alike. It seems, with reference to a town, to be used of streets, and of quarters of a city. In the country, it is used as the part of a 'pagus.' See Forcellini on the word. The Italian is 'borgo.'

180. 'Tuscan images;' 'little bronze images of the gods.'

181. 'African,' in the original 'Gætulian,' the people to the south of Mauritania.

184. 'palm groves of Herod,' the Great, the friend of Antony; he had groves of palms about Jericho, 'the city of palms,' which brought him wealth. Compare Virg. *Georg.* III. 12.

187. 'the genius-god,' partly identified with the man, partly independent. Yonge compares Spenser *F. Qu.* II. 12, 47. See *Ep.* II. 1, 144.

197. 'in the holidays;' the Quinquatria, five days sacred to Minerva, beginning on the 19th of March. See Ovid, *Fasti*, 809—850: where we see the goddess is at once a goddess of learning and of scholars, and also of war and blood.

210. 'do you count your birthdays;' as we should say, 'are you thankful for the years you have had, and looking forward to the end of life with contentment?'

THE ART OF POETRY.

18. 'river Rhine.' It is likely here the reference is to Furius, who made the Rhine so muddy. *Sat.* I. 10, 37.

19. 'can paint a cypress.' Said to allude to a Greek proverb: 'What, do you want a cypress too?'

32. 'near the school of Æmilius.' A school of gladiators.

'an ordinary artist.' Others read 'imus,' the 'lowest;' either in skill, or having his shop lowest down.

45, 46. These two lines are transposed in the editions.

50. 'old-fashioned,' literally 'girt' in the lower part of the body, with the arms free. 'Cethegi.' See *Ep.* II. 2, 117.

54. 'Cæcilius.' See *Ep.* II. 1, 59.

56. 'Cato.' See *Ep.* II. 2, 117.

60. 'at each year's fall.' But others take it 'as the years swiftly pass.' See *Odes*, IV. 6, 39.

64. 'Neptune be received,' alludes to the 'portus Julius' made by Agrippa in honour of Augustus, near Baiæ, before the expedition against Sextus Pompeius, B.C. 37.

65. 'the marsh;' perhaps the Pomptine marshes.

67. 'the river;' perhaps an exaggeration of what Augustus did in clearing out the Tiber.

77. 'who was the inventor of these elegiacs.' Tyrtæus was one of the earliest writers of elegiacs.

79. 'Archilochus.' See *Epod.* 6. 13.

83. 'to the lyre.' Here, as in *Odes*, IV. 2, he seems to refer to the subjects of Pindar's *Odes*, most of which are lost. (1) mythology, (2) the games, (3) love, (4) wine: to which is to be added the 'dirge for the dead;' 21st line of *Ode* IV. 2.

91. 'Thyestean banquet.' Varius wrote a tragedy called *Thyestes;* which Quintilian. X. 1, 98, thought would stand comparison with any Greek author, but Niebuhr not unnaturally doubts this. See *Odes*, I. 6, 8.

94. 'Chremes,' the father in the comedy.

96. 'Telephus.' Of him said Euripides, in his play laughed at by Aristophanes:

'For I to-day must needs for beggar pass,
And, being what I am, another seem.'

'Peleus.' At this play also Aristophanes laughs.

101. 'As human countenances,' &c. Comp. Rom. XII. 15.

114. 'god.' Others read 'Davus.' But Horace appears here to be speaking only of tragedy. Compare 227.

A 'god' would be further removed from the world than a hero. Compare Hercules, a hero in the *Trachiniæ*, with Hercules, a god in the *Philoctetes*.

116. 'bustling nurse,' a favourite character on the Greek stage. In the *Choephoræ* the nurse is natural and half comic, and is like one in ordinary life. So in *Romeo and Juliet*.

120. 'illustrious Achilles.' Bentley proposes to read 'Homeric Achilles.' This emendation is a good sample of the great cleverness and great rashness of Bentley.

121. 'as one restless,' &c. Mr. Gladstone, on Homer, objects to this description of Achilles: but the Achilles of Mr Gladstone is taken, not from Homer, but from Mr Gladstone's own inner consciousness.

123. 'Ino' with her son, Melicerta, threw herself into the sea. About 24 short fragments of Euripides' *Ino* are extant.

124. 'Ixion.' Æschylus, Sophocles, Euripides, all wrote a play of this name. In the play of Æschylus was this line, 'Death is more glorious than an evil life.'

129. 'dividing the subject of the *Iliad*.' The only remaining Greek play taken directly from the story of the *Iliad* is the *Rhesus*.

132. 'trite and obvious circle of events,' i.e. generalities open to any poet.

135. 'shame.' Keightley explains it 'of respect for the original poet;' Orelli, of being laughed at by the audience. It may mean simply the shame of confessing a failure.

136. 'Cyclic writer.' The Cyclic writers were so called by the grammarians of Alexandria in the second century before Christ. The *Iliad* and *Odyssey* were in the cycle. But, as most of the poems were inferior, they

were separated from the two great poems, and became a byword for badness.

140. 'acted he,' i. e. Homer, at the opening of the *Odyssey*.

145. 'Antiphates,' &c.; all of these are parts of the *Odyssey*.

146. 'return of Diomede,' as in the Cyclic poem called 'The Returns.'

147. 'the twin eggs' of Leda, as in the *Cypria* of Stasinus.

148. 'into the middle of events.' Homer is followed in this by Virgil, Tasso, Milton, Camoens.

155. 'Please, sirs, to applaud.' So always end the plays of Plautus and Terence. 'chants;' for the actors used to chant. See Livy, VII. 2. So Cicero, speaking of the actors in the play of *Afranius*, calls them 'chanters.'

156. 'characteristics of each age.' Horace here seems to follow Aristotle, *Rhet.* II. 12, and is closely followed by Boileau, *L'Art Poetique*, Chant III. 390: 'Le temps, qui change tout,' &c. Shakspeare, *As you like it*, II. 7, is of course original, and far superior to the Greek, Latin, and French writers.

161. 'guardian.' the pædagogus, or slave who accompanied the boy, and from whom he was freed, when he put on the toga virilis. See Galat. III. 24, 25.

175. 'Many blessings.' This is added in a melancholy tone, and in keeping with Horace's turn of mind.

179. 'reported.' Hence the important part which the 'messenger' held in Greek plays, in this point very unlike ours.

180. 'Now, less keenly,' &c. It is as if Horace felt the truth on this point, but did not venture to go against the established custom.

186. 'Atreus.' Of this play of Sophocles only one fragment is extant.

187. 'Procne,' in the play of Sophocles called 'Tereus,' alluded to in the *Birds* of Aristophanes, l. 100. One fragment, describing the unhappy lot of women, has merit in it.

'Cadmus.' According to Probus on Virg. *Eclog.* 6. 31, there was a play of Euripides of this name.

189. 'five acts.' The plays of Euripides are so divided in the Variorum Edition, Glasguæ, 1821, but Aristotle's division was into the prologos, epeisodia, and exodos; and the 'five acts' is altogether a later idea.

191. 'Nor let a god intermeddle.' In the plays of Euripides, the gods are often most unnecessary and undignified intermeddlers.

195. 'save what advances,' &c. Here too Euripides is an offender, but his choruses are often so very beautiful, that we may well pardon his offence.

196. 'let the chorus support the good.' A remarkable exception to this precept is found in the *Antigone*, no doubt to bring out more strongly the pious courage of the maiden.

197. 'and restrain the angry;' as in *Œdipus Rex*.

'and love those that fear to sin.' But another reading gives 'and love to appease the haughty.' This reading of Bentley's is followed by Orelli, Keightley, Yonge.

200. 'let it keep secrets,' as in the *Choephoræ*, *Electra*, *Medea*, *Hippolytus*.

202. 'The flute,' &c. It is hard to tell here how far Horace follows history.

203. 'with few holes.' Macleane says those in the British Museum have six.

208. 'embraced the city.' What city? Athens, or Rome? It is hard to say. But some MSS. have the plural 'cities.'

210. 'his Genius.' See *Ep.* I. 7, 94, note, and *Ep.* II. 1, 144.

215. 'train,' called 'syrma,' from the Greek word 'to draw.'

219. 'saws of wisdom,' found often in the chorus in Æschylus, Sophocles, and Euripides: in the two first rather religious, in the last rather philosophic.

221. 'wild Satyrs.' The Satyric dramas, entirely different from comedies, were very likely the oldest form of the drama, and were afterwards joined to the tragic trilogy. See Paley's introduction to the *Cyclops* of Euripides, the only Satyric drama now extant.

227. 'any god or hero.' As Silenus, the Satyrs, Ulysses, in the *Cyclops*.

232. 'as matron bid to dance.' Keightley quotes the Scholiast: 'for there are certain holy rites in which matrons dance, as in those of the Mother of the gods.' *Od.* II. 12, 17.

237. 'Davus,' the slave of Comedy. 'Davus am I, no Œdipus.'

239. Silenus, 'god of the wine-vat,' was bald, old, red-faced, head of the Satyrs; Bacchus was his darling and trouble. When his ass brayed, the Titans fled.

244. 'The Fauns,' 'the speaking gods,' here are confounded with the Satyrs, Latin gods with Greek. Horace says they should not on the stage either mince like city fops, or talk in low language, like rabble.

249. 'roasted chick-peas.' Keightley says 'cecio fritto,' 'fried chick-pea,' is a term of abuse, as we use 'chaw-bacon,' and Sancho is called 'harto de ajos,' stuffed with garlic.

252. 'a rapid foot.' Comp. *Od.* I. 16, 24. Horace says the swiftness of the foot made it seem a trimeter, though it really had six feet. But the iambic 'metre' = 2 feet.

254. 'But not so very long ago.' This is puzzling, as spondees appear in the verses of Archilochus, 600 years before Horace.

256. 'The Iambic.' It is here personified, as one light and airy, together with its grave steady friend the Spondee.

259. 'much vaunted trimeters.' This is spoken ironically.

262. 'The Iambic lays upon them.' The Iambic speaks as one, whose feelings are hurt by the neglect of spondaic Ennius, who was satisfied with one iambic in a line; such a line is this of Ennius, 'Cur talem invitum invitam cogis linquere?' of which the Iambic has good grounds to complain.

265. 'Shall I then write loosely?' &c. Yonge well explains it thus: 'Shall I write carelessly, because readers have no ear, or

because they are indifferent, and will excuse it?'

270. 'rhythm and wit of Plautus.' Varro, Cicero, Gellius, judged verydifferently. Niebuhr says 'how Horace could have been blind to the merits of Plautus, is inconceivable;' not more so, than how Niebuhr could have judged Horace and Virgil as he has done. We are but bad judges one of another, even in literature.

275. 'Thespis.' This drama was made up of hymns in honour of Bacchus, with one or two monologues inserted to give the chorus a rest. Solon was a spectator, when Thespis herself gesticulated, using the trochaic metre. Horace has omitted Phrynichus, who first wrote plays on graver events, as on 'the capture of Miletus.'

277. 'faces smeared with lees of wine;' the τρυγοδαίμονες of Aristophanes. 'des diables barbouillés de lie.' See the note in Delphin edition.

280. 'magnificent diction.' The 'grand words,' Aristoph. *Frogs*, 1004.

283. 'the law was submitted to.' Schlegel says he cannot agree with Horace; but thinks that the old comedy flourished and died with Athenian freedom.

288. 'tragedies or comedies on Roman subjects.' Such were the *Brutus* and *Decius* of Accius. Ennius' tragedies were all on Greek subjects, as were the comedies of Terence and Plautus of a Greek character.

291. 'the blood of Numa.' For the Pisos claimed descent from Numa Pompilius, as a gentleman in England, now alive, does from the Emperor Maximinus.

301. 'the barber Licinus,' of whom, the Scholiast says, it was written 'of marble is Licinus' tomb; Cato has none, Pompey a humble one: who can believe in the gods?'

302. 'as spring comes on.' So, blood used to be let in spring.

304. 'of a whetstone.' Isocrates used the same simile.

322. 'prettily sounding trifles.' So Aristoph. *Frogs*, 1005, 'tragic trifles.'

327. 'Albinus.' The Scholiast says he was an usurer.

332. 'oil of cedar,' 'cypress.' Pliny says that thus things were protected against decay and moths.

340. 'ogress,' 'Lamiæ.' They had the face of a lady, the feet of a donkey. The word is connected with Lemures, larva, λαμυρός. See Paley on Ov. *Fast.* V. 41, who compares 'goblin' and 'gobble.'

342. 'knights,' 'Ramnes.' See Livy, I. 13.

345. publishers = 'Sosii.' See *Ep.* I. 20, 2.

357. 'a second Chœrilus.' See *Ep.* II. 1, 232.

359. 'Homer sometimes nods.' What parts of his poems Horace alludes to, it is hard to say. Glaucus' speech in *Iliad* 6th, and Æneas' in the 20th book are wearisome and long-winded.

366. 'O elder youth.' This is the one who was assassinated when prætor in Spain.

371. 'Messala,' Corvinus. See *Od.* III. 21, 7; *Sat.* I. 6, 42; *Sat.* I. 10, 28, 85.

'Aulus Cascellius.' He refused to draw up the legal form for the proscriptions of Antony and Augustus. He was famous for law, bons mots, freedom of speech. But there were two, father and son. See Walckenaer, vol. I. 461.

373. 'booksellers.' Literally 'columns.' See *Sat.* I. 4, 71. Judging from Martial, I. 117, 11, it would seem that these columns, pillars, or door-posts, were covered with the names of books sold in the shop.

375. 'bitter honey.' Literally 'Sardinian;' the opposite of that of Hybla.

385. 'against the bent of your genius.' Literally 'with Minerva unwilling:' so the Romans said 'coarse Minerva,' 'heavy Minerva,' 'my Minerva,' 'a man of every Minerva.'

387. 'before Mæcius.' See *Sat.* I. 10, 38.

388. 'kept back for nine years.' So Cinna did not publish his *Smyrna* for nine years: Cat. 95: and Isocrates kept back his *Panegyric* for the same time; Quintil. X. 4. Perhaps this accounts for its artificial style. Menage, a witty Frenchman, speaking of a book long kept back, said, 'long has the maiden been expected, and now that she appears she is quite an old lady.'

394. 'Amphion.' See *Odyss.* XI. 261, where Amphion and Zethus are builders of the common kind, not to the sound of the lyre. Pausanias, IX. 5, 4, says he had been taught the Lydian harmony by Tantalus.

399. 'tablets of wood;' on which, called ἄξονες, were written Solon's laws.

402. 'Tyrtæus,' B.C. 680, the lame schoolmaster, whose spear was his song. But it is a great fall from Homer to Tyrtæus.

403. 'oracles were delivered in verse,' usually hexameters, as so often in Herodotus. Pliny says 'we owe the heroic verse to the Pythian god,' not to Homer.

404. 'of princes;' as those at Syracuse, Larissa, &c.

418. 'and to confess,' &c. 'So,' says the Delphin editor, 'the troublesome and fatal race of bad poets multiplies among the children of men.'

431. 'as hired mourners.' So Lucilius: 'the women hired weep much at the funeral of a stranger, and tear their hair, and cry louder and louder.' See St Mark v. 38. This is the Irish 'keening.' Our mutes are mute, as becomes the English character.

434. 'Patrons.' Literally 'kings.' They are so called as early as the time of Plautus. *Stich.* III. 2, 1. So Mart. II. 18, 8. 'A man who is a king, O greatest of kings, ought not to be under another king.'

438. 'Quintilius.' He had a villa at Tibur, and was a friend of Virgil. He had probably been dead nearly 20 years, when Horace thus remembers him. We may imagine that Virgil and Horace both consulted him on their verses, as did other poets of a different kind. This simple sincerity (*Od.* I. 24, 7) would help to make him a good critic.

450. 'second Aristarchus,' 160 B.C. At Alexandria he educated the sons of Ptolemy. He

did not spare Homer himself, and time has not spared one of his 800 commentaries. He was the Scaliger of antiquity. See the excellent Delphin note.

453. 'the jaundice.' Literally the 'regal malady.' ἴκτερος.

454. 'Diana's wrath.' As the goddess of the moon, the reputed cause of madness.

465. 'Empedocles,' of Agrigentum, the Greek Lucretius. B C. 440 a Pythagorean, who was first a girl, then a boy, a shrub, a bird, a fish, and finally Empedocles. So he had a wide experience. Milton, *P. L.* III. 469.

'cold blood.' Either knowing what he did, or with an allusion to his own opinion, that cold blood makes men dull, or, simply, because he was cold, and wanted to be warm; or the word is merely used to make a comic antithesis to 'burning Etna.'

471. 'accursed plot,' 'bidental.' A place struck by lightning, 'fulguritus.' It was purified with the blood of sheep, 'bidentes,' on which word Aulus Gellius gossips much. *Od.* III. 23, 14, note.

474. 'kills by his recitation.' The bores of these days, of whom Horace had a special dread. See Martial, III. 44, of one Ligurinus, round whom there was a solitude.

INDEX.

[*The references are to the pages.*]

N.

O.

P.

Q.

R.

S.

T.

U.

V.

www.ingramcontent.com/pod-product-compliance
Lightning Source LLC
Chambersburg PA
CBHW030343270326
41926CB00009B/947

9783337372040